Instrument of Culture

The structure of language; how it is formed and changed . . .

A review of the modern spoken languages . . .

Language and its relation to religion, politics and economics, science and literature, superstition and intolerance . . .

Dialects, place names, family names . . .

Problems of language learning and how they can be solved . . .

Slang, cant, jargon . . .

Evolution of writing . . .

The controversial problem of an international language . . .

These are just a few of the subjects Mario Pei discusses in this enlightening and entertaining study of language—that most basic and marvelously complex instrument of culture. Albert Guerard said in *The New York Herald Tribune:* "There are many introductions to linguistic studies. . . . I do not hesitate to rank Mario Pei's among the most comprehensive and the best balanced." Horace Reynolds wrote in *The New York Times:* "This is a book good for both reading and reference." After reading *The Story of Language* George Bernard Shaw observed that Professor Pei's "prodigious memory and knowledge remind me of Isaac Newton."

Other MENTOR Books of Related Interest

LANGUAGE, A MODERN SYNTHESIS *by Joshua Whatmough*
A fascinating discourse on the structure, mechanics, and evolution of language through the ages, and its role today. (#MT642—75¢)

THE CREATIVE PROCESS
edited with Introduction by Brewster Ghiselin
Some of the greatest minds (including Einstein, Nietzsche, Yeats, and Jung) reveal how they begin and complete creative works. (#MP383—60¢)

BOOKS THAT CHANGED THE WORLD *by Robert B. Downs*
Histories of sixteen epoch-making books, from Machiavelli's *The Prince* to Einstein's *Theories of Relativity*. (#MP400—60¢)

ADVENTURE OF IDEAS *by Alfred North Whitehead*
A history of mankind's great thoughts, tracing the development of crucial ideas from ancient times to the present. (#MT551—75¢)

THE STORY OF
LANGUAGE

by MARIO PEI

Revised Edition

A MENTOR BOOK

Published by The New American Library, New York and Toronto

CONTENTS

THE STORY OF
LANGUAGE

PART ONE

The History of Language

— Chapter One —

NONLINGUISTIC SYSTEMS
OF COMMUNICATION

There was speech in their dumbness, language in their very gesture.
—Shakespeare, The Winter's Tale

YOU are traveling along a motor highway. At the side of
the road there appears an octagonal signpost, with no let-
tering on it. If you do not know the code, you will go right
on past it, into the arms of a traffic policeman or, more
tragically, into a crash. If you know the code, you will come
to a full stop. In like manner, a round disk with a cross tells
you you are approaching a railroad crossing, a diamond-
shaped sign tells you to slow down, a square sign indicates
that you are entering a school zone. Most states have now replaced these symbolic signposts with lettered signs, because illiteracy is rapidly diminishing. They depended upon a visual
symbolism of shape and served their purpose well when a
segment of the driving population was still semiliterate. But
the nations of Europe make use of a system of visual road
signs that is designed to surmount the language barriers of a
continent where over twenty languages are official. The European round sign with a horizontal bar across it means "no
entry" or "one way." The transversal bar through a bent arrow
that points left means "no left turn." A triangle standing on its
apex means "main road ahead." Similar in nature is the international "snow language," used in Canada and other countries
where heavy snows present a problem; here there are visual
symbols for snow that is smooth, sun eroded, rain eroded,
wind eroded, that has a film crust, a wind crust, a feltlike
structure, rounded grains, or crystal facets.

The red, green, and yellow lights and "blinkers" which
are now so common are equally effective, save in cases of
color blindness. They depend upon a visual symbolism of

color, in which red arbitrarily stands for "stop" or "danger," green for "safety" or "go," yellow for "slow" or a transitional signal, a blinking light for "caution."

You are trying to pass a truck on a narrow highway at night. In response to the tooting of your horn, the truckman flashes his rear outline lights off and on. If you know the code, you know that you can pass him safely. But if instead of signaling with his lights he waves his arm up and down, you know there is a car coming in the opposite direction and drop behind till he gives the welcome flash. Here we have a symbolism of light and one of gesture.

In none of the cases outlined above has there been an interchange of language, spoken or written. There has, however, been an interchange of meaning, a transfer of significant concepts. If we accept only the narrower etymological definition of language as that which is produced by the human vocal organs and received by the hearing apparatus, we shall have to deny the name of "language" to these transfers. If we accept the broader definition of language as any transfer of meaning, they are forms of language differing in degree but not in kind from a spoken or written message.

In their anxiety to restrict language to a pattern of sounds, too many linguists have forgotten that the sound symbols of the spoken tongue are neither more nor less symbolical of human thought and human meaning than the various forms of activity (gestural, pictorial, ideographic, even artistic) by which men have conveyed significant messages to one another since the dawn of history. It is a commonplace among linguists that the spoken language antedates the written language by thousands, perhaps millions, of years. Insofar as the written language is a symbolical replica of the spoken tongue, this is undoubtedly true. But there is little or no assurance that organized sound language, as distinguished from mere animal cries, antedates pictographs painted on the walls of caves or petroglyphs carved on rocks, whose purpose undoubtedly was to convey a significant message or establish a permanent record.

Some scientists claim that certain animal species communicate by nonlinguistic devices; that bees, for example, convey significant messages to one another by odor and by dancing in their hives, or that ants use their antennae in a significant way. Some of the stories in this connection are impressive. The American nighthawk is said to emit varieties of sounds which convey significant messages to its fellows. Dolphins are claimed to possess a mysterious form of communication (extrasensory, perhaps) which permits quasi-human collaboration between two or more of the species. Attempts to get animals and birds to "talk," or at least to understand human speech, range all the way from experiments with the anthropoid apes (a chimpanzee is said to be able to pronounce "papa," "mamma," and "cup" in a hoarse whisper) to the speaking crow, parrot, and mynah bird, whose vocabulary can be quite extensive. Professor Eckstein, of the University of Cincinnati, claims that higher forms of animal life, such as the bird, dog, or chimpanzee, are capable of changing man's words into symbols and thus understanding them. But even in the best-attested cases, there is no evidence that any of the animals in question are able to project their "language" into nonimmediate situations, which is a characteristic of all human speech. The dog or bird can give warning of a present, immediate danger or notice of a present, immediate desire; it cannot warn you, as the most primitive human being can, that there is a danger lurking in wait many miles away, or inform you that it desires to do or have something, not now but tomorrow. This nonimmediate feature seems reserved to the systems of communication of human beings, be they oral, gestural, symbolic, pictorial, or written.

Meaning may be transferred by devices that have nothing to do either with the spoken language or with its written counterpart, and this basic proposition few will be so hardy as to deny. A logical corollary is that language as we know it did not necessarily have to become the great thought conveyor that it is. Granted a different historical development, it is conceivable that the human race might have reserved its oral passages for purposes of eating and breathing only and developed an entirely different machinery for the transfer of meaning. That this might have been so is proved by the truly vast number of auxiliary meaning conveyors that the human race has actually devised and employs side by side with the spoken and written language. Our justification for discussing them here lies partly in the fact that they *are* auxiliaries to language, partly in our partiality for the broader definition of language as that which serves to convey meaning, partly in the fact that a historical discussion of language would be incomplete without them.

In the written language, as will be seen in a subsequent chapter, there are two possibilities: the written language may follow the spoken language, symbolizing its sounds, or at least its words; or it may avoid any connection whatsoever with the spoken language and symbolize thoughts, ideas, and objects. In the former eventuality, the written language is, of course, a handmaiden to the spoken tongue; in the latter, it is altogether free of spoken-language restrictions. In either case, it resembles the spoken tongue in that it depends upon symbols which require common acceptance. The same is true of any nonlinguistic system of communication. There must be common agreement upon a symbol before the latter can become meaningful, serve the purposes of transfer, and be dignified, even figuratively, with the name of "language." We may assume that common acceptance of the symbol takes place through a process of individual innovation and piecemeal acceptance rather than through mass creation. The innovator is one who enjoys prestige and is therefore imitated. If the leader of a group decides upon the use of a certain symbol, oral or otherwise, with a given value, a few of his followers will imitate his usage, which later spreads from individual to individual until it becomes universal within the group.

The systems of communication that have been devised by man's fertile brain since the inception of civilization are numerous, not to say innumerable. An interesting question that arises in connection with them is that of historical priority; namely, whether and to what extent the mutual acceptance that characterizes them is based on a previous understanding depending upon spoken language. The story of the fall of Troy, for instance, tells us that the news of the final victory was relayed from Asia Minor to Greece by a series of signal fires. Signal fires have been in use ever since and are believed to have led to the use of the heliograph, whereby the sun's rays are reflected from a mirror at significant intervals. But was not the meaning of the signal fires of Troy previously agreed upon through the agency of the spoken tongue?

The same question arises in connection with the tom-tom used by African natives as a long-distance telephone. Its significantly spaced beats antedate the Morse code by several centuries, and their rate of transmission by a skilled operator is as speedy as that of the telegraph. It was once thought that there was no connection between the tom-tom and the spoken language, but more recent research indicates that the two-toned tom-tom imitates the tones of the native words, to which additional "qualifying" words are added to avoid confusion between two or more words having identical tones. This gives us practical assurance that the tone signals were originally arranged at a series of spoken-language conferences. The same may be said of the smoke signals of the

American Indians. If it could be proved that all non-linguistic systems of communication were originally systematized through the spoken-language medium, the historical priority of the spoken language would be established. While this proof is readily forthcoming in the case of many systems, it is lacking in others, notably in the field of gestural language.

Certain nonlinguistic forms of communication come close to the spoken, others to the written language. The "uh-huh" uttered in three distinct tones, and without accompanying gestures or nods, to signify "yes," "no," and "maybe" in some sections of the South is so close to spoken language that one is left in doubt whether it should be mentioned in this chapter. Very close to the spoken language is also the whistling language used by the natives of Gomera, in the Canary Islands, who communicate by means of it over very long distances (some say six miles); it seems established, however, that this whistling language is based on Spanish rhythms and pitch. A similar type of whistling language is employed by the natives of Kusnoy, a village in Turkey. The sounds are described as formed with tongue curled around the teeth and lips not puckered but tensely drawn, with the palm of the left hand cupped around the mouth, and high pressure applied from the lungs. The villagers are said to speak, argue, and even woo in whistles.

Volumes have been written on the imitation of animal and bird calls to convey signals, particularly in warfare. In the production of the film *Home of the Brave,* a birdcall specialist was employed to identify and reproduce the twelve Pacific island bird calls used by the Japanese in their surprise attacks, to keep liaison among the advancing units.

Other auditory forms of communication not based on human speech or the vocal organs include U. S. Army bugle calls, over forty in number, each invested with its own peculiar significance; the applause which may take the form not only of hand clapping but also of stamping the feet, banging canes or umbrellas on the floor, or even rushing up to the front and beating the palms of the hands on the stage. There are the long and short blasts of the locomotive whistle, which engineers often use in various combinations for special messages (one short toot for "I'm coming to a stop"; three shorts for "I'm about to back up"; four shorts as a request for instructions; two longs to indicate a start).

Symbols of this sort, however, serve to express only one basic emotion or information and are therefore to some extent disqualified for the status of language, which must express a variety of things. On the other hand, they share one important characteristic of language; they are based on mutual agreement and become quite meaningless if the requisite general acceptance is not there. In World War Two, American WACS were quite bewildered by Italian clucks, and Italian girls by American wolf whistles, until the meaning was explained. In like manner, the American hiss in token of disapproval and loud whistling in sign of enthusiastic applause are quite misunderstood in many European countries, where violent disapproval is expressed by whistling and the hiss is never heard. In Japan a variant of the hiss, a loud sucking-in of the breath, betokens polite recognition. Among quasi-vocal sounds that hold different meanings in different lands may be mentioned the "tsk-tsk" which we use to deplore something but which means "no" in the Mediterranean countries and the Near East; our shushing sound to demand quiet, which means "hurry up" in Germany; the "pst-pst" which some countries use to call a cat, others to draw the attention of people. There is even an account of a joint American-Yugoslav attack that failed during the war because the Americans did not use the right noises to the Yugoslav mules that carried their supplies and so could not get them started.

Laughter can be a language of limited powers. By it we can express friendliness, agreement, flattery, derision, unbelief, surprise, and many other emotions. A giggle may indicate embarrassment or humility and is so used by the Japanese. There are other noises produced through the instrumentality of the vocal organs that do not qualify as standard speech yet carry a burden of meaning. The uncouth "Bronx cheer" is elevated by the Neapolitans, under the euphonic name of *pernacchio,* to a full-fledged semantic post.

One of the most elaborate meaning codes, involving both visual and auditory devices, appears in a pamphlet issued by the Civil Air Patrol for the guidance of owner pilots of private planes. A series of colored lights, red, white, and green, indicates to the pilot while still on the ground a clear take-off, a clear runway, return to ramp, stop; while similar light signals tell the pilot in flight to return and land, to give way and circle, to use caution. In radio communication, pilots use distinctive words as an audible language code to spell out letters (Bravo for B, Juliet for J, X ray for X, Zulu for Z). Then there are visible ground to air signals, eight feet long, where a single L means "require fuel and oil," a double L means "all's well," two L's back to back mean "not understood." Lastly, there are panel signals, given with two- or three-colored cloths, which can also be used at sea, where they have different meanings (yellow-blue-yellow in parallel bars indicates on land the direction of the nearest civilization, at sea the direction of rescue craft). All this is in addition to radio, mirrors, fires built from piles of kindling wood, flares, and smoke grenades.

Other varieties of nonlinguistic forms of communication come close to the written language and are supposed by some to have given rise to it. Under this heading fall firstly the pictographic drawings of prehistoric groups concerning whose ability to speak there is some doubt; secondly the knotted ropes and notched sticks of the ancient Chinese, the South American Indians, and the West African and Australian natives. For the first, the question of priority in time appears insoluble. Did the Cro-Magnons and other still more primitive men who developed a very effective rudimentary form of pictorial art, whereby they left significant messages and records, possess speech? Or are their efforts indicative of an abortive tendency to communicate by means of pictures before connected language began? For the second, the problem that poses itself is to what extent the mutual understanding of the symbols in question rested upon a previous linguistic understanding. All we can say with definite assurance is that the meanings conveyed by the ropes and sticks are independent of the spoken languages of their users and of such a nature as to afford the possibility of international use among speakers of different languages. The *quipu,* or "knots," used by the Peruvian Incas, for instance, included red ropes to symbolize soldiers, yellow ropes for gold, white ropes for silver, green ropes for grain, with a single knot signifying 10, two knots 20, a double knot 100, and so forth. The messages conveyed by means of the *quipu* were so complicated that special officials called *quipucamay-ocuna,* or "keepers of the knots," were ordained to interpret them.

Another curious form of visual symbolism is the Zulus' "language of the beads," where brightly colored beadwork in various patterns can be used to transmit even love letters. Receipt of a beadwork necklace bearing many white beads assures the young Zulu that his bride-to-be thinks highly of him and that all is well. The addition of a few red beads indicates that her heart is full and she is in good health. Purple, symbolical of the sunrise, and yellow, symbolical of the sunset, mean that the young lady misses him particularly at dawn and dusk. But deep yellow means "I'm jealous," and beige-gray means "You are too poor in livestock for me to marry you." "Wish I were with you" is betokened by nut-brown beads.

Before we smile at this symbolic "language" of largely il-literate groups, let us recall that in our own highly de-veloped civilization in a day, not too remote, when only one out of five could read the written sign, figures of Indians were used to indicate tobacco shops, while carved Chinese stood for tea shops, Beau Brummels for tailors. Our brightly colored barbershop poles and the three-ball insignia of pawn-shops are in the same class (the latter was in origin a group of three pills, from the coat of arms of the Medici family, which started its existence with medicine as its pro-fession but later shifted to banking and moneylending). The visual symbolism of advertising is not as widespread as it used to be; but who does not recall the old-fashioned phonograph and the listening dog, with or without the caption "His master's voice," or lovely Phoebe Snow traveling in immaculate white along a "Road of Anthracite" which is today run by electricity and Diesel engines?

Hoboes and gypsies have a way of carving symbolic mes-sages on the bark of trees, or scratching them on rocks, for the benefit of their fellows who may follow. A pair of spectacles, in gypsy symbolism, means "Beware! Danger and trouble here!"; but a small circle inside a larger one spells out "Very kind people. Don't impose on them." As early as the seventh century A.D., the Chinese used fingerprints as distinctive signatures on documents, while the illiterate's cross or mark runs through the Middle Ages and down to the end of the nineteenth century.

Perhaps the most elaborate visual code of all is that of medieval heraldry, now widely adopted by our automobile manufacturers. The designs and colors used in the various coats of arms of noble families not only served the purpose of positive identification (in fact, the medieval terminology was "to read someone's arms"), on the battlefield and else-where; they also told a complete story. The arms of France's heir to the throne, called Dauphin or Dolphin, for obscure reasons, show a field of black with red diamonds on which are three dolphins diving over a crown. Could anything be plainer than the coat of arms of the city of Oxford, an ox above two wavy lines, to record the fording of the Thames by an ox at the city's present site? In the static "language" of Persian rugs, singing birds portray happiness, brooks sym-bolize the life force, and trees are indicative of contemplation.

With so many partial systems of visual symbolism in use, it is not to be wondered at that the idea of a system of elaborate picto-ideography for international communications should repeatedly have arisen in the course of the last few centuries. The first serious attempt was made by Leibnitz. More recently, Charles Bliss, an Australian, devised what he called "semantography," a system of one hundred basic visual symbols which could be combined to produce all sorts of complicated meanings. Margaret Mead favors a code of glyphs, or visual symbols, for use at the UN and other international gatherings, and this idea is being actively sponsored by internationally minded groups in Washington and New York.

Another great division of nonlinguistic communication is gestures, which have no connection, save in a few specific instances, with either the spoken or the written language. Here the problem is more complicated. Granted that many conventional modern gestural signals, like those of a baseball umpire, football coach, boxing referee, or traffic policeman, are based upon previous linguistic understanding, the fact nevertheless remains that gestural language is commonly conceded to have preceded oral speech, some say by at least one million years. It is further estimated that some seven hundred thousand distinct elementary gestures can be produced by facial expressions, postures, movements of the arms, wrists, fingers, etc., and their combinations. This imposing array of gestural symbols would be quite sufficient to provide the equivalent of a full-blown modern language. It is quite conceivable: first, that a gestural system of communication could have arisen prior to and independently of spoken language; second, that such a system, had historical conditions been favorable, might have altogether supplanted the spoken tongue; third, that it could today supply the world's needs for an international common system.

The third part of this proposition requires no proof. Many North American Indian tribes are known to have developed a system of sign language whereby members of different groups, speaking dissimilar languages, could carry on lengthy conversations about any topic (the northern tribes generally used two hands, the southern tribes one). The Indian system of sign language has been repeatedly described in books from as far back as the early nineteenth century. It is unaccompanied by facial expressions and characterized by rich imagery. To indicate that one is sad, for instance, one points to oneself, makes the sign for "heart," then draws the hand down and away in the direction of the ground. A question is indicated by rotating the raised hand in a circle by wrist action; a lie by two spread fingers, showing "double talk," or a man with a forked tongue; "friend" by the two forefingers raised together, symbolizing brothers growing up in each other's company.

The International Boy Scout movement, with a courage based on ideological conviction, resolutely adopted the Indian sign language and proceeded to develop a science of pasimology, or gestures, which serves the Jamborees in perfect fashion. Representatives of as many as thirty-seven different nations have met at various times and carried on both general business and private conversations in pasimology. The use of Indian sign language for international purposes has repeatedly been advocated. Sir Richard Paget and the American Tourist Association, in recent times, have both advanced the possibility of "handage" to replace language.

The gesture-language idea was carried on by teachers interested in the training of deaf-mutes. Here, however, we have a secondary ramification. Some deaf-mute language systems express gesturally and by means of facial expressions only ideas and states of mind, in which case they can be internationally used. Others spell out words, which means that a particular language is called into play, whereupon the gestural system becomes a mere auxiliary of the spoken tongue. Still other systems combine both approaches. A fourth approach is that of lip reading and the consequent reproduction of audible speech by the "deaf oralists," but this, of course, is merely a phase of the spoken language.

It is interesting that the American Indians should have contributed to the world's civilization their own particular form of pasimology, used for the avowed purpose of avoiding international language difficulties. Their systematic reduction of meaning to gestures, however, has less developed counterparts in other portions of the world. It has been noted by students of pasimology that many gestural forms are universal. For example, the gestures describing a beard, a headdress, and a cupped hand raised to the mouth denote respectively a man, a woman, and water in Armenia, Russia, among the Australian Bushmen, and among the deaf, while American Indian signs for "child," "man," "no," "tear," and "night" have been traced in Egyptian, Chinese, and Mayan symbols on monuments, representing the same ideas. Both ancient Egyptian and ancient Chinese monuments represent "no" by a pair of outstretched arms or hands.

Gesticulation used as an aid to the spoken language is universal, but to different degrees and with different symbolisms. Southern Europeans use many more gestures than the inhabitants of northern Europe. There is a story that King Ferdinand of Naples, coming back to the city after the 1821 revolt, tried to address the crowd from the balcony of the royal palace but found it impossible to make himself heard above the shouting of the multitude, whereupon he lapsed into a gestural harangue, in which he gave a silent but eloquent series of reproaches, threats, admonishments, and pardons, thus winning over a mob to which those gestures were a part of daily life.

Differences in gestural symbolism are often striking. To the ancient Greeks, a downward nod of the head meant "yes," an upward nod "no." The modern Neapolitans express "no" by an upward jerk of the head, coupled with the sticking out of the lower lip. Americans usually wave good-by with the palm of the hand down, but many Europeans give the same wave with the palm of the hand up and the fingers moving back and forth, which gives their signal a come-hither look. An Italian downward motion of the forearm, with the extended fingers sweeping down past the chin, which they barely touch, means "nothing doing!," while a wave of the forearm, with the fingers and thumb cupped close together and coming to a point, means, "What is it all about?" Wolf whistles and clucks to express admiration of feminine charms give way, in many parts of the world, to visual gestures, such as pressing the forefinger into the cheek, or even both forefingers into both cheeks, while at the same time rolling the eyes. South Americans will often open one eye wide with thumb and forefinger; a word translation of this gesture would probably run: "My, but you're an eyeful!"

Among ancient gestures that have given rise to language clichés is the *pollice verso* ("thumbs down," in our parlance, but the thumb was actually turned up) of the ancient Romans, which meant death to the gladiator who had been overcome. The Romans' expression for "to applaud" was *pollicem premere* ("to press the thumb"), but actually they displayed their approval by clapping, snapping their fingers, and waving the flaps of their togas.

A few special gestures have interesting historical origins. Our military salute goes back to medieval times, when knights raised the visors of their helmets on meeting so they could recognize one another. The Fascist salute, with extended arm and outstretched hand, goes back to the days of ancient Rome; its significance was in origin a peaceful one, indicating that there was no concealed weapon, and the

American Indians used a very similar greeting. The clenched fist of the Communists arose in opposition to the Fascist salute.

Gesticulation used for a specific, even professional, purpose is an ancient phenomenon. In the traditional dancing language of Japan, China, Korea, Indo-China, and Indonesia there is a series of conventionalized gestures which serve to convey both the narrative and the emotional states that are to be symbolized. Among the latter, there are said to be some two hundred symbols to express various phases of love. The flirt language of the fan, widely used by lovers in past centuries, conveyed very complicated messages.

The casino croupiers of Monte Carlo also have developed a complete system of sign language. Finger tips touching the table mean, "There's a chiseler here"; a finger behind the ear is a distress call for the head man; the finger of one hand touching the thumb of the other means, "O.K.; let him play"; crossed index and third finger is "please take over"; palm and fingers extended downward means, "They are cleaned out."

In all these phases of gesturing, however, previous understanding achieved by linguistic means is implicit. The same may be said of scientific and semiscientific systems of communication such as semaphores, flags, cable codes, and the universal weather-reporting code, intelligible in all parts of the world, devised by the meteorological division of International Civilian Aviation and based upon the use of groups of five figures.

To the question why did gestural language not become generalized in the place of spoken language, a fairly satisfactory, though somewhat mechanistic, answer was given by Darwin. Gestural language requires use of the hands, while the spoken language leaves the hands free for other tasks; gestural language requires light and unobstructed view, while the spoken language can operate in the dark and around obstacles. On the other hand, the international advantages of gestural language are more apparent than real, since spoken language could, if desired, be made equally international, while gestural language, as has been seen, is not necessarily international in scope. Even the greater expressiveness and emotional release of gestural language is largely hypothetical, in view of what can be and is achieved along these lines by the spoken tongues.

In sum, systems of communication not based on speech, while extremely useful on specific occasions, are generally inferior to the spoken tongue as meaning conveyors. The one great exception to this general statement is writing, which by sublimating and multiplying symbolical values has succeeded in implanting itself by the side of the spoken tongue, of which it is a substitute and an auxiliary, to the point where some prefer it and consider it an instrument of transfer superior to its oral counterpart.

— Chapter Two —

THEORIES OF LANGUAGE ORIGIN

God, that all-powerful Creator of nature and architect, of the world, has impressed man with no character so proper to distinguish him from other animals, as by the faculty of speech.

—Quintilian

Language,—human language,—after all, is but little better than the croak and cackle of fowls, and other utterances of brute nature,—sometimes not so adequate.

—Hawthorne

IF there is one thing on which all linguists are fully agreed, it is that the problem of the origin of human speech is still unsolved.

Theories have not been wanting. Some are traditional and mystical, like the legends current among many primitive groups that language was a gift from the gods. Even as late as the seventeenth century, a Swedish philologist seriously maintained that in the Garden of Eden God spoke Swedish, Adam Danish, and the serpent French, while at a Turkish linguistic congress held in 1934 it was as seriously argued that Turkish is at the root of all languages, all words being derived from *güneş*, the Turkish word for "sun," the first object to strike the human fancy and demand a name.

Other theories may be described as quasi-scientific. One hypothesis, originally sponsored by Darwin, is to the effect that speech was in origin nothing but mouth pantomime, in which the vocal organs unconsciously attempted to mimic gestures by the hands.

Several theories are current among linguists today, but with the distinct understanding that they are as yet unproved and, in the nature of things, probably unprovable. They have been given picturesque names, which proves that linguists, too, can be imaginative on occasion.

The "bow-wow" theory holds that language arose in imitation of the sounds occurring in nature. A dog barks; his bark sounds like "bow-wow" to a human hearer. Therefore he designates the dog as "bow-wow." The trouble with this theory is that the same natural noise is, apparently, differently heard by different people. What is "cock-a-doodle-doo" to an Englishman is *cocorico* to a Frenchman and *chicchirichì* to an Italian.

The "ding-dong" theory maintains that there is a mystic correlation between sound and meaning. Like everything mystical, it is best discarded in a serious scientific discussion.

The "pooh-pooh" theory is to the effect that language at first consisted of ejaculations of surprise, fear, pleasure, pain, etc. It is often paired with the "yo-he-ho" theory to the effect that language arose from grunts of physical exertion, and even with the "sing-song" theory, that language arose from primitive inarticulate chants.

The "ta-ta" theory that language comes from imitation of bodily movements is further exemplified in the Darwinian belief described above.

The ancient Greek philosophers, who gave some attention to the problem of the origin of language, allowed themselves to be led afield by their speculative leanings. Pythagoras, Plato, and the Stoics held that language had come into being out of "inherent necessity" or "nature," which is begging the question, while Democritus, Aristotle, and the Epicureans believed it had arisen by "convention" or "agreement." How this agreement had been reached by people who had no previous means of mutual understanding they did not trouble to explain.

Leibnitz, at the dawn of the eighteenth century, first advanced the theory that all languages come not from a historically recorded source but from a protospeech. In some respects he was a precursor of the Italian twentieth-century linguist Trombetti, who boldly asserted that the Biblical account of the Tower of Babel is at least figuratively true, and that all languages have a common origin. A contemporary linguist, E. H. Sturtevant, presents a novel theory which, though slightly paradoxical, has its merits. Since all real intentions and emotions, he says, get themselves involuntarily expressed by gesture, look, or sound, voluntary communication, such as language, must have been invented for the purpose of lying or deceiving. People forced to listen to diplomatic jargon and political double talk will be tempted to agree.

On at least three recorded occasions, attempts were made to isolate children before they began talking to see whether they would evolve a language of their own. One such attempt was made by the Egyptian king Psammetichos, the second by Frederick II of Sicily about 1200, the third by King James IV of Scotland around 1500. These attempts, lacking scientific controls, proved inconclusive. More recent cases of children who had allegedly grown up among wolves, dogs, monkeys, or gazelles have added little to our knowledge, save that the human child, though ignorant of human language when found, takes to it readily and with seeming pleasure, something that his animal playmates are incapable of doing.

Animal cries, whether we choose to describe them as language or not, are characterized by invariability and monotony. Dogs have been barking, cats meowing, lions roaring, and donkeys braying in the same fashion since time immemorial. The ancient Greek comic poets indicated a sheep's cry by Greek letters having the value of "beh"; in modern Greek, those letters have changed their value to "vee." The sheep's cry has not changed in two thousand years, but the Greek language has.

Human language, in contrast with animal cries, displays infinite variability, both in time and in space. Activity and change may be described as the essence of all living language. Even so-called dead languages partake of this changeability, as evidenced by the ingenious combination devised by the Vatican to express the modern concept of "motorcycle" in Latin—birota ignifero latice incita ("two-wheeled vehicle driven by fire-bearing juice").

In one sense, the reason for the changeability of language is as mysterious as the origin of language itself. In another sense, it is crystal clear. Language is an expression of human activity, and, as human activity is forever changing, language changes with it. It seems at least partly established that language changes least rapidly when its speakers are isolated from other communities, most rapidly when they find themselves, so to speak, at the crossroads of the world. Among the Romance languages, a tongue like Sardinian, comparatively sheltered from the rest of the world, has changed little from the original Latin, while French, exposed to all inroads, invasions, and crosscurrents from the rest of Europe, has diverged the most. Arabic, long confined to the relative isolation of the Arabian peninsula, preserves the original

Semitic structure far better than Hebrew, located in much-visited Palestine.

Many linguists hold that agricultural and sedentary pursuits tend to give stability to language, warlike and nomadic life to hasten its change. Lithuanian, the tongue of a population of peaceful farmers, has changed little during the last two thousand years, while Scandinavian evolved very rapidly during the Viking era. An influence exerted on language by climate has often been claimed but never fully substantiated.

Whether much or little, all languages change in due course of time. A modern English speaker encounters some difficulty with the English of Shakespeare, far more with the English of Chaucer, and has to handle the English of King Alfred as a foreign tongue. A French speaker finds the fifteenth-century language of François Villon a little difficult, has considerable trouble with the eleventh-century *Chanson de Roland,* barely recognizes the tongue of the ninth-century Oaths of Strasbourg, and if he goes further back has to view the documents he finds from the Latin rather than from the French standpoint; yet there was never a break in the continuity of the spoken tongue of France or its speakers.

Two main theories have been advanced concerning the breaking up of an original tongue into separate languages or dialects, and here again there is evidence of secret imaginative, even poetic, leanings on the part of supposedly unemotional linguistic scientists. One is the "tree-stem" theory, whereby the parent language is supposed to act as a tree trunk, while new languages are branches or offshoots. The other is the "wave" theory, in accordance with which new languages and dialects arise and spread like ripples when you throw a stone into the water.

Two different modes of change in language sounds are recognized: the change may arise very gradually, almost imperceptibly, and be as gradually and unconsciously adopted by the speakers; or it may arise suddenly, as the result of an innovation made by one speaker who has prestige in the community and is therefore widely imitated.

It is estimated by scientists that some tens of thousands of years elapsed between the beginning of society and art (and, probably, speech) and the first appearance of writing. During these long centuries language continued to evolve, but we unfortunately have no record of that evolution. Linguistic records properly described as such are almost exclusively in writing. The oldest such records at our disposal are those of

Sumerian, a language spoken in the Mesopotamian valley between about 4000 B.C. and 300 B.C., when it became extinct. The affiliations of Sumerian are undetermined, but it seems unrelated to the Semitic Akkadian spoken by the Babylonians and Assyrians, who invaded the Sumerian territory about 3000 B.C.

Sumerian and Akkadian lived side by side for a long period. Almost contemporaneous with Akkadian are written records of ancient Egypt and China, both of which go back to almost 2000 B.C.

After this beginning, language records come thick and fast. Many languages of antiquity have disappeared, leaving few and scanty remains. Etruscan, Cretan, Iberian, and Gaulish, to cite a few better-known examples, are among the fallen. Other languages, like those of the North American Indians, are similarly disappearing today. For some dead languages our only records are a few inscriptions on coins or tombstones, or names of people, rivers, and mountains that have come down to us, like the Delaware Indian "Manhattan" and the Iroquois "Adirondack," which survive their originators. Hesychius, a Greek lexicographer of the fifth century A.D., cites words from many ancient languages, including Egyptian, Akkadian, Galatian, Lydian, Phrygian, Phoenician, Scythian, and Parthian. It is a favorite pastime among comparative linguists to reconstruct extinct languages from a few words or inscriptions, in much the same fashion that paleontologists reconstruct extinct animals from a few fossil bones.

No document of the original parent language of our western tongues, Indo-European, has ever been found or is likely to be found, since the language probably broke up into separate Indo-European languages before the invention of writing. By a comparison of the known daughter tongues, however, linguists are able to present a hypothetical but quite plausible facsimile of this unknown tongue.

The oldest languages of our Indo-European family of which we have records are Sanskrit, Greek, and Latin, in the order given. The approximate dates for each are 2000, 1400, and 500 B.C. The original homeland of the Indo-European speakers is unknown, but the Iranian plateau and the shores of the Baltic are the places most favored. From a study of words common to all the Indo-European languages, it can be argued that the original Indo-Europeans knew snow, the birch, willow, and pine, the horse, bear, hare, and wolf, copper and iron. This would place them in the Copper-Stone Age, about 2500 B.C.

The oldest Sanskrit records are the Vedic hymns, a series of religious poems. The Homeric poems, *Iliad* and *Odyssey*, mark the undisputed beginning of Classical Greek, while for Latin we have a series of inscriptions, the oldest of which, *c.* 500 B.C., appearing on a belt buckle from the city of Praeneste, reads: *Manios med fhefhaked Numasioi* ("Manius made me for Nummerius").

Among all the world's languages, Greek and the Latin-Romance group are the ones of which we have the most complete unbroken history. Latin records run from *c.* 500 B.C. to the end of the Roman Empire and beyond, merging with nascent French in A.D. 842 and with nascent Spanish and Italian in 950 and 960, respectively. Greek, starting with the *c.* 1400 B.C. Linear B of the Minoan inscriptions, goes on through the Homeric poems (*c.* 800 B.C.) and Classical and Byzantine Greek to the present-day modern Greek.

Anglo-Saxon and Old English are synonymous terms. The Anglo-Saxon period lasted until the middle of the twelfth century, when the Middle English period began. Modern English begins about 1400. Approximately the same periods apply to Old, Middle, and Modern German. It is perhaps of interest to note that, as late as the sixteenth century, English, today the tongue of nearly 300 million people, had less than five million speakers, being surpassed in point of numbers by German, French, Spanish, and Italian.

Words in our modern languages that can be traced directly back to the pre-Classical tongues of antiquity are relatively few. Our "wine" comes from the Latin *vinum* which Latin seems to have borrowed previously from Etruscan or some earlier Mediterranean language; the word *vinum* appears frequently in Etruscan inscriptions. "Mules" for "house slippers" may go back to Sumerian, which called such slippers *mulus.* Our word "gum" comes from the Greek *kommi,* but Greek appears to have borrowed it from ancient Egyptian, where it appears in the form *qmit;* Coptic, Egyptian's closest modern descendant, has *komi.* "Cream" may have originally come from the Gaulish or Aquitanian *krama,* though some authorities ascribe its origin to Greek *chrisma.* The "eeny meeny miney mo" used in childish games goes back to numerals used by the ancient Welsh tribes, and the Indo-European word which gives rise to our "ten" is said to have been originally a compound of "two" and "hand," while "five" seems connected with "finger."

Animal call words have a long and interesting history. *Dil,* which was originally a call word for geese, became in Irish the word for "dear." "Hog," originally a pet name for a pig, which in sections of England is used for pet lambs and bullocks, gave rise in Irish to *og* ("young" or "little"). The use of "puss" or some very similar word or sound (*bis, pss,* etc.) to call a cat is common to the British Isles, Arabia, North Africa, Spain, Brittany, Italy, Scandinavia, Germany, and Holland. Such forms as *pusei* in the Tamil of southern India, *pisa* in Rumanian, *piso* in Albanian testify to the widespread use of the form.

What are the chances that modern linguists, equipped with the powerful aids of present-day science, may one day break down the veil of mystery that enshrouds the origin of language? Frankly, very slight. The mightiest searchlight cannot cast a beam on what is not there. When man first began to speak, he left no material records, as he did when he first began to write. Hence, the truly scientific study of the origin of language can properly begin only with the beginning of written-language records.

All that the scientist in the linguistic field can do in connection with the beginning of speech is to observe what is observable around him (the speech of infants, the languages of primitive groups, etc.), compare his observations with the earliest records and known historical and anthropological facts, and, basing himself upon those observations and comparisons, make surmises which will be more or less plausible, more or less complete, but never scientific in the true, full sense of the word.

The languages of primitive groups do not cast too much light upon the problem. They are, as a rule, anything but primitive, save with reference to the vocabulary of modern civilization. Linguists who explore these tongues regularly find in them refinements of distinctions and complexities unknown to our own languages, even though circumscribed by the primitive group's experience and environment.

As for the speech of infants, observers are still unable to agree. Professor William Entwistle, for example, claims that the infant becomes conscious of the sound of the human voice after twelve weeks, starts prattling more language sounds than he will ever use after sixteen, and after thirty-two begins to form syllables, regularly with *m, p, b,* or *n, t, d* followed by a vowel sound, with the result that a labial or dental regularly gets into the baby's designation for his two parents. This accounts for the fact that *ma* has the same meaning in English, Chinese, and Quichua, while Arabic has *umm*, and that "father" or "dad" have counterparts in Gothic *atta*, Latin and Greek *pater*, Gaulish *tatula*, Welsh *tad*, Russian *otyets*, Italian dialectal *tata*, as well as Quichua *tayta*, Chinese *fu* (from an earlier *b'iu*), Arabic *abu*, Swahili *baba*. The preference in consonants is occasionally interchanged, as where Georgian has *mama* for "father" and *deda* for "mother," or Russian *baba* for "old woman" or "grandmother" (but Russian *dyadya* for "grandfather" and *dyed* for "uncle" fall into line). Entwistle's conclusion is that the coincidence of first sounds with first things noted has given rise to the idea of a natural connection between the word and its meaning.

Professor Orvis Irwin, of the Iowa Child Welfare Research Station, gives an altogether different account: the child starts with only eight language sounds, of which five are vocalic, while the only consonants are *h, l,* and the glottal stop; and it is only at the end of his first year that the child starts using *mama* and *dada*. The child's recognition vocabulary runs from three words at the end of his first year to over two hundred at the end of his second, at which point, however, he is still unable to form one third of the phonemes used by his language group. Whichever view we choose to accept (and there are many others), this is far from solving the problem of the origin of speech, save for what concerns the baby's obvious imitation of language sounds.

But what about the process of association of sounds and sound sequences with ideas and concepts, which seems basic to human language? Some mechanically inclined scientists claim that the development of the human being's relatively larger brain was a necessary prerequisite for the rise of language, but this is somewhat like the question of the priority of the chicken or the egg. Could not the larger brain have developed in consequence of the rise of language, and the impressive possibilities language afforded of putting the brain to good use?

If all that is needed for language is a process of imitation, why are apes, who imitate humans so well in other respects, inferior to birds, who imitate us only in respect to language? Why do cats and dogs, who have been living with us and observing us for many centuries, fail to imitate our language when we imitate theirs so well?

— Chapter Three —

THE FAMILY RELATIONSHIPS
OF LANGUAGE

. . . Philologists, who chase
A panting syllable through time and space,
Start it at home, and hunt it in the dark,
To Gaul, to Greece, and into Noah's Ark.
          —Cowper, *Retirement*

THE world's languages have been, in their majority, very imperfectly studied and classified. Far too little is yet known about the structure and affiliations of the tongues of the American Indians, the African Negroes, the natives of Australia and New Guinea, and a large number of the tongues spoken by Asia's teeming millions.

The languages of Europe, the Mediterranean basin, and the Near East, being the most readily accessible as well as the ones of which we have the longest unbroken records, have been definitely and satisfactorily assigned to groups and families, on the basis of certain definite resemblances.

It has long been the dream of certain linguists to trace all languages back to a common source. Attempts to do this have so far proved largely fruitless. The variability of language in the course of time is such that in the absence of definite historical records of what a language was like five thousand, one thousand, or even three hundred years ago, classification becomes extremely difficult.

A fundamental unity, indicating a common ancestry, underlies such diverse tongues as English, Russian, Irish, Spanish, Greek, Albanian, Armenian, Persian, and Hindustani. Another separate and distinct unity definitely appears for such tongues as Arabic, Hebrew, the Amharic of Ethiopia, and the ancient tongues of Babylonia, Assyria, Phoenicia, and Carthage. Finnish, Hungarian, Turkish, and most of the languages of Asiatic Russia are grouped together in a third

unit; but while all linguists admit the kinship of Finnish and Hungarian, some doubt their relationship to Turkish. Other similar groupings cover the tongues of southeastern Asia, including Chinese, Burmese, Thai, and Tibetan; the Dravidian languages of southern India; the Malayo-Polynesian tongues of the far-flung Pacific. Japanese stands in a class by itself, unless we accept its doubtful link with Korean; so does Basque; so does a group of languages spoken in the Caucasus, of which Stalin's Georgian is one. Such terms as "African Negro languages," "American Indian languages," "native Australian languages" represent geographical rather than linguistic concepts. There are within those groups separate language characteristics apparently as distinct as those differentiating English from Arabic or Turkish from Chinese.

Indo-European is the name given to the family of languages to which English belongs. The name is based on the fact that this family covers most of Europe and extends eastward as far as northern India, with a total body of speakers of nearly one and a half billion. Indo-Germanic is a synonymous term preferred by German linguists, based (outside of reasons of national pride) on the fact that it includes the easternmost and westernmost members of the family.

In most Indo-European languages, the numerals from one to ten and the words of close family relationship (father, mother, sister, brother, etc.), as well as a number of other fundamental words, are recognizable as coming from the same roots. "Brother," for example, is easily discernible in the German *Bruder,* less easily distinguishable in the Irish *bhrathair,* the Latin *frater,* the Greek *phrater,* the Russian *brat,* the Sanskrit *bhrātā,* the Persian *birādar.*

As far back as the sixteenth century, an Italian writer, Filippo Sassetti, who visited India commented on the fact that there were startling resemblances between Sanskrit and Italian. "Six," "seven," "eight," "nine," "god," "snake" are in Italian *sei, sette, otto, nove, dio, serpe,* in Sanskrit *sas, sapta, astau, nava, deva, sarpa.* Much earlier, in the first century B.C., a Roman grammarian, Marcus Terentius Varro, had noticed the similarities between Greek and Latin but had come to the erroneous conclusion that Greek was the mother language, Latin the daughter tongue. Noah Webster, of dictionary fame, believed "Chaldee" to be the original universal language, but he also noticed the kinship between Greek, Latin, and the Germanic languages before it was generally recognized. It remained for Bopp and the Grimm brothers, at the beginning of the nineteenth century, to create the com-

parative method by which the exact nature of the relationship among the Indo-European languages was definitely ascertained.

Within the great Indo-European family (which, incidentally, includes about half of the world's population) there are subgroups, some of several hundred million speakers, like the Germanic, Romance, Slavic, and Indo-Iranian; others like the Celtic, Greek, Albanian, and Armenian, which are quite small.

The justification for these subgroups is obvious. Languages like French, Spanish, and Italian, stemming directly, in historical times, from one common ancestor, Latin, show closer resemblances to one another than to related but more distant Indo-European tongues like Hindustani, German, or Welsh.

It is supposed that in prehistoric times, before writing appeared, the speakers of the original Indo-European parent language formed one closely knit group and that, by successive waves of migration, bodies of speakers detached themselves from the original homeland and the other groups, losing contact with them and allowing their speech to turn into a dialect of the original, still recognizable as coming from one source but becoming more and more different as time wore on, to the point where it would not occur to the man in the Moscow or New York street to imagine that the Russian of the one and the English of the other were once the same tongue. The modern language which is supposed to be closest to the original parent Indo-European speech is Lithuanian, the tongue of about three million people on the shores of the Baltic.

English belongs to the Germanic branch of Indo-European, though with qualifications. The Anglo-Saxon that forms the backbone of our tongue, particularly in its spoken, everyday aspects, was once very close to the Low German dialects of the Dutch and German North Sea coastal areas. But as a result of the Norman conquest of England in 1066, the English language acquired such an extensive body of French and Latin words and grammatical forms that present-day English is best described as a fundamentally Germanic tongue with an imposing Romance superstructure.

The national language that is the closest relative of English is Dutch, with its Belgian variant, Flemish, and its South African variant, Afrikaans. Next comes standard German, while the Scandinavian languages are slightly more remote. Frisian, a variant of Dutch spoken along the Dutch and German North Sea coast, is the foreign speech that comes closest to modern English, as shown by the rhyme:

"Good butter and good cheese is good English and good Fries." Icelandic, a Scandinavian tongue with less than two hundred thousand speakers which has undergone very little change since its inception as a branch of old Norse, carried by Viking explorers to the land of the geysers, is the modern tongue that most resembles our ancestral Anglo-Saxon as spoken in the days of King Alfred and Canute.

Since English, German, Scandinavian, and Frisian can be traced back uninterruptedly to the seventh or eighth century, and since the farther back we go the closer these languages come together in structure and vocabulary, it is not unreasonable to suppose that there was a primitive Germanic tongue which had broken up into our known languages not too long before the appearance of the latter. This primitive Germanic, in turn, had broken away from the parent Indo-European stock an undetermined number of centuries previously.

The Romance tongues are so called because they stem directly from Latin, the language of the Romans. They include French, Spanish, Portuguese, Italian, and Rumanian, along with nonnational tongues like Provençal, Catalan, Sardinian, and the Romansh of Switzerland. Latin had at least two ancient relatives, Oscan and Umbrian, which formed with it the Italic branch of Indo-European; but Oscan and Umbrian were swallowed up in the course of Roman expansion. The Logudorese spoken in central Sardinia today is by far the closest to ancient Latin of the Romance languages, though this honor is often erroneously claimed by Rumanian and Romansh. "Romania" was a term devised in the fifth century to describe those parts of the former Roman Empire where Latin had become and continued to be the popular spoken tongue. The Rumanians, who had been separated from their Latin-speaking brothers of the west by the Slavic invasion of the Balkans, retained the name and appropriated it for their exclusive use. Rumanian is indeed the descendant of the Latin brought by Trajan's legionaries to Dacia, around A.D. 100, but is differentiated from the western Romance languages by abundant infiltrations of Slavic, Hungarian, Turkish, and Greek words and constructions, which give it a distinctive flavor.

The Slavic tongues show perhaps closer connections among themselves than most of the other Indo-European branches. An Italian and a Spaniard, or a Spaniard and a Portuguese, each speaking his own tongue, will understand each other with difficulty. None will understand a Frenchman or a Rumanian without special study. A German, a Hollander, an

Englishman, and a Swede will be unable to carry on intel-
ligibly if each insists on using his own tongue. But a Russian,
a Pole, a Czech, and a Yugoslav can manage to achieve a
fair degree of understanding.

The Slavic languages are sometimes grouped with the Baltic
tongues (Lithuanian and Lettish) to form a Balto-Slavic group,
but while Lithuanian and Lettish are fairly close to each
other, they are comparatively remote from the Slav tongues.

The Celtic languages are divided into two branches:
Goidelic, including Irish, Scots Gaelic, and Manx; and Brythonic, composed of Welsh, Breton, and Cornish. A third
Celtic branch was Gaulish, once spoken extensively on the
European continent and even in Asia Minor (St. Jerome, in
the fourth century, remarked that the Galatians speak like the
Gauls). Such names as Galicia, appearing in Spain and in Poland, bear witness to Gaulish wanderings. But today Gaulish
has become extinct, while its smaller brothers live on.

Greek, Armenian, and Albanian form separate small
branches of Indo-European, with approximately ten, two, and
one and a half million speakers, respectively.

The easternmost member of the Indo-European family is
Indo-Iranian, which comprises the Persian of Iran, the Pashto
of Afghanistan, and a host of languages and dialects of
northern and central India, from ancient Sanskrit through
the medieval Prakrits and Pali, to the modern Hindustani,
Bengali, Oriya, Rajasthani, Punjabi, Marathi, and many others.
Between three and four hundred million people speak
Indo-Iranian languages today.

Equal in historical importance, though not in numbers, with
Indo-European is the Semito-Hamitic family of North Africa
and the Near East. Most widespread among the modern
Semitic tongues is Arabic, most influential upon the history
of civilization is Hebrew. The Hamitic branch includes,
among others, the ancient Egyptian of the hieroglyphic inscriptions, the medieval Coptic that issued from it, the
Berber tongues that are intermingled with Arabic in North
Africa, and the Cushitic tongues of Ethiopia.

Ural-Altaic includes such tongues as Finnish, Estonian,
Hungarian, and Samoyed, in its Uralic branch; Turkish,
Mongol, Tungus, and Manchu in its Altaic branch.

The Sino-Tibetan languages of southeastern Asia (Chinese,
Thai, Burmese, Tibetan) enjoy the distinction of having the
world's second largest body of speakers, well over six
hundred million, being surpassed in numbers only by Indo-
European.

Japanese and Korean; the Caucasian languages; the Dravidian tongues of southern India; the Malayo-Polynesian tongues of the Pacific are separately classified, while for the tongues of the African Negroes, the North and South American Indians, and the natives of Australia and Papua classification is difficult and incomplete.

Of picturesque interest are many small language groups that have no apparent affiliation. The Ainu of the Japanese island of Yezo, spoken by a white-skinned race of perhaps twenty thousand, shows a mysterious, though probably chance, affinity to the Celtic languages, Danish, and French in saying "four-twenties" for "eighty"; it may be related to some dying tongues of eastern Siberia. Basque, a mysterious tongue spoken by about one million people in northeastern Spain and southwestern France, is said to be the descendant of ancient Iberian, the language of Spain before the coming of the Indo-Europeans. Attempts have been made to link it with Berber and ancient Egyptian, with certain African Negro languages, with the tongues of the Caucasus, even with the Iroquois of North America, but with little success. The ancient Etruscan of central Italy has left us some nine thousand inscriptions, some quite lengthy, but no satisfactory interpretation of them has been achieved.

Is there a possibility that our present classification of languages will be improved? More light is being shed upon language affiliations all the time, as more material is discovered. It is even possible that one day the dream of some linguists will come true, and all languages be proved to have a common origin.

— Chapter Four —

THE EVOLUTION OF LANGUAGE

Stability in language is synonymous with rigor mortis.
— Ernest Weekley

We ain't what we want to be, and we ain't what we're goin' to be, but we ain't what we wuz.
— South Carolina mountain proverb

MANY years ago, I was requested to tutor in French a young girl who had to take College Entrance Examinations. Knowing that she had had four years of Latin as well as three years of French, I spared no occasion in the course of the tutoring to remind her that certain French words which she had difficulty in remembering came from Latin words which she knew. For a time she took it patiently, though with a somewhat bewildered air. But one day she finally blurted out: "Do you mean to tell me that there is a *connection* between Latin and French?" In the course of four years of one language and three of the other, it had never occurred to any of her Latin teachers to inform her that Latin had descendants, or to her French teachers to tell her that French had a progenitor!

This episode is not meant, at least at this point, to be a reflection upon some of our language-teaching methods. It simply illustrates certain widespread areas of ignorance in our general linguistic knowledge and at the same time serves as an example of how languages evolve.

Languages change as human beings do, but the changes are spread over periods of centuries instead of years. Save at special times, the change is all but imperceptible to the speakers. As you look in the mirror each morning you are not aware of having changed from the day before. Yet the times comes when you are no longer a child, but a man; no longer a young man, but a middle-aged, then an elderly, man. Yes, languages die, too, like individuals. They may decompose into fine dust or a heap of bones from which it is difficult to reconstruct the image of the living organism that once was there. They may be embalmed and preserved for posterity, changeless and static, lifelike in appearance but unendowed with the breath of life. While they live, however, they change.

The language stream of which we have by far the most complete, unbroken record is the Latin-Romance. From the fifth century B.C. until today this stream unfolds before our eyes like a majestic river whose course can be explored from the source to a point beyond which nothing can be explored, because the future is inscrutable. If it is our purpose to follow the evolution of language, it will be far better served by following this stream than any other. Yet, as we do so, we shall have the assurance that save for matters of historical detail we are following the stream of language in general. Differences in linguistic history are of degree and detail, not of kind.

Latin issues from the subsoil as a tiny rivulet about 500 B.C. Its prehistory is unknown because of the lack of written records before that time, but we can assume that a group of Indo-European speakers, striking southward and westward from their original homeland and making changes in their language as they went, finally found their way across the Alps into the Italian peninsula, where they found people of different racial and linguistic stock. When Latin first appeared, it was the tongue of a small body of speakers settled around the mouth of the Tiber River in west central Italy. To the south and east of them were close relatives: Faliscans, speaking a kindred tongue; Sabines and Sabellians, who spoke Oscan, a language of the same Italic subdivision of Indo-European as Latin, but already strongly differentiated. Another group of Italic-speaking people, the Umbrians, had settled to the northeast, while the immediate northern neighbors of the Latins were the non-Italic, non-Indo-European Etruscans, a powerful, mysterious race whose untranslated records appear throughout northern Italy, in isolated localities of the south, and even in some of the remote islands of the eastern Mediterranean. The valley of the Po in the extreme north of Italy was held by Celtic-speaking Gauls; the cities of southern Italy and western Sicily were for the most part Greek settlements. In both north and south we have traces of other prehistoric races, speaking vanished languages (Ligurian, Rhaetic, Venetic, Messapian, Sicel) of which only a few fragmentary and undecipherable inscriptions have come down to us.

The history of the Latin speakers and their language was from the first a record of bitter struggle for survival; against the Etruscans, who at one time conquered Rome and established their own dynasty of Tarquinian kings, later expelled by the popular movement that set up the Roman Republic; against the Gauls, who swept down to the very gates of Rome on repeated occasions; against Rome's own Sabine and Sabellian kinsmen. By the middle of the third century B.C. Rome had established her hegemony over the Italian mainland. The Etruscans were subjugated, the Gauls driven back to the foothills of the Alps, the Umbrians, Oscans, and Greeks of central and southern Italy absorbed or turned into allies, and Rome was ready to embark upon a career of overseas conquest and to grapple with Carthage, the great seafaring power of the Mediterranean.

The Latin language as it first emerged in the fifth century B.C. was a rough, elemental tongue, indicative of a military-agricultural civilization, lacking most of the refinements of syntax and vocabulary which were later to distinguish it, yet endowed with all the morphological complexities of typical Indo-European structure. It was a language of case endings and verbal terminations, making scant use of prepositions or fixed word order. From the standpoint of sounds, the archaic Latin language does not seem to have differed greatly from its later Classical counterpart: vowel sounds were distinguished by long and short quantity, and a good many diphthongs appeared which the later language turned to simple long vowels (*deicō*, "I say," for instance, later became *dīcō*, and *oinos*, "one," became *ūnus*). Consonant sounds displayed the same lack of certain groups which appears in later Classical Latin: the sounds represented in English by *ch* of "church," *sh* of "she," *j* of "joke," *s* of "pleasure," *th* of "thing" or "this," *li* of "million," *ni* of "onion," were absent from the Latin sound scheme.

Fair samples of this early Latin language are the fifth century B.C. inscription on the belt buckle found near Praeneste (*Manios med fhefhaked Numasioi*, "Manius made me for Nummerius," for which the Classical Latin equivalent would be *Manius me fecit Nummerio*), and the third century B.C. inscription appearing on the tomb of Scipio (*honc oino ploirume cosentiont Romai duonoro optumo fuise virom Luciom Scipione*, "The majority in Rome agree that this one man, Lucius Scipio, was the best of the good"; the Classical equivalent would be *Hunc unum plurimi consentiunt Romae bonorum optimum fuisse virum Lucium Scipionem*).

Rome's victorious series of wars against Carthage served on the one hand to carry Latin to such distant lands as Sicily, Sardinia, Spain, and North Africa, on the other to bring Latin in closer contact with the more polished Greek of the southern Italian and Sicilian cities. These Greek contacts were shortly expanded by the conquest of Greece itself, as well as Asia Minor and the Balkans. At this point, Latin begins to take on its Classical aspect. Unwieldy sounds are discarded, the morphological structure is regularized, syntax assumes a more sonorous and rhythmical outline, and Greek loan words dealing with all phases of more graceful living, like *hora* ("hour"), *theatrum* ("theater"), *machina* ("machine"), *cathedra* ("seat"), *schola* ("school"), *thesaurus* ("treasure"), begin to pour in, mingling with an older, earthier layer of foreign borrowings from Etruscan and Oscan which had included such forms as the words for "wine" (*vinum*), "ox" (*bos*), and "wolf" (*lupus*).

Classical Latin finally emerges in all its brilliancy about 100 B.C. and holds undisputed sway for three hundred years and more. This is the language of Caesar, Cicero, and Virgil, a smooth, polished tongue, capable of expressing the most complex notions, the loftiest of poetic and philosophical thought, the keenest of legal and juridical expression. Remembering that the language of poetry and oratory exemplified by Virgil and Cicero is always to some degree artificial, we may nevertheless accept Caesar's military communiqués as typical of the cultured language of the period:

Gallia est omnis divisa in partes tres, quarum unam incolunt Belgae, aliam Aquitani, tertiam, qui ipsorum lingua Celtae, nostra Galli appellantur. ("All Gaul is divided into three parts, one of which the Belgians inhabit, another the Aquitanians, the third those who in their own tongue are called Celts, in ours Gauls.")

This language of Classical Rome still reveals an overwhelming predominance of ancient Indo-European features. Vowel quantity persists; so does the relative paucity of consonant sounds. The grammatical structure hinges almost completely on inflectional endings that indicate gender, number, case, person, tense, mood, and voice. The syntax has become supple and graceful, with involved constructions partly imitated from the Greek, partly developed by the Romans themselves. The vocabulary is greatly expanded, by means of word formation, word coinage, and word borrowing, to the point where it satisfies all the requirements of a highly complex civilization.

Some linguists claim that this Classical Latin tongue which we still learn in the schools was largely an artificial device, used merely by a literate and literary *élite* for purposes of writing, and that the language of the masses at this period had already undergone a vast amount of transformation in the direction of the modern Romance tongues. For this view there seems to be little justification. While we can readily grant that the involved subordinate clauses and choice vocabulary of the writers, particularly the poets, did not extend to the lower classes, and that a great amount of slang was bandied about which did not find its way into the literary records that have come down to us (which are, by the way, only a small fraction of the total output of those centuries), still there is little reason to suppose that the sounds and the grammatical forms which constitute the real backbone of a language diverged noticeably from the Classical standard. People who think the Latin cases and verb forms were too difficult for the Roman gladiators and slaves forget that similar linguistic complexities appeared until recently in the mouths of illiterate Russian and Lithuanian peasants who, having learned them from childhood in given contexts rather than out of grammar books, experienced no apparent difficulty with them. There has come down to us a marching song of Caesar's legionaries, of which a few lines are given for purposes of comparison:

> *Ecce nunc Caesar triumphat qui subegit Gallias. . . .*
> *Brutus quia reges ejecit, consul primus factus est;*
> *Hic quia consules ejecit, rex postremo factus est.*

(Behold now Caesar triumphs, who subdued the Gaulish provinces. . . . Brutus, because he threw out the kings, was made the first consul; He, because he threw out the consuls, has now been made king.)

The charge of excessive literary influence can hardly be raised in the case of a military marching song, and there is nothing in its language, particularly its morphology, to distinguish it from Caesar's own bulletins.

But new historical factors were soon to inject themselves into this picture of a seemingly stabilized, universalized tongue. First came the leveling impact of Christianity, with its emphasis on spiritual equality and the importance of the individual, imparting a new dignity to the speech habits and speech tendencies of the lower classes and breaking down Classical standards of linguistic "purity," admiration for Classical pagan models, and the refinements of Classical syntax and vocabulary at the same time that it brought into Latin a new wave of word importations: some, like *abbā* ("father," "abbot") from the Aramaic, but the majority, like *presbyter* ("elder," "priest") and *baptizein* ("to baptize") from the Greek of the New Testament and the earliest Christian writers.

The force of this impact can hardly be overstressed. The official language, hitherto kept within traditional bounds by literati and grammarians, began to throw off its aristocratic shackles and to vulgarize itself. As a tool of Christian propaganda and conversion, it had to be revised downward so as to reach masses of people in the distant provinces who had never been touched by Classical literary influences. The result was that Latin began to change, imperceptibly at first, then more and more rapidly.

The vowel quantities of the Classical language were among the first casualties. The language of the lower classes tended toward stressful, emphatic utterance, and a strong accent almost inevitably lengthens the accented vowel of a word and shortens and obscures those vowels in the word which are not accented. By the end of the fourth century A.D., written Latin had not greatly changed its appearance save in matters of elegant style and vocabulary, but spoken Latin had developed a new sound pattern, wherein stressed vowels were drawled, unstressed vowels dulled, weakened, and often dropped. Probus, a grammarian of the period, warns his readers that they should pronounce *oculus* ("eye"), not *oclus, calidus* ("warm"), not *caldus.* The drawing and mouthing of stressed vowels led to changes in the nearby consonants, and we find words having unvoiced consonants like *p, t, c* between vowels shifting these consonant sounds to their voiced counterparts, *b, d, g* (*pagare* instead of *pacare,* "to appease," "to pay"; *amadus* instead of *amatus,* "beloved"). New palatal sounds arose which had not appeared in the language previously. A word like *centum* ("hundred"), pronounced *kentum* in Caesar's times, now became *tsentu* or *chentu* in pronunciation, though the spelling did not change (even today, French, Spanish, and Italian use *c* in *cent, ciento,* and *cento,* though the first pronounces it like *s,* the second like *th,* and the third like *ch*).

Most important of all, the weakening of final vowels began to undermine the system of case endings, causing in the minds of the speakers a confusion that had to be repaired by new syntactical devices. A Roman of Caesar's day found no difficulty in distinguishing between *Petrum* ("Peter," direct object) and *Petrō* (dative case, "to Peter"). But as the final *-um* of *Petrum* and the final *-ō* of *Petrō* became indistinct, the two forms merged in sound, and confusion of meaning arose. There was only one thing to do: put the merged form immediately after the verb if it was meant to be the direct object of that verb, or use a preposition along with it if it was meant to convey the meaning of "to Peter."

With the fifth century came the great barbarian invasions and the final downfall of the Roman Empire. What part the newcomers may have played in the process of linguistic transformation they found going on is still a matter of controversy. The majority of significant sound and grammar changes were already in progress when they arrived, and they may or may not have added to them. But there is no controversy about the great contribution they brought to the vocabulary of the period. Latin, which by this time was becoming definitely a Vulgar, as distinguished from a Classical, tongue, accepted hosts of new words from the Germanic invaders. A lexicon of words and forms which do not appear in the Classical period, but are to be found in later Latin writings, consists of eight large volumes. Many of these words are artificial coinages based upon existing Latin and Greek roots, prefixes, and suffixes, but an even greater number consists of importations brought in by the barbarians. Among them we find words like *wadjo*, whose Anglo-Saxon cognate is "wed," and which gives rise to the later French *gage*, from which English still later borrows "gage" and "engage"; *wîsa*, Anglo-Saxon *wise* of "in wondrous wise," which in French later turns to *guise* and is borrowed back by English; *hatjan*, which is cognate to the English "hate" and later develops into French *haïr; marah-skalk* ("horse groom"), which later becomes the French *maréchal* and is reborrowed by Germanic English in the form "marshal," which no one thinks of associating with our native "mare"; *kausjan*, later to become the French *choisir*, whose Anglo-Saxon form was *cēosan*, from which we get "choose."

Between the fifth and the eighth centuries, the process of linguistic fermentation went on, powerfully aided by the new Germanic leaven. The language, nevertheless, continued to be Latin, a Latin farther and farther removed from Classical standards and already revealing a strong trend toward Romance. A sample of this breakdown Latin, taken from a deed of sale of the eighth century composed in Gaul, is instructive: *Constat nus at alliqua fimena nomine Nautlindo, vindemus tibi pecia de maso probrio jures meo.* ("It is stated that we are selling to you, a certain woman Nautlinde by name, a piece of farmland of my own property.")

In this passage, the Classical cases have all but disappeared. Prepositions are used which the Classical language would have dispensed with. Words that are either not Classical or not Classically used are of frequent occurrence. The state of the Latin language in these final centuries of its existence as a vernacular may be and frequently is described as Proto-Romance. In spite of this, it was still fairly unified. Little if any reference is made during the centuries preceding the ninth to any linguistic differences or difficulties in the lands that had once formed the western provinces of the Empire, Iberia, Gaul, Italy. The numerous documents that have come down from that period bear extremely few traces of the divergences that were later to arise among the various Romance languages. The natural centrifugal force of language, tending to dialectalize a unified tongue once the artificial controls of a common government and institutions, education and communications are removed, was indeed at work, but it had to fight against a deeply rooted tradition of Roman unity that had been in operation for many centuries, as well as against the more recent and perhaps even more powerful consciousness of a western Christian unity fostered by the Church, whose everyday language was the Latin it had inherited from the Empire.

The break, however, had to come. The growing feudal system, making every community economically self-sufficient, tended more and more to dissolve the traditional sense of unity, at the same time that lack of schooling and deepening ignorance caused the spoken language of each community to degenerate faster and faster from Latin standards, independently of the innovations going on in neighboring communities. Shortly after the beginning of his reign, Charlemagne urged the bishops and priests of his realm to use a more correct, grammatical language in their sermons and homilies, thereby revealing that he did not yet have a clear-cut realization of the fact that Latin was giving birth to new languages. But by 813, reversing his earlier edict, he ordered the sermons to be preached henceforth not in the *lingua latina,* but in the *lingua romana rustica,* thus acknowledging that a new language, which was no longer Latin, had been born. From this point on, the story of the spoken language of the western regions of the former Roman Empire is no longer the story of Latin but that of the Romance tongues. Yet it is the same language, proceeding in an unbroken stream that shifts its course but does not at any time cease flowing.

A first sample of the new *lingua romana rustica* announced by Charlemagne appears in 842 in the Oaths of Strasbourg, a treaty of alliance sworn by two of Charlemagne's descendants in the presence of their troops, who in their function of witnesses had to be addressed in their own spoken popular tongue. It began as follows:

Pro Deo amur et pro christian poblo et nostro commun salvament, d'ist di in avant, in quant Deus savir et podir me dunat, si salvarai eo cist meon fradre Karlo, et in aiudha et in cadhuna cosa, sicum om per dreit son fradra salvar dift. ("For the love of God and for the Christian people and our common salvation, from this day on, insofar as God grants me the knowledge and the power, so will I help this my brother Charles, both in aid and in all things, just as one by right ought to help his brother.")

In this first document of the new French language, we see on the one hand the continuation of many features of Latin, both Classical and Vulgar, on the other the emergence of new characteristics which set it apart even from the late Latin of the previous century. The six cases of Classical Latin have merged into two, a nominative-vocative distinguished by a final -*s*, the survivor of the -*us* of Classical Latin, and a genitive-dative-accusative-ablative, or oblique case, characterized by the absence of a final -*s* (the -*ī*, -*ō*, -*um* endings of the Classical cases having merged or completely fallen away). This two-case system is the predominant morphological trait of Old French, a language which continued in use from the ninth to the fourteenth century, when even these two surviving cases finally merged into the single case form of present-day French.

By way of contrast, Spanish and Italian emerged (at least in recorded written form) more than a century later, in 950 and 960 respectively. They were more conservative than French in the matter of sounds, retaining the Latin final vowels, but less conservative as to morphology, since they merged all the Latin cases into one from their very inception.

Continuing on French soil the history of the language that once was Latin, we find the Old French language coming into full bloom around the end of the ninth century and giving rise to a flourishing epic literature by the eleventh. Here is an excerpt from the first great epic poem of the Old French period, the eleventh-century *Chanson de Roland:*

Dist Oliviers: Paien ont grant esforz;
De noz Franceis mei semblet aveir poi:
Compaign Rodlanz, kar sonez vostre corn,
Si'l odrat Charles, si retornerat l'ost.

(Said Oliver: The pagans have great numbers;
Of our Frenchmen it seems to me there are few:
Comrade Roland, pray, sound your horn,
So Charles will hear it, and the army will return.)

The language of the eleventh century shows further deep-rooted transformations from that of the ninth. Accented vowels, already lengthened by the stress accent in the Vulgar Latin period, are now hammered out into diphthongs (Latin *bene*, "well," becomes *bien;* Latin *novum*, "new," becomes *nuef;* Latin *me*, "me," becomes *mei;* Latin *florem*, "flower," becomes *flour*). Latin unstressed vowels are frequently dropped, so that a word like *dormitorium* turns into *dortoir*, *duodecim* into *douze*. Consonants undergo drastic changes, *amata* becoming *amede*, then *aimée*, *ripa* turning to *rive*, *pacare* to *paiier*, then *payer*. *Sacramentum*, which was still *sagrament* in the ninth-century Oaths, becomes *sairement*, then *serment*. Structurally the language preserves a measure of Latin elasticity by reason of the retention of a double case, so that a construction like *lo pedre veit li filz* (Latin *illum patrem videt ille filius*) can still be used to mean "the son sees the father." Old French vocabulary shows resiliency, resourcefulness, and vigorous growth, along with the loss of certain segments of the old Latin lexicon. New words like *hommage* and *bachelier* are formed by grafting new and old suffixes on existing roots. Numerous Germanic and other loan words appear, many of which the language has since discarded. Semilearned words borrowed from the language of religion abound. The Old French of this period is a tongue of strong stress, harsh and full-mouthed sounds, comparatively little phonetic grace, but powerfully effective, more similar in rhythm to present-day English than to present-day French, the language of a race of hardy warriors and farmers, uncouth and unrefined but earnest and sincere even to the point of fanaticism.

Beginning with the twelfth century, however, as the differences among social classes deepen and the cultural standards of the aristocracy and bourgeoisie begin once more to rise in a civilization that had regained some measure of stability and equilibrium, a tendency becomes noticeable to abandon some of the more violent stress features, to reduce heavy diphthongs and triphthongs to monophthongs (the diphthong *ue* of *nuef,* for instance, becoming the middle rounded simple vowel now indicated by the *ue* spelling of *neuf;* the three vocalic sounds of *beau* merging into the single vowel sound of the present pronunciation), to develop lengthier and more elegant syntactical constructions as an aid to clarity and expressiveness, and ultimately to reduce the two-case system to a single case form. This process of transformation is fully completed by the fifteenth century, as indicated by a stanza from François Villon, the author who, more than any other, marks the inception of modern French:

> *Povreté tous nous suyt et trace;*
> *Sur les tumbeaulx de mes ancestres,*
> *Les ames de quelz Dieu embrasse,*
> *On n'y voyt couronnes ne sceptres.*

> (Poverty follows and tracks all of us;
> Upon the graves of my ancestors,
> Whose souls may God embrace,
> One sees neither crowns nor scepters.)

The language, having regained a measure of grace and refinement, now falls once more into the hands of a cultivated upper class, paralleling the experience of Classical Latin in the days of the late Republic and early Empire. From its foreign contacts, especially with Italian, it receives hosts of new words and new concepts. The Renaissance and Humanism begin to have their effect, and a large portion of the Latin and Greek lexicons is poured into French in the form of cultivated loan words, often without regard for the fact that they already appear in the language as popular words. *Fragile,* for instance, enters as the learned doublet of *frêle,* the historical French development of Latin *fragilis,* while the learned *monastère* drives out the popular *moustier* which French had directly inherited and developed from Latin *monasterium.* Writers conscious of the Latin origin of their language give old popular words etymological spellings which are often ridiculous, sometimes erroneous (*vingt,* for example, from Latin *viginti,* "twenty," was *vint* in Old French; the *g* was at no time pronounced; *chevaux* from Latin *caballos,* "horses" was *chevaus* in Old French; *x* replaces *s* because at one time scribes wrote a final *-s* with a long flourish, crossing the end of the preceding *u,* and this flourish was erroneously interpreted by later scribes to be an *x* and slavishly imitated).

As for the cultured influences of the centuries following the fifteenth, French may be said to share them with the other great languages of western Europe. Phonological changes since the time of Villon have been relatively few (one might mention the group *oi,* as in *roi, froid,* which was still pronounced like the *we* of *"wet,"* and the *ill* of such words as *fille,* still pronounced like the *lli* of "million" at the end of the eighteenth century). Morphologically, the structure of Villon still fundamentally holds. In the matter of syntax, the French of the seventeenth century developed a conscious, deliberate regularity and exactness which made it and still make it today one of the finest linguistic tools of precision and expressiveness in the world. The vocabulary of French has marched side by side with that of the major western tongues, acquiring the myriad terms of modern science and modern life. The standard French of today, elaborated by Vaugelas and Racine, Rousseau and Voltaire, Hugo and Chateaubriand, Gide and Camus, is, like the Latin of Horace, Livy, and Juvenal, a language of dazzling refinement and deep-rooted culture, fully capable of infinite self-expression, fully equipped to take care of all the needs of the civilization it represents and typifies.

Yet in the French of today there are underground rumblings almost, if not quite, as perceptible as the stirrings of linguistic change that must have annoyed people like Cicero in the first century B.C.

To begin with, there is slang, a slang that seeps upward and outward from the language of the *banlieue* into that of the *élite.* Consider, for instance, the following passage taken from Robert Brasillach's *Six heures à perdre,* published in 1953:

> *Elle ne vous a pas dit que nous étions du dernier bien ensemble, non? C'est aussi vrai qu'elle a été en carte, en maison. Mais elle s'est mariée avec un client, de façon tout ce qu'il y a de plus regulière. Elle vous tracasse, hein? Le genre malingre, vous voyez ça?*

> (She didn't tell you we were together quite a lot lately, no? It's also true that she has been registered as a prostitute and has done time in a house. But she married a customer, in the most regular way there is. She bothers you, hey? The slender type, you see!)

Here we have slang expressions like *du dernier, en carte, en maison;* semislang words like *tracasser, malingre;* colloquialisms like *de façon tout ce qu'il y a,* incorrect forms like *regulière* for *regulier.* Elsewhere we encounter dialectal and patois forms which are occasionally heard where one would least expect them, even a morphology wherein the real distinction between singular and plural is made not in the noun but in the article (*le mur* is distinguished in speech from *les murs* not by the *-s* or *les* or *murs,* which is not heard, but by the vowel sound of *les,* which differs from that of *le*), and a phonology in which the vowel sounds of *pâte* and *patte* tend to merge, as do the nasal sounds of *vin* and *un.* These and other characteristics of modern spoken French probably point to the shape of French to come, a language which may differ as much from the elegant language of La Fontaine as the Oaths of Strasbourg differ from Virgil's *Aeneid,* and which may not be called French at all but go by an entirely different name in the roster of the world's future tongues.

— Chapter Five —

DIALECTS

England and America are two countries separated by the same language.
— G. B. Shaw

THE question is often asked: "Just what is the difference between a language and a dialect?" Politically speaking, one might answer that a language is what is officially accepted as the national form of speech, and a dialect is what does not have such acceptance. This definition would eliminate as languages such tongues as Welsh and Breton, while Lithuanian and Lettish, not having been languages under the Czars, would have become languages with the creation of the Lithuanian and Lettish Republics at the close of the First World War and then would again have ceased to be languages as soon as these nations were absorbed by the Soviet Union.

From the literary standpoint, one might say that a language is a form of speech that has given rise to a literature, a dialect one that has not; this would establish Sicilian and Neapolitan, Ozarkian and Brooklynese as languages, while it would eliminate Sardinian and most of the languages of the African Negroes and American Indians.

A third reply is that there is no intrinsic difference between a language and a dialect, the former being a dialect which, for some special reason, such as being the speech form of the locality which is the seat of the government, has acquired pre-eminence over the other dialects of the country.

Actually, there is no clear-cut reply to the question. Even linguists shrink from answering it, and rightly. When a language is examined under the microscope, it is found to be infinitely diversified. There is one form of cleavage and stratification along social and cultural lines, which leads to the infinite gradations of standard tongue, vernacular, slang, cant, and jargon. There is also a local, geographical division which extends not merely to regions and sections of a country but also to towns and quarters of towns. Some linguists go so far as to assert that each speaker may be said to have a dialect of his own, as evidenced by the fact that his friends can identify him by his speech.

A language is often a conglomeration of, and compromise among, several forms of speech. Often the conglomeration and compromise fail to occur or take place only partially. It may be easy enough to describe the British standard as "the King's English," based largely upon the pronunciation of the educated classes of London, which in turn represents a sublimation of southern English dialectal forms; or the Italian standard as the tongue of the educated classes of Florence; or the French standard as the speech of cultured Parisians. In reality, how many Englishmen use the King's English without trace of local intonation or peculiarity? How many Italians use Florentine? How many Frenchmen use Parisian?

Linguistic reality shows us that, while it is fairly simple to set a written-language standard for a region or nation, it is quite another thing to impose a universal spoken-language standard. It further shows us that localisms of intonation, enunciation, grammar, and vocabulary crop up everywhere and are extremely difficult to eradicate.

There is, of course, another and more optimistic side to the picture. Once a unified language has been established, dialects tend to sink lower and lower in the social scale, becoming what the French call *patois,* and to give way to the standard language. The movement, however, is somewhat like that of a line stretching out into infinity; it never is really completed. The Roman Empire succeeded in establishing written-language unity in all those of its provinces which accepted Latin as the popular tongue. But many scholars suspect that this unity was not paralleled by spoken-language unity, and that the local intonations and dialectal forms of the various provinces formed the basis for the later emergence of the diversified Romance tongues.

A similar movement is observed today in many countries that have achieved a measure of national unity. The local dialects are repressed, suppressed, discouraged. More and more members of the younger literate generations acquire the national language with few, if any, traces of the strong localisms of their parents. Yet the dialects somehow manage to survive, leading a sort of underground existence from which they may at any moment re-emerge.

Among the chief factors that tend to destroy dialects and unify language are education, military service, trade, a common religious background, common political institutions, a national consciousness, and a good system of communications and transportation. What is often forgotten is that a breakdown in any or all of these factors tends to have the opposite effect—to break up a unified language into dialects. Nationwide linguistic unity is historically revealed to be largely a man-made, deliberately willed state of affairs. The natural tendency of language is centrifugal, not centripetal, and this means that language tends to break up into local varieties whenever contacts are lost and political unity ceases to exert its pull toward the center.

This means in turn that in the course of history we are faced with the alternation of the two movements, one of which temporarily prevails in accordance with historical, social, cultural, political, religious, and economic conditions. Our Indo-European parent language found it easy to break up into numerous diverging "dialects" (Celtic, Italic, Germanic, Slavic, Greek, Indo-Iranian, etc.) at a time when there was no community of political institutions, no cultural bond, no national consciousness, and when communications among the branches, once severed, could not be restored. But whenever historical conditions tended toward civilization, as in the days of the Roman Empire, the tendency of the official chosen tongue to impose itself over the other speech forms became manifest, only to break down again when the artificial controls of civilization were removed. The tongue of the Anglo-Saxon invaders of England was identical with the Low German dialects of the mainland from which those Anglo-Saxons came; but within a century or two, by reason of lack of common institutions and communications, the Anglo-Saxon of England and the Old Frisian of the continent became differentiated. The tongue of the English settlers who came to America was, of course, identical with that of the Englishmen who remained behind. The migration to America took place at a period when education, trade, religious, cultural, and political bonds all existed. But such were the difficulties of communication across the Atlantic that the English of England and that of the American colonies soon began to diverge, and the divergence continues to the present day, though it may well be obliterated in the future by reason of vastly improved means of communication which bring one nation's speech habits to the other nation by fast steamer, plane, radio, television, and spoken films.

Americans are fond of discussing their own dialectal differences. Actually, these differences are trifling when compared with the tremendous divergences one finds in countries only a fraction of the size of the United States. It is easy to account for this. America was born and grew up in an atmosphere of modern, artificial conditions, under which localisms could not flourish with the ease with which they had blossomed in Europe's Middle Ages, when a mountain barrier like the Apennines proved far more impassable than the three thousand miles separating our eastern seaboard from our west coast.

Our comparative language unity should not, however, lull us into the erroneous belief that these conditions are fixed and immutable. Granted a change in historical conditions, a natural or man-made cataclysm whereby our railroads, highways, airplane routes, and broadcasting were disrupted, along with our unified political, social, and educational institutions, our American language would inevitably succumb to the inexorable centrifugal force inherent in all language, and localisms would quickly arise that would make the speech of California as unintelligible to the inhabitants of New York within a few generations or even decades as is the speech of England to the inhabitants of the German North Sea coast.

Dialectal divergences, like all language changes, are directly due to innovations. If the innovation has nationwide or language-wide acceptance, no dialectalization will result. But if the innovation spreads over one portion of the speaking area and not over others, we have the creation of a dialectal feature. At this point it is up to the people who direct the nation's linguistic policies (or think they do) to determine whether the innovation shall be considered as forming part of the standard language (whereupon the noninnovating areas become to some extent dialectal) or whether it shall be rejected by the official national tongue, in which case the innovating areas are described as having developed dialectal features. The tendency among modern American linguists is to assume an attitude of neutrality with respect to dialectalization, at least for what concerns American English, and to avoid labeling the dialect of one section of the country the "standard" or "official" speech. This criterion is, of course, not followed in Britain, where the King's English is official, or in the overwhelming majority of foreign countries, where the dialect of the capital has usually become or given rise to the standard language.

With regard to innovations that lead to dialectalization, two interesting observations have been made. The first is that dialects of isolated regions often tend to preserve old forms to a greater degree than the literary language, the speech of the Ozarks, for instance, coming closer in many respects to Elizabethan English than does the present-day speech of London. For this there is a valid reason: national literary languages are far more exposed to the world's linguistic cross-currents than are remote dialects, and their tendency to innovate is correspondingly greater.

The second observation is that when people migrate from their homeland they are more likely to keep intact the language of the period of migration than do those who stay behind. The English of the Appalachian mountaineers is closer to seventeenth-century English than any present-day English dialect; the French of Canada is closer to seventeenth-century French than is the Parisian of today; Yiddish is closer to fifteenth-century German than is present-day German; while the Portuguese of Brazil reflects the pronunciation of the period of discovery and colonization better than Lisbonese. This phenomenon, which is not universal, hinges to some extent upon the preceding one. Insofar as the mother country is exposed to linguistic and literary crosscurrents, while the colony remains comparatively isolated, the latter will naturally tend to be more conservative than the former. French-speaking Canadians, cut off from France and surrounded by English speakers, whom they regard with suspicion if not antipathy; Jews segregated in the ghettos of eastern Europe; Brazilians with an ocean between themselves and Portugal, would naturally tend to conserve their older speech forms. On the other hand, Americans come closer than Englishmen to seventeenth-century English only when they happen to be isolated Appalachian mountaineers; the rest of the American population, having placed itself at the crossroads of the world fully as much as the British, have proceeded to make innovations of their own. Nevertheless, in the matter of sounds at least, many linguists hold that "General American" comes closer to the English of Shakespeare than does the King's English of today.

For what concerns the English of America, three main dialectal varieties are recognized: Eastern, Southern, and Midwestern (or General American), with about 30, 40, and 110 million speakers, respectively. However, more careful investigation, such as is being carried on in connection with Professor's Kurath's *Linguistic Atlas of the United States,* reveals the presence of at least twenty-four well-defined regional dialects, most of which are located east of the Mississippi.

The following list of words, pronounced by an American speaker and listened to by an expert, usually suffices to place the speaker within twenty miles of his home locality: "merry," "marry," "Mary"; "wash," "water," "Washington"; "on," "off," "dog," "oft," "lot," "log," "sorry"; "about the house"; "greasy"; "father," "park," "part"; "first," "bird"; "can" (verb), "can" (noun); "ash," "ask." Each of these groups of words places the speaker east or west, or north or south, of a certain line, until he is restricted to a given small area. "Greazy," for example, would place the speaker south of Philadelphia, while "greassy" would place him north of Trenton. The pronunciation of r after vowels ("father" as against "fathah") distinguishes between a Philadelphian and a New Yorker. Most American speakers distinguish in pronunciation between "horse" and "hoarse," "for" and "four," "morning" and "mourning," but the local dialects of Philadelphia and New York, among others, do not.

One authority, claiming three major and eighteen minor dialect areas for the continental United States, graphically illustrates the differences of the three major areas by means of the sentence "My father was born here," which sounds like "moy fawder z bawn heeah" in the mouth of an Eastern speaker, "mah-ee fah-thuhr wuz bawrn hiuhr" in that of a Midwesterner, and "mah faathuh whuz bohn hiuh" in that of a Southerner. Other examples given for New England include the dropping of final r and the intrusion of a so-called "parasitic" r in "Asiar" and "Idear"; "sapawt" for "support," "caw" for "corps," "viga" for "vigor," "jes" for "just," "lahst" for "last," a diphthong in "he'ah" and "awaya" ("aware"), a faint palatalization of sibilants in "cauzh" ("cause"). Upper Southern traits include a diphthongization of oo in "fiud," "miun," "spiun" ("food," "moon," "spoon"); a raising of front vowels, so that "pen" becomes "pin" and "catch" becomes "ketch"; "wahter" and "wush" where the East has "wawter," "wahsh" (but this trait appears also in parts of the Midwest). The claim is made that some Southerners distinguish between "yawl" for one person addressed and "yew all" for more than one, but this is difficult to prove. For the mountain dialect, the sample comes straight out of the comic strips: "Jughaid Smif, how kin ye be so forwards? When I hol' yore han', my pore ol' haht does flipflops and skins the cat."

According to some authorities, the Southern drawl and the New England twang are in danger of disappearing, while

Midwestern speech, or General American, is spreading. This is due to the many Midwesterners who move to other parts of the country and impose their type of speech. The process, however, is a very slow one.

In addition to regional dialects, the speech of the United States is characterized by special localisms typical of a single city or even borough, and by immigrant dialects.

Among the first may be mentioned the perhaps overemphasized Brooklynese, which is in part straight slang, more or less common to all the large cities of the East. A humorous *Language Guide to Brooklyn* spoke of such expressions as *pahrmee* ("pardon me"), *lemeawf* ("let me off") and *aniain-foolin* ("and I ain't fooling"). From the standpoint of dialect, these examples are hardly to be classed with the answer given by an Ozark mountaineer to an inquiry about the score of a baseball game: "Nary-nary in the seventh, with us'uns to bat." On the other hand, there are phonetic features in the Brooklyn speech which are said to arise from the influence of early Dutch settlers in Greenpoint. Chief among these is the interchange of *oi* and *er* ("boid" for "bird," "erl" for "oil"). Another is the use of *t* and *d* for the two sounds of *th,* as exemplified by "tree of dem bums struck out." But the matter of Dutch influence is viewed with suspicion in many reputable quarters, while the phonetic features in question seem to be common to other cities and boroughs, notably the Bronx.

Pamphlet dictionaries have been issued for at least two of America's most colorful local speech forms. The one published by the *News and Courier* of Charleston, South Carolina, as a guide to local speech includes such definitions as: "abode—wooden plank"; "rah chair—where you are at"; "sex—one less than seven, two less than eh-et, three less than noine, foe less than tin." Self-explanatory is: "When you make toe-est, doan' bun the braid."

Not to be outdone, the linguistic guide to Brooklyn offers: "fodder—male parent"; "earl—a lubricant"; "oil—an English nobleman"; "tree—the numeral that precedes four"; "wader —one who waits on you"; "doze—the ones yonder"; and, of course, "Long Guy Land—the island on which Brooklyn is situated."

Immigrant dialects, while quite picturesque, have a tendency to die out with the first or at most the second generation, surviving as a matter of humor on the stage. Linguists are agreed that there is very little chance that the sounds of American English will be permanently influenced by the pronunciation of immigrants. One notable exception to the mortality of immigrant dialects is the "Pennsylvania Dutch" of certain regions in Pennsylvania, which is not Dutch at all, but a direct descendant of the seventeenth-century Rheno-Franconian dialect of German. A chair of Pennsylvania German language and literature was established by Muhlenberg College at Allentown, but the continued vitality of the dialect under modern American conditions is doubtful. Of particular dialectal interest are some of the expressions that have crept into local English from Pennsylvania Dutch, like "the milk is all" for "there is no more milk," "outen the light" for "put out the light," and "the paper wants rain" for "the paper predicts rain."

The dialects of Britain are far more numerous and divergent than anything we have in America. There are nine principal dialects in Scotland, three in Ireland, thirty in England and Wales—this outside of Scots Gaelic, Irish, and Welsh, which are in no sense dialects of English but completely separate languages of the Celtic branch of Indo-European. Among the chief English dialects are: Cornwall, Devon, Somerset, Dorset, Gloucestershire, Oxfordshire, Shropshire, Lancashire, Westmoreland, Northumberland, Yorkshire, Lincolnshire, Norfolk, Cockney, and Sussex. Cockney, the lower-class dialect of London, seems to be linked with Cockaigne, an imaginary country where the rivers flowed with wine and the streets were paved with pastry and roast geese. The Cockney tendency to play with initial *h* is on a par with the Bostonese tendency to play with final *r*; both are dropped where they should be sounded and inserted where they are not supposed to exist. An account of the way an exasperated Cockney tried to spell out the name of the town of Ealing for the benefit of the telephone operator runs as follows: "E for 'eaven, A for wot 'orses eat, L for where you're going, I for me, N for wot lays eggs, and G for gawd's sake keep your ears open!" It is also claimed that the town of Hepworth, Ontario, was named by a Cockney after Epworth, England.

Some of the English dialects still use "thou" and "thee" instead of "you," a practice which in America is followed only by a few conservative Quakers. "Thik" is Wexfordshire dialect for "this"; Gloucestershire uses "thak" for "that"; "hoo" is Yorkshire dialect for "she," and it may be added that the Yorkshire speech is normally quite incomprehensible to the average American. In Sussex they use "Hastings ladies" for "large clouds," "scrump" for "apple," "butterfly day" for "bright day," and "drythe" for "drought." Ulster, in Ireland, uses "dayligone" for "twilight," while from Scotland we have imported "curmudgeon," said to come from the French *coeur méchant* ("evil heart"). Lancashire has "nobbut a tuthry" for "only two or three pence"; East Anglia, still under Scandinavian influence, offers "Hesta clap yat dahn lonnen?" for "Have you shut the gate down the lane?" From Gloucestershire four words for pear are reported: "frum," if the fruit is ripe and perfect; "mawsey," if it's soft and woolly; "sapy" if it's sodden; "roxy" if it's thoroughly decayed; but "daddocky" is used in connection with decayed wood, and "rasty" in connection with spoiled bacon. Picturesque Yorkshire supplies us with "Ah'm laikin wi' ma thoom" ("I'm not working because of my thumb"); "Yon's gawmless" ("That guy is a dope"); "Shoot thi gob or Ah'll pause thee" ("Shut your mouth or I'll slug you"); "mawngier nor owd hell" ("madder than hell"). Widely scattered among the British dialects are "book" for "magazine" ("I've been reading your book in a book"); "hogget" for "lamb"; "kittle" for "to neck"; "starve" for "to die of cold"; "mooch" for "to approach with evil intentions." While some of these expressions merely sound strange, others point to the possibilities of misunderstanding among people speaking what is officially the same language.

The dialects of other important languages show even greater diversity. Ancient Greek, unlike Latin, had many definitely recorded dialects (Doric, Achaean, Ionian, Attic, etc.). Only one of them survives as a separate dialect, the ancient Laconian of Sparta, which comes down in the form of the modern Tsaconian. The others all merged into the national language, or *koine* (literally "shared," "common," "popular"), a term that arose in the fourth century B.C. to denote the common Greek tongue which had evolved out of the earlier dialects. The *koine* is the Greek form that appears in the New Testament, and the word is still used today to denote a common language in general use among people speaking different dialects.

French has numerous dialects, including Picard, Norman, Lorrain, and Walloon, the last-named of which is spoken in southern Belgium and parts of northern France. The Provençal spoken in southern France is rated as a separate Romance language, rather than a dialect of French, and had a flourishing literature in the Middle Ages.

In addition to its numerous dialects on its own home soil, a few of which were literary in the Middle Ages,

French has also evolved overseas varieties. A sample of Canadian Quebec French runs as follows: *"B'jou, Pi-yire, c'mesva?" "Paw pire. Twee?" "Toujours pareil, no change."* (Standard French would run: *"Bonjour, Pierre, comment ça va?" "Pas pire. Toi?" "Toujours pareil, pas de change-ment."*) Characteristic of this dialect is the tendency to change a French open *e* to the sound of an English "long" *i*, so that *cher* sounds like "shire." From the Antillean French of Guadeloupe come these samples: *On n'a que parti* ("I'm leaving"); *Da mi a bé* ("Give me a drink"); *Chiemoun* (*mon chien*, "my dog").

Medieval Spanish had three main dialects, but two of them, Leonese and Aragonese, have almost disappeared before the encroachments of Castilian. The last, however, has given rise to new dialectal forms, including the Andalusian of southern Spain, on which most Spanish-American varieties are based. The dialects of Italy are, in proportion to population and area, probably the most numerous and widely divergent of any language; they include Sicilian, Neapolitan, Roman, Tuscan, Venetian, and the Gallo-Italian dialects of northwestern Italy, so called because the Gauls are supposed to have had something to do with their formation. German has two great divisions, High and Low German, but each is subdivided into innumerable local varieties. Russian shows comparatively little dialectalization, less perhaps than its kindred Slavic languages, like Serbo-Croatian, which is divided into the *shto, cha,* and *kaj* dialects, depending upon which of the three words they use for "what."

The minor "dialects" of China have bodies of speakers larger than many of the national tongues of Europe. Among the principal Chinese dialects are the Wu of Shanghai, the Min of Fu Kien province, and Cantonese, each of which has between 40 and 50 million speakers. Cantonese, which has more complicated tones than Mandarin and permits consonant sounds like *t* and *p* at the end of words, is the Chinese dialect most often heard in the United States. The difference between Mandarin and Cantonese is illustrated by the expression for "paper tiger," scornfully applied to the United States after our Korean fiasco: *chih lao fu* in Mandarin, *gee lo fu* in Cantonese, with additional differences in tones.

The official literary languages of most countries are based upon a local dialect which assumed the leadership either because it was spoken in the region where the capital was located, or because its speakers gained political and military predominance, or because they set a cultural pattern for the entire country. These three possibilities are well illustrated by the three major Romance languages, French, Spanish, and Italian. Standard French is the original dialect of the Ile-de-France, the region centering about the capital city of Paris; during the Middle Ages it fought a long and hard struggle for predominance with other northern French dialects, particularly Picard, which in the twelfth and thirteenth centuries was employed side by side with Francien as a literary tongue. But the fact that Francien was the dialect of the French court gradually set it in first place, and by the beginning of the fifteenth century the speech of cultured Parisians became the official tongue of all of France. In Spain, Castilian predominance was assured by the fact that the inhabitants of the Castilian provinces took the lead in the war for the reconquest of Spain from the Moors, so that it was Castilian rather than Leonese or Aragonese that spread southward with the advancing Spanish armies that finally threw the Moors back into Africa in 1492. In Italy, where no political or military factor was involved, the predominance of Tuscan in its Florentine variety became established after Florence had given to Italy, in the first half of the fourteenth century, the mighty literary output of Dante, Petrarch, and Boccaccio.

Standard Russian is based on the Moscow dialect, and standard Japanese on the Tokyo dialect. The "National Tongue" of China represents largely the North Mandarin prevalent in the region of Peking. But in Germany, where political unity did not exist until a comparatively late date, it was the cultural factor that won out, with Luther's High German translation of the Bible setting the pattern.

Most of the local speech peculiarities of the countries of the New World, outside of the United States, were brought to America from the various regions of France, Spain, and Portugal. Canadian French is close to the French of the seventeenth century as spoken in the northern French provinces. Many Spanish linguists assert that there is not a single speech peculiarity in any part of Spanish America, outside of local vocabulary borrowed from the native Indian tribes, which does not have its counterpart in some section of Spain. However, even outside of Indian borrowings, many vocabulary divergences have arisen in Spanish America for which the dialects of Spain are not responsible, and the same holds true for the Portuguese of Brazil in relation to the dialects of Portugal. Though all of Spanish

America theoretically speaks the same Spanish, automobile tires are *illantas* in Peru, *gomas* in Cuba; an illiterate farm hand is a *peón* in Mexico, a *guaso* or *roto* in Chile, a *guajiro* in Cuba, a *jíbaro* in Puerto Rico, a *pongo* in Bolivia.

The vocabulary divergences which can arise in various localities, even under circumstances most favorable to standardization, are often startling. Most of us are aware of the New York "block" and "sidewalk" *vs.* the Philadelphia "square" and "pavement"; the New York "thruway" or "parkway" *vs.* the California "freeway," the Illinois "tollway," the Pennsylvania "turnpike"; the New York "bag" *vs.* the Midwestern "sack" and the Southern "poke." There is a whole series of subtle linguistic divergences in the nomenclature for soft drinks, which in the Boston area are "tonics." The "coke" of the North is often the "dope" of the South. A Midwestern "milkshake" is a New York "frosted," a Boston "cabinet," a South Carolina "blizzard." If you ask for a "chocolate soda" in New York, you'll get chocolate syrup and chocolate ice cream; in the Midwest you'll get the chocolate syrup with vanilla ice cream, and if you want chocolate all the way through, you must ask for a "double chocolate soda"; conversely, if you want the mixture in New York, you should ask for a "black and white."

For linguistic differences between America and Britain, see the chapter "King's English and American Language."

In other languages such differences are often far more extensive. Various sections of Portugal call a man's sock by the following names: *peúga, meia de homem, meia curta, miote, mieta, tornuco.* The *esquadra* ("police station") and *mercearia* ("grocery store") of Portugal are the *delegacia* and *venda* of Brazil. The *bodega* which is normally "wineshop" in Spain is "grocery store" in Latin America, the *cigarro* which in Spain is "cigar" becomes "cigarette" in Cuba, where *tabaco* ("tobacco" in Spain) means "cigar."

Dialects, like the poor, are always with us. Attempts to eradicate them and standardize the language often meet with signal success, but new dialects will then arise out of the unified, standardized language. Like other local differences of food, dress, and customs, dialects are often a nuisance. Yet they lend picturesque variety to language, and variety is the spice of life.

— Chapter Six —

THE SAGA OF PLACE NAMES

No nation knows itself until it knows its past.
                                        —Ben Ames Williams

HISTORICAL linguists usually make much of place names, and rightly. When a given territory changes hands, the spoken language of the former inhabitants may completely give way to that of the newcomers, but the place names normally remain as a perennial monument to the people who first lived there, though they may change to the point where they are practically unrecognizable, like the Celtic or pre-Celtic Eboracum that ultimately became York. (The original Celtic name is lost, but it was recorded by the Romans as Eboracum, which the Anglo-Saxons later changed, on the basis of resemblance of sound, to Eoforwic, or "Boar's Town." Later, under Danish influence, this became Jorvik, and still later York.) Often a few place names are all that remains of an ancient and vanished language.

Toponymy, the study of place names, is a science in itself. The Department of the Interior has a special bureau, staffed by competent linguists, whose task it is to make an accurate study of the place names of America, the varied nomenclature of the states and cities, towns and hamlets, hills and mountains, rivers and lakes that constitute our country's physical self.

Our linguistic prehistory is well outlined in extent, though not described in depth, by the host of American Indian names that survive in our toponymy. Half of our states bear Indian names, with the remainder showing Spanish, French, English, and Latin origin. Among the former, Dakota means "leagued" or "allied," having once been the home of the confederated Sioux tribes; Tennessee is "the vines of the big bend"; Iowa "the sleepy ones"; Oklahoma "the red people"; Kansas "a breeze near the ground"; Michigan "great water"; Kentucky "the dark and bloody ground"; Illinois "the tribe of perfect men"; Texas "Friends!," and Idaho "Good morning!" (Had New Jersey retained its Indian name instead of assuming an English one, it would today be Scheyechbi, "the land by the long water.") Among the names of European origin, some perpetuate the names of queens, virgin or otherwise (Virginia, Maryland); of kings, like Charles or George of England (Carolina, Georgia) or Louis of France (Louisiana); of regions of the Old World or the New (New York, New Jersey, Rhode Island, named after the island of Rhodes in the Mediterranean, New Mexico); or of men prominent in history (Washington). Most historical in point of time, perhaps, is California, which seems to be derived from Californe, an imaginary land appearing in the eleventh-century French epic *Chanson de Roland*.

Our land is studded with names like Ossining ("place of stones"), Hoboken ("tobacco pipe"), Oswego ("place of flies"), Katonah ("sickly"), Ticonderoga ("brawling water"), Biloxi ("worthless"), Shenandoah ("daughter of skies"), Peoria ("place of fat beasts"), which pay tribute to the poetic and practical sense of the original inhabitants. Lake Success, which was once the temporary seat of the United Nations, had nothing to do with hopes concerning that organization, but comes from an Indian word *Suksat* whose meaning is unfortunately lost. The Mississippi ("father of waters") was called in its lower course *Malbanchya* ("place of foreign languages") by the Choctaws, who were bewildered by the mixture of tongues spoken in the early French, Spanish, and English settlements on its banks. Adirondack ("bark-eater") is the name bestowed by the Iroquois upon the Algonquins, for whom they had no love. Chicago comes from the Piankashaw Indian *chi-kak-quwa* ("place of skunk smells"), a name fittingly bestowed upon a locality where many wild onions grew. Manhattan is said to mean, in the language of the Delaware Indians, "the place where we all got drunk," in reference to a drinking bout in which the natives polished off a barrel of Henry Hudson's rum, though according to another authority the name has the more sober meaning of "town on an island."

But these American place names, picturesque and descriptive as they are, tell us little of prehistoric wanderings and happenings. It is otherwise in Europe and Asia, where almost every place name contains a record of migrations and conquests, far-flung trading posts and garrison towns. Many of the place names of Britain are neither Celtic nor Roman nor Anglo-Saxon nor Norman but were left behind by the vanished, mysterious dark-skinned race of the Picts who lurked on the further side of Hadrian's wall and who seem to have been related to the Iberians of Spain. The Celtic-speaking Gauls have left records of their wanderings in the Galatia of Asia Minor, the Galicia of Poland and the Galicia of Spain, as well as in numerous localities of western Germany and northern Italy. The *-dunum* and *-acum* suffixes of many localities of Roman Gaul (Lugdunum, later Lyon; Cameracum, later Cambrai), even the *-lanum* of Mediolanum ("in the middle of the plain"), modern Milan, are Gaulish. Many of the towns, streams, and mountains of the Italian peninsula bear the imprint of the Etruscans, Ligurians, and Messapians. Gascony's ancient name, Vasconia, shows that its former inhabitants were Basques. The fact that at one time the Slavic world reached the eastern banks of the Elbe, whence it was driven back to the Vistula by the Teutonic Knights of the Middle Ages, is revealed by the Slavic origin of the name Prussia (once Borussia) and by the names of such cities as Berlin (Slavic for "wasteland") and Leipzig (from Slavic *lipa,* "linden tree").

Historical events are confirmed and often clarified by place names. Early Greek settlers, moving from their original home to Hesperia ("the land of the west"), fittingly called their new Italian surroundings Magna Graecia, or Greater Greece. They founded, among various cities, Naples and Palermo; the former was Neapolis, or "new town," an anachronism today; the latter was Panormos, or "all-harbor," a tribute to the Sicilian capital's ship-sheltering qualities. Greek seafarers also gave its name to Malta (Melita, or "land of honey") and to the Balearic (or "slingers' ") Islands (the root is the greek verb *ballo,* "to hurl," which gives us "ballistics"; the inhabitants of the Balearics were the most skillful slingers of ancient times).

The Romans were among the great place-name givers of antiquity. Provence was named by them; it was Provincia, the best-loved province of the Empire, therefore the "province" *par excellence.* Many of their settlements were named in honor of Caesar Augustus; it is Caesarea Augusta that later became the Spanish Zaragoza, while Caesarea alone produced the French, English, and American Jersey. Germany is probably not a German word at all, as proved by the native Deutschland; it is said to come from a Celtic root, meaning "neighboring," seemingly cognate to Latin *germanus* ("brother"), from which we derive our "germane" and Spanish its *hermano*. Germany, according to its Roman etymology, would be a "brotherly" country. Many cities in western Germany bear Roman names; Köln, which we know by its French name of Cologne, is Colonia or "colony"; Münster is *monasterium;* München, or Munich, is *monachos* ("monks"), with a German inflectional suffix.

Medieval history is illustrated by two place names of Spain: Castile, which originally meant "castles," pointing up the fact that the center of Christian resistance against the Moors was studded with fortresses; and Gibraltar, from the Arabic *Jebel Tarik* ("Tarik's mountain"). Tarik was the leader of the Moslem hordes that swept into Spain in the eighth century and overthrew the Spanish Visigothic kingdom. The Latin name of Gibraltar had previously been "the Pillars of Hercules," which reminds us of the role played by mythology in toponymy.

Albion, poetic name for England, seems to be derived from the Greek *Alouion,* linked with Celtic *alp,* "height." The name, however, may also go back to an Indo-European root meaning "white" (Latin *albus*), and the term "white island" may have been suggested by the chalk cliffs of Dover. The Amazon River of South America was so named by the explorer Orellana after a battle with the natives in which the women fought more bravely than the men, after the fashion of the legendary Amazons of antiquity. Nippon, whose literal meaning is "sun-origin," sums up the legend about the descent of the Japanese race from the sun goddess Amaterasu. The name Cipango for Japan which Marco Polo brought back to the West is a Chinese translation, *jê pên kuo* ("rising-sun land"), whence also "Japan." The Brahmaputra River of India is "the son of Brahma," and the Solomon Islands were so named because their discoverer, Mendana, created the legend that they had yielded gold for King Solomon's temple, itself somewhat legendary.

Commercial products are responsible for a vast number of place names. Cassiterides is the name by which Herodotus mentions the British Isles in the fifth century B.C.; the name means "tin islands." The name of the Andes means "copper" in the tongue of the Incas. Italy, in its Latin form Italia, goes back to an earlier Vitelia, "land of calves," "land of cattle." The Faroe Islands are the "sheep islands" in Danish; Java is the Malay *jawa* ("barley"), and our own United States is to the Japanese *Bei-koku,* or "rice land." Argentina is "silver land," though the silver came from Bolivia. The name of Barbados

Island means "bearded" and refers to the bearded fig trees growing there. Brazil got its name from the fact that its coastal forests are rich in trees containing a dye known in Portuguese by that name; the dye had previously been named *brasil* after *brasa* ("live coal").

Geographical and physical characteristics enter into many names of localities. Ecuador reminds us that the Equator traverses the country. Piedmont is "at the foot of the mountains," and the Dodecanese, to which we sometimes add a redundant "Islands," means "twelve islands" in Greek. The French name for the English Channel is *La Manche* ("the sleeve"), by reason of its shape and function (an arm of the sea passes through it). The Chinese name for China, Chung Kuo, means "middle country." Eritrea is "red" and owes its name to the adjoining Red Sea, which in turn got it from the minute red plant and animal life that abounds in its waters. Bab el Mandeb, at the Red Sea's entrance, is "gate of tears" and was so called because so many ships were wrecked in its treacherous waters. Volcanoes are usually graphically named: Popocatepetl, in Mexico, is Aztec for "smoke mountain"; Haleakala in Hawaii, the largest extinct volcano in the world, means "home of the sun"; and Japan's Fujiyama is "fire mountain." Louisiana's Baton Rouge ("red stick") was so named because at the time of its founding a large red cypress reminded one of the founders of an enormous walking cane.

Names of races and peoples often appear in the names of countries, sometimes adding to our historical stock of information. The ancient name of France, Gaul or Gallia, must have sounded to the Romans like "land of roosters" (the Latin word for "rooster" is *gallus*), and the boastful habits of the Celtic inhabitants may have contributed to this impression; at all events, the crowing Chantecler is still the emblem of France. The country's name, however, was changed after the coming of the Franks, a Germanic tribe that crossed the Rhine and overran the northern part of Roman Gaul, setting up its own Merovingian dynasty about A.D. 500. *Français* ("French"), *François* ("Francis"), "Frank," and "frank" all come from the name of this tribe. The original meaning of "frank" is "free," whence *franc-tireur*, a guerrilla sniper, free from the inhibitions of military discipline, and *lingua franca*, the "free tongue" of the Mediterranean or, in another interpretation, the "tongue of the Franks" or westerners.

Belgium is named after the Belgae, an ancient Gaulish

tribe inhabiting that region. Their name seems to derive from the fact that at one time they dwelt on the banks of the Bolga or Volga. The Bulgars appear to have derived their name from the same source, but they were accused of homosexual practices in the Middle Ages, and their national name gave rise to French *bougre* and English "bugger."

The name of Russia seems to come from the Scandinavian tribe of Rus, which overran the northwestern part of what is now the Soviet Union and set up a "Russian" dynasty. The Slavs, however, have a legend about three brothers, Rus, Lech, and Czech, who are said to have founded the three north Slavic nations of Russia, Poland, and Bohemia. The Hungarians have a similar legend about two brothers, Hun and Magyar, who gave rise to the two kindred races, the Huns and the Magyars; the western name of Hungary commemorates the Huns, but the Hungarians call their country Magyarország, or "Magyar land."

Rumania is the "land of the Romans," and the Rumanians proudly trace their ancestry to Trajan's Roman legionaries who settled Dacia, a Roman province roughly corresponding to modern Rumania, at the beginning of the second century A.D.

Three Germanic tribes are responsible for Lombardy, Normandy, and the French name for Germany, *Allemagne*. Lombardy, in northern Italy, is the land of the Lombards or Longobards ("long beards"), fiercest and most uncouth of all the Germanic invaders who penetrated the former Roman Empire. In the Middle Ages the Lombards were great bankers, whence London's Lombard Street; they were also dealers in old furniture, whence "lumber." "Norman" is the French development of "Northman"; in the ninth century the Northmen invaded France, then made peace with the French kings and settled down in the region which bears their name; they soon gave up their Scandinavian tongue in favor of French, which they already spoke when they conquered England in 1066. Scandinavian, however, continued to be spoken in the city of Bayeux until the twelfth century. *Allemand*, the French word for "German," is in origin the name of a single Germanic tribe, the Alemanni, who used to be located in what is today Switzerland, southern Bavaria, and the Tyrol.

So far as the Near East is concerned, Palestine is not the land of the Jews but that of the Philistines or "wanderers." The Hebrew name for it is *Eretz Yisrael* ("land of Israel"), and Israel itself means "alerted of God."

Names are often bestowed upon lands not by their own inhabitants but by neighbors. Hindustan is not Hindustani but Persian and means "land of the river Sindhu"; the original Sanskrit name for India is *Aryavarta* ("dwelling place of the Aryans"); India is also known as Bharat, "supported" or "maintained," presumably by its ancient gods. Neither Abyssinia nor Ethiopia is a native name for the kingdom of the Lion of Judah; the first is Arabic and means "mixture of races"; the second, officially selected by the Ethiopians, is Greek and means "land of the burnt faces." Manchukuo was the name bestowed by the Japanese upon the former Chinese province of Manchuria, but the name itself was appropriately Chinese for "Manchu land." Neither Korea nor Chosen is Korean; the former comes from Japanese *Kōrai*, which in turn comes from Chinese *Kao Li* ("lofty-beautiful"); the latter is the Chinese *Ch'ao Hsien* and means "morning freshness"; the Koreans call their country *Hankuk*. Siam is a Malay name; the native name for Thailand is *Muang hai*, "land of the free." To the Indonesians, Borneo is *Kalimantan*, New Guinea is *Irian*, and their capital, which the Dutch had named Batavia, has been rechristened Jakarta, "important city."

Localities are frequently named after individuals. Bolivia is named after Simón Bolívar, who led in the struggle to liberate South America from Spanish rule. Bermuda is named after its discoverer Juan de Bermúdez. Saudi Arabia is named after the Saud family, which has been reigning since 1766, but the adjective also means "fortunate"; thus, by a strange coincidence, we have a modern Arabic literal translation of the ancient Roman name Arabia Felix, which was not applied, however, to the same section of the Arabian peninsula.

Changes in place names frequently reflect historical transfers of power and political events as well as nationalistic aspirations and ambitions. In ancient times, a city called Urusalim by the Babylonians became Jebus when occupied by the Jebusites, then Yarushalayim when selected by David as the capital of his kingdom; it is now Jerusalem.

More recently, two regions called Austrasia ("eastern realm") and Lotharingia ("land of Lothair," one of Charlemagne's descendants) developed into Alsace-Lorraine; but that is the French name. Whenever the Germans held the region, they called it Elsass-Lothringen, and the name of the capital changed from Strasbourg to Strassburg. The city called Bratislava by the Czechs is Pressburg to the Germans and Pozsony to the Hungarians. The island called Karafuto by the Japanese is Sakhalin to the Russians. The islands called Falkland by the British are the Malvinas to the Argentinians, who claim them, the name being derived from St. Malo, home port of the original French settlers. A section of what we call Antarctica is called Graham Land by the British and O'Higgins Land by the Chileans, who named it for their national hero, Bernardo O'Higgins.

Rivers, being more mobile than towns or even countries, are far more subject to name changes along their courses. The Danubium Flumen of the Romans is the Donau to the Germans, the Dunaj to the Czechs, the Duna to the Hungarians, the Dunav to the Yugoslavs, the Dunarea to the Rumanians, and the Dunai to the Russians. Equally startling are changes in river names in other continents. India's Brahmaputra, before it reaches the Indian plain, is the Matsang, the Tamchok, the Tsang-Po, the Dihang. The Congo River of Africa bears along its course such varied names as Chambezi, Luapula, Luwa, Lualaba. On the North American continent, the Athabaska becomes the Slave before it ends its life as the Mackenzie, and the Saskatchewan continues from Lake Winnipeg as the Nelson. The Yadkin of North Carolina becomes the Pee Dee in South Carolina; it is believed that this is the river Stephen Foster had in mind, but it sounded better as Suwanee. The New River of North Carolina turns into the Kanawha of West Virginia, while in Georgia the Okmulgee becomes the Altamaha.

The strangest discrepancies in place names occur on the eastern coast of the Adriatic, where the old Italian names are giving way to Yugoslavic: Zara, Sebenico, Spalato, Ragusa, Meleda, Lesina, Curzola, and Veglia have become Zadar, Šibenik, Split, Dubrovnik, Mljet, Hvar, Korcula, and Krk: but Zadar has again been changed to Titograd, in honor of the Yugoslav dictator.

Russian place names underwent a thorough overhauling when the Soviets came to power. Petrograd, formerly St. Petersburg, became Leningrad; Samara became Kuibyshev; Nizhni Novgorod became Gorki; Vyatka turned into Kirov; Tsaritsyn became famous under the name of Stalingrad; Tver became Kalinin. But Stalingrad, now that Stalin is out of favor, has turned into Volgograd. Since East Prussia was occupied by the Russians, Königsberg has been rechristened Kaliningrad, Tilsit has become Sovetsk, Friedland was turned into Pravdinsk, Preussisch Eylau into Bagrationovsk, Gumbinnen into Gusev, Insterburg into Chernyakhovsk.

Even street names reveal political trends. How else to interpret the change in the name of a street in Riga from

Street of Jesus to Street of the Godless? Or Bratislava's Molotov, Bakunin, and Kropotkin Streets to Obchodna (Business Street), Rjazanska, and Pri Dvore? Or the exquisite change of New Delhi's Kingsway to Raj Path, which is an exact translation, and of Queensway to Jan Path, which is "People's Road"? In Paris, the Avenue du Maréchal Pétain became the Avenue de la Division LeClerc after the liberation, while the Avenue de Tokyo and the Avenue Victor Emmanuel III became the Avenue de New-York and the Avenue Franklin D. Roosevelt, respectively. A street that had borne the name of Henri Heine had been changed during the German occupation to Rue Jean Sebastien Bach; it was changed back, but the Parisians didn't want to stop honoring Bach and are looking for another street to name after him.

Other changes in street names have different motivations. Toronto, which boasts such picturesque street names as Baseball Place, Drum Snab Road, The Wishbone, Baby Point Road, Thermos Road, and Industry Street, turned its Cherry Pie Road (named after a little girl whose name was Cherry) to the more impressive York Valley Crescent. Several London boroughs were merged and renamed not long ago, but only after discussion in Parliament. Among the changes made were Hampstead, Holborn, and St. Pancras to Camden; Bethnal Green, Poplar, and Stepney to Tower Hamlets; Wanstead, Woodford, and Ilford to Redbridge.

Toronto is not the only city to have picturesque street names. Peking boasts, among others, of Jade Street and Velvet Paw Lane. Moscow has its Sharikopodshipnikovskaya Ulitsa, which is the Street of the Ball Bearings. The prize, however, seems to go to Lisbon. Here we have the Rua da Saudade (The Street of Longing), the Rua do Chão Salgado (The Street of the Salty Floor), Beco Lava-Cabeças (Alley of the Head Washers), Travessa de Mata Porcos (Hogbutchers' Alley), Travessa dos Ladrões (Highwaymen's Alley), Travessa da Horta de Cera (Wax Orchard Alley), Rua do Imaginario (Street of the Imaginary), Beco Espera-me Rapaz (Wait for Me, Boy, Alley), Travessa de Fala Só (The Alley Where You Speak to Yourself), Rua do Bemformoso (Handsome Man Street), Rua da Triste e Feia (Street of the Sad Ugly Woman).

There are a few general facts concerning the place names of our own and other lands that ought to be more widely known. The *Minne-* in Minnesota, Minnehaha, Minnetonka, etc., is a Dakota Indian word, meaning "water." The *los* and *las* of place names of Spanish origin both mean "the" (Los Angeles, "the angels"; Las Vegas, "the plains"). The suffixes

-*wich* and -*wick* are akin to the Latin *vicus* ("village"); hence Greenwich Village is redundant. The suffixes -*cester*, -*caster*, -*chester* of Leicester, Lancaster, Portchester, etc., come from Latin *castra* ("encampment," "fortified place"). The *Aber-* and *Inver-* so common in Scottish place names (Aberdeen, Inverness) are Celtic terms for "estuary," "river's mouth."

Spanish place names, and many place names of the New World given by the Spaniards, are frequently of Arabic origin, by reason of the long domination of Spain by the Moors. Those beginning with *Al-* contain the Arabic definite article: Alcántara means "the bridge"; Alcázar, "the palace." Others begin with *Guad-,* from the Arabic *wad* ("river"); Guadalquivir, Guadalajara, Guadalupe all contain this prefix.

The prefix *Alt-* in place names means "high" if the place name is Romance: Altamura ("high walls"); "old" if the place name is Germanic: Altdorf ("old village"); "gold" if the place name appears in one of the tongues of northern Asia: Altai ("golden mountains"). The -*holm* of Swedish names means "island" (Stockholm, "pile island"); the *Bel-* or *Byel-* of Slavic names means "white" (Belgrade, "white city"; Byelorussia, "white Russia"); while the ending -*gorod* or -*grad* means "town" (Novgorod, "new town"; Leningrad, "Lenin town"). The suffix -*var* of Hungarian place names means "fortified place," and the -*dam* of Dutch names is "dike."

In Hebrew names, *Beth-* means "house" (Bethlehem, "house of bread"; Bethel, "house of God"). The -*abad* so frequent in the place names of India and Persia is a Persian suffix meaning "city." The -*pore*, -*pur*, and similar forms appearing frequently in India and Malaya have the same meaning; Singapore is "lion city"; Jaipur is "pink city." The -*stan* of Hindustan, Afghanistan, Pakistan, etc. is a Persian word meaning "country"; the Moslem generic term for the infidel lands of the west is Feringhistan ("country of the Franks"), a tribute to the role played by the French in the Crusades, where Islam and Christianity clashed.

A place name that seems directly taken from a linguistic manual is the southern French region of Languedoc, which means "tongue of *hoc*"; it is derived from the southern French (Provençal) habit of using the Latin *hoc*, literally "this" as an affirmation, in contrast to the north of France, which used *hoc ille* ("this he"; with a verb like "did" or "said" understood); *hoc ille* later became *oil,* and still later the modern French *oui.*

Certain place names are indicative of historical errors. Even though Columbus' name is immortalized in Columbia,

Colombia, etc., America was named after Amerigo Vespucci by a map maker who erroneously thought Vespucci had discovered the new continent. The theory has lately been advanced in France, however, that America comes from Armorica, the ancient Latin name for Brittany, and that Vespucci took his first name from the name of the new country rather than the reverse.

An even greater linguistic blunder occurred at the same time. Columbus, thinking he had reached the Indies, called the inhabitants of the New World "Indians," a term which until then had been properly reserved for the inhabitants of India. When the error was discovered, all sorts of distinctions were resorted to; the English thought of using "Red Indian" or "American Indian" as against "East Indian"; but plain "Indian" was a term that stuck like a leech to the unfortunate inhabitants of the Western Hemisphere. To avoid confusion, people began to cast about for a new name for the Indians of India, and got into a worse morass by using "Hindu" to describe both a religious and an ethnic group. "Hindu" might be etymologically correct to describe the inhabitants of Hindustan, but it is also used to denote those inhabitants of India who are of Aryan stock, or those who speak Indo-Iranian languages (the stock and the languages do not all coincide). Religiously speaking, "Hindu" covers those inhabitants of India and Pakistan (roughly two thirds) who believe in the religion of Brahma, Vishnu, and Shiva, as opposed to the Moslems, Sikhs, Jains, and all the other minority faiths of India.

Other historical misnomers are our use of "Dutch," which comes from German *Deutsch* and means "German," to describe the Hollanders, who call themselves *Nederlandsch* or *Nederlands;* and our term "Midwestern" which, however correct it may have been in the 1800s, is an anachronism at a period when the Midwest lies in the eastern part of the country.

There is an abundance of poetry in the world of place names. Ceylon is from the native *Sindhaladwipa* ("lion island"), but among more poetic names bestowed upon it by Hindu writers are "Garden of the Sky," "Land of Dusky Leaves," "Island of Jewels," "Land without Sorrow." Formosa, the name bestowed by the Portuguese explorers on the island of Taiwan, means "beautiful." The Chinese name for America is *Mai Kuo* ("beautiful land"). Tel Aviv, capital of Israel, is "hill of spring," and Addis Ababa, capital of Ethiopia, is "new flower." Vladivostok is "eastern might," Madras is "university," Chungking is "repeated congratulations" and

Curaçao, capital of the Dutch West Indies, is a Portuguese word that means "healing." Rajasthan, in India, is "Royal Land"; its alternate name, Rajputana, is "Land of Kings' Sons," "Land of Princes," and every Rajput considers himself a prince. The Azores derive their names from the *açores*, or hawks, found there by the first Portuguese explorers to set foot on the islands; according to latest accounts, the hawks are still there.

Translations of place names are often curious. Montenegro is an Italian translation of Serbian *Crna Gora* ("black mountain"), while Bosporus is an exact Greek translation of the English "Oxford." Cairo, in Arabic, means "the conqueror," but the form is feminine, so that it might be translated "the triumphant female" (actually, the word is the Arabic designation of the planet Mars, which was in the ascendant when the city was founded). Patagonia is "land of the big feet," coming from Spanish *patacón*, "big foot"; when Magellan first set foot on Tierra del Fuego in 1520, enormous footprints were discovered in the sand. Yucatán, in Mexico, means "what do you say?" in the language of the local Indians; this was the answer given by them to inquiries as to the name of the country. One Sicilian town bears the Greek name of Calimera, which means "good morning"; another, Linguaglossa, bears a name which is a repetition of the word "tongue," first in Latin, then in Greek; Mongibello, the name of a mountain, means "mountain mountain," first in Latin ("mons"), then in Arabic ("jebel").

Large, important, or historically known European cities usually have their names translated when they appear in foreign languages; *Venezia*, for instance, is "Venice" to the English, *Venise* to the French, *Venedig* to the Germans; "London" is *Londres* to the French and Spaniards, *Londra* to the Italians, *Londinon* to the Greeks, *Lontoo* to the Finns, *Londyn* to the Poles; *Roma* of the Italians becomes *Rom* to the Germans, *Rzym* to the Poles, *Rooma* to the Finns, "Rome" to us; *Moskva* is "Moscow" to the English, *Moscou* to the French, *Mosca* to the Italians; the Germans' *Wien* is "Vienna" to us, *Viyana* to the Turks, *Wieden* to the Poles. Smaller or less famous centers are generally left untranslated. American cities are normally untranslated, save for the "New" of "New York" and "New Orleans"; but the Vatican's Latin translation has *Petricula* for Little Rock, *Sinus Viridis* for Green Bay, *Campifontis* for Springfield.

When it comes to names of countries, the situation is more serious. We barely recognize ourselves in the French *États-*

Unis, the Spanish *Estados Unidos,* the German *Vereinigte Staaten;* but what American would recognize his own country from the Serbo-Croatian *Zjedinjene Drazave,* the Finnish *Yhdysvallat,* the Arabic *Alwellat Almotaheda,* the Gaelic *an t-oileán úr* (literally, "new island"), the Japanese *Bei-koku* (literally "rice land")?

The matter of the pronunciation of place names sometimes leads to divergences, not only when the names are foreign but even when they are indigenous. Great controversies arose during the war about the radio pronunciation of such Russian and Polish towns as Orel and Lodz, which in their native languages sound like "Oryol" and "Wudge." To get the G.I.s to pronounce with even approximate correctness the name of the French city of Rheims, someone devised the spelling "Rhance," while French railroad conductors occasionally pronounced it "Reems" to get themselves understood by American soldiers on leave. Even here in America we have New Orleans stressed on the first syllable by its inhabitants but on the last by most Easterners; Houston, which is Hewston in Texas but House-ton when it appears as the name of a New York City street; St. Louis, which is a source of offense to Missourians if you don't sound the final *-s.* On the Pennsylvania Railroad run from New York to Columbus, you pass through Newark, New Jersey, and Newark, Ohio; the trainmen always make a careful distinction between the two; the first is stressed on the first syllable and the *-ark* sounds like *-erk;* the second is definitely New Ark, with both syllables equally stressed.

For a corruption of a retained foreign place name, none better can be found than Key West, which in no way resembles a key nor is particularly west of anything; it is simply the English sound adaptation of the Spanish *Cayo Hueso* ("bone island").

American place names show endless variety but also some wearisome repetition, particularly of Old World counterparts. Where England has one Manchester, the United States has twenty-six. There are in America no less than thirty-seven Berlins, twenty-one Romes, nineteen Viennas. Cairo, Alexandria, Moscow, even Russia's discarded St. Petersburg have their namesakes in America. Athens, Sparta, Troy, Ithaca, Utica, and Syracuse are only a few of the American representatives of Classical antiquity.

But, by way of contrast, we have also novel, highly imaginative names. Whose heart will fail to warm to What Cheer, Iowa; Social Circle, Georgia; Harmony, Pennsylvania;

Friendship, New York; Humansville, Missouri; Helper, Utah; Loyal, Wisconsin? Plain Dealing, Louisiana; Commerce, Georgia; Enterprise, Alabama; Export, Pennsylvania; and Emporia, Kansas, sound as though they were taken from the terminology of the National Association of Manufacturers. Mathematicians will like Oblong, Illinois; Circleville, Ohio; and Crossville, Tennessee, while geographers will be pleased with North East, Maryland; Due West, South Carolina; and Meridian, Mississippi. Other picturesque American place names are Wink, Texas; Sleepy Eye, Minnesota; Hominy, Oklahoma; Frostproof, Florida; while to H. L. Mencken's list of comical place names in the United States one might add Boneyard Hollow, Polka Dot, Getaway, Greasy Ridge, and Hogskin, all located in southern Ohio. And what shall we say of those two congenial and sports-minded Ohio towns, Basil and Baltimore, which decided to merge even to their names, with a resultant Baseball, Ohio? Santa Claus as the name of an American town brings much business to the post office. California offers, among other things, Wiskeytown, Bourbon, and Peanut, while Pennsylvania, probably the most linguistically creative state in the Union, has Pig's Ear, Bird-in-Hand, Dogtown, Pancake, Live Easy, and Bedbug Hollow. A foreign land, Chile, gives us a mountain with the name of Quisapué. This is analyzed into "¿Quién sabe, pues?" and means, roughly, "Who the devil knows?"

Another important variety of United States place names has been supplied by the strong Christian faith of early Spanish and French settlers, particularly in our Southwest. Sangre de Cristo Range in New Mexico means "Blood of Christ"; Corpus Christi in Texas is "Body of Christ"; Santa Cruz and Santa Fe mean "Holy Cross" and "Holy Faith." The original name of Los Angeles, bestowed in 1781, was "El Pueblo de Nuestra Señora la Reina de los Angeles de Porciúncula," "The Village of Our Lady the Queen of the Angels of Little Portion."

Still others of our place names are indicative of the nationality of the early settlers: witness Swedesboro and Finns Point, New Jersey; Germantown, Pennsylvania (also Illinois); French Lick, Indiana; Frenchville, Maine; Frenchtown, New Jersey; Russiaville, Indiana; Spanish Fork, Utah.

The names bestowed upon inhabitants of various localities often reflect foreign or dialectal origin. The correct name for a citizen of Los Angeles, for instance, is Angeleño, which is pure Spanish. A citizen of Monaco, the tiny principality whose capital is Monte Carlo, is a Monegasque, reflecting the local dialect. Other such names for inhabitants reflect cultured Latin forms of the place name itself: the adjective for Oxford is Oxonian; for Exeter, Exonian or Exon; for Cambridge, Cantabrigian.

Gotham means "the hamlet of the Goths"; but what connection can the Goths have with New York, to which the name is so often applied? It was bestowed, it seems, in 1807 by Washington Irving, who knew the history of the original Gotham in England. In the days of King John, the inhabitants, having learned that the king was planning to establish a hunting lodge near their village and fearing high taxes and other nuisances, acted by preconceived plan in such a strange, nonsensical fashion that the king's messengers reported the spot unsuitable. Gotham since then assumed the meaning of a town with method to its madness.

— Chapter Seven —

THE STORY OF PERSONAL AND FAMILY NAMES

The myrtle that grows among thorns is a myrtle still.
—Talmud

What are names but air?
—Coleridge

NAMES are the badge of individuality. So long as the individual is nameless, he is amorphous. When he receives or creates a name by which he can identify himself, he enters upon a truly subjective existence. By acquiring the names of objects, animals, and people around him, he acquires also an objective consciousness.

The distinction between proper and common nouns, or names, is largely a product of civilized thought. More primitive is the distinction between animate and inanimate objects, a distinction which still forms part of the grammatical structure of many languages.

Little if any distinction must have been made at first between human beings and animals. The free interchange of names between the two animate classes is characteristic of most primitive groups. "Little Bear" is a perfectly sound primitive name for an individual. But "bear" itself is originally the "brown one" or, if we take it in its more common Indo-European variant typified by Latin *ursus,* it is the "harmer" or "bruiser." Such names could serve equally well for animals or people. Once they became regularly associated with animals, they could easily be transferred to people by reason of a real or fancied resemblance, or the desire for resemblance.

The single name is found associated, even in many primitive groups, with a tribal or clan name, often with a nickname, or honor name as well. There is little doubt that this piling-up of names is an outgrowth of social living. Among the Mohawks, for instance, we find the existence of a birth name like Morning Cloud, a confirmation name like Hungry Wolf, an honor name like Scalp Raiser, and the tribal name, Mohawk. The ancient Romans bore a personal name like Marcus, a hereditary family or clan name, such as Tullius ("of the Tullian clan"), and a personal nickname, such as Cicero ("chick pea"), from a wart on the nose. This nickname, however, often became hereditary.

Among many primitive tribes personal names are not divided into male and female, and the same name can be indifferently applied to a man or a woman. A similar tendency is noticeable in present-day America, where names like Lee, Beverly, and even Marion and Leslie are used for people of both sexes.

The Christian, and particularly the Roman Catholic, tradition calls for first names which are taken either from the Bible or from the saints' calendar. Some European countries actually used to limit by law the possibility of first names to these two categories, to which they later grudgingly added the personages of antiquity. The custom of using saints' names in baptism, however, did not come into full vogue until the tenth century. During the four preceding centuries, there was a vogue of Germanic proper names in the countries penetrated by Germanic invaders after the fall of the Roman Empire. Their pagan, often totemistic origin, however, is clearly perceptible. Germanic names like Adolph and Rudolph mean "noble wolf" and "famous wolf"; Bernard is "bold as a bear"; Eberhard, "bold as a boar." The Latin name Lupus ("wolf"), which became extremely common in those centuries and which survives today in place names like Saint-Lô ("saint wolf"), was probably a loan translation from the Germanic. But the Romans themselves had previously used such totemistic animal names as Ursus and Leo.

The vogue of Germanic names in medieval Europe is attested by the fact that of the five leading recorded first names in England after the Norman Conquest (these five names rose from 38 per cent of the total in the twelfth century to 64 per cent in the fourteenth) four, Henry, Robert, William, and Richard, are of Germanic origin; the fifth, John, is Biblical. Throughout the entire period, William kept its absolute lead over the others.

A Germanic suffix that acquired and still holds great vogue is *-bert,* etymologically related to the English adjective "bright." Albert is "bright in honor," Robert (or Rupert or Rupprecht) "fame bright," Lambert "land bright." The pure root appears in the feminine Bertha, whose exact Latin counterpart is Clara ("bright").

Ludwig, Lewis, Louis are all variants of an originally Germanic name meaning "bold warrior." Chlodovechus is the form the name assumes in the Latin documents of Gaul after the Frankish occupation, and Clovis, the first Merovingian king of France, is simply the namesake of his remote Capetian succesor, Louis XVI.

The process of name forming does not vary its pattern greatly from language to language. Latin Valentine is simply "valiant," Latin Agnes (or its Spanish descendant Inez) is "lamblike." Greek Napoleon is "forest lion," Greek Philip "horse lover." Celtic Arthur is "noble," Celtic Owen is "young warrior." Persian Cyrus is "sun," Persian Esther "star."

Hebrew names are often distinguished by a religious note which is largely absent from those of other origins. The -el appearing in such Hebrew forms as Emanuel, Gabriel, Michael means "God" or "of God." Daniel, for instance, is "God is my judge."

Jesus is a Greek rendering of the Hebrew Joshua, "savior." The use of Jesus as a first name for men, without the least trace of irreverence, is widespread in Latin-American countries.

Unfamiliar and strange are the forms which some very common names assume in different languages. John is easily recognizable in French Jean, Spanish Juan, German Johannes (Johnny is Hans or Hansel), even in Italian Giovanni, Russian Ivan, and Serbian Jovan; but Irish Sean and Finnish Juhana require a translation. Joseph causes no trouble in its Spanish, German, and Slavic variants, José, Josef, and Josip; but it becomes more difficult in Italian Giuseppe and practically unrecognizable in Irish Seosmh. Stephen, a Greek name meaning "victor's wreath," becomes Étienne, Esteban, Stepan, Istvan, and Stiobhan in French, Spanish, Russian, Hungarian, and Irish, respectively. Few people would recognize the familiar Helen in the Hungarian Ilona or its diminutive Ilka.

Names peculiarly lend themselves to distorted, shortened, or diminutive forms, many of which become so unrecognizable as to cause confusion. Ted, which in America serves for Theodore, is Britain's diminutive for Edward, along with Ned. Ed can stand for any of the names beginning with a prefix which in Anglo-Saxon meant "wealth" (Edmund, Edgar, Edwin, etc.). Mandy is a short form of Latin Amanda ("lovable," "loveworthy"). Mamie, which many think a diminutive, is a full name, taken from Old French *m'amie* ("my lady friend") or *m'aimée* ("my beloved"). Tabby, so often incorrectly applied to she-cats alone, was originally the Syriac Tabitha ("gazelle"). Similar situations arise in other languages. Spanish José becomes Pepe or Pepito, Italian Giuseppe turns into Beppo or Peppino, and an apparently harmless Italian name like Dino may conceal a much more impressive Aldobrandino, Germanic in origin, meaning "old brand" or "old sword," with a diminutive ending which is practically all that survives.

"Nickname" is "an ekename," an additional name bestowed usually for purposes of precise identification. This is clearly illustrated in the Bermuda telephone directory, where people are listed not only with their names and addresses but also with the appellation by which they are known to their intimates. Alfred Smith of Longford Mews, Warwick, for instance, is "Smudge" Smith; but O. C. Smith of St. George is "Slim" and another Smith is "Happy." Feminine nicknames include "Tiny," "Buster," and "Sweets." Residences, too, have their nicknames: "Wits' End," "The Ruin," "Kum-n-si-us," "The Last Shilling." A merry, hospitable, informal place is Bermuda.

A few names are unflattering to their owners. Among these are Calvin (Latin "bald"), Claude (Latin "lame"), Ulysses (Greek "hater"), Priscilla (Latin "somewhat old"), Mary (Hebrew "bitter"), Barbara (Greek "foreign"). Ursula ("little she-bear") is a matter of taste. So also are George (Greek "farmer") and Algernon (Old French "bewhiskered").

Many of the names bestowed by the Pilgrim Fathers upon their offspring strike a humorous note today. Among them we find such gems as Humility, Hate-Evil, and Kill-Sin.

Another humorous note is supplied by those feminine names of recent American adoption which are taken from foreign languages (usually Italian or Spanish) without regard for their meaning in their tongues of origin. Lana is "wool" in Latin, Spanish, or Italian. Gretta, supposedly an improvement on an original German Grete, becomes Italian for "mean," "petty." Unforgivable are Buffa and Natica. The first is Italian for "funny," the latter for "buttock."

Mencken, in his second *Supplement*, offers a remarkable list of girls' names spreading from Oklahoma to Texas and the deep South, among them Alapluma, Vaughncille, Wymola, Xmay, and Zzelle. One masculine name, reported from Kentucky, which seems to have escaped his notice, is Tootall; its fortunate possessor actually grew to the stature of six and a half feet. The dwellers of the Amazon valley, about two decades ago, became fascinated by Frigidaire, with the result that many girls in that area bear that name. In Nyasaland, Africa, a native tribe got into the custom of taking names from a publisher's catalogue which had somehow fallen into their hands. Their chieftain took for himself the sonorous name of Oxford University Press. A grateful mother in the Congo, impressed by the organization's educational work, named her infant son Unesco.

The custom of family names, as distinguished from the primitive clan or tribal name which fell into disuse after the fall of the Roman Empire, did not generally arise in Europe till the twelfth century, when Venetian patrician families began to hand down a second name from father to son. Previously, there had been a sporadic use of patronymics, like Walter, John's son, which ultimately developed into Walter Johnson; of trade names, like John the Baker, which resulted in John Baker; and of location names, such as Thomas-at-well, which finally became Thomas Atwell. Along with these came nicknames, like Long John, later transposed into John Long. Confusion over the use of such names lasted for centuries and still endures today in a few localities, notably Iceland, where a son assumes his father's first name with the added suffix -son; thus Olaf the son of Gudman Thorwaldsson becomes Olaf Gudmansson, but Olaf's son Erik is Erik Olafsson. A similar system has been in use since time immemorial among Semitic speakers; in Arabic countries Abdul ibn Hussein is Abdul son of Hussein, and among nonwesternized Jews Yakub ben Abraham is Jacob son of Abraham. The Ethiopians, too, betray their Semitic origin by a series of alternate patronymics. Abebe Tadessa automatically names his son Tadessa Abebe, and the latter in turn must name his son Abebe Tadessa. But the Ethiopian government, succumbing to modernization, is taking steps to halt this practice and institute a permanent surname for each family.

Crystallized patronymic forms supply us with perhaps a plurality of our family names: Nelson, Jones, or Johnson, Williams, Harrison, Davis, etc. Almost equal in number are the petrified trade names: Baker, Smith, Collier, Taylor, Butler, etc. Some of these names have connotations different from the ones you might suspect. Fuller and Walker, for instance, both indicate descent from a fuller, or thickener, of raw cloth, who was called *wealcere* in some sections of Anglo-Saxon England. Crowder is from the name of a player of a Welsh musical instrument called *crwth*. Location names like London, Berlin, Woods, Craig, Downs are only slightly less numerous.

Identical processes in name forming have occurred in most western languages. A name like Smith has an exact counterpart in French Ferrier, Spanish Herrero, Italian Ferraro, German Schmidt, Dutch Smit, Hungarian Kovacs, Polish Kowalczyk, even Syrian Haddad. Russian Kusnetzov, however, is more literally Smithson. Jones and Johnson are paralleled by Italian Di Giovanni, Spanish Juánez, Norwegian Hanssen, Russian Ivanov. Woods has a counterpart in French Dubois, Italian Bosco, Spanish Madera, German Walde. Atwell is translated by French La Fontaine.

As we well know from the abundance of foreign names in our midst, family names of one country often get into another and become, so to speak, naturalized there. Many third-generation Brazilians bear such names as Williamson, Green, Wright, Garner, Cook, Ferguson, Thatcher, Matthews, Moore, and Lee. They are the descendants of some ten thousand die-hard Confederates who could not resign themselves to Yankee carpetbagger domination after Appomattox and emigrated to South America, where they were very well received. One of the colonies they founded is still named Vila Americana, and these Brazilian Americans are living proof that we, too, can on occasion be a nation of emigrants for political reasons.

Smith, the most common family name in both Britain and America, has a three-to-two lead over its nearest competitor, Jones or Johnson. In Russia the situation is reversed. Ivanov holds a three-to-one lead over Kusnetzov. On a par with the widespread use of Smith in the Anglo-Saxon countries is that of Chen as a family name in China.

Among the patronymics must be reckoned the numerous Celtic forms in O', Mc, Mac, Ap, P, and the Norman-French Fitz. Mc (or Mac) and Ap are respectively the Gaelic and Welsh forms of "son," while Fitz is the Anglo-Norman variant of French *fils*. McHugh, Aphugh (or Pugh), and Fitzhugh are therefore the same name, which might be anglicized into Hughson.

Not all family names, of course, belong to the three classes mentioned above (patronymics, trade names, location names). Some describe a personal characteristic or habit of some long-forgotten ancestor. Drinkwater (or French Boileau or Italian Bevilacqua) is a reminder of teetotaling tendencies somewhere along the line. White (French Leblanc, Italian Bianchi, German Weiss, Russian Byelov, Welsh Gwynne) was first applied to some member of the family who was unusually fair or prematurely gray. The name of the Czech composer Smetana means "cream"; Gorky is "bitter"; Tolstoi is "fat"; Colombo (Columbus) is "pigeon"; Machiavelli is "bad nails"; Bonaparte is "on the right side."

Endings and prefixes in family names are often indicative of national origin. The suffix -ian (Kalenderian, Bagramian) is Armenian; -quist, -rup, -holm, -strom, -dahl, -gren, and -sen (Linquist, Northrup, Lindholm, Bergstrom, Liliedahl, Kilgren, Johannsen) are Scandinavian; -ez (Pérez) is Spanish; -berg, -burg, -stein, -sohn are German, Scandinavian, or Yiddish; -ich or -ić (Karageorgeovich, Adamić) is Yugoslav; -yi (Perenyi) is Hungarian; -poulos (Stavropoulos) is Greek; -oglu (Yegenoglu) is Turkish; -i (Petri) is Italian; -off or -ov (Molotov, Rachmaninoff) is Russian; -eff or -ev (Gheorghieff, Andreiev) is Russian or Bulgarian; -enko (Kravchenko) is Ukrainian; -wicz (Sienkiewicz) is Polish; -ski (Paderewski) is Polish, but its variant -sky (Kerensky, Radetsky) is Russian or Czech.

Among the prefixes, van (Van Houten) is Dutch or Flemish; von (von Hindenburg) is German; de may be French, Spanish, Portuguese, or Italian (de Musset, de Avila, de Vasconcellos, de Amicis); di and da are Italian (di Parma, da Feltre). The French de may appear in such variants as du, de la, des (Duhamel, de la Falaise, Desgranges); the Spanish variants are del, de los, de las (del Río, de los Ríos); the Portuguese are do, da, dos, das (Davega, dos Passos); Italian variants are too numerous to mention (del Giudice, delle Colonne, etc.). These prefixes do not necessarily betoken aristocratic lineage.

Not all languages give names the same arrangement. A Russian name consists of the given name; a real patronymic, ending in -vich or -ich for men, -vna for women; and a family name, usually ending in -ov or -ev, which is a petrified patronymic and turns to -ova, -eva in the feminine: thus, Ivan Nikolaievich Semyonov (John, son of Nicholas, of the Simons) or Olga Nikolaievna Semyonova (Olga, daughter of Nicholas, of the Simons).

It is perfectly polite and proper to address a Russian by his or her given name and patronymic (Ivan Nikolaievich, Olga Nikolaievna), omitting the family name, just as it is perfectly polite and proper to address a Spaniard by his or her first name, prefixing Don or Doña (Don Manuel, Doña Inez) and omitting the family name.

The Burmese use prefixes before their names; a young woman has the prefix ma, which changes to daw when she grows older; young men carry the prefix maung, while older men have *u*, literally "uncle": thus, "Ma Thein," later "Daw Thein," and "Maung Thant," later "U Thant."

In many Catholic countries three first names are given at christening, one by the father, one by the sponsor, and a third by the priest. Despite this, the use of a middle name in life is far less customary than it is in America. The "Jr." so common in the United States is practically nonexistent elsewhere, and a Budapest newspaper recently voiced an inquiry by one of its readers as to why so many Americans append Jr. to their names and whether the suffix has any historical significance.

Spanish-speaking countries often combine the paternal and maternal family names (Menéndez y Pelayo, Rico y Fraga). In many lands, notably Hungary, China, and Japan, it is customary to place the family name before the personal name at all times and not merely on index cards: Chiang Kai-shek is Kai-shek of the Chiang family.

The alias which in most social groups is slightly questionable is an accepted social custom among the Gypsies, who use a *nav romanes* (Romany name) for use among their own people and a *nav gajikanes* (foreign name) for use among non-Gypsies.

Curios in the field of names abound. To begin with, there are unusual spellings, as in the family name Eggerss. Then there is the matter of transcription into other writing systems, notably the Chinese. The name of Kennedy, for instance, came out in Taiwan newspaper transcriptions as Kan Nai Dai, with three characters that spell out "willing-endurance-bliss." Long and short family names tend to go to extremes in some lands. China's widespread Ng and Sz are surpassed for written-form brevity by France's O, the name of a family living in Neuilly, while India's Tiruvalyanguidi Vijayaraghavacharya (the first name means "village of prosperous rice fields" and the second breaks up into a synonym for Rama and the name of a fourteenth-century religious leader) is outstripped by the 55-letter name of a Fijian cricket player: Talebuamaineiilikenamainavaleniveivakabulaimakulalakeba (meaning unknown to this writer).

Names bestowed upon breeds of dogs can be picturesque. A recent dog show boasted of Affenpinschers, Basenjis, Borzois, Bouviers des Flandres, Dandie Dinmonts, Keeshonden, Lhasa Apsos, Alaskan Malamutes, Puliks, Rottweilers, Samoyeds, Schipperkes, Tervurens, Vizslas, and Weimaraners, not to mention references to two extinct breeds, Ruttanfungers and Wunks (the latter are, or were, Chinese). A French canine society, seeking new names for new breeds at the end of the alphabet, came up with a suggestion for Xenophons, Yaltas, Yosemites, Zeuses, and Zanzibars.

The names of some flowers, like the narcissus, iris, gentian, and peony, go back to classical mythology. Others, like the dahlia, poinsettia, zinnia, and lobelia, record the names of their creators or discoverers. Others show derivation from a multitude of diverse languages, like the Latin calendula and gladiolus, the Greek chrysanthemum and anemone, the Persian-Arabic lilac, the Dutch daffodil, the French pansy and dandelion, the Anglo-Saxon mistletoe and daisy. Even weeds have their poetic names: Creeping Jenny, Bouncing Bet, Snow-on-the-Mountain, Panic Grass, Lamb's Quarters.

Poetic names are also given to the most unlikely objects. Some of our rockets bear the names of Atlas, Tiros, Thor, Zeus, Apollo, Explorer, Ranger, Mariner, and even Dyna-Soar, an ingenious re-etymologizing of a word that means "fearful lizard" into one that means "power rise," even if the latter is a hybrid. Computing machines and electronic brains have been baptized with such names as Bark, Besk, Perm, Informatik, Gamma, Ural, Pegasus, Mercury, Petra, and Zebra.

But recently names have fallen upon evil days. The tendency is visible to replace them, possibly altogether as time goes on, with numbers. To Internal Revenue, we are Social Security numbers; to banks, depositor numbers; to the telephone company, a ten-digit series; to organizations that issue credit cards, a credit number; to the Motor Vehicle Bureau, a license number; to the military authorities, a draft number; to our employers, employee numbers. It is little wonder that a columnist suggests that we give up our names, allow all these numbers to be merged into one, which will appear on a single card, to be known as the "Social Obscurity Card," and that we be henceforth known as Mr. 789–432–2831, with perhaps the last number changing from 1 to 2 for Mrs., and *a, b, c, d,* etc., added on for children until they come of age, when they turn into full-fledged numbers in their own right.

— Chapter Eight —

THE LANGUAGE OF POLITENESS AND INSULT

"Mend your speech a little, lest it mar your fortune."
—Shakespeare, *King Lear*

INTIMATELY connected with names, and to some extent arising from them, are the superabundant titles and expressions which social living has forced practically all races to subscribe to. The "Mr.," "Mrs.," and "Miss" of English, the *Monsieur, Madame,* and *Mademoiselle* of French, the *Herr, Frau,* and *Fräulein* of German, and all the other myriad prefixes for proper names have a long and interesting history.

"Mister" is originally the Latin *magister,* "headman," "commander," "steersman" (the root is *mag-,* "great"). The educational, intellectual, or occupational headman becomes the "master," the *maître, maestro,* and *mastro* of the Romance languages, even the *Meister* of German. Socially, he turns into a person who is respected because of his prominent position. "Mistress" is the same word, to which is added the Greek feminine suffix *-issa,* which in French becomes *-esse.* "Miss," an abbreviation of "Mistress," was used under Charles I to denote a woman of ill repute but later began to be applied to an unmarried woman, with the spelling "Mis." In Shakespeare's days, "Mistress" was used for both married and unmarried ladies.

In Victorian days, the proper British gentlemanly form of postal address was "So-and-so, Esquire." "Esquire" comes from Latin *scutarius* ("shield-bearer"). The shield-bearer or *écuyer* was in medieval times a young man of noble birth who had not yet won his knight's spurs and still served his apprenticeship. He was the companion of the prince, noble, or knight. There was only one lower rank in the social scale of those who counted, the "gentleman," one descended of gentle lineage. The use of "Esquire" to a distinguished correspondent is, from the etymological point of view, somewhat condescending.

Madame and *Mademoiselle*, along with *Monsieur*, are normally used by the French in direct address *without* a following name; where an American would say "Good morning, Mrs. Jones" the Frenchman simply uses *"Bonjour, Madame."* *Madame* comes from the Latin *mea domina* ("my lady"), and *mademoiselle* is a diminutive or youthful form (*-illa* was a Latin feminine diminutive ending). On the contrary, Spanish *Señora, Señorita* and Italian *Signora, Signorina* contain an implicit charge of old age. The base form is the Latin masculine *senior* ("elder," "older"), from which Spanish *Señor,* or Italian *Signore,* French (*Mon*)*sieur* and *Seigneur* and English "Sir," "Sire" are derived. As applied to a man, the appellation "elder" is a token of respect; as applied to a woman, the compliment is somewhat dubious; when it comes to a young unmarried woman, it is downright paradoxical, since it makes her a "little old woman."

German *Herr* is "Lord," in the most comprehensive sense of the word. *Frau,* on the other hand, is simply "woman," and its use for spinsters as well as married women is authorized by a German court decision. In this polite usage of "woman," German is paralleled by Italian *donna,* applied to a lady of high estate, and by English "queen," which originally simply meant "woman." German *Fräulein* is "little woman."

Pre-Soviet Russia used *gospodin* and *gospozha,* both based on the Indo-European word that gives us "guest" and "host." But since the 1917 Revolution it is no longer stylish, and may even be unwise, to use these words. "Comrade" (*tovarishch*), "citizen" (*grazhdanin*), and "citizeness" (*grazhdanka*) are preferred. But the Yugoslavs, who had also adopted "comrade," have been showing a distressing tendency to go back to the old words for "sir" and "madam." The French Revolution tried to introduce similar words at the end of the eighteenth century, but the French were far too fond of their polite appellations to give them up permanently.

While most languages use titles of politeness, there is infinite diversity in usage. Some foreign languages are far more prolix than English in their use of honorific titles in correspondence. A German letter, for instance, is addressed to *"Hochwohlgeboren Herrn Professor So-und-so"* (literally, "High-well-born Mr. Professor") and starts: *"Sehr verehrter Herr Professor!"* ("Greatly honored Mr. Professor"). By way of contrast, there is a tendency in French to eschew all titles save *Monsieur, Madame,* and *Mademoiselle* in direct conversational address, and a society was formed at the University of Virginia in 1925 "for the encouragement of the use of 'Mr.' as applied to all men, professional or otherwise."

Some languages carry the husband's title over to the wife. *Frau Professor* in German is used not only to a lady professor but to a professor's wife. In Italian a title like "Professor" is used in connection with anybody holding any teaching position beyond elementary school, or to an orchestra player.

Conventional formulas for "I" and "you" abound in many languages. English is the only language that capitalizes "I" in writing, whereas many languages capitalize "you," and this has been interpreted, rightly or wrongly, as a sign of an exaggerated ego on the part of English speakers. A few languages, including Siamese and Hungarian (the latter only in flowery speech), use "slave" for "I." The Hungarian term is *szervusz,* taken from Latin *servus,* the word that gives us "serf," "servant," and "servitude." "Your humble servant" in English is not too far removed. Malay uses *sahaya* or *patek* ("slave") when addressing a superior; *tean* ("companion") in addressing an equal.

In most languages there are at least two forms for "you," one more familiar, the other more polite. Often the plural form of "you" serves also as a polite singular. The English use of "ye" and "you," originally plural forms, to replace "thou" and "thee" in the singular has led to the practical extinction of the latter.

The rising of the polite plural for the singular has a curious historical origin, if we are to believe the more picturesque of the two theories on the subject. The less picturesque is that "you" for "thou" arose by imitation of editorial "we" for "I," a current practice in the ancient world. Cicero tells the Romans "We have saved you from Catiline," when it is fairly obvious that he means "I have saved you." But editorial "we" is essentially a plural of modesty, while "you" for "thou" is a plural of reverence, and it is difficult to see how the one could arise from the other.

The second theory is that the use of "you" for "thou" arose in the later days of the Roman Empire, when there were two emperors, one sitting in Rome, the other in Constantinople. Persons addressing one of the emperors would use "you" on the theory that they were addressing the totality of imperial authority. Later, when the Empire had fallen, barbarian chieftains demanded imperial honors for themselves, including the "plural of majesty." Ultimately, every petty official required the honorific form of address which, by reason of too frequent use, gradually lost some of its effectiveness. At this point, new devices began to come into being for use with those whom one really wished to honor. Spanish, for example, evolved a *Vuestra Merced* ("Your Grace" or "Your Honor") which ultimately contracted into *Usted*. Grammatical logic, however, required the verb to be in the third, not in the second, person (in English we say to a judge: "Your Honor *is* mistaken"). *Usted* is consequently construed with a third person singular verb.

Italian went further than Spanish. After developing such forms as *Vostra Signoria* ("Your Lordship") and *Vostra Eccellenza* ("Your Excellency"), it went on to replace them with a short pronoun. But since "Lordship" and "Excellency" are feminine nouns in Italian, it was the feminine pronoun *lei* ("she") that was used to replace them. Accordingly, the form "she," duly capitalized in writing, is used in Italian with a third person singular verb as a polite "you" (*Lei scrive*, literally, "she writes," for "you write"). The Fascist Government, during the years of its existence, tried, but quite unsuccessfully, to abolish "she" and bring back the earlier "you." "You" appeared in office, commercial, and even private correspondence, but "she" continued to be used in conversation.

Portuguese and Polish have a polite usage which is reminiscent of Congressional practice. Instead of saying "you" one uses "the gentleman," "the lady."

French, which uses a simple "you" for polite purposes, has a special expression, *tutoyer*, which means "to thou-and-thee" somebody, to address familiarly instead of politely. There was an abortive tendency to *tutoyer* during the French Revolution, but Robespierre viewed it with disfavor and even spoke in approval of the generalization of "you." A French revolutionary writer described the habit of using the familiar form of address as "characteristic of absolute monarchies."

There is considerable embarrassment in languages that use a polite and a familiar form of address about passing from the former to the latter when a change in the nature of the relationship between two persons warrants it. Hesitation, confusion, relapses, and apologies are the result before the new form of address becomes stabilized. It has been claimed that the English equivalent of the French transition from *vous* to *tu* is the passing from "Mr. So-and-so" to the use of the person's last name, then to the use of his first name; but it is not quite the same thing. One can always avoid pronouncing a name, but it is not easy to avoid "you."

Titles bestowed upon national leaders, as often as not by themselves, are frequently picturesque and definitely betray a state of mind. We can begin with the inscription on the tomb of Seti I, an Egyptian Pharaoh who ruled in the fourteenth century B.C. and whose appellations include "Mighty of Bows, Lord of Diadems, Beloved of Ra, Rich in Captives, Speaking with His Mouth, Acting with His Hands, Encompassing the End of Those Who Transgress against His Ways." Peru's Inca was the "Child of the Sun." China's emperors were styled "Son of Heaven," and the title of the ruling British monarch has included since the days of Henry VIII "Defender of the Faith." There have been along the course of history titles bestowed upon monarchs (no doubt by others) that were not too complimentary: the *rois fainéants* or "do-nothing kings" of medieval France, or such epithets as Louis the Fat and Ivan the Terrible. Seti's nomenclature is paralleled in recent times by some eastern rulers. The Dalai Lama is described as "Tender Glory, Absolute Wisdom, Ocean-Vast." A maharajah of Gwalior was the "Ultimate Authority, Light of the Age, Richest of the Rich, Bravest of the Brave, Gentlest of the Gentle," and Siam's Chulalongkorn, believed to be the hero of "The King and I," called himself in a letter to President Lincoln "the Great Rising-Forth from Mankind" and "the Jeweled Head of a Pin." *Führer, Duce, Caudillo,* and *Vozhd'* (the last means "leader" and was applied to Stalin) are of recent vintage. So is Pakistan's *Qaid-e-Azam,* "Great Leader" or "Great Guide." Trujillo called himself "Benefactor of the Fatherland" and "His Illustrious Superiority," and Fidel Castro is sometimes known as "Maximum Leader." Nkruma of Ghana bears the title of *Osagyefo* ("Redeemer"), but he is also known as "His High Dedication, the Quencher of Fires, Fount of Honor, Renewer of All Things." This, however, is not surprising in Africa, where tribal chieftains have such titles as "One Who Deflects Arrows" or "One Who Speaks But Once and Is Heard."

Polite expressions are often instructive as to origin, meaning, or both. Our own "thank" is akin to "think" and German *danken* to *denken.* One directs one's thought with gratitude toward the person one thanks.

The Latin expression for "to give thanks" was *gratias agere.* The *gratias* survives today in Spanish *gracias* and Italian *grazie,* both related to "grace" and "gratis," which in Latin means "for thanks" and nothing more. French *merci,* on the other hand, comes from Latin *merces* ("reward"), which is connected with "merchant" and "commerce" and reveals a material turn of mind.

There are two Russian expressions for "thank you," both highly unsuited to an atheistic society. *Spasibo* is *spasi Bog* ("God save"), while *blagodaryu Vas* is "I bless you." The Japanese "thanks," *arigatō,* literally means "it is difficult," referring to the hardship encountered in your service by the one you thank or possibly to the difficulty of appropriately thanking him. A more polite Japanese expression of gratitude, *makoto ni go shinsetsu de gozaimas',* literally means "in truth, an august, special, lordly amiability is here honorably placed."

For "you're welcome" or "don't mention it," German says "pretty please"; Italian says "nothing" or "I beg." French, Spanish, and Portuguese say "there is not whereof," with "to speak" understood. Russian says "not for that."

Equally curious are formulas of greeting and leave-taking. "Good-by" is originally "God be with you." Our "hello" is in the original Anglo-Saxon "be whole" or "be healthy." We use it in opening a telephone conversation, and so do many other tongues which have borrowed it from us. German, however, also uses "Here Mr. So-and-so." The British and Portuguese use "Are you there?" Spanish says "What is it?" or "At the phone." Italian says "Ready!" Russian says "I'm listening." Japanese says "Say, say!" the implication being "By all means speak up, if it so pleases you."

The Japanese do not say "good morning," "good evening," but simply "it is morning," "it is evening." The Russians say "be healthy." The Chinese use "morning peace," "evening peace." "Peace be with you" is the beautiful salutation of the Semitic languages, to which the equally beautiful reply is "And unto you be peace."

By way of contrast, the language of insult is what you choose to make of it. As a British court ruled not too long ago, "Whether language is foul or not depends on where it is used; something that is foul in the south may be a term of endearment in Yorkshire." If you use in Sweden the term that literally translates "darling" (*älskling*) you may get your face slapped; it means "darling," but only between lovers, and bears the implication of existing sexual relations. In Italy the exclamations *Che gambe!* ("What legs!") and *Che bbona!* ("How good!") drew the equivalents of fifteen-dollar fines; the first was deemed too open an expression of admiration, while the latter, in the Roman dialect, is a term often used to or about prostitutes or women of low morals.

The 1961 issue of *The Table,* which is further described as *The Journal of the Society of Clerks-at-the-Table* of the British Parliament, contains a full manual of expressions whose use is permissible or not permissible in the various Parliaments of the British Commonwealth. To begin with, "liar" is barred; but it may be paraphrased in such fashions as "trifler with the truth," or Churchill's "guilty of terminological inexactitude." (There are 125 ways, it is claimed, to call a man a liar without using the word itself.) Other expressions disallowed by one or another Commonwealth Parliament include "wicked," "half-witted," "mongrel," "idiot," "dishonorable member," and just plain "fool." Churchill at one time or another used "boneless wonder," "countrified businessman," "modest man with plenty to be modest about," "merchant of discourtesy," and "squalid nuisance." In return, he was called "bogyman of the country" and "political chameleon," while Anthony Eden was described at the time of the Suez incident as "an overripe banana, yellow outside, squishy inside."

Again proving the point that the insulting connotation depends on your location are those animal and vegetable names which are so freely bestowed. "Wolf" may not be too complimentary an epithet in English, but *mon loup,* "my wolf," is a term of endearment in French. "Monkey" in Italian (*scimmia*) is not too good a word to use to a woman, but its Russian equivalent, *obyazanka,* has endearing connotations. *Pollo,* "chicken," is "coward" to us, "sucker" in Italian, "handsome young man" in Spanish. *Kraut* ("cabbage") was applied by our troops to the Germans in an uncomplimentary fashion, but *mon petit chou,* "my little cabbage," is used by a Frenchman to his best girl, as is *kleine Lausbube,* "little louse baby," or *kleine Maus,* "little mouse," by a German. Other terms of endearment unconnected with animals or vegetables include most frequently a word that is not much favored in English, "treasure" (Italian *tesoro,* French *mon trésor,* German *Schatz,* Russian *tovarka*). But Italian also favors "love" (*amore*), as does French (*mon amour*). Russian has a poetic "little sun" (*solnichno*), Spanish a majestic "beloved of my heart" (*querida de mi corazón*). Strangely, two of our favorites, "honey" and "sweetheart," fail to appear in other languages, at least to this writer's knowledge.

But generally, the animal and vegetable worlds fare ill at the hands of language-using man. "Pig," "dog," "skunk," "cat," "cow" have generally evil connotations. German combines two of them into the picturesque *Schweinehund,* "pig-dog." We have even coined adjectives like "catty" and "bitchy." Horned animals, notably the goat and the ox, are symbolical of the deceived husband in many languages. The donkey, or ass, symbolizes stupidity; the mule symbolizes stubbornness. French *chameau*, "camel," is a term of opprobrium, and *veau*, "calf," is "sucker" or "greenhorn" (but Italian *vitellone*, "big calf," means "playboy"). Only a few animals, like "lamb," "lion," and "eagle," have flattering connotations attached to their names.

Plain cuss words are often of mythological or religious origin. Typical of the first are "by Jove" and "by Jiminy" (Gemini). For the second, we have the English "Gorblimey" ("God blind me") and all those attributes of the Deity that proper elderly ladies use ("Goodness," "Gracious," "Mercy," even "Dear me," which is probably a corruption of Italian *Dio mio*, "my God"). The various uses of "hell" have been grammatically classified as follows: 1) negative adverb ("The hell you are!"); 2) super superlative ("hotter than hell"); 3) general adverb ("fight like hell"); 4) intensifier ("Who the hell is he?"); 5) literally used noun ("Go to hell!"); 6) synonym for "uproar" ("to raise hell"); 7) combination word ("hell's bells," "hell and high water").

— Chapter Nine —

THE HISTORY OF WRITING

The palest ink is better than the most retentive memory.
—Chinese proverb

LANGUAGE is a completely arbitrary symbol of thought. Writing is a symbol of the spoken language, less arbitrary than the language itself, since in most systems of writing there is an attempt to make characters correspond to sounds. A system of writing is a symbol of a symbol, just as a check is symbolical of paper money, which is in turn symbolical of gold.

The symbolic character of writing has been partly lost sight of in the most advanced systems, which strive to make characters correspond to spoken sounds, while it stands out most starkly in the more primitive systems, where the spoken-tongue intermediary is omitted and the character is symbolical not of a sound but of a thought concept.

When a written form is achieved, the result is generally greater stability in the spoken tongue. Many languages of primitive groups are unwritten and consequently highly fluctuating, with many dialects, a rapid rate of change, and an undetermined standard form. Similar high variability in the spoken language is to be observed in tongues like Chinese, in which the written symbol for the thought rather than for the sound still persists. An ideographic system of writing places little restraint upon the spoken language. A phonetic system constricts the spoken tongue into a mold, forces the speakers, to a certain extent, to follow the traditional pronunciation, as indicated in the equally traditional orthography, rather than their own whimsical bent, and gives rise to "correct" and "incorrect" forms of speech which, were the spoken language unrestrained by a written form, would be equally "correct" variants or, at the most, conservative or innovating forms.

Many peoples believe their language or system of writing to be of divine origin. The name of the Sanskrit alphabet is Devanagari, which means "pertaining to the city of the gods." Hieroglyphic, used by the ancient Egyptians for their formal documents, carved in stone, means "sacred stone writing" (the Egyptians also had the hieratic and demotic scripts, more generally used on papyrus). They believed that writing had been devised by Thoth, god of wisdom, and the Egyptian name for writing was *ndw-ntr* ("the speech of the gods"). The Assyrians had a legend to the effect that the cuneiform characters were given to man by the god Nebo, who held sway over human destiny. Cuneiform was produced by pressing wedges into wet clay tablets (the name means "wedge-shaped"); it was used by the Sumerians, Assyrians, Babylonians, Persians, and other peoples of the Mesopotamian region from about 4000 B.C. to the time of Christ. The Mayas attributed writing to their most important deity, Itzamna. The lost prehistoric writing of Japan was styled *kami no moji* or "divine characters." As late as the Christian Middle Ages, Constantine the Philosopher (another name for Cyril, apostle to the Slavs) is described as having had Slavic writing revealed to him by God.

Primitive systems of writing like the Egyptian and Assyro-Babylonian, as well as the present-day Chinese, were originally based on pictorial representation pure and simple, like the systems also developed by still more primitive groups like the American Indians and the Australian natives. (There is at least a suspicion that writing may have gotten beyond the purely pictorial stage in the Mayan hieroglyphics and the Bolivian Aymará petroglyphs, flanked by such subsidiary evidence as the Aymará words *kelkata,* "writing," and *khaweera kelkata,* "river of writing.") A pictograph is a symbol denoting a definite object, like a fish or tree or man. Sumerians, Egyptians, and Chinese alike, when they wanted to indicate in permanent pictorial form the concept of "sun" or "moon," merely drew a picture of the sun or moon. These pictures became conventionalized in different ways, depending partly on the nature of the writing materials, partly on the bent of the individual races.

But the number of picturable objects is definitely limited, far outstripped by both thought concepts and spoken-language words. As soon as they became aware of the shortcomings of their pictographs, the devisers of early writing ingeniously developed ideographs, which are symbols of non-picturable things, actions and ideas. The Chinese, for instance, combined their pictographs for "sun" and "tree" into an ideograph signifying "east" (the sun rising through the trees). "Sun" and "moon" were put together to form "light"; "eye" and "water" to form "tear"; "woman" plus "child" gave "good." The process could go, and went, much further. Two or more ideographs, once contrived out of pictographs, could be combined to denote still more complicated or abstract concepts: "green" and "year," themselves ideographs originally contrived out of earlier pictographs, mean "youth"; and "faith" plus "piety" plus "temperance" plus "justice," all ideographs, represent "virtue."

There is one great advantage in a picto-ideographic system of writing. No matter how much individual users may diverge in their speech, all will be able to understand one another's written messages. NaCl means the same to the Italian chemist, who says *cloruro di sodio,* and to the American, who says "sodium chloride." In China, people who speak mutually unintelligible dialects are able to read one another's writing with no difficulty whatever. The spoken word for "man" may vary widely, according to the dialect; but the written symbol for "man" is the same throughout the vast Middle Kingdom.

To judge from what happened in the west, however, the disadvantages of such a system must have outweighed the advantages. Sumerians, Assyro-Babylonians, and Egyptians, having started with a picto-ideographic system, soon began to isolate certain characters and give them a phonetic value. The Egyptian symbol for "sun" was a picture of the sun. The spoken Egyptian word for "sun" was *re.* The sun picture is often found in hieroglyphic inscriptions standing not for "sun" but for the spoken syllable *re* occurring in a longer word.

It remained for the Phoenicians and Hebrews finally to use their symbols with the exclusively phonetic value of single syllables or consonants, dropping the ideographic connotation altogether. At this point, we have the beginning of a true phonetic alphabet.

Curiously, however, the very word "alphabet" betrays its pictographic origin. It is the Greek version of Semitic *aleph, beth,* the first two letters of the early Semitic alphabet. *Aleph* means "ox," and the letter which ultimately developed into our *A* was at first a picture of the head of an ox. *Beth* is Semitic for "house," and the original *B* was the picture of a house. At least seventeen of the letters of the Semitic alphabet have similar pictographic connotations. Dr. Hugh Moran claims to have established a definite link between the shapes of the Semitic letters and those of the Chinese twenty-eight-symbol lunar zodiac, but his findings are unconfirmed.

Once the system of using symbols to represent sounds rather than objects or ideas became established, it spread with relative rapidity. The Greek legend says that Cadmus of Thebes first brought the alphabet from Phoenicia to Greece about 1500 B.C. The Greek alphabet, derived from the Phoenician, gave rise to the Etruscan, which in turn gave rise to the Roman, in use among western nations today. The names of the Greek letters (*alpha, beta, gamma,* etc.) are phonetic imitations of the meaningful Semitic names (*aleph, beth, gimel*) but with their connotation gone, while the Romans simply named the letters by their sounds, as we do.

Another variant of the Greek alphabet was adapted for the use of the Goths by their bishop Ulfilas in the fourth century, but it fell into disuse when the Goths were absorbed into the Roman Empire of the west. Still another version of the Greek alphabet was devised by two bishops from Constantinople, Cyril and Methodius, for the Slavs to whom they brought Christianity in the ninth century. Faced with Slavic sounds which did not exist in Greek, they stretched the Greek alphabet as far as it would go, then drafted one or two Hebrew characters and invented others. The result was the Cyrillic alphabet used today by those Slavic nations which followed the Eastern Church—Russians, Ukrainians, Serbs, and Bulgars. The Poles, Czechs, Slovaks, Croats, and Slovenes, who accepted the western version of Christianity, adopted the western Roman alphabet.

The Roman alphabet had a long and intricate development. Written at first exclusively in the characters which today appear in our printed capitals (A, B, C, D, etc.), it was soon modified for purposes of more rapid writing. The ultimate result was the large variety of printed and hand-scripts in use today. Variants of the Roman alphabet are the graceful characters of Irish and the German Gothic or Black Letter alphabet, first developed around the twelfth century from the earlier Carolingian script used by scribes at the court of Charlemagne and his successors. Black Letter was used in English till the sixteenth century, when it was replaced by the plainer Roman.

The parent Semitic alphabet of the Phoenicians and Hebrews had, however, a far larger number of descendants than the Greek, Roman, Cyrillic, and Gothic of the west. Spreading southward and eastward, it gave rise to the beautiful

Arabic alphabet which, like the Hebrew, consists exclusively of consonants. Vowel values are indicated in Arabic by dots and dashes above or below the line, in Hebrew by vowel points usually beneath the consonant. Both scripts frequently omit the vowel symbols altogether, leaving it to the intelligence of the reader to supply the vowels. This works out as if we were to spell "heart" HRT; there might be confusion with "hurt," but in a context this danger would be minimized. In addition, the consonants of the Arabic alphabet regularly assume four different forms, according as they are initial, medial, or final in the word, or stand by themselves.

Just as the alphabet of the Romans was adopted by such diverse nations as the English, Irish, Czechs, and Swedes, so likewise the Arabic alphabet spread with the Koran to an infinite number of races and languages. The Fula, Hausa, and Swahili of central Africa, the Malay, Javanese, and Sundanese of the Dutch East Indies, the Moro of the Philippines, the Urdu and Punjabi of India, the Persian of Iran, and several of the Turkic languages of the Soviet Union in Asia use some form or other of the Arabic alphabet.

It is perhaps worth while noting at this point that Hebrew and Arabic are read from right to left. The left-to-right reading arrangement of the west arose through a strange process. The earliest Greek, appearing in Homeric times, has an arrangement called *boustrophedon,* or "as the ox plows": left to right, then, for the next line, right to left, then left to right again. Why this system, so restful for the eye, was not permanently adopted is one of the unsolved mysteries of language.

Other developments of the original Semitic alphabet appear in the Armenian alphabet and in the ancient Devanagari of India, in which Sanskrit is written. From the Devanagari stem practically all the myriad scripts of India, Burma, and Thailand. But in the case of many of them we have to note a regression. The Semitic symbols are consonants, with the vowels either separately indicated or left to the understanding of the reader. Many of the alphabets of India and southeastern Asia turn a single consonant into a large number of symbols, each of which carries the consonant value plus a separate vowel value, and since the number of possible vowel values in some of these tongues is large, this multiplies the symbols to the point where they become unmanageable and difficult to learn. Tamil, the leading Dravidian language of southern India, has a syllabic script of 312 characters, while other languages of India range up to 500 and 700 characters.

The major civilized languages of the earth may thus be said to have two main systems of writing, drawn from separate sources: the Chinese picto-ideographic, which also serves Japan; and the Semitic phonetic alphabet, derived from an Egyptian hieroglyphic which was also originally of a pictographic nature. The Chinese system has remained static. The Egyptian-Semitic-Western system has proved its dynamism and power of adaptation.

Japan received the Chinese system of writing along with Chinese literature about A.D. 300. The Japanese use the same symbols as the Chinese, but since the spoken languages are totally different the symbols are differently read; the symbol for "man," for instance, pronounced *jên* in Chinese, reads *hito* in Japanese.

The Japanese, however, like the ancient Egyptians, proceeded to devise auxiliary syllabic alphabets by the simple process of taking certain Chinese ideographs and giving them not a meaning value, but a sound value. There are two such syllabaries, the *hiragana* and the *katakana,* each consisting of forty-eight syllabic characters. If either syllabary is read completely through in the order given in Japanese, it spells out a brief poem on the frailty of human affairs. The Japanese make use of these syllabaries to represent case endings and verb endings, which their language has and Chinese has not. They also use them alongside of the ideograms, in much the same fashion that we write "$10 (ten dollars)."

It seems strange that, having progressed that far on the road to complete phonetization, the Japanese did not proceed to discard the Chinese ideograms altogether and further develop their syllabaries into complete phonetic alphabets. They give as an excuse the fact that there are in their language large numbers of homophones (words sounding alike but having different meanings), which in ideographic writing are distinguished by completely different symbols but which in phonetic script would be indistinguishable. That this argument does not hold too much water is indicated by words like our own "post," which is both pronounced and spelled the same way despite its wide variety of meanings ("army post," "post this letter," "post a guard," "post a notice," "fence post"). The Japanese, however, point to a word like the spoken-language *kami,* which means "good taste," "hair of the head," "paper," "lord," "governor," "seasoning," "god" or "above." They even claim that their spoken-language word *ka* has 214 separate meanings, each indicated by a separate character.

Chinese and Japanese, when printed on a page, are read

from top to bottom, with the vertical columns running from right to left, though other arrangements are possible.

Of all the phonetic alphabets in existence, the Roman is the most widespread as well as the one providing the possibility of greatest simplicity. This possibility is not always fully exploited, as shown by the spelling difficulties of our own English. Under the circumstances, it is not surprising that movements tending to conversion from more complicated scripts to the Roman alphabet should have arisen in such widely separated countries as Turkey and Japan. The Turks, who had been using the Arabic alphabet since their adoption of Mohammedanism, turned to the Roman alphabet in 1928 under the guidance of their leader Kemal Atatürk. The Japanese established a society for the use of the Roman alphabet as far back as 1885. Even the Chinese have recently experimented with the Roman alphabet, in modified form, for their tongue. In addition, they have simplified about 1,000 of their commonest characters, drastically reducing the number of strokes needed to write them in order to make them more accessible to the illiterate. Lastly, they have adopted Roman-form alphabets for their minority groups (Uighur, Kazakh, Mongol, Tibetan) to replace the complicated alphabetic forms previously used in those languages. The Russians modified their Cyrillic alphabet somewhat in the early days of Soviet rule, but since Cyrillic offers equal possibilities with Roman of symbol-for-sound correspondence, there is no great urgency upon them to turn to the west for a new script. Such urgency appears in the case of many languages of India and southeastern Asia, and missionaries, chief among them the Reverend Frank Laubach, have been hard at work devising phonetic systems of writing to replace the cumbersome, illiteracy-fostering scripts of the east.

The Roman alphabet is probably the best among historically developed devices for recording sounds. But it is far from perfect. The fact that it came into being to serve the linguistic needs of the Romans, but was later adopted by other nations with widely different speech habits, accounts for part of the trouble. An added feature of difficulty resides in the fact that language sounds change, often rapidly and radically, while spelling tends to remain traditional.

Spelling reform of languages like English and French, designed to bring the written form in line with present-day pronunciation, is often advocated, but, like Mark Twain's weather, no one ever does anything about it. Shaw's famous bequest, offering large money prizes to people who would devise a rational system of English spelling, has so far led to no satisfactory solution (Shaw himself often used a system of shorthand). For this there are a few good reasons, in addition to hidebound traditionalism. If we were to reform our spelling, all our existing books would have to be scrapped and reprinted in the new spelling (this argument, by the way, was also advanced by the Japanese when some American educators suggested to them that they get rid of their Chinese ideographs and syllabic characters and use Roman script instead). Also, a word like "nation," which is now easily recognized in written form by French, Spanish, Portuguese, Italian, German, and even Russian speakers, would be far less recognizable if spelled, more or less phonetically, NEJSHUN or something similar. Lastly, orthographic reform runs into heavy opposition from printers and typists, who are thoroughly used to standard twenty-six-letter linotype machines and keyboards and resent the injection of the additional characters that would be necessary to represent the forty-four or forty-five phonemes of English on a straight sound-for-symbol correspondence.

One suggestion, offered by this writer and based upon linguistic phonemic transcriptions, is for a series of foolproof digraphs (two-letter combinations representing a single sound, like the *th* of *think*) that would permit us to use our twenty-six letters without any additions (by foolproof we mean such simple rules as the use of *th* to represent only and invariably the unvoiced sound of *think,* *dh* for the voiced sound of *this,* a hyphen to separate *t* from *h* when two separate sounds are to be represented, as in *hot-house*).

English makes use of no subsidiary characters, save for the apostrophe. Many other languages use accent marks, umlauts, cedillas, tildes, hooks, and bars over vowels and consonants to indicate a modified pronunciation of the symbol in question. This is again due either to the fact that the language has changed since the alphabet was adopted or that, at the time of the adoption, the language had sounds that did not very well fit into the scheme of the Roman alphabet. Some of these subsidiary characters have interesting histories. The tilde of Spanish (ñ) was in origin a small *n* written over a larger *n* to replace the double *n* of earlier times (we still have a survival of the earlier Spanish spelling in our *duenna,* which modern Spanish spells *dueña*). The cedilla (ç), as its name implies, was used in Spanish before it was used in French, and has the literal meaning of "little z"; it was originally a small-size *z* written under a *c* to indicate that the latter was to have a palatal instead of a velar sound.

It is a curious fact that there is no language which has absolute symbol-for-sound correspondence, though Finnish comes quite close, using a single letter of the alphabet for each sound of the language and indicating a long vowel or consonant by writing it twice.

Phoneticians, who are concerned with language sounds, have devised an International Phonetic Alphabet, a chart consisting of some hundreds of characters, designed to represent all the sounds occurring in all known languages. But even phoneticians are occasionally pessimistic about their labors, for there is practically no sound represented by the same symbol in two different languages which absolutely coincides. French and English, for instance, both use what looks in writing like *D*, but the French sound is produced by pressing the tip of the tongue against the back of the upper teeth, the English sound by touching the tip of the tongue to the gums immediately back of the upper teeth—a trifling difference, perhaps, but one that serves to distinguish a native speaker from a foreigner trying to speak the language. As one phonetician puts it, "it is difficult, not to say impossible, to obtain an idea of speech from phonetic symbols." Another phonetician had previously stated that "it is almost impossible for one person to express to another by signs the sound of any word."

Yet attempts are made all the time. Some of them are deliberate products of conscious thought, like the so-called "phonetic transcriptions" that purport to convey to the speakers of one language the correct pronunciation of words in another: "voo-lay voo?" for French *voulezvous?* or, worse yet, "kes-ker-voo-za-vay?" for "qu'est-ce que vous avez?" The full impact of this system does not strike us until the tables are turned; a French manual for the guidance of French speakers trying to order a meal in an American or English restaurant offers such gems as *chéque rhoume* for "check room," *ouétresse* for "waitress," *mille* for "meal," *ouitte quéques* for "wheat cakes," and *lambe tchoppe ouid peautéteaux* for "lamb chop with potatoes."

Others are innocent products of the semiliterate, people who try to spell as they pronounce. This phenomenon goes all the way back to antiquity: vulgar Latin inscriptions carved on tombstones by ignorant stonecutters often betray to detectivelike linguistic investigators the trend of the spoken language away from Classical Latin standards and toward the nascent Romance languages.

Perhaps the phonetic system of writing is not the acme of perfection after all. There is at least a talking point in the arguments of those who advocate that we go back to the picto-ideographic system of our remote ancestors or simply adopt the ideographic writing of the Chinese. At least all the peoples of the earth, regardless of their spoken tongues, would understand one another in writing.

PART TWO

The Constituent Elements of Language

— Chapter One —

THE COMPARTMENTS OF LANGUAGE

Who climbs the grammar-tree, distinctly knows
Where noun and verb and participle grows.
                                        —Dryden

TO the question: "What is language?" many and varied an-
swers have been given. Some linguists, fastening upon the
phonetic aspects of speech, have defined language as being
basically a series of sounds produced by certain human organs and received by others. Another school replies that
since the main characteristic of language is meaningfulness,
and since a transfer of meaning can take place without the
medium of sound, as witnessed by semaphoric or gestural
systems of communication, the phonetic aspect of language
is secondary to the semantic feature.

To the grammarian, language is primarily a series of grammatical forms, roots, and endings. To the literary specialist,
language is a series of words so arranged as to produce a
harmonious or logical effect. To the lexicographer, language
is fundamentally a list of words with their separate derivations, histories, and meanings. To the man in the street,
language is what he uses, quite unconsciously, to communicate with his fellow man.

Obviously, these partial definitions are all correct. But
precisely because they are *all* correct, the sum total of language amounts to something greater than any one of them.

Sounds in themselves do not constitute language; yet the
spoken language consists of sounds. Meaningfulness may be
achieved in a number of nonlinguistic ways, therefore meaningfulness alone does not constitute language; yet language,
to be worthy of the name, must be meaningful. Grammatical
forms and grammatical categories, taken by themselves, are

dead things, as will be attested by many former students who "went through" Latin or French in certain educational institutions; yet language is characterized by their presence to the extent that there is no language, however primitive, that does not possess some system of grammar. Spoken and written language consists of separate words; but unless these words are arranged in certain sequences, they will not only fail to convey beauty or logic but will even fail to convey complete meaning. Lastly, a language that does not serve as a medium of communication is a traitor to its function.

Let us for the moment fasten our attention upon the aspects of "language" which the name itself implies ("tongue," "speech"). It is the spoken medium, with its written auxiliary, that serves to an overwhelming degree the communication needs of the human race.

This spoken-language machinery, developed and improved over countless centuries, consists of sounds, produced by the human vocal organs and received by the human auditory organs. In the case of the written counterpart of speech, the sounds are replaced by written symbols, which represent either the sounds themselves or the ideas that the sounds are intended to convey and which are perceived by the visual organs.

This is the purely mechanical setup of language. Obviously, the broad definition above must be restricted before a satisfactory description of language is achieved. The human vocal organs can, and often do, utter nonsense sounds which are received by the human ear but convey no specific meaning. A pencil in a human hand is likewise capable of producing signs which will be seen by the human eye but will carry no particular message.

It is only when the sounds are grouped into words, and the written signs into letters or significant symbols, that they begin to acquire the true character of language. The word is an arbitrary sequence of human voice sounds which has gained general acceptance in a social group as conveying a certain concept, idea, or meaning. The word is meant to arouse in my hearer's mind a concept similar to that which I am endeavoring to express. Hence, the word is a fundamental part of language. It consists of sounds, but the sounds must be arranged in a certain order and must, above all, convey a given meaning.

The word by itself is a very incomplete bearer of meaning. A word like "dog," uttered alone, begins to convey a message to my hearer, but unless I accompany it with other words, or with gestures, all that my hearer will gather is that I have my mind occupied with a dog. On the other hand, when I say, "Look at the pretty little white dog running up the street," my hearer does not even have to follow my request to have in his mind a fairly complete picture of what I have in mine. Just as the sequence of sounds completes the word and gives rise to the beginning of an image, so the sequence of words completes the mental picture.

But while my language is now made adequate to complete my meaning, there is still another element involved. Had I said, "Look at the pretty little white *dogs* running up the street," my hearer would have obtained a somewhat modified picture. Here I have not added words or shifted their order. I have made a simple sound modification in a single one of my words, adding a significant sound-and-meaning element whereby the message is transformed. My addition in this case is a grammatical or morphological element whereby I join the auxiliary notion of number to the fundamental notion of "dog." My language is now complete, since I have fully succeeded in transferring from my own mind to that of my hearer a complete and complex notion, through the instrumentality of my speech organs and of his organs of hearing. The transfer may as yet be imperfect, since I may have in mind poodles running up a broad street and he may visualize the scene as involving terriers running up a narrow street. But the meaning may be further clarified by means of additional sounds, words, sentences, and grammatical forms. The linguistic principle and method are established.

Four primary elements have entered my demonstration, plus one determining over-all concept and purpose. The latter is, of course, meaning and its transfer, to which the four elements are subservient. The elements are sounds, words, sentences, and grammatical forms, all of which are, to a greater or lesser degree, necessary to serve my ultimate purpose, language.

The transfer of meaning, in linguistic terminology, is "semantics," from Greek *semainō* ("to mean"). Without semantics there is no true language. Semantics may be served by speech, by writing, by gestures, by signs, by anything that conveys meaning, which means that semantics transcends the narrower etymological definition of language as "oral speech" though not the broader definition of language as "means of communication."

Sounds, produced and received by human organs, are indispensable in the spoken language, which accounts for the greater part by far of meaningful transfer. The investiga-

tion of spoken-language sounds forms the object of a large
number of related fields of study (phonetics, phonology,
phonemics, etc.), all of which have in common the element
phonē, or "sound."

The word, consisting of an orderly, conventional sequence
of sounds, constitutes the minor unit of language. It may be
placed under the heading of vocabulary or lexicology, primarily concerned with the meaning and use of words, or of
etymology, which goes into the origin, development, and history of individual words.

The sentence, consisting of an orderly sequence of words,
constitutes the major unit of speech. Here the problems involved are placed under syntax (orderly arrangement) and
style.

The grammatical forms, or variants of individual words,
which serve to convey accessory notions of number, gender,
time, mode of action, etc., form the morphological division
of language (Greek *morphē* means "form" or "shape").

Each of these four primary divisions of language, as well
as the all-embracing field of semantics, presents its own peculiar and fascinating problems, its own historical and geographical development, its own complex ramifications. As
each one is taken up in detail, various questions will arise
to trouble not only the layman but even the expert.

It is a commonplace that words are borrowed from one
language by another, as when we appropriate *éclat* from
French, *spaghetti* from Italian, *fiesta* from Spanish. But to
what extent and under what circumstances is this borrowing
process operative? Does it extend to sounds, grammatical
forms, and sentence structure as well as to individual words?
How much can a language borrow without, so to speak,
going into receivership?

All languages possess sounds, words, and sequences of
words. But do they all possess grammatical forms—terminations similar to our -*s* marker that forms the plural of most
of our nouns or the -*ing* that forms our gerunds? If not,
what replaces them?

All languages have sounds. But to what extent do different languages have the same sounds? How great is the
possible range of speech sounds?

"Semantics" is a lovely sounding word, and one that has
recently been somewhat overworked. To what extent do the
semantics of different languages coincide? Does "liberty"
or "democracy" mean to a Russian not merely approximately,
but even remotely, what it means to us?

"Esthetics" is another overworked term. Is there an esthetics of language? Are some languages inherently beautiful, others ugly? Are words in the same language beautiful or ugly, or is the impression of beauty or ugliness simply a by-product of their semantics?

Above all, is there a "philosophy" of language, a system whereby we may reduce all languages to a least common denominator, permitting us to generalize and reach universal conclusions? Or is each language a law unto itself? Or are there divisions of language which follow universal rules, others which escape regimentation?

Not all of these questions can be fully answered, here or elsewhere. But an awareness of the problems of language is the first necessary step toward their eventual solution.

— Chapter Two —

THE SOUNDS OF LANGUAGE

The spoken word is the foundation of all language.
—Linguaphone motto

SPOKEN language is characterized by language sounds, produced by the human voice, received by the human ear, and interpreted by the human brain.

Speech sounds, like all other sounds in nature, are subject to certain physical laws. Sound waves travel at a given rate, which varies with the nature of the sound and the medium; they also have certain frequencies of vibration. Since speech sounds are produced by certain human organs and received by others, physiology also enters the picture of the sounds of language. Spoken language therefore functions in harmony with two of the most important physical sciences, physics and physiology. This double physical-science aspect of language has caused some linguists to view their subject as a primarily mechanical or physical activity. That this is erroneous is proved: 1) by the fact that language, to answer its definition, must not only be produced, transmitted, and received but also interpreted; 2) that "language," unless we wish to quibble on the ground of the etymological derivation of the term, can exist also where sound is not involved—in a written message or a meaningful symbol.

Since, however, the most widespread form of language is the spoken one, the importance of sound and its dependence upon physical relationships must not be minimized. Without entering into a complicated technical discussion of the speech organs, it may be pointed out that the main organs participating in the production of speech sounds are the lungs, which serve as a bellows for the breath stream; the glottis, pharynx, and larynx; the vocal cords; the mouth and nose, which act as resonators; the uvula, soft and hard palate, tongue, teeth, and lips.

Very roughly speaking, a speech sound is produced by allowing the breath stream, as it issues from the lungs, to resonate at some point along the throat, mouth, or nose, at the same time subjecting it to some sort of modification or constriction produced by juxtaposing two or more of the organs enumerated above. The technical terminology used in defining the various kinds of speech sounds is involved and precise but of little interest to the layman. Two of the more widely known terms are "vowel," a sound produced without friction or stoppage, and "consonant," a sound characterized by friction, squeezing, or stoppage of the breath in some part of the vocal passage. Vowel sounds are always accompanied by vibration of the vocal cords; consonant sounds may or may not have this vibration, the presence or absence of which we can easily perceive by putting our fingers to our Adam's apple and uttering in turn the sound of *d* and that of *t,* or *b* and *p* or *v* and *f.* Vowel sounds are often described as front, middle, and back, according to the part of the mouth where they are articulated. Consonant sounds, in addition to being voiced or unvoiced (that is, accompanied or not by vibration of the vocal cords), are also said to be plosive (where the breath stream is gathered up behind a complete obstruction, then suddenly released, as when we pronounce *p* or *b*) and fricative (where the obstruction is only partial, and the breath stream escapes gradually, as in the case of *f* or *v*). They may also be subdivided, according to the point of articulation, into dental (where the obstruction is produced at the teeth), labial (at the lips), etc. A sound like that of *p,* for example, is plosive (full obstruction, suddenly removed), labial (the obstruction is produced by the lips), and unvoiced (unaccompanied by vibration of the vocal cords).

From the standpoint of transmission, the sound waves produced when you speak travel through the air at the rate of approximately twelve hundred feet per second, with consonant sounds generally having more vibrations per second than vowel sounds. Differences of high and low pitch are caused by lengthening or shortening the vocal cords; women, whose cords are normally shorter than men's, have higher-pitched voices. Volume can be accurately measured in decibels, which are the standard unit of measurement for all noises. Forty decibels is average for normal conversation. For individual sounds, measured in microwatts, vowels range between 9 and

47, consonants between 0.08 and 2.11, attesting the higher sonority and carrying power of the vowels.

The receiving apparatus, the human ear, is too complicated to be described in a work of this scope. Of interest, however, is the fact that, acoustically, the five basic vowel sounds (*a* of "father," *o* of "more," *e* of "let," *i* of "machine," *u* of "sure") are perceptible by the ear in the order given, while, among the consonant sounds, *k, g, ch*, and *j* are more perceptible than *p, b, f, v, t, d, s*, and *z*. It is fairly well established that in a normal conversation the hearer really hears only about 50 per cent of the sounds produced by the speaker and supplies the rest out of his own sense of the context. This explains why foreign languages are often easier to speak than to understand and why unfamiliar words, especially proper names, must be spelled out.

This basic imperfection of the hearing apparatus is also responsible for the distortion of speech sounds by babies and foreigners and is believed to be the fundamental cause of sound change within a given language.

As we begin to investigate the nature and variety of speech sounds, we are struck by two seemingly contradictory features. The first is that most languages, to judge from their *written* appearance, seem to have approximately the same sounds. The western languages, in particular, all have what amounts to the same alphabetic notation. But this superficial impression is corrected the minute we begin listening to the actual sounds. The written notation may be the same, but the spoken sounds for the most part diverge, sometimes slightly, sometimes to an astounding degree. The grammars of foreign languages are the first to put us on our guard against confusing sound and spelling; but they seldom do so to a sufficient degree. Actually, almost every sound in every language is a trifle different from what appears to be, in written notation, the same sound in another language.

Furthermore, precise recording instruments show that no two native speakers of a language pronounce any word or sound of that language exactly alike. There is always a tiny spread between your pronunciation and mine, which is fortunate, since it enables us to recognize a person by his voice. These infinitesimal differences arise from the different power of the lungs, the different length of the vocal cords, the different shape of the vocal organs, and a different point of articulation of the sound in question.

Little control can be exercised over the first three of these factors. The point of articulation, on the other hand, can be accurately described and controlled by the individual. There is no difference based on race or nationality that can be detected in lung power, length of vocal cords, or shape of vocal organs; consequently any belief that racial factors control speech sounds is founded on unscientific premises. As for the point of articulation of a given sound, that can be imitated to perfection by anyone willing to devote sufficient time and labor to the effort. This means that the sounds of a foreign language can be acquired to the point of native-speaker perfection by anyone who cares to do so.

Outside of lack of time, patience, interest, and effort, there are two basic causes for the imperfect acquisition of the speech sounds of a foreign tongue. One is that the sounds are imperfectly heard—something that can and does happen to native speakers as well as to foreigners. The other is deliberate imperfect reproduction, due to one of two causes or a combination of both—laziness and self-consciousness.

Linguistic laziness causes us to spare ourselves the effort of reproducing a sound that calls for a position of the speech organs which is unfamiliar to us. This means that the English speaker, even after he has been informed of the difference between an English and a French *t* sound, will nevertheless substitute his familiar gum *t* for the French tooth *t* when speaking French. His unspoken justification for this is precisely the one offered by the grammar: the two sounds are *approximately* the same, and one is ever so much easier than the other! In reality, it is easier only in the sense that whatever has become familiar is easier.

As for self-consciousness, that is something that goes deep down into the roots of human, particularly adult, psychology. The child has no self-consciousness when he imitates. He is not afraid of sounding ridiculous. The child will consequently imitate the spoken sounds of a language (his own or another) to the very limit of his faculties of hearing and pronunciation; the adult fears he will sound funny when he pronounces a sound to which he is not accustomed, and this fear causes him to use in its place the nearest sound to which he is accustomed and which he can pronounce without fear of making himself ridiculous. Young children, of course, learn the spoken sounds of foreign languages infinitely better than their elders.

The basis of a foreign accent is a series of sound substitutions in which the foreigner uses his own sounds instead of the sounds of the language he is trying to speak. A trace of foreign accent is present in about 99 per cent of cases where a person of one linguistic background tries to speak another tongue.

This leads to another consideration. If there are some fifty recognized sounds in a language like English, a more or less equal number in French, German, Spanish, Italian, and Russian, and these sounds seldom exactly coincide, then what is the total number of possible speech sounds in all the existing tongues? No one has ever counted them, but, as may be surmised, they run into the thousands. This is not as strange as it sounds. When we consider the many infinitesimal or major shifts in the point of articulation of any given sound—the fact that we can form an obstruction between, say, the tongue and any part of the teeth, gums, or hard palate, and that the sound that issues forth when the obstruction is suddenly removed will be somewhat different in each case—we can perceive how many varieties of *t* can be uttered. An *f* can be pronounced by juxtaposing the lower lip and the edge of the upper teeth, as we do; it can also be uttered by using both lips, as the Japanese do when they want to pronounce what passes in an English transcription of Japanese for an *f*; to us, that is not a speech sound at all but only a noise we make when we blow out a match. Nothing could be more different than the French *r*, produced by vibrating the uvula, the Spanish *r*, pronounced by trilling the tongue, and the American *r*, made by cupping the tongue. Yet these diverse sounds are all represented in writing by the same symbol, which misleads Americans into pronouncing French *au revoir* with two Midwestern cupped *r*'s, and Frenchmen into saying "crush" with a trill of the uvula.

Linguists have long been aware of the insufficiency of the ordinary alphabet to denote even the major variations of sound occurring in the major languages. In the nineteenth century, Lepsius, a German Egyptologist, undertook to construct an alphabet designed to represent the sounds of many languages. His early attempt was expanded within more recent decades into the International Phonetic Alphabet in use among linguists today, which supplies symbols for various shades of sound in practically all tongues. But these symbols are extremely numerous and unwieldy. At the same time, they are far from adequate to record, in written form, the too-numerous variations of the sounds of language, of which no individual language exploits more than a small fraction, fifty or sixty at the most, as against a possible total running well into the hundreds and constantly growing.

Under the circumstances, it is not surprising that some linguists should have practically abandoned the phonetic approach (that is, the description of the sounds of a language with reference to the vast field of all possible sounds) to go over to the phonemic approach, whereby the sounds of a language are studied, so to speak, in a vacuum, without reference to or comparison with the sounds of any other language.

These linguists choose to speak of the "phonemes" rather than of the "sounds" of a language. The phoneme is defined as a variety of sounds in a given language which the speakers of that language choose to regard as a single sound. The sounds of *k* in "kin" and "skin" are quite different; "kin" has a puff of breath after the *k*, "skin" has not. In many languages, these two sounds of *k* would be considered as separate and would give rise to semantic confusion if they were interchanged (Sanskrit *kala*, for instance, with the puffless *k* of "skin," means "indistinct"; Sanskrit *khala*, with a puff of breath after the *k*, means "threshing floor"). English speakers, however, are not aware of a distinction, even though they make it when they speak. The two sounds of *k* never occur in words that might cause confusion. Therefore, the two *k* sounds are a single phoneme in English, while in Sanskrit they are represented by two different letters of the alphabet and constitute two distinct phonemes. Two different sounds within one phoneme, like the two sounds of *k* in "kin" and "skin," are called allophones (Greek for "other sound") or positional variants of the same phoneme, it being tacitly, even unconsciously, understood among English speakers that the *k* sound, if initial in the word, shall be accompanied by a puff of breath, but that it shall have no such puff if it follows an initial *s*.

One interesting feature about the phonemic description of a language is that it links sounds to meaning, recognizing the essentially semantic character of language. Another is that it permits the use of ordinary alphabetic symbols over and over again as we pass from one language to another, since the phonemes of one language are never compared to the phonemes of another language. French *t* and English *t*, being different sounds, would have to be differently designated in a complete phonetic alphabet. But since the phonemic alphabet of French serves only French, and that of English only English, there is no difficulty about using the symbol *t* for the French sound in the French phonemic pattern and for the English sound in the English. Phonemics, like phonetics, is still far from perfected, and there are still many points of controversy among its followers. But great strides have been made in the phonemic description of languages.

All living languages are characterized by sound changes which have occurred and are occurring in the course of their history. The *ch* sound of "cheese," "church," "churn," for instance, frequent as it is in present-day English, was nonexistent in Anglo-Saxon. On the other hand, Anglo-Saxon had a sound, similar to the harsh guttural of German *ach,* which was once designated by the combination *gh* that we still see in "night" and "through" and which has disappeared from modern English. Modern Spanish has a similar guttural, represented by *j* in words like *Méjico, Quijote, jugar.* This sound arose in comparatively recent times out of two earlier sounds which Spanish has utterly lost, the *sh* sound of "she" and the sound of *s* in "pleasure."

"Phonology" is the study of sound transformation along the historical course of a language. The reasons for these transformations are still partly obscure. Some linguists choose to view a part of them as due to the mixture of two or more linguistic stocks, a blend or compromise between two or more sets of speech-sound habits. Others like to bring in the environmental factor; a new cold climate that encourages greater energy of articulation or causes you to keep your mouth as closed as possible, a warm climate that leads to laziness or relaxation of the speech organs. These theories are debatable and are constantly being debated. One plausible theory accounting for a majority of sound changes is that they are due to imperfect hearing and imitation of one generation's speech by the succeeding generation, leading to a slow, gradual transformation. A variant of this theory is that the majority of sound changes occur abruptly, as the result of deliberate imitation by the community of an innovation made by someone who has prestige or authority in the group. This personal innovation, in turn, may be deliberate, accidental, or forced by circumstances. An excellent example of the last type, were it not for the fact that it seems not to be true, would be the story to the effect that Philip II of Spain had a lisp which was imitated first by his courtiers, then by other segments of the population, and which gave rise to the lisped *th* sound of Castilian *cielo, decir* in the place of the original *ts* and *dz* sounds of those two words.

An example of a deliberate innovation is the abortive attempt made in sixteenth-century France by literary circles to replace the *r* sounds of the French language with *z* sounds which they deemed more graceful. A phrase like

"Mon mari est allé à Paris acheter une chaire" was turned into *"Mon mazi est allé à Pazis acheter une chaise."* *Mazi* and *Pazis* were rejected by the bulk of French speakers, along with most forms containing *z* for *r*. *Chaise,* however, struck the popular fancy and remained, along with the original *chaire,* which soon took on the more learned connotation of a professorial chair. English, which had borrowed the word from French long before the attempted innovation, has only the older form, "chair," unless we wish to accept *chaise longue.*

Some linguists choose to consider the sound-change process as something operating with the regularity of physical laws. *Lautgesetz* ("sound law") is a term devised by the German nineteenth-century linguist Leskien to describe this supposed absolute regularity. The formulation of his "law" is to the effect that in a given area and at a given period, if a sound changes, the change will be universal and will have no exceptions. This iron-clad rule is robbed of some of its inflexibility by amendments to the effect that, if apparent exceptions appear, they are due to some extraneous factor, such as learned influence, foreign or dialectal borrowing, analogy, etc.

While not all linguists are disposed to accept this ruling, it has interesting and even useful applications. Beginners in the study of German are often fascinated by the working out of Grimm's Law, whereby it is possible to predict that a Latin or Greek *d* will appear in English as a *t* and in German as a *z* or *ss* (*dentem,* "tooth," *Zahn; pedem,* "foot," *Fuss*). Romance beginners like to watch the working out of a Latin *ct* group which regularly becomes a *tt* in Italian, an *it* in French and Portuguese, a *ch* in Spanish, a *pt* in Rumanian (*noctem, notte, nuit, noite, noche, noapte; lactem, latte, lait, leite, leche, lapte*).

On the other hand, the "no exception" clause in the sound law runs squarely into fully observable facts that contradict it. The French *chaise* appearing above is a case in point: a few French words containing *r* went through with the shift; others did not.

In addition to their characteristic sounds, languages are distinguished by certain subsidiary features. Chief among these is what is commonly known as "accentuation," a term which in most modern languages is synonymous with stress. A certain syllable of the word is pronounced with greater vocal force than the rest. The same occurs with a certain word within the sentence or phrase. In the Germanic languages, including English, the stress is usually on the initial syllable of a word of two or more syllables. English, by reason of its many loan words from foreign sources, presents numerous exceptions to this generalization. (In the sentence just read, there are nine words of two or more syllables, and in three of them the stress is not on the initial syllable.) The Romance languages, outside of French, more often stress the penult. French is said to stress the last syllable of the word, but in reality the stress is fairly evenly distributed throughout. The Slavic languages show great diversity in this respect, Czech having initial accentuation, Polish regularly stressing the penult, while in Russian the place of the stress is unpredictable. Interesting experiments have been carried on by Professor Roman Jakobson and his associates to determine in what way the accentual habits of speakers of various languages influence their impression of sound. Knocks given at regular intervals, with every third knock louder than the preceding two, are perceived by Czech speakers as separated by a pause *before* the louder knock, by French speakers *after* the louder knock, by Polish speakers *between* the two less loud knocks. If the loudness is made equal but a longer interval is placed between the knocks, the Czech speaker calls the first knock the loudest, the Polish speaker the second, the French speaker the third. When it is recalled that Czech invariably puts its stress on the initial syllable of a word, Polish on the next to the last, French on the last (if at all), this difference of opinion is seen to be directly influenced by the stress habits.

That the accent was not always a matter of relative stress or vigor of utterance is indicated by the etymology of the word itself (*ad-cantum,* "upon-singing"). The earlier accentuation of the languages of our Indo-European group seems to have been largely a matter not of stress but of musical pitch, with the accented syllable pronounced on a higher note than the surrounding syllables. This musical pitch is still discernible in languages like Swedish and Serbo-Croatian. In languages of other families, such as Chinese, the voice pitch is utilized to convey semantic distinctions: *ma* pronounced in one tone means "mother," in another tone "flax," in a third tone "horse." This means that pitch in Chinese becomes phonemic and must be observed under penalty of our being misunderstood. With us, pitch serves at the most to convey emotion or emphasis, but not in accordance with any set rule generally accepted by the speakers.

Another factor that enters consideration under the heading of sounds is the relative rapidity of speech. All languages may, of course, be spoken more or less rapidly. It has been observed, however, that the average rate for French is about 350 syllables a minute; for Japanese, 310; for German, 250; for English, 220; while most languages of the South Seas do not go beyond 50 syllables a minute. Those who think Frenchmen speak too fast are therefore not altogether wrong, at least from the standpoint of an English speaker. Familiarity or unfamiliarity with the language that is being spoken naturally has a great deal to do with the impression of rapidity that one receives. Within the same language, there are different rates of speed for different groups of speakers. It has been estimated that the normal American woman speaks at the rate of 175 words per minute as against 150 for the average male. This difference has been linked with greater emotional instability, but the connection is as yet unproved.

With the sounds of language running into the hundreds or even thousands, curios in the field of speech sounds naturally abound. Some tongues, like Hawaiian, are extremely poor in sounds; the only consonant sounds of Hawaiian are *h, k, l, m, n, p,* and *w,* and none of them may be used without a following vowel, with the result that a Hawaiian trying to say "Merry Christmas" will come out with "Mele Kalikimaka."

Among the widespread languages, Arabic is the one having the greatest variety of guttural sounds; but the tongues of the Caucasus are generally conceded to be the ones having the richest assortment of consonant sounds.

The Hottentot-Bushman languages of southwest Africa use grunts and clicks as normal parts of their speech sounds. Some European languages seem to be able to get along without vowels; the Yugoslav name for Trieste is *Trst,* while in Czech "a hill full of fog" is *vrch pln mlh;* actually, the *r* and *l* in these words serve as vowels.

Japanese lacks the sound of *l,* and a Japanese speaker pronouncing a foreign word with *l* usually substitutes a lightly trilled *r.* Chinese reverses this process, saying "lice" for "rice."

In Spanish, no word begins with *s* followed by another consonant, and a Spanish speaker trying to pronounce "Spanish" will normally say "Espanish."

Jakobson and his associates report that they have found no language where the syllable cannot begin with a consonant or end with a vowel, but there are many where the syllable cannot begin with a vowel or end with a consonant.

Two of the questions asked in the preceding chapter come

to mind at this point. They concern the "dynamism" and the "philosophy" of language.

Does our survey of language sounds cast any light upon the problem of language change? Some languages transform their sound pattern at a relatively rapid, others at a relatively slow, rate. Physical and psychological activity, climate, racial mixture, linguistic blending have all been suggested as possible causes for rapid sound shifts, isolation and sedentary life for linguistic conservatism. It is quite possible that any or all of these factors play a role, but the role is difficult to prove. It is, incidentally, equally difficult to disprove.

As for the philosophy of language, what do language sounds have to teach us? We have seen in them infinite diversity, coupled with a fundamental similarity hinging on the fact that they are produced by basically identical vocal organs and received by basically identical auditory organs. Fundamental divergences, if any, would seem to reside rather in the semantic division of language, the interpretation that is given by the human brain to conventionalized sounds. The first conclusion which we are able to attain appears to be that the philosophy of language must be sought rather in language taken as a whole than in language taken in a single one of its compartments.

— Chapter Three —

WORDS

The word makes men free. Whoever cannot express himself is a slave. Speaking is an act of freedom; the word is freedom itself.

—Ludwig Feuerbach

THE word may be defined, from the mechanical standpoint, as a succession of speech sounds conventionally arranged; it may also be defined from the semantic end as the most elementary speech unit of meaning.

A language is essentially an array of words, each of which is accepted by the social group as conveying a given meaning or meanings. This fact is occasionally lost sight of by some language educators, who concentrate their efforts on grammatical forms and syntactical arrangement to the detriment of vocabulary, with the ludicrous result that some of their students are able to conjugate irregular verbs but unable to form a sentence in the foreign language because they don't know enough words.

The quality of inarticulateness, or floundering about for the appropriate word, is by no means limited to those trying to speak a foreign language. It can be and very often is characteristic of native speakers. Orators, political and otherwise, are frequently at a loss for a word.

This need not surprise us. While the speakers of a given language normally share all of the language's limited number of speech sounds or phonemes, all of the language's basic grammatical forms, likewise limited in number, and all of the language's elementary syntactical combinations, they are far from sharing all the language's stock of words.

The complete English vocabulary is said to consist of close to a million words. It is doubtful if any individual knows more than one fifth of this number. Hundreds of thousands of words, though they are listed in the large dictionaries, belong to special scientific, professional, or trade parlances and are not used or even recognized by the average speaker. Every field of modern activity has its own specialized vocabulary. There is a special vocabulary of medicine, one of psychology, one of botany, one of music, even one of boilermaking and cattle raising.

The question therefore is not so much how many words there are in a language as how many of these words the average speaker knows.

It is here that we run into widely divergent figures and opinions. Several years ago, an Englishman named D'Orsay produced a study based on the everyday speech of a group of fruit pickers, in which he presented the rather startling conclusion that the use vocabulary of the illiterate and semiliterate does not exceed 500 words. Very recently, the president of the Linguaphone Institute estimated, from a study of subway conversations, that the average person uses about 1,000 workable words in his lifetime and seldom exceeds 1,200.

Many reputable linguists have challenged these estimates. A very careful study made by a group of psychologists presents the following figures: an average four-year-old child knows over 5,000 words; at six, he reaches a vocabulary of 14,000 words; at eight, of 26,000 words; at ten, of 34,000.

Still another estimate places the average two-year-old vocabulary at about 300 words, the six-year-old at between 2,000 and 3,000, the stupid adult at 10,000, and the average adult at between 35,000 and 70,000.

The discrepancy in these estimates may be partially due to confusion between use vocabulary and recognition vocabulary. For every word that we constantly use in our everyday speech, there are perhaps ten words that we are able to recognize when we hear them or see them in print. Some of these we are also able to use when the occasion calls for them. This would mean that even the child or adult having a normal use vocabulary of 1,000 words would "know" 11,000.

Frequency of use of certain words partly resides within the individual, his calling and his interests. But to an even greater degree, it depends on the nature of the words themselves. Certain words will occur dozens of times in the course of a very brief conversation on any topic whatsoever. Others will be used very occasionally, and under special circumstances. The most frequently used word in the English vocabulary, both in speech and in writing, is "the." The articles "a" or "an"; common prepositions like "of," "to," "in," "for"; common pronouns like "I," "me," "you," "him," "she," "they"; common verb forms like "am," "is," "are," "had," "have" naturally tend to occur again and again. What-mough reports that, in a study of 100,000 running English words, 3,000 accounted, with their constant repetition, for 95 per cent of the total. The Institution for Basic German of the University of Pittsburgh has prepared a basic list of 1,300 German words guaranteed to account for 85 per cent of ordinary conversation (the study, incidentally, revealed that 3 per cent of the recorded conversations consists of "wast-age": the "ah's," "well's," and "er's").

It is this frequency of occurrence, perhaps, coupled with the nature of the ordinary casual conversation, that fosters the legend of the extremely limited vocabulary of the less-educated speakers.

It may also be forgotten that speakers naturally tend to acquire and use those words which fit into the picture of their everyday lives. An illiterate peasant knows the names of plants, shrubs, trees, insects, animals, and farm tools of which a highly educated and cultured city dweller may be almost totally ignorant. Education and culture have a great deal to do with vocabulary range, but not inevitably so; illiterate speakers sometimes reveal an amazing range of spoken vocabulary.

The point must also be made that recognition, or even use, of certain words does not always indicate an accurate knowl-edge of what those words really denote. Words like "atomic" and "cyclotron" are used by speakers and writers who have a very hazy idea of what they stand for. Even simpler, "picturable" words are often used with a vague understanding of their meaning. If you are inclined to doubt this, try to give a nontechnical definition of an "elm" that will serve to dis-tinguish it from other trees or of a "thrush" that will set it apart from other birds.

The question of vocabulary possession is further compli-cated by semantics. A given word, even of the picturable variety, seldom elicits quite the same mental image in any two individuals, because each is tied up in our consciousness with an entire series of subconscious associations. "Lion" may evoke in one mind the picture of Metro-Goldwyn-Mayer's snarling Leo; in another it may be associated with the memory of the calm, majestic stone lions of the New York Public Library.

The matter of individual vocabulary range depends on sev-eral complex factors: frequency of use, use vs. recognition, specialized vocabularies, greater or lesser accuracy in use or recognition, even semantic connotation. Under the circumstances, estimates as to the probable vocabulary range of various classes of speakers are bound to be divergent and unsatisfactory.

Greater precision can, of course, be achieved in the matter of vocabulary range for literary purposes. But even here we run into striking discrepancies. One authority, for example, estimates that Shakespeare used 16,000 different words in his works, another 20,000, while a third places the figure at 25,000. Racine is said to have used only 6,000 different words, Victor Hugo 20,000. Milton's literary vocabulary is variously estimated at 8,000 and 11,000 words. For newspaper usage we are informed that a single issue of the French *Le Temps* contained 3,800 different words.

Here again the suspicion is aroused that different standards may account for the discrepancies. Even in a little-inflected language like English, morphological variants of the same word ("ox," "oxen"; "foot," "feet"; "book," "books"; "I," "me"; "go," "goes," "going," "went," "gone") bring up the question whether such variants should be counted as individual words or lumped together as forms of a single word. Such a difference of standard might easily explain the 16,000- to 25,000-word count for Shakespeare. In the case of a more highly inflected language like French, where a single verb can have several dozen morphological variants, it might account for Racine's 6,000 vs. Hugo's 20,000 words. Lastly, literature is always open to the charge that it neglects certain classes of words which are of rather frequent occurrence in speech. This double standard rises to plague linguists every time they are asked, as often happens, which of two languages has the more extensive vocabulary. Should only root words be considered or should all morphological variants be taken into account? If the latter system is followed, highly inflected tongues like Russian or Latin will far outstrip in total number of words languages like Chinese, which has no flectional endings at all, or English, which has discarded many of them.

Basing ourselves upon the standard of root words regardless of morphological variants, which seems more scientific and practical, we find that there is almost as much variation in the vocabulary range of individual languages as there is among the speakers of a single tongue. This, however, should not deceive us into making easy generalizations concerning the vocabulary range of so-called "primitive" languages. It is true that they lack the scientific, technological, and occupational word apparatus of the more "civilized" tongues, but they very often make up for this deficiency with an amazing complexity of objects, concepts, and terms for which we, from our supposed vantage point, have no equivalent. The best proof of this is that we are sometimes compelled to borrow such terms just as they stand instead of translating them into our language, as has happened with the "taboo" of the South Sea Islands, the "totem" and "wampum" of the American Indians, and the "boomerang" of the Australian natives. Elsewhere we are forced to give a conventional translation of a term of which we have picked up the semantic connotation, as when we copy the Chinese and speak of "saving face." Then there are those very numerous cases where a less developed language makes fine distinctions essential to its speakers and their activities but not to us (Javanese, for instance, has ten words for "to stand" and twenty for "to sit," according to posture, attitude, and symbolism; Eskimo has nearly a dozen words for "snow," indicating that it is soft, loose, hard-packed, frozen, crusted, melting, etc.; on the other hand, Hawaiian is said to have no word that precisely means "weather"). All in all, people who explore a "primitive" language with the idea that they will have to learn a very limited vocabulary are often in for strange surprises.

Again, it is amazing to what extent languages, even of the primitive variety, possess the machinery for borrowing, adapting, or creating words once the object or concept denoted by these words is brought to their notice. This mental machinery, which all languages seem to possess in approximately equal measure, will be discussed at length under the appropriate headings.

The vocabularies of Classical languages, like Sanskrit, Greek, and Latin, naturally lacked all the expressions of modern technology as well as thousands of other modern words. In spite of this, they were remarkably extensive. A fairly complete vocabulary of ancient Greek lists well over 100,000 words while one of Latin has over 80,000, and these figures leave out of account the fact that there must have been thousands of Greek and Latin words in the more popular spoken tongues which did not find their way into the literary records that have come down to us. The Classical vocabularies include thousands of words denoting objects and even concepts which have since become obsolete. While less complicated than our own, the Classical civilizations were nevertheless formidably complex.

Words, to a far greater degree than sounds, grammatical forms, or syntactical arrangement, are subject to change. Some of the major divisions of vocabulary change are loss by obsolescence, usually brought about by the disappearance of an object, activity, or concept; quasi-mechanical growth by morphological or structural devices, as when an adjective like "Congressional" is built out of "Congress" plus two separate suffixes; growth by combination, as when "railroad" is composed out of two separate words, neither of which has the meaning of the composite word.

Of a less mechanical nature in the process of vocabulary growth are word borrowing, word coinage, and semantic shift, with their concomitant extension into slang, cant, jargon, and, ultimately, the vernacular and even the literary tongue.

These processes of growth and development are common to morphological forms and syntactical structure as well as to the individual word, though the latter generally offers by far the best and most striking exemplifications. Their discussion will therefore be left in abeyance until the other two great compartments of language have been described.

— Chapter Four —

THE STRUCTURE OF LANGUAGE

The minimum grammar is no grammar at all.
—Giuseppe Peano

"GRAMMAR" is a term devised by the Greeks, in whose language it literally means "that which pertains to writing." The modern tendency, however, is to regard grammar as the study of speech rather than of writing, or at least of both.

The Romans had a saying, *Verba volant, scripta manent* ("What is spoken flies away, what is written endures"), which perhaps serves to illustrate the point of view of the Greeks, as well as of grammarians generally: the written word, remaining as a permanent record, is worthy of greater consideration than the fleeting spoken word.

Yet the spoken word antedates and forms the basis of the written word. Consequently, those modern linguists who care little about the prescriptive grammar of languages, which is concerned with how people *should* speak, and devote most of their attention to descriptive grammar, dealing with how they actually *do* speak, have some measure of justification. To avoid misunderstandings, they generally avoid the word "grammar" and use instead "structure" or, more precisely, "morphology."

That this is a modern trend is amply indicated by the older grammars on record, which are almost without exception of the prescriptive, normative type. The first known grammar is Panini's *Sutras,* a fourth-century B.C. treatise on the Sanskrit language, consisting of some 4,000 very brief statements of linguistic phenomena.

Numerous grammars of the prescriptive type have been left to us by the Greeks and Romans, and it may be said that the prescriptive type of grammar predominates down to the beginning of the twentieth century.

Yet there are exceptions. One Roman grammarian, Probus,

has left us a list of over 300 terms commonly mispronounced or otherwise misused in his day, along with the "correct" forms. Needless to say, it is the "incorrect" variants, revealing spoken-language trends, that interest the present-day linguistic researcher.

During the early Middle Ages, brief glossaries for the use of travelers and missionaries were the vogue. One such glossary from the eighth century A.D., giving a list of Romance words and phrases for the use of German speakers, reminds one of a modern army phrase book; it contains such expressions as "Give me a haircut" and "Shave the back of my neck."

Modern grammars continue largely in the classical tradition, giving the forms of the language under consideration as they should be rather than as they are spoken. Notable strides have been made of late in presenting both usages, the more strictly literary and the broader colloquial, but since the latter includes all the gradations of vernacular, dialect, jargon, and slang, linguists are still divided as to just where to draw the line.

In a narrower definition, structure includes those significant variations in the form of words (like "ox," "oxen"; "foot," "feet"; "go," "goes") which add accessory notions to the basic meaning conveyed by the root word. More broadly, structure includes also such word arrangements as may likewise serve to modify meaning. To illustrate: in "Peter sees Paul" there is nothing in the form of "Peter" or "Paul" to indicate that Peter does the seeing while Paul is seen; it is only their relative position that shows us that. But since matters of word arrangement pertain to the domain of syntax, the boundary line between what is strictly morphology and what is strictly syntax is often hard to draw or distinguish.

The Sanskrit, Greek, and Latin grammarians, basing themselves upon their own languages, which were all of a highly flexional type, evolved first and foremost a series of parts of speech, a very limited number of pigeonholes into which all the words of their languages would fit without difficulty or confusion. The Greek philosophers, particularly, are credited with the creation of such terms and concepts as "article," "noun," "adjective," "pronoun," "verb," "adverb," "preposition," "conjunction," and "interjection." This classification of words, while very well suited to the ancient Indo-European languages and the modern ones which have retained the ancestral structure, does not work at all well for languages of different types, like the Chinese, American Indian, or African Negro. It does not even altogether suit those Indo-

European languages like English which have largely gotten rid of their flexional endings and gone over instead to a system of position and prepositions.

In Latin (and this applies also to our ancestral Anglo-Saxon) it was not at all necessary to adhere to a word order like "Peter sees Paul." One could place "Peter" and "Paul" anywhere in the combination because *Petrus* carried a -*us* ending which marked him as the doer of the action, *Paulum* a -*um* ending which marked him as the receiver of the action. When English evolved out of Anglo-Saxon and the Romance languages out of Latin, these distinctive endings were for the most part lost, with the result that position in the sentence became a prime factor if the meaning was to be retained. In addition, Latin would say *Paulī* for "of Paul," *Paulō* for "to Paul." The Romance languages here are forced to use the prepositions "of" and "to," while English gets along either by using those prepositions or by pressing into service the only case ending it has not discarded ("Paul's"), while at the same time using position as a substitute for "to" ("I gave Paul the book," where it is conventionally understood that if there are two objects the first carries the accessory notion of "to," the second does not).

In the matter of verbs, the ancient Indo-European languages would use a form like *amābō* with the sense of "I shall love." Here *ama-* conveys the basic notion of "love," -*b-* indicates futurity, and -*ō* indicates the first person singular, "I," as the doer. Modern English isolates the three concepts into three separate words, with the result that while Latin had many dozens of individual forms from the same verb, each conveying all sorts of accessory notions of person, number, time, mode of action, etc., English uses a series of subject pronouns ("I," "you," "he," "they"), a relatively limited number of auxiliaries like "shall," "should," "had," "may," "might," and is then left with the need of very few inflected verb forms; a weak verb like "love" has only four ("love," "loves," "loving," "loved"), while a strong verb has five ("see," "sees," "saw," "seeing," "seen").

This means in turn that the distinction between a verb, a noun, an adjective, etc., so easy to make in languages where the ending shrieks out the name of a part of speech, becomes quite difficult once the endings are no longer there. Is "mail" a verb, a noun, or an adjective? ("Mail the letter"; "Send it in the mail"; "Put it in the mailbox.") Is "up" an adverb, a preposition, a verb, a noun, or an adjective? ("I am getting up"; "Let's go up the street"; "I'll up you five dollars"; "the ups and downs of life"; "i am going uptown.") Needless to say, each of these words began its career as a definite part of speech, and the other uses are later "functional changes," facilitated by the fact that our words have few or no distinctive endings and can therefore easily pass from one category to another.

Languages which have retained the ending-system can, of course, transfer words from one category to another, but usually the transfer is attended by a change of label. Italian has *posta* for the noun "mail" but *postale* for the adjective and *impostare* for the verb.

Chinese, on the contrary, has carried the process of functional change farther than English. While some Chinese words, by virtue of their meaning, can be said to be specific parts of speech, the majority have the greatest freedom of movement from one category to another, depending upon their use and position in the sentence. A Chinese root like *ta* can be used as a noun to mean "size" or "greatness," as an adjective to mean "big" or "great," as a verb meaning "to be great" or "to make great," as an adverb meaning "greatly." The exact meaning is made clear by where it stands in the sentence.

Even in Hungarian, which normally has clearly outlined and separate parts of speech, you can have an expression like *fagy* which means indifferently "frost" or "it is freezing."

On the other hand, there are languages which incorporate into a single verb form a far larger number of concepts than even the most ambitious Indo-European tongue. A single verb form in Japanese means "to desire to sleep," while in Turkish one single verb form has the meaning "to be impossible to be made to be loved."

Two misconceptions which frequently beset the layman are that all languages must necessarily work out in somewhat the same fashion, and that the structure of the languages of primitive groups is necessarily simple. Nothing could be further from the truth.

We not only take for granted the similarities we note in such languages as English, French, Spanish, German, even Russian and Latin, but wonder with some resentment why there are not more. These similarities are due simply to the fact that these languages are closely related, in fact were at one remote time a single language. As we wander out of the Indo-European field, we shall note vast and fundamental differences in linguistic mentality, accompanied, strangely enough, by a sufficient number of sporadic yet essential similarities to indicate that all human beings are subject to similar basic experiences and can, though not of necessity, evolve similar thought-and-language processes.

As for the simplicity of primitive languages, that is totally a figment of the imagination. In some Eskimo languages a "noun" can have more than one thousand forms, each with its own precise meaning. In a language of Guatemala any verb can have thousands of different forms, by the addition of various endings. In the tongue of the Kwakiutl Indians, you cannot say "the man lies ill" but must phrase it somewhat like this: "This-visible-man-near-me I-know lies-ill-on-his-side-on-the-skins in-the-present-house-near-us."

A comparison of our own grammatical concepts with those of other languages and groups will begin to reveal some of the fundamental differences.

With us, the concept of grammatical gender is basic. We divide up nouns into "masculine," "feminine," and "neuter" according as they denote males, females, or inanimate objects. We do not, however, carry this concept beyond the point of replacing the noun by "he," "she," or "it." There is nothing left today in our nouns to indicate their gender, though there once was. "Man," "woman," and "table" are respectively masculine, feminine, and neuter by reason of their meaning, but not of their termination. Other tongues often give an excellent clue to gender in the endings of their nouns; in Latin and Russian, for example, nouns ending in -a are feminine, though with exceptions, and adjectives used with them must "agree in gender"; that is, also take on a feminine ending.

Some languages of our group, like Latin, Greek, German, and Russian, divide nouns as we do into masculine, feminine, and neuter but with seeming lack of logic make many inanimate objects masculine or feminine, and a few animate objects neuter (we have some remnants of this "illogical" classification, as when we call a ship "she" or a baby "it").

Other languages of our group have discarded the neuter gender, leaving only a masculine and a feminine, as is the case in French, Spanish, and Italian, where you must refer to a table as "she" and a pencil as "he." The same two-gender system appears also in the Semitic tongues, but only by coincidence.

The minute we leave the Indo-European and Semitic groups, we are struck by the radically different concepts appearing elsewhere. Some languages make no gender distinction whatsoever. In Hungarian the same word means "he," "she," "it." In Chinese and Japanese, gender does not enter the language picture at all, save insofar as one may specifically want to indicate sex by an appropriate word (the "bull-child" and "cow-child" of Chinese-English pidgin is a good illustration).

Many languages divide words into animate and inanimate, but here again strange exceptions appear. The Algonquian languages include in their animate class such words as "kettle," "knee," "maize," "bean," and "tobacco."

Other tongues make classifications which correspond to our genders only to the extent that they show the desire to classify. Some of the Dravidian languages of southern India lump females with inanimate objects into an "inferior" gender but place goddesses with males in a "superior" caste.

In sum, it may be said that while few languages classify objects and persons in exactly the same way, most of them indicate some measure of desire for classification, based, however, on the most diverse factors.

Another concept essential to us is that of number. We insist on defining persons and things as singular or plural. In this respect, English, which has discarded gender terminations, retains an ending for the plural, at least for nouns. There are a few exceptions, like "deer," "sheep," "grouse," which will at least serve to explain to us in what manner some other languages manage to get along without distinctive plural forms.

The actual use of the plural form, where it definitely exists, does not always follow what seems a logical system to us. That we ourselves are not too logical in its application is illustrated by such time-honored expressions as "a six-foot pole," "ten head of cattle," "two dozen eggs." Finnish and Hungarian always use the singular instead of the plural after numerals, so that a sentence like "I see five man" is natural to them. Arabic uses the plural with numerals from three to ten, the singular from eleven on. Russian has the genitive singular of the noun after two, three, and four, the genitive plural from five on ("one house," "two of house," "five of houses").

The original Indo-European parent language seems to have had eight cases: nominative or subject case; genitive or possession case; dative or indirect object case; accusative or direct object case; vocative or direct address case; instrumental or "with" case; locative or "in" case; ablative or "from" case. Each of these had its own appropriate, distinctive endings, which permitted the language to dispense with fixed word order on the one hand, with prepositions on the other. As the case endings fell away in some divisions of Indo-European, syntactical position and the use of prepositions grew in importance. But it would be a mistake to attribute the use of these devices exclusively to the falling-off of the ancient case endings. Russian today still retains seven of the original eight case forms of Indo-European but has concomitantly developed a full array of prepositions and a fairly fixed word order.

The total number of possible grammatical cases has been estimated at thirty-six, which is probably an understatement. Tongues like Finnish, Hungarian, and Turkish still have many of them (the official Finnish grammar speaks of fifteen, including such forbidding names as "inessive," "allative," "translative," and "comitative"). In these tongues the case marker is added to the noun, with the plural marker, if any, inserted between the two. All of the words which with us are prepositions ("of," "by," "from," "in," "with") appear in these languages as postpositions. In Hungarian *a ház* is "the house"; *a házban* "in the house"; *a házak* "the houses"; *a házakban* "in the houses." A somewhat similar system appears in Japanese, where *Tōkyō kara* means "from Tokyo" and *Tōkyō ni* "in Tokyo."

From the standpoint of the spoken language, it would seem to make little difference whether the postposition is kept separate from the noun, as in Japanese, or treated as a case ending and attached to the noun, as in Latin. Yet there are two important structural differences. The first is that in Latin the root *Paul-* and the endings *-us, -ī, -ō, -um,* etc., can under no circumstances be used by themselves, while in Japanese *Tōkyō* and *kara* can. Secondly, Latin and similar Indo-European languages use two entirely different sets of endings for the singular and the plural (even three in those languages where there is a dual number), whereas in Finnish, Hungarian, Turkish, and Japanese the same set of postpositions serves both numbers. Under the circumstances, many linguists reject the application of the terms "case" and "case ending" when speaking of the tongues that use postpositions.

English has kept only one of its former noun cases separate from the general form into which all the others have coalesced. This is the genitive or possessive, which is marked by *'s* or a mere apostrophe. The Romance languages, with the exception of Rumanian, have not saved even that much. By way of contrast, most Slavic languages have seven cases, and if we go outside of the Indo-European field we find that the Georgian of the Caucasus has twenty-three forms of the noun that may be compared to cases.

The personal pronouns have done better in saving their

ancient forms. We still retain a nominative "I," a genitive "my," and an accusative "me," while German goes us one better in distinguishing between a dative *mir* and an accusative *mich*.

One grammatical category which some languages enthusiastically accept, to the point of making it the most frequently used word in the language, and others absolutely reject, is the definite article. Ancient Greek had a word for "the," Latin did not. Quintilian, a Roman first-century grammarian, writing about his language which he compares with Greek, says: "*Nostra lingua articulum non desiderat*" ("Our language does not desire an article"). That he was wrong is proved by the later development of the Romance languages, all of which, without exception, developed a word for "the" out of the earlier words for "that," a process in which they were accompanied by the Germanic languages, including English. The Slavic tongues, with the exception of Bulgarian, refused to go along this road, and the result today is that a Slav who has acquired an insufficient amount of English says: "I see book on table." Outside the Indo-European group, some languages use an article, others don't "desire" it.

The languages that use an article generally put it before the noun, but several append it in the form "boy-the." Among the tongues that have a postposed article are Rumanian, Bulgarian, Swedish, Norwegian, Danish and Icelandic.

The question arises at this point whether the article is necessary or "desirable." Its semantic function, where it exists, is to convey to the listener the impression that the object named has already been mentioned. A Slav can easily retort that if the object has been mentioned your listener should be perfectly aware of the fact. The article therefore takes its place among those grammatical forms which can be dispensed with if one wishes to save time and space. Actually, we omit "the"s, "a"s, and "an"s in telegrams.

Historically, the growth of the article seems to be the result of an emphatic or concretizing tendency. The object is pointed to and described as "that book." But constant repetition weakens the emphatic force of the demonstrative, and it insensibly turns into a mere indicator of objectivity. Its original emphatic, concretizing, even glorifying function can be discerned in the tendency of some languages to use it with proper names, as when French says *la Boncour* for "Mrs. Boncour," or Italian *il Petrarca* for "Petrarch."

The adjective is defined as a word that limits or describes a noun. In many languages the adjective has no separate existence from the noun. In one Dravidian language of southern India a concept like "strong man" is expressed by "strength-man," making a universal rule of our occasional performance in "mailbox." That the noun itself is not an indispensable concept is indicated by the Aranta of Australia, in which things have to be turned into actions or states, so that "man" is literally rendered by "being-more" (man is a superior being).

Great variety of forms and concepts appears in pronouns. Many languages make a distinction between "we" including the person spoken to and "we" from which the person addressed is excluded. The distinction of gender which we make in the third person singular ("he," "she," "it"), but not in the plural ("they") is carried on by some languages to the second and even the first person. In Arabic a different "you" is used according to the sex of the person addressed.

Demonstrative pronouns have great range. Archaic English used to make a threefold distinction between "this" (near the speaker), "that" (near the person addressed), and "yon" (far removed from both). This distinction still exists in many modern languages, notably Spanish (*este, ese, aquel*).

Numerals are generally stable and more or less inter-equivalent, which Entwistle attributes to the fact that they are not affective, like the nouns, verbs, and adjectives. If we accept this view, it would be further proof of the validity of the interplanetary "language" of mathematics. (It has been suggested in some quarters that if we are ever to initiate communications with beings from other planets or solar systems, they will have to start with mathematical principles, such as $2 + 2 = 4$, which have universal validity, at least at the present stage of our knowledge.)

In Indo-European, the verb is subject to the grammatical concepts of person, number, tense, mood, and voice. These distinctions in the original Indo-European tongue are very clear-cut. A form like Latin *amarentur* is third person plural, imperfect subjunctive passive, and means "they might be loved," something which it takes us four words to express.

Any or all of these concepts may be dispensed with in individual languages. Chinese refuses to make any distinction whatsoever in the verb itself, which is an immutable root. All one can do in Chinese to express "I am writing," "I wrote," "I shall write," etc., is to use the word for "I" and the root "write," preceded, if one wishes, by an expression like "now," "yesterday," "tomorrow."

Certain languages are extremely poor in time distinctions, others extremely rich. As against the timeless "write" of Chinese, one Indian language of the Pacific Northwest distinguishes between recent past, remote past, and mythological past, while a native Australian language has five future tenses, two for things that will happen today, the others for more indefinite future periods.

There is reason to believe that the only two true tenses of original Indo-European were a present, doing service also for the future, and a past. From these two fundamental time notions there developed in the course of centuries the multiplicity of tenses which harass today's speakers. Some linguists hold that the distinction between present and past was originally not a time distinction at all but one of manner of action, incomplete vs. completed, or instantaneous vs. durative, a distinction which still appears in the aspects of Slavic verbs. But since incomplete action is normally in the present or future, and completed action in the past, the sense of time in the verb gradually crept in to supplant the earlier concept of aspect.

Our moods, which present an action as definitely occurring (indicative), conceived of as possible (subjunctive), ordered (imperative), or noncommittal (infinitive), are extended by other languages into optative (wished for), causative (made to take place), inceptive (beginning), etc. Some languages have a complete negative conjugation, running side by side with the affirmative (Japanese *ikimasu*, "to go," *ikimasen*, "not to go").

In the matter of voice, there is strong reason to believe that our active (subject acts) and passive (subject is acted upon) were originally an active and a middle (subject acts on or for himself). Sanskrit and Greek, which have all three voices, indicate the transition from the middle to the passive concept. The Latin passive (*amatur*, "he is loved") seems to be merely an extension of an originally impersonal form (*itur*, "it is gone," "there is a going," "someone goes," very similar to the Japanese *ikimasu*).

Many languages have verb compounds to render what to us would be a single verb. The Chinese "look-see" for "see" has even been loan-translated into colloquial English. The language of the Paiutes has such formations as "eat-stand" ("stand while eating" or "eat while standing") and "several-travel" (idiomatic for "to give birth while traveling").

If there is one general conclusion to be drawn from these few illustrations of grammatical forms and concepts, it is that they have almost infinite multiplicities of which no one language exploits more than a small fraction. No grammatical concept seems to be *per se* sacred or universal, far less indispensable. The system of separate parts of speech, so beautifully suited to the early Indo-European tongues, falls by the wayside in many other languages. Gender, number, case, person, tense, mood, voice, so meaningful and important in our linguistic system, are either extended *ad infinitum* or utterly effaced in other systems. Each language is a law unto itself in the matter of what it considers meaningful or necessary in the way of grammatical distinctions.

Yet by widely diverging devices, by a structural equipment no part of which is necessarily the same, all languages manage to fulfill their fundamental function, which is the transfer of meaning. It is almost as though it were not the structural device that mattered but only the ultimate purpose.

Perhaps mankind's language runs parallel with mankind itself. The human being manages to live, whether his food is fish, rice, and seaweed or bread, butter, and steak. He achieves transportation, whether by oxcart, camelback, horse, motorcar, or airplane. He trades, whether by barter, wampum, cocoa beans, gold, banknotes, or checks. He communicates with his fellow man, whether by parts of speech, roots, inflected forms, or polysynthetic sentence words.

Mechanically, the essential part of man is the human form, which all men hold in common. Linguistically, the essential part of language is the sound-making machinery we call speech. But what gives significance to man is the purposeful breath of life itself. What gives significance to language is meaningful transfer.

The means by which human life and activity are sustained are secondary to the purpose of life itself. They may vary and diverge infinitely in manner, but they inevitably converge in their aim. The means by which language achieves its purpose are just as infinite. It is the semantic purpose that never changes and is common to all tongues.

— Chapter Five —

THE ARRANGEMENT OF WORDS

Order is Heaven's first law.
                                        —Alexander Pope

THE unit of speech is neither the individual sound nor the individual word but the sentence, conveying a complete concept. Consequently, the unit of speech corresponds roughly to the unit of thought.

Syntax deals with the arrangement of words in this longer, more complete unit of thought and speech. Its importance is usually greater in languages that are poor in flexional endings, lesser in tongues where the word endings carry a considerable share of the semantic burden. In Chinese, which has no flexional endings whatsoever attached to its monosyllabic root words, the role of word order is paramount. "I see he" differs from "he see I" only in the relative position of the words. In a tongue like English, where some flexional endings survive, morphology and syntax may be said to play complementary roles in bearing the burden of meaningfulness. In highly inflected tongues like Sanskrit and Latin, word order plays a somewhat secondary part, though it is frequently utilized to indicate relative emphasis on words. In a combination like *Petrus Paulum videt,* it is immaterial in what order the words are arranged; but conventionally whichever word comes first bears a larger portion of the sentence-stress. *Petrus Paulum videt* stresses the doer of the action: "*Peter* sees Paul." *Paulum videt Petrus* stresses the receiver of the action: "Peter sees *Paul.*" *Videt Paulum Petrus* stresses the action itself: "Peter *sees* Paul."

Some languages, however, seem to combine a more or less fixed word order with a full set of word endings. It is probable that the word order of these languages arose rather as a matter of habit and convention than out of necessity. Yet these languages, more rigidly bound by their morphological structure, preserve a measure of syntactical freedom which may be used at will for purposes of stress, rhetorical effect, or poetic license.

Syntactical inversion is still effectively used in some modern western languages to reveal emotional content. A Spanish-language film, for example, bears the title *Vuelven los García* (*The Garcias Come Back*). Spanish could just as easily place the subject before the verb, which is, indeed, the more common construction; but the inversion lends a feature of suspense and animation, of barely suppressed excitement, that would be lacking in the more sober subject-verb arrangement. In like manner, French exceptionally says: *"Ton frère, je l'ai vu hier"* ("Your brother, I saw him yesterday") in the place of the ordinary: *"J'ai vu ton frère hier."*

The syntax of the common man is of an elementary variety as contrasted with that of the more cultured person. Spoken-language syntax is normally less involved than written-language syntax. The ultimate in syntactic complexity is achieved by the political, literary, or scientific writer who needs precise linguistic distinctions to represent involved thought complexes. It is probable that at the time when Cicero and Virgil were composing their long-winded orations and verses the Roman man in the street was speaking for the most part in short, simple sentences, encumbered with a minimum of complicated modifiers and subordinate clauses.

A distinction must therefore be made in syntax, far more than in phonology or morphology, between what is popular and what is learned, what is colloquial and what is literary. The complexities of syntax as we know them from English or Latin grammar pertain rather to the written, cultured, even literary and poetic language than to everyday speech. It is for that reason that syntactical studies are often avoided by "pure" linguists, who want to concern themselves with what is truly and properly language, preferably of the spoken, colloquial variety, whereas they are favored by philologists, whose domain ranges over literature as well as language.

It is customary among "pure" linguists to assert that, since the normal flow is from the spoken to the written language and from the popular to the literary language, their interest in literature as a reflection of language is necessarily limited. What they forget is that the current of language is more often alternating than direct. Very many terms, expressions, even syntactic constructions, not to mention figures of speech, of which Shakespeare is said to have known and used two hundred, have their beginning in some form of literary composition and find their way thence into the spoken popular language. This process of language change has its best exemplifications in the field of vocabulary, but there is enough of it in syntax to permit us to discuss it in this chapter.

Students of Romance languages often wonder at the fact that, while French, Spanish, and Italian show very clear and unmistakable similarities of syntactical usage, they nevertheless diverge on such points as the use of "to have" or "to be" with certain intransitive verbs (French and Italian say "he is come" while Spanish and Portuguese say "he has come"), the agreement of past participles with a direct object, or the use of a progressive construction like "I am speaking," which is permissible in Spanish or Italian but not in French. In the older period of these languages, there was equal confusion and fluctuation in all of them with respect to these points. The confusion still exists today among the more untutored speakers, but only to a limited degree. For the most part, the speakers of these languages have, in the course of generations, adapted themselves to the pronouncements of their respective Academies, which came out at different times with different and often arbitrary rulings. These pronouncements were at first followed only by the literary; then by the literate; ultimately, as education spread, by an actual majority of the speakers of each language. Examples of this kind could be multiplied. If, in the long run, constructions like "I ain't got none" and "Them's them" disappear from our own spoken language, they will justly be said to have bowed to the written, even to the literary, tongue.

This interchange between the spoken and the written language takes place wherever a written language exists. The only spoken tongues that escape literary influences are those that have no written counterpart, and these are growing fewer all the time.

The written-tongue tradition brings a stabilizing influence to language, slowing its rate of change by creating standards which both writers and speakers feel impelled to follow and by giving rise to concepts of "correct" and "incorrect" speech which, however arbitrary they may be at the outset, soon receive the sanction of tradition and social custom.

The language of poetry frequently reflects a syntactical freedom which the colloquial tongue has relinquished. Old King Cole may call for his fiddlers three in poetry, but not in prose. Poetic license, which many take to be the occasional violation of the traffic rules accorded to writers otherwise bound by the regulations of rhythm and rhyme, may also be viewed as a modern extension of archaic conditions, when the abundance of flexional endings permitted a greater range in word order.

Syntax, popular or cultured, shows at least as much diversity from one language to another as does morphology. What is correct usage in one language is often incorrect in another, even of a closely related group. "It is me" is perfect, indeed compulsory, syntax in French, though English grammarians frown upon it. But Spanish and Italian, the sister-languages of French, say: "(It) am I," a construction which French once had but later discarded.

English morphology is relatively simple; English syntax is correspondingly involved, though this may not be apparent to the speaker who has grown up with it. It makes quite a difference whether we "see through something" or "see something through," as was discovered by the French translator who rendered H. G. Wells' *Mr. Britling Sees It Through* by *M. Britling y voit clair*. To such purely syntactical instances may be added those combinations in which morphology enters to confuse the semantic issue, like "look over" and "overlook," "take over" and "overtake," "stand with" and "withstand."

In morphology, we discovered that no grammatical concept or form is universal or indispensable. This also holds true of syntax. An elementary subject-verb-object arrangement, while common to a large number of languages including such widely separated ones as English and Chinese, is rejected in many parts of the world. The subject regularly follows the verb in the Celtic tongues. The Caucasian languages turn what to us is an active construction into a passive one: "I make my father happy" becomes, in Georgian, "Through me contented makes self father." The relative clauses which are among the most common of the subordinate clauses in our western languages are often avoided in others through the use of participles: "He looked like a man who had lost all hope" would in many tongues appear as "He looked like a man having lost all hope." There is nothing sacred about our custom of putting adjectives and adverbs before the nouns or verbs they modify, as is well known by anyone who has studied a Romance language ("the house white," not "the white house"). Even the definite article, as has been seen, is subject to being placed after instead of before the noun, while prepositions can easily turn into postpositions, of which we have a few in our own language, though we don't like to admit it ("lengthwise," "skyward" are simple illustrations). The verb may assume any position in the sentence, or be relegated to a fixed post which may come at the beginning, in the middle, or at the end of the sentence, or absorb most of the other elements of the sentence (in Arabic the object pronoun is appended to the verb, while in Basque and some American Indian languages the verb incorporates both subject and object).

The morphologico-syntactical forms of the verb take on extremely delicate shades of both usage and meaning in the various tongues. Parallel past tenses, like "I saw" and "I have seen," occur in most of the western languages, but there are no two languages in which they are used in precisely the same fashion.

Stress upon a certain portion of an extended period of time is conveyed by different devices. English says: "I have been here for two hours," emphasizing by the tense used the fact that the action began in the past; but most other languages say: "I am here since two hours," stressing the fact that the action still goes on, and this syntactical arrangement is commonly offered by foreigners speaking English.

The forms of negation and interrogation are particularly interesting by reason of their diversity. One of our own syntactic slogans is to the effect that "two negatives make an affirmative." This is not at all true in the Romance languages, where such expressions as "I didn't never see nobody" are standard.

Many languages, including our own, invert the order of the subject and verb to make the sentence interrogative ("Is John here?"). Chinese and Japanese never do this, but use instead an interrogative particle at the end of the sentence, which is like a spoken question mark. Esperanto uses an interrogative particle at the beginning of the sentence, while Spanish, in written form, indicates both questions and exclamations by the use of inverted question and exclamation marks at the beginning of the sentence. Russian uses both inverted order and an interrogative particle, unless a clearly interrogative word like "when," "where," or "who" starts the sentence.

Some of our so-called rules of syntax are highly artificial, as illustrated by "This is nonsense up with which I shall not put," coined in derision of the "rule" that sentences should not end with prepositions.

The foregoing examples, few and scattered as they are, indicate the range and diversity of the syntactical devices that have been elaborated by the world's many languages in the course of their history. As in the case of sounds, words, and grammatical forms, the conclusion is forced upon us that there is no standard syntax, even of the most elementary variety, that is common to all tongues. The possiblities of syntactical arrangement are as endless as are those of sound combinations or morphological forms.

Syntax, more than any other compartment of language, lends itself to the purposes of connected, complex thought and its communication. It is an essential part of that physiological-psychological machinery whereby man transfers his ideas to his fellow man. But where phonology, morphology, and vocabulary are of particular interest to the linguist, syntax transcends the narrower field of linguistics and acquires paramount importance in the more elaborate divisions of communication—rhetoric, literature, prosody. Syntax is the essential ingredient of that elusive literary element called style. It is primarily by his syntax that the stylistic speaker or writer distinguishes himself from his fellows.

At the same time, language, even in its more elementary reaches, cannot exist without syntax. The delicate shadings of literary syntax, like the broader, general outlines of the word arrangement of the popular spoken tongue, serve the one essential aim of conveying meaning, which reveals itself more and more to be the primary function and purpose of language.

— Chapter Six —

SEMANTICS AND SEMANTIC CHANGE

Language exists only when it is listened to as well as spoken. The hearer is an indispensable partner.
—John Dewey

Upon the ability to translate ideas and political policies into terms that have the same meaning to all who use them depends the outcome of the peace of the world for all time.
—EDITORIAL, *"In the Beginning Was the Word,"*
Saturday Review of Literature (October, 1941)

AS the science of meaning and its transfer, semantics naturally includes all of the compartments of language: spoken, written, gestural, or symbolic. Semantics is "language" in its broadest, most inclusive aspect. Sounds, words, grammatical forms, syntactical constructions are the tools of language. Semantics is language's avowed purpose.

There is nothing illegitimate about selecting one of the compartments of language as a field of special study; but all specialization in phonetics, phonemics, or phonology, in morphology and grammatical forms, even in lexicology, word history, and literary style should be accompanied by a realization that from the standpoint of language these fields are necessarily incomplete and complementary, each of them contributing only a share to the ultimate picture of language.

Meaning and its transfer are indissolubly linked with psychology, both of the individual and of the mass. The science of mental processes being still in its infancy, we ought not to be astonished to find that there is a great deal about language, its past origin and growth, even its present evolution, that is not yet clear and perhaps never will be. The true linguist avoids, to the best of his ability, the know-it-all attitude, since he realizes that in his field, as in all fields of human knowledge, what is definitely known and provable is only a very small portion of the entire truth.

As a leading linguist has rightly remarked, a truly complete system of meaning involves an analysis of the universe. All that the linguist can do is to deal with language, based only upon that analysis of the universe which is completed during the life of the individual speaker or, at the most, of the speaking community.

The meanings of all the utterances of a linguistic community are said by the same authority to include the total experience of that community: arts, sciences, practical occupations, amusements, personal and family life.

Here, however, we run into certain difficulties. To begin with, no two individuals have precisely the same life experience. Even granting that they have at their disposal the same equipment of semantic expression (sounds, words, grammatical and syntactical forms), these means of expression will fail to coincide, to approximately the same degree as the individual experiences differ. A word or sentence is not merely a bundle of sounds; it is also a bundle of associations. These associations are not quite identical for any two speakers; neither will the words or sentences hold for them exactly the same semantic content.

In this, there is a striking parallel to speech sounds, the mechanical tools of language, and to vocabulary, the word equipment of the individual. No two individuals produce precisely the same sounds; no two individuals have precisely the same stock of words; no two individuals derive precisely the same shade of meaning out of the same utterance.

The strictly historical process of semantic change, whereby words and expressions vary and even reverse their connotations in the course of time, will be discussed farther on; special mention may be made at this point, however, of those linguistic forms which are knowingly and deliberately invested with certain meaning associations for the purpose of turning them into vehicles of specialized, directed, or distorted thought.

Theodore Roosevelt once spoke of "weasel words." Since his time, we have had "pacification" used in connection with the destruction of defenseless towns, "liberation" for indiscriminate bombings followed by forcible occupation, then "transfer of populations" or "rectification of frontiers" for mass deportations, "elimination of unreliable elements" and "liquidation of the opposition" for imprisonments and shootings. Still later have come "collective security," "peaceful coexistence," "non-committed nations" and "global commitments." Such words and expressions have multiplied, particularly in the field of politics and international relations but, to a surprising and generally unsuspected degree, in other fields as well. In the former, they go to swell the vocabulary of propaganda for or against a certain principle or idea. In the latter, they become part and parcel of the jargon of individual trades, professions, and walks of life, but, again in a measure that few realize, they also go to swell whatever propaganda content those professions or walks of life may contain.

The process whereby this is accomplished varies according to circumstances but is almost always the same in substance. A word or expression is lifted out of its usual context, charged with a new meaning or set of meanings, and placed once more in circulation in an entirely different context. Such words as "liberty," "liberalism," "democracy," expressions like "freedom of the press" and "People's Republic," are glaring examples of difference in semantic content, brought about naturally, by reason of the different experience of different individuals or groups, or deliberately, to create a particular frame of mind. Often the two factors converge. It could not, for example, be expected that two nations with such widely different backgrounds and past experiences as America and Russia would naturally fall into the same definition of "liberty" or "democracy." When to the natural semantic differences are added deliberately instilled variations of a government-sponsored variety, it is not at all surprising that the same word should not hold the same meaning for both. American "democracy" is said to emphasize the complex concept of government "by" the people; Soviet "democracy," of government "for" the people. The word "liberty," which has to us certain connotations involving individual freedoms, used to appear in the Nazi and Fascist anthems, where its semantic connotation revolved around the freedom of the national or racial group to expand at the expense of others. The situation is occasionally complicated by the fact that in one language two meanings are combined in a single word, while another language keeps them separate. The Russian *"My trebuyem mira"* may signify "We want peace," but also "We want the world."

Within our own political life, attention has been repeatedly called to the growth of a vocabulary of clichés, each of which bears its own load of specialized and often complex meaning. Back in the days of Theodore Roosevelt, such expressions as "Malefactors of great wealth" and "merchants of death" were current. The international scene has resounded to such terms as "Fascist," "reactionary," "progressive," "bourgeois," "colonialism," "satellites," "Iron Curtain," while the home front has offered other gems: "Red-baiting," "book burning," "witch hunt," "McCarthyism," "hatemongers." Such rigidly formalized, ritualistic adjectives as "forward-looking," "clear-thinking," "peace-loving," "freedom-seeking," expressions like "to further positive, constructive aims" or "to engage in irresponsible, destructive criticism," have become part of the verbal ammunition of some of our political parties, to the point where some groups accuse others of carrying on a semantic war and creating a state of mind described as "logophobia," the fear of being labeled with a certain word.

But this is far from being a merely political process. The field of commercialized hygiene has given extended connotations to "B.O.," "halitosis," and other sloganized expressions. The field of art has its semantically charged words, like "abstract," "objectivism," "formalism," "decadent." Even a seemingly harmless combination like "modern art" had to be changed to "contemporary art" because, in the words of those who made the change, "modern" used in connection with "art" "lent itself to double talk, opportunism, and chicanery." In other fields we find meaning-charged words and expressions, like "unfair," "maladjusted," "underprivileged" (or "disadvantaged"), "insecure," "racial minorities," "tensions," "frustrations," "discrimination," "unscholarly," "unscientific," "education for leadership," the use of each of which normally carries implications as to the user's background and point of view that far outstrip the dictionary definitions of the words themselves. The situation is described by a contemporary writer as one of "loyalty to words." But "loyalty to words" is anything but a recent phenomenon. Historical terms, like "God-fearing," "Popery," "transubstantiation," "iconoclasm," or "Tory," "Jacobin," "Cavalier," and "Ghibelline," carried in the past an equally high charge of semantic dynamite.

The semantic overcharge sometimes leads to the dropping of a word, as when a noted politician rejected for himself the term "liberal" and chose instead "libertarian," or when the Veterans of Foreign Wars decided to drop "comrade" from their terminology because of its supposed Communistic associations and use "buddy" instead; interestingly, the East

German Communists, worried about the semantic charge attached to "comrade," suggested that it be replaced by "colleague," which would have a professional rather than a political aura.

Instances of this sort abound historically. In both the French and Russian Revolutions, the word "soldier" was generally discarded as being associated with the old regime and replaced by the term "warrior." The word "army," associated with the army of the Czars, was replaced by "Red Guard" in the early days of the Soviets, though it later returned to favor (*Krasnaya Armiya,* "Red Army"); and a word was coined from it which means, all by itself, "Red Army soldier" (*krasnoarmyeyets*). The terminology associated with the Czarist police was replaced by an entirely new set of words when the Soviets came to power, while "patriotism," a term which, an early revolutionary writer said, "has become, in the hands of the reactionaries, a pretext for robbery and murder, and a term of opprobrium," was a few years later reinstated with all honors in such expressions as "the lofty patriotism of the Soviet defenders of the frontiers of their native land." The very words "Russia" and "Russian" were for a time avoided almost completely and even today are somewhat cautiously used, while Soviet writers occasionally debate whether Biblical clichés, like "the Gospel of the Revolution," "the Herods and Pilates of the people," "to crucify the masses," should or should not be used in a movement meant to be godless.

Closely connected with the natural or deliberate semantic charge which gets attached to words and expressions is the matter of the relativity of meaning. This is illustrated by references to be found in nineteenth-century books to the "fantastic" and "terrific" speed of trains running twenty miles an hour, or by the arbitrary definition of "antique" as something produced before 1830, as well as by the use of "free," for a time threatened with banishment by the Federal Trade Commission, to describe an object given in connection with the buying of something else.

Even outside these rather glaring instances, it is seldom that words and expressions are endowed with absolute meanings. "Hot" applied to a day in August is quite different from "hot" describing the condition at the center of the sun. "Young" is well applied to a man of forty running for President but inappropriate for a heavyweight contender of the same age.

There is even a geographical relativity that affects such commonplace prepositions as "up" and "down," and for which only occasionally there is a logical explanation. "Up North" and "Down South" are undoubtedly due to relative positions on the map, but what of "Down East"? In Egypt, you "go up" when you are heading south, because you are going up the Nile. But why are you invariably invited to "come down" to Martha's Vineyard?

The relativity of meaning becomes paramount as we pass from one language to another. This is due to the more varied backgrounds of speakers of different languages, as well as to what French writers often refer to, rather vaguely, as the "genius" of the individual languages.

The point is often made that reading works of literature in translation fails to convey the beauty, charm, etc., of the original. What is probably meant is that the areas of semantic correspondence fail to coincide, even approximately, in any two languages. This is not surprising, in view of the lack of coincidence of sounds, grammatical forms, or syntactical concepts among the various tongues.

Each language has its own precise distinctions, its highly meaningful terms, which to be made clear to speakers of another language require not a translation but a full definition accompanied by explanatory notes. A business term like the American "overhead" is to some extent covered in other languages by such expressions as "general expenses" or "miscellaneous expenditures," but the meaning is far from the same. A prize was once offered in a group of language teachers for an exact and concise Italian equivalent of "wishful thinking," but no one got the prize. A similar prize should be offered for an English rendering of the Romance *antipatico*. The recently coined and sycophantic "senior citizen" is only a pale rendering of the concept conveyed by the French *vieillard*, the German *Greis*, the Latin *senex*. A semantic distinction like the one existing in English between "house" and "home" cannot be made in many languages without having recourse to five lines of explanation or an excursion into the language of poetry where expressions like "domestic fireside" are available. The distinction between "sky" and "heaven" is difficult to make in French or Italian unless one has recourse to "paradise." Which figure of speech is more cogent, the English "dead end" or the French *cul-de-sac?*

Every language is laden with idioms, constructions peculiar to that language, which cannot be literally translated into another, and the meaning of which cannot be gathered from their component parts. English "look out" for "be careful," if literally translated into other tongues, will convey only its literal meaning of "look outside." English "to run out of something," "to catch up with someone," "to be well off" are highly idiomatic. When a house "burns up" in English, it also "burns down." All of this goes to show that language is anything but logical, and that semantics cannot by any stretch of the imagination be turned into an exact science.

Add to this that language is replete with words which are throwbacks to an earlier stage of civilization, like "manufacture" (literally, "making by hand"), "manuscript" (literally "hand-written"), "to sail" for a certain destination (usually by steamer), "to ship" goods by rail or truck. Even our "sunrise" and "sunset," in the light of modern science, are semantic misnomers.

Words like these are striking but actually far from unusual. Very few words, except those recently coined, retain their original meanings throughout their history and migrations from one tongue to another. Out of one hundred Latin words, less than half retain in the Romance languages or in English anything like the same meaning they had in Latin. Approximately the same proportion holds for the Anglo-Saxon part of our linguistic heritage. As the experience of existence changes from one generation to another, words change their meaning. A few examples will suffice to illustrate this.

"Infant" is originally "nonspeaking," still partly true in the new connotation, but with a restriction of meaning to the young. The original meaning of "foyer" is "fireplace." A "secretary" was once a "separator," and a "secret" was what is set apart; both words come from *secretus,* the participle of the Latin *secerno* ("to separate"). "Noble" is originally "knowable"; it comes from the Latin root *gno-* ("to know"). A "person" was once a "mask"; *persona,* which can be analyzed into "through-sounding" (the sound of the voice comes through the mask), was the mask worn by Roman actors; but this mask gave them a character and a "personality." "Rival" originally meant "pertaining to a river bank"; its present meaning is due to the concept of two landowners contending for water rights on the bank of a stream. A "comrade" is originally one who shares a room with you; a "companion," one who eats bread with you. "Meat" was once food of any kind, as evidenced by terms like "meat and drink," "sweetmeats," and "flesh meat." "Intoxicated" once meant "poisoned," and "incensed" is etymologically "burned up." "Hose" changed its meaning from "tights," in Shakespeare's times, to "stockings" today. "Typewriter" once meant the typist, not the machine, and "naughty" was "poor," one who had naught. The original application of the term "automobile," in 1883, was to streetcars.

Some words manage to come close to reversing their original meaning in the course of their histories. "Brave" comes from the same root as "depraved," Latin *pravus,* which originally meant "crooked," then "scoundrelly"; but a thoroughgoing scoundrel has to have some physical courage, hence the ultimate meaning of "brave." The Romance languages have here gone even further than English, since "brave" used before the noun has in French and Italian acquired the meaning of "good," "worthy"; in fact, in both languages it may be ironically applied to indicate one who is so good that he is good-for-nothing. And what could be more semantically contradictory than "atomic fission," which is the "division of the indivisible," or the splitting of the unsplittable?

Our English "silly" has as its cognate the German *selig* ("blessed"), which retains the original meaning; the English transfer went from "blessed" to "blessed fools," then to "fool" pure and simple. A similar development appears in French *crétin* (from which we get "cretinism") from the Latin *christianus* ("Christian"), while in Italian *cristiano* is often used for "human being," but in a disparaging or pitying sense.

"Nice" comes from the French *niais* ("silly"), which in turn goes back to the Latin *nescius* ("stupid," "not knowing"); the English change in meaning seems to have arisen with the use of the word in expressions like "a nice distinction," meaning first a silly, hair-splitting distinction, then a precise one, ultimately an attractive one.

Latin *domina* ("mistress," "lady") largely retains its meaning in French *dame* and in the "dame" of England, which is used as the feminine counterpart of "knight" or "sir." In American slang, however, "dame" has become attached to "girl," with a somewhat free-and-easy connotation.

Studies of the earliest appearance of certain words in the language often bring to light startling semantic changes. "Measles," for example, appearing in the thirteenth century, first had the meaning of "leper" or "leprous"; both the word and the meaning came in from Old French, which had derived the word from Latin *misellus* ("wretched"). "To stump," which first appears in a document of the year 1250, has there the meaning of "to stumble over a stump." "To neck" and "to table" first appear as verbs in the year 1450, but at that time meant "to strike in the neck" and "to enter on a table." The original meaning of "face" used as a verb (1440) is "to present a bold face," while "souse," appearing in the sixteenth century, is originally "hit." "Brash," now used as an adjective, first appeared in the sixteenth century as a verb with the meaning of "to attack."

Semantic divergences occur naturally between two languages that undertake to use the same word. The two or more words appearing in different languages from the same source but with different meanings, like English "silly" and German *selig*, or English "nice" and French *niais* already mentioned, are called cognates. Deceptive cognates constitute one of the most effective stumbling blocks in the study of a foreign language. German *Lust* is a cognate of English "lust" but has the harmless meaning of "pleasure," while our semantically attractive "gift" has in its German cognate *Gift* a word that means "poison." English "knight" and German *Knecht* are also related, but the German word means "serf." In the broader Indo-European field, the specialization of meaning is shown by the fact that the cognates of the English "chin" mean "cheek" in Latin, "jaw" in Sanskrit, "mouth" in Breton; and the restriction of meaning by the fact that a "deer" was originally any animal, as it still is in the German cognate *Tier;* Shakespeare speaks of "mice and rats and such small deer," but the animal we now call "deer" being particularly the object of the chase in England, the word became restricted to a single genus.

Words can easily change their rank in the course of their histories. A "constable" was originally a "stable companion," while a "marshal" was a "horseboy" or "horseshoer." In medieval times, however, a constable (*connétable*) became an officer of high rank, to revert later to a mere police officer, while both high and low rank appear in "marshal" today ("Marshal of France," "town marshal"). The lofty Arabic *al-wazir,* or vizier, becomes in Spanish an *alguacil,* or policeman, and in Italian an *aguzzino,* or hangman's assistant. "Harlot" and "lewd" did not always have the evil connotations they bear today. The former was used by Chaucer in the sense of "maidservant," while the latter once meant merely "ignorant."

Other words that have undergone what the philologists

call pejoration of meaning are "knave," "villain," and "churl." "Knave" was once "young man," as still borne out by its German cognate *Knabe* or by its use in card playing as a synonym for "jack." "Villain" was in origin "pertaining to a villa or estate," then was applied to the peasants attached to the estate; in an aristocratically dominated civilization, peasants were invested with all sorts of unpleasant characteristics, and French *vilain* finally got to mean "ugly," Italian *villano* "unmannerly," "impolite," and English went farthest of all with "villain of the piece." "Churl" started out in life as "strong fellow," as evidenced by German *Kerl* and King Harold's housecarls, a Scandinavian equivalent of the Anglo-Saxon *ceorl;* after the Norman Conquest he sank to the same level as the French *vilain* and, by the same process of mental association, became a "churl" with a corresponding adjective "churlish" which is an excellent translation for the Italian *villano*. "Crafty" was once "knowledgeable," at a time when all our sciences now ending with Greek *-ology* terminated in the Saxon *-cræft*.

Overworked words undergo heavy semantic shifts. This fact has been noted in connection with "disinterested" (once "unbiased," now often used as a synonym for "uninterested"); with "darling" (put into vogue by certain actresses as a form of address for practically anybody, including the stagehands); and, most recently, "literally," now often used where its opposite, "figuratively," should appear (among examples from contemporary writings are: "rooms literally bursting at the seams with huge enrollments," "the book is literally a garbage heap," "outraged members literally blew their tops with indignation").

Other examples of semantic confusion are reported from such diverse fields as the military and the medical. From the former we have a report that millions of dollars are wasted because, in the words of Naval Commander Curtis W. Bunting: "Semantics plays a big part in trying to buy things. When one manufacturer calls it a bracket, another a hanger, and still another a strap, it isn't easy." One medical man complains about the medical use of "normal" and "abnormal" to indicate healthy and diseased, respectively; an individual with one brown eye and one blue eye, he states, is abnormal but neither physically nor mentally diseased. Another medical man objects to the ill-defined use of the term "shock" to describe the condition of disaster casualties and warns us that misinterpretation of the term may cost lives, as shock may at one time apply to great loss of blood and at another to mere pain or fright.

One of the oldest words in the Germanic languages is "corn." But semantically "corn" has become specialized to mean "wheat" to the British, "oats" to the Scots, and "maize" to the Americans. Not knowing this fact, a government agency during the war bought "corn" for European famine relief at the request of the British Government, and this bit of linguistic ignorance cost a few million dollars to repair.

There are words which take on new meanings without relinquishing the old ones. "To escalate," for instance, is given as recently as 1961, in *Webster's Third International*, with the sole meaning of "to ascend" or "to carry up, as on a conveyor belt," and "escalation" with the sense of "to raise prices in order to correct an unjust discrepancy." But it has become quite common, in a very short time, to speak of "escalating" a war, raising it from the status of a brush conflict fought with minor forces to a major conflagration.

Semantics is utilized by the world of commerce, and particularly of advertising, in various ways, most of them legitimate. There can be no real objection, for instance, to dubbing a type of crayfish "rock lobster" or using such terms as "journal" for "magazine," "library" for "set of books," "program" for "sales campaign." The situation becomes more dubious when we come to the overnumerous coinages of the commercial world ("power-pak" and "hydramatic" come to mind) and to the use of hyperbolic adjectives of the type of "colossal," "fabulous," and "screen classics."

The question is often asked: "What makes for semantic change?" Far more than syntax, grammatical forms, or even sounds, the semantics of language is subject to all the forces, overt and obscure, of individual and mass psychology. Each word, as has been seen, has its own semantic history, and for each change in the meaning of that word there is a definite cause, which it is usually impossible to ascertain with any degree of accuracy a few years after it has taken place. Yet the process of language change is fundamentally the same. In the case of each semantic shift, as in the case of each sound shift or each change in the grammatical pattern, there is usually an innovation made by an individual, deliberately or accidentally, and accepted by the group. Language is forever changing, and semantics changes with it.

The essential part of semantics is acceptance of a given meaning. Meaning, like all else in the realm of language, is a matter of convention. From the subjective standpoint, a language we do not understand is no language, however objective its reality may be. Human progress is based upon cooperation; cooperation can be based only on understanding; understanding, in turn, is based upon the conventional acceptance of meaning. Semantics is therefore at the very heart and core not merely of language but of human civilization.

— Chapter Seven —

THE INTERNATIONAL LANGUAGE BANK

What we frankly give, forever is our own.
—Granville

LANGUAGE sounds and grammatical forms have their own peculiar, often slow, process of evolution, which is generally of an internal character. It is comparatively seldom that a language borrows a sound or a morphological ending from another tongue, though there are among linguists some confirmed believers in the "ethnical substratum" who hold that when speakers of two different languages come in contact they are bound to influence one another's pronunciation and even grammar. In the latter field, the theory is fairly easy to disprove, since the written language normally affords a good record of grammatical change. In the matter of sounds, the question whether languages borrow from one another is still controversial. Substratum supporters believe, for instance, that when the Romans conquered Gaul they taught the Celtic-speaking Gauls the Latin language but were never able to make them pronounce it Roman fashion, and that it is the mixture of Celtic sounds with Latin words that laid the groundwork for the ultimate development of French and its distinctive sound pattern, as differentiated from Italian or Spanish, which had different racial and linguistic backgrounds. English, in the same manner, is said to have been to some extent influenced in its sound pattern by the coming of the French-speaking Normans. Even the peculiar intonations of our own South are supposed to be the result of a blending of the speech habits of English colonists with those of Negro slaves who originally spoke West African languages. Nonbelievers in the theory of the ethnical substratum and linguistic sound blending, on the other hand, point to the fact that in South America, where the American

Indian languages are still very much alive, there is no noticeable influence of these languages upon the sound pattern of the Spanish imported by settlers from Spain. They also point out that in the United States immigrant accents tend to die out completely within a generation or two, leaving no trace on the English of the localities where immigrant groups abound.

With regard to the other two great compartments of language, syntax and vocabulary, there is unanimity among linguists as to the mighty validity of the borrowing process. Numerous examples are on record where syntactical constructions have been borrowed by one language from another, particularly in cases where the latter had achieved a higher degree of civilization and development. The first document of a Teutonic language, Ulfilas' fourth-century Gothic translation of the Bible, displays wholesale borrowing of syntactical constructions and arrangements from the original New Testament Greek.

Far more than sounds, grammatical structure, or syntactical patterns, languages tend to borrow individual words. This process of word borrowing is so extensive and general that it has become a familiar commonplace to all, specialists and laymen alike. No one needs to be reminded that *Blitzkrieg* and *Gemütlichkeit* have come into our language from German, *hors d'oeuvre* and *à la carte* from French, *fiesta* and *sombrero* from Spanish, *obbligato* and *ravioli* from Italian. The operation of the word exchange has been likened to that of a vast international bank, which places the currencies of all countries at the disposal of all the rest, with the added ideal feature that what is borrowed need never be repaid, save perhaps in kind.

Of special interest are the many loan words that are shunted back and forth from one language to another. The Italian *palla* ("ball") came into Italian as a loan word from the Germanic Longobards and is cognate to our own word; as part of the name of a game, *pallamaglio*, it found its way back to one of the Germanic countries, England, where it assumed the form "Pall Mall"; then it came to Italy once more as the name of an American cigarette.

Some languages show a certain amount of resistance to foreign loan words. German, for example, prefers the loan translation, adopting the idea of the foreign word but substituting its own equivalent roots for the foreign roots, as when *Ausdruck* is coined on the mold of Latin *expressio*, or when *Fernsprecher* ("far speaker") replaces an earlier *Telephon* (from the Greek for "distance sound"), or *Was-*

serleitung ("water leading") an earlier *Aquaedukt,* borrowed from Latin. English occasionally uses the loan-translation process, as when "shorthand" goes side by side with "stenography" (Greek for "narrow writing"). But English is definitely among the languages that welcome all comers from abroad.

There are many such languages. Persian has borrowed over half its vocabulary from foreign sources. Albanian has only about 8 per cent of native Albanian words, with the rest taken from Romance, Turkish, Greek, and Slavic. Armenian has only 23 per cent of native words, with the rest from Parthian, Greek, Arabic, and Syriac. In a count of 551 Turkish words, 251 only were found to be of native Turkish origin; of the rest, 235 were Arabic, 51 Persian, and 14 Romance.

Even the Romance languages, which boast of their direct descent from Latin, are studded with non-Latin words. In a French etymological dictionary listing 4,635 root forms of the French language, 2,028 are Latin, 925 Greek, 604 Germanic, 96 Celtic, 154 English, 285 Italian, 119 Spanish, 10 Portuguese, 146 Arabic, 36 Hebrew, 4 Hungarian, 25 Slavic, 34 Turkish, 6 from African tongues, 99 from assorted Asiatic languages, 62 from American Indian languages, and 2 from Australian and Polynesian. Despite the Romance classification of French, Romance, including Latin, Italian, Spanish and Portuguese, has contributed a bare majority of the words.

All of the western Romance languages borrowed many words from the Germanic invaders, including the names of the cardinal points of the compass (east, north, south, west), which might indicate that the Germanic invaders had a better sense of direction than the Romans, and, for some mysterious reason, the names of most colors, though the Romans were far from color-blind.

The original basis of English is Anglo-Saxon, a language of the Germanic or Teutonic branch of Indo-European. Yet a straight vocabulary count from the dictionary will show that barely 40 per cent of English words are of Anglo-Saxon origin. The rest are borrowed, primarily from French, Latin, and Greek, but also from practically every tongue under the sun. On a straight vocabulary count one would therefore have to classify English as a language of international origin. But here another factor comes into play, the relative frequency of occurrence of words, and it is under this heading that our Anglo-Saxon heritage comes into its own. The Anglo-Saxon element in English comprises a large number of extremely high-frequency words, like the articles "the" and "a" or "an"; prepositions, conjunctions, and adverbs like "of," "to," "for," "by," "in," "and," "but," "if," "fast," "slow," "well"; common verbs, adjectives, and nouns like "go," "come," "eat," "see," "bad," "good," "high," "low," "bread," "hand," "sea," "land." The over-all result may be gleaned from the following random examples:

In an ordinary English letter, words of Latin or Greek origin are about 15 per cent of the total; in a literary or scientific work, they run up to over 30 per cent. The Preamble to the Constitution contains twenty-five words of Latin and twenty-eight of Anglo-Saxon origin; the latter, however, include five repetitions of "the," two of "to," two of "for," two of "of," and three of "and." A count of words used in subway advertising and directional signs shows 70 per cent to be of Anglo-Saxon origin, 30 per cent from other sources; the Anglo-Saxon words include the usual connective words of very frequent occurrence; if the count is restricted to nouns, verbs, adjectives, and adverbs, the proportion is closer to fifty-fifty.

We should not be misled into thinking that all short, pithy, common words are Anglo-Saxon, and that only three- and four-syllable words come from foreign sources. Words like "very," "air," "hour," "cry," "oil," "cat," "pay," "piece," "box," "face," "poor," "dress," "push," "fine" are of foreign origin, despite their native appearance and common use.

Such examples arouse questions. Do words, when they migrate from one language into another, behave as people do under similar circumstances? Do they remain alien in appearance, or do they take out citizenship papers? Some do one thing, others the other. Generally speaking, words that enter a language at an early period, before conscious cultural influences begin to make themselves generally felt, are quickly and thoroughly assimilated. "Cheese," "street," "mint," "kiln," place-name endings like "-minster" and "-chester," came into Anglo-Saxon from Latin long before the Norman Conquest, mingling with such native words as "wassail" and the *hal beo thu* ("whole be thou") which ultimately gave us "hello." Most laymen would set such words down as native English, even if they knew the Latin equivalents from which they once sprang (*caseus, strata, moneta, culina, monasterium, castrum*). In early, popular, noncultural borrowings, the tendency of the borrowing language is not merely to appropriate the foreign words but to make them conform to its own speech habits and sound patterns, even to its own laws of accentuation; Old French *verai*, for instance, was stressed on the last syllable, like most French words, but the English "very" to which it gave birth shifts the stress to the initial syllable, in accordance with the general custom of the Germanic tongues.

Later borrowings were often less popular and spontaneous, and occurred under the influence of learned people: clerics and monks in the Middle Ages, scholars and lexicographers in the Renaissance, scientists and educators in modern times. At this point, a definite attempt is usually made to retain some of the foreign flavor of the appropriated word, which remains more or less an alien in our midst. "Bishop," for example, is a thoroughly anglicized, naturalized version of Greek *episkopos*, but "episcopal," coming from the same source, retains its Greek appearance. "Frail" is naturalized, "fragile" is alien; both come from Latin *fragilis*. "Palsy" and "paralysis," "minster" and "monastery" are other sets of doublets, twin words coming from the same source, of which one has acquired native form while the other remains somewhat foreign in appearance. Occasionally we find triplets ("spice," "specie," "species"), quadruplets ("jaunty," "gentle," "genteel," "Gentile"), and even quintuplets ("desk," "dish," "dais," "disc," "discus").

It is but natural that words should have the greatest chance of being adopted when the object they denote does not already exist as a word in the borrowing language, as is the case with Zulu "assegai," Australian "boomerang," and American Indian "wigwam." Very often, however, a language gives up its own native word in favor of an adopted alien, as when Latin speakers renounced *galea, albus,* and *bellum* ("helmet," "white," and "war") in favor of Germanic *helm, blank,* and *werra.* In England, before the coming of the Normans, "despair" was *wanhope* and "library" was *book-hoard.* Anglo-Saxon *ynwit* was replaced by Latin-French "conscience" in the thirteenth century, but not till a book entitled *The Agenbite of Ynwit* ("The Remorse of Conscience") had appeared. Still more frequently, both the alien and the native word remain, becoming synonyms that enrich the language's vocabulary, like Anglo-Saxon "shun" and Norman-French "avoid," or "knighthood" and "chivalry."

Languages often borrow words used as prefixes and suffixes and then proceed to use them in their own fashion, often producing "hybrids" against which the purists rant until they are in such common use that it is vain to rant any longer. "Automobile" is such a hybrid. Its first part is "self" in Greek, its second portion "movable" in Latin. On a higher plane is the objection to "genocide," which combines the Greek root for "race" with the Latin root for "kill"; "genticide" has been suggested as a nonhybrid, all-Latin substitute. A lovely hybrid is "tenderoni," coined by an American firm by combining English "tender" with the suffix of Italian *macaroni*. A good example of a hybrid in a foreign language is the Russian word for "barber," *parikmakher*, in which the *makher* is the German *Macher* ("maker"), while the *parik* is French *perruque*, from which we get our own "periwig," later shortened to "wig."

The story of English word borrowings would easily lead us into a full-fledged dictionary of word origins. The Anglo-Saxons began borrowing words as soon as they settled in England, and "bald," "crag," "crock," "down," "glen," "ton," "druid," and "bard" are among the words they took from the ancient tongue of the Celtic Britons. Danish raids and settlements on the English coasts led to an intermingling of two closely allied Germanic tongues; among words of Scandinavian origin in English are "cake," "call," "curl," "die," "dirt," "get," "happen," "ill," "kid," "root," "skin," "sky," "ugly," "wing," and "want," as well as the verb form "are" and the pronouns "they," "them," and "their." "Skirt" and "shirt" were in primitive Germanic the same word, but while "shirt" developed from the Anglo-Saxon, "skirt" was brought in by the Danes. Similar Scandinavian-Saxon doublets are "loose" and "-less," "scrub" and "shrub." But English also has plenty of synonyms of which one represents the Danish importation, the other the original Anglo-Saxon word: "anger" and "wrath," "cast" and "warp," "ill" and "evil."

Latin words and expressions, as we have seen, began streaming into English when it was still Anglo-Saxon and have been continuing their inroads ever since. A few that have remained most thoroughly alien are *verbatim* and *passim, inter nos, modus vivendi, persona non grata, non sequitur, lapsus linguae, summum bonum,* and *terra firma.*

The Norman-French element, itself largely derived from Latin, made a vast contribution in the centuries that immediately followed the Norman Conquest, but French words have never ceased crossing the Channel. Often it is a dialectal form of French that reaches English, as is the case with most English forms in *-oon* ("saloon," "cartoon," "pontoon"), which betray their Anglo-Norman dialectal origin by their ending. "Cattle" and "chattel" both come from the French, which had derived them from Latin *capitalis*; however, "cattle" is from the Picard dialect of French, while "chattel" is from the standard language. Among older English words from French sources are "challenge" and "chance," "gun" and "engine," "jolly" (from French *joli*) and the "boon" of "boon companion" (simply *bon compagnon,* "good fellow"), "puppy" (from French *poupée,* "doll") and "assets" (from *assez,* "enough"), "taste" (from *tâter,* which means not to taste, but "to grope"), and "flirt" (from *fleurette,* "little flower"), "alas" (from *"Ah, las!"* in which the *Ah* is merely an interjection, and the *las* means "weary" with "me" understood), "kerchief" and "curfew" (from *couvre-chef,* "cover head," and *couvre-feu,* "cover fire"), "bayonet" (from the city of Bayonne, where the weapon was first manufactured) and "sabotage" (from *sabot,* a wooden shoe; the reference is to the delightful practice of disgruntled workers of throwing a shoe into the machinery, similar to our "throwing a monkey wrench"). *Chiffonier, blasé, ennui, de trop, noblesse oblige, belles lettres, par excellence, de rigueur, savoir faire, comme il faut, fait accompli, laissez faire, cherchez la femme* are among French expressions that have not taken out naturalization papers.

The Renaissance brought three great language streams, Greek, Arabic, and Italian, in contact with English. The Greek contribution has increased rather than diminished with the passing of time, turning in recent decades into an imposing scientific and technical vocabulary which bids fair to make our language among the richest in the world. These scientific terms consist not only of words like "atom," "cyclotron," "telegraph," and "hydrotherapy" but also of prefixes like *hyper-* and *hypo-,* whose Latin counterparts are *super-* and *sub-,* and which often lend themselves to the formation of hybrid words, as when *hyper-* is attached to "tension," which is of Latin origin. But the total Greek contribution is not merely scientific and technological. Numerous Greek words appear in the popular speech. "Idiot," for example, is Greek for "private" (a thoroughly private person is abnormal and belongs in an institution); "adamant" is Greek for "unsubdued"; "cyclone" is Greek for "coil of a snake"; "cheer" in the expression "to be of good cheer" goes back to the Greek *kara,* "face"; "paper" comes from *papyrus,* the Greek name of a sedge grass whose pith was used as a writing material by the ancients; "Bible" comes from another Greek name for the same material, *biblos.* Among recent Greek additions to our vocabulary which have not become naturalized is *hoi polloi,* Greek for "the many." Many words that come to us from Greek are claimed to have been borrowed by Greek from earlier Cretan or "Mediterranean" sources; among them are "asphodel" and its Dutch derivative "daffodil," "absinthe," "hyacinth," "labyrinth," "triumph," "mint" (the herb), "rose," "narcissus," "sandal," "purple," "cithara" (with its later Arabic derivative "guitar"), "sack," "cane," and "paean."

Arabic contributions usually, but not always, bear a distinguishing mark, the *al-* prefix that represents the Arabic definite article ("alcohol," "algebra," "alkali," "alcove," etc.). From the Arabic come "dragoman," "minaret," and even such semislang terms as "ballyhoo" and "so long" (the former is *b-Allah hu,* "by Allah it is"; the latter is *salaam,* "peace," borrowed by Malay in the form *salang,* then brought to Britain by colonial troops).

Italian offers us the names of most of our military units and ranks, coined by the Italian *condottieri* of the Renaissance ("battalion," "regiment," "brigade," "infantry," "cavalry," "artillery," "corporal," "captain," "colonel," "general," and "generalissimo," even the loan translation "free lance"), along with a wealth of words dealing with all fields of life, art, literature, and music, like "ballot" and "garble," "balcony" and "façade," "sonnet" and "gazette," "burlesque" and "cavalcade," "dilettante" and "replica," "miniature" and "sketch," "model" and "studio," "falsetto" and "a cappella," "staccato" and "scenario," "piccolo" and "viola," "farina" and "semolina," "fiasco," "vista," "bravo." Two curious Italian importations are the seeming loan translation "skyscraper" (the English term first appears in America in 1891; the Italian equivalent, *grattacielo,* applied to a person, not a building, goes back to 1252), and the exclamation "Dear me!," which seems to be an adaptation of the Italian *Dio mio.* The suffix *-esque* of "picturesque," "arabesque," etc., is also of Renaissance Italian origin.

The centuries of the modern era have brought to the English language words from practically every language in the world, often in exceedingly roundabout fashion. "Grippe," for instance, comes to us from French, but the word seems to be originally Russian, where *khripota* is "hoarseness" and *khripyet'* is "to have a rattle in one's throat"; the word appears to have traveled westward in the eighteenth century, when Russian troops occupying Berlin brought the disease with them. On the other hand, "knout" (*knut*), the whiplash, comes to us from Russian, but the word originally came to Russia from Germany, as evidenced by the German diminutive *Knüttel* ("cudgel"). "Ghetto" is an Italian word but seems to come from a Rabbinical Hebrew *get* ("divorcement"), indicating the isolation of the Jews from the rest of the population (another theory is that it is a shortened form of *borghetto,* small city quarter).

From kindred Germanic languages of the Scandinavian group there have come to us words like "geyser," "saga," "ski," and "slalom." Dutch has contributed such expressions as "blunderbuss," "veld," "spa," and "forlorn hope" (*verloren hoop*, "lost troop"). Yiddish has given us "fooey" and "kibitzer"; German naturalized words like "kindergarten" and "liverwurst," "meld" and "sauerkraut." These lists could be extended indefinitely, as to both words and languages.

To the question: "What have others borrowed from us in return?" the answer is long indeed. French has taken, without change of form or meaning, our "baby," "bridge," "club," "film," and "sandwich"; "wagon" has acquired in French the meaning of "railway coach," while *boxe* and *bouledogue* are the forms assumed by "boxing" and "bulldog." Among latest accretions to the French vocabulary from English are *niou louque* which will be recognized by some as "new look," *rocanrole* ("rock and roll"), *bar snack* (our "snack bar" in reverse); slightly changed but still recognizable words like *pin-up, best-seller, hot-dog, shampoing, kidnappé, strip-tease, knock-outé;* accompanied by another host of words and expressions that are completely unchanged, at least in written form (what French pronunciation does to them is an entirely different matter): *automation, surprise party, cocktail, football, mixer, standing, pep* (for which there is also, however, the loan translation *piment*), *living room, week end, knock-out, parking, smoking* (used only in the sense of "dinner jacket"), *camping, sweepstake, crawl, clubhouse, uppercut, chewing gum, jeep, under dog, night club, business man, up-to-date, bungalow, hold up.* This writer was once stumped by a word occurring in the recording of a French popular song of which he was trying to transcribe the script; the word sounded like *graw-GHEE*, and it did not resemble any French word I had ever heard; it ultimately turned out to be the English "groggy." There is even one word, *brassière,* whose basic meaning in French is "shoulder strap" but which was borrowed by English with a meaning which in French would be rendered by *soutiengorge* or *bustier,* and which has now been reborrowed by French with its well-known American connotation. It is no wonder that Etiemble writes an entire book to condemn what he calls *Franglais,* the weird combination of French and English which, he claims, American commercialism has foisted on France; but Daninos comes to the rescue of loan words from English and reiterates the proposition, so familiar to all linguists, that languages in contact are bound to mix.

Fears similar to Etiemble's are voiced by Spain's foremost linguist, Menéndez-Pidal, who expresses deep concern over the influence exerted on the Spanish language by the English —and particularly the American—press, radio, TV, cinema, publicity, and brand names. Since some Spanish-speaking countries are in more direct contact with us than others, the American-English penetration is richly varied. To cite but one example, Mexican Spanish calls a rail bus powered by an old engine *calamazo*, because the name of its place of manufacture, Kalamazoo, appears on it; the man who runs it is a *calamacero*, and a collision in which it may become involved is a *calamazazo*.

Italian has taken "cold cream," "football," and "nylon" and turned them into *colcrem, futbol,* and *nailon*. The latest edition of Panzini's *Dizionario Moderno* of Italian neologisms, containing about 20,000 recently admitted words, shows English, and more specifically American English, to be responsible for a great many of them.

Russian is perhaps more partial to loan words from the British side of English, though they are not always flattering to the lenders. *Khuligan* and *khuliganizm* are the forms given by Russian to English "hooligan" and "hooliganism" (the name was originally that of a very ill-behaved Irish family living in Southwark, London). The Russian slang *loder'*, "lazybones," is taken from the English "loader" (stevedore); the Russians were apparently impressed by the slowness of the work on English docks. But in addition, Russian is replete with English words, particularly of a technical nature.

The sporting, and especially the baseball, terminology of foreign languages displays a curious blend of the twin processes of word borrowing and loan translation. French *single, double, triple,* Italian *straik,* Spanish *beisbol* and *jonrón* (which is pronounced and means "home run") illustrate the first. French *but sur balles, arrêt-court, cambrioler* are loan translations for "base on balls," "shortstop," "to steal."

Language blending at times takes strange forms. The Pittsburgh area reports two conglomerations in use among its immigrants of Italian and German origin; one is *formaikäse* for "cheese," blending Italian *formaggio* and German *Käse* in a form reminiscent of French *choucroute* for "sauerkraut" ("cabbage" twice, first in French, then in German); the other is *muss pagarlo*, "I've got to pay for it," with a German "must" and an Italian "pay for it."

Is a language better or worse off for admitting all comers to citizenship? Here perhaps again a parallel with human beings is instructive. No language is "pure," as no race is "pure," with the possible exception of a very few minor and backward tribes and their tongues. Among western European groups whose known histories indicate maximum racial and linguistic intermingling are the British, the French, the Italians, and the Spaniards. To judge from their achievements, culture has suffered no setback from either racial or linguistic intermingling.

Yet at various times, purists have tried to purge the English language of words of foreign origin, replacing them with Anglo-Saxon roots. One slogan created by these linguistic nationalists was: "Avoid Latin derivatives; use brief, terse Anglo-Saxon monosyllables." The joke is that the only Anglo-Saxon word in the entire slogan is "Anglo-Saxon."

— Chapter Eight —

THE GREAT LANGUAGE MINT

Language is not an abstract construction of the learned, or of dictionary makers, but is something arising out of the work, needs, ties, joys, affections, tastes, of long generations of humanity, and has its bases broad and low, close to the ground.
— Walt Whitman, *"Slang in America"*

THERE is a Greek word, "onomatopoeia," which literally means "name-making." The term has been, rather unfortunately, appropriated by some linguists to designate the creation of words which are supposed to imitate sounds heard in nature, like "buzz," "chug," "clang," "coo," "fizz," "gurgle," "purr," "zip," and "zoom," or the recent and still slangy "yakity-yak" and "blah" for "idle chatter." The word "unfortunately" is used on two separate counts. First, the connection between the sound and the word is often more imaginary than real, as shown by the widely divergent forms that the same natural sound takes in different languages; in French, for instance, a dog does not go "bow-wow" but *"oua-oua,"* while in Italian he goes *"bu-bu"*; a turkey in France goes not "gobble-gobble," but *"glou-glou"*; an owl does not "hoot" but *"hulule"*'s; a cat does not purr but goes *"ron-ron"*; the English mouse "squeaks," but the French mouse *"couic"*'s. The second and more important objection to the current use of "onomatopoeia" is that etymologically the term should mean simply "word creation," without reference to the imitation of sounds. If this view were accepted, onomatopoeia would come to be recognized as perhaps the most important of the processes of linguistic change, because of all the words that exist in any language only a bare minority are pure, unadulterated, original roots. The majority are "coined" words, forms that have been in one way or another created, augmented, cut down, combined, and recombined to convey new needed meanings. The language mint is more than a mint; it is a great manufacturing center, where all sorts of productive activities go on unceasingly.

Linguists recognize a variety of processes whereby new words are added to the language. Not the least important among these is the process of sheer creation, whereby a word that did not previously exist is suddenly thrust into the spoken tongue. English lexicographers are often troubled by words for which no satisfactory etymology can be found; these words normally appear in the dictionary without the genealogy that adorns their more fortunate fellows, which are labeled as proceeding from an Anglo-Saxon or Latin or Greek or French forebear. These words are the illegitimate children, the bastards of the lexicological family. All that word historians can tell us about them is that they first appeared in the twelfth or fourteenth or twentieth century; they have no seeming cognates, no apparent source, often no clear-cut *raison d'être*. Someone invented them; somewhere or other along the language's course they met with popular favor, spread in the spoken tongue, got into literary records, and ultimately became part and parcel of the language. We may reasonably surmise that they were at first considered slang; that later they became colloquialisms; and that lastly they gained full standing, like the "blab," "tot," and "chat" which first appear in fifteenth-century English documents. Only exceptionally, in modern times, are the circumstances of the coinage known, as is the case with "Shangri-la," a place name invented by the author of *Lost Horizon* and popularized by Franklin D. Roosevelt.

Few people realize how many such words manage to arise, gain temporary popularity, then sink back into desuetude and oblivion. There is a long list of words current in the sixteenth century which did not come down to us: "pingle" (for "fight"), "yerk" (for "hit"), "snudge" (for "be miserly"), "sdeign" (for "disdain"), "ghost" (for "die"), "daw" (for "fool"), "yuke" (for "itch"), "begeck" (for "cheat"). There are many words in Shakespeare concerning whose precise meaning we are uncertain: "aroint," "ronyon," "bubukles," "coystril," "bisson tears," "riggish," "ribraudred," "wappened." There is a "maupygernon," representing a highly spiced dish of hog's kidneys, popular in medieval England but long since vanished. There are words still used in British dialects but no longer in standard English, like "cog" (to cheat at lessons) and "mich" (to play truant).

Those expressions which fall by the roadside and fail to

bloom are nonce words. The New York Transit Authority, having enjoyed a measure of success with "litterbug," tried to go on to "litter critter" but did not meet with public favor. "Poorthink," a term devised by the advertising magnates to describe the mentality that sends a high-priced executive by tourist class to negotiate a million-dollar deal, is still in the balance. Personal creations like Louis Sobol's "knocktail hour," "whooper-upper," "New Year's Weave," Richard Kostelanetz's "sensumentality" (defined in the book review where it appears as "an erotic undertone excessive for the actions described"), have definite merit, but will they ever enjoy the popularity of Delcevare King's "scofflaw" or of other creations now so thoroughly grounded in the language that one wonders why they ever had to seek admission: "global," "blueprint," "imbalance," "brash," "off-beat," "teenager," "chain store," "southpaw," "filibuster"? That onomatopoeia, in the narrower sense of the word, still functions is proved by a columnist who claims that "Arghoof" is the way your name sounds when it is spoken outdoors by several hundred people at once; but if the performance is indoors, then it sounds like "Yulkuks."

Other processes of word formation and vocabulary growth have been properly catalogued and given technical names by linguists grateful that they offer possibilities of thorough investigation. There is derivation, the process whereby an existing root is combined with established prefixes and suffixes to form new words, as when "protest" gave rise to "Protestant" and the latter in turn to "Protestantism," or when "defenestration" was coined to describe the process of putting to death by throwing from a window. A more recent example is the creation by New York Zoo authorities of "platypuserie" and "platypusorium" to describe the residence of the Australian duckbill, whose Greek name simply means "flat-footed." Other recent products of derivation are "automation," "luncheonette," "atomry," "overkill," "survivability," "supersonic," "superette" (a small supermarket), "animage" (John Hubley's term for the process whereby he gives life to cartoon films), and "dialathon" (a system of progressive phone calls set up by merchants to catch swindlers). A pretty and very recent Italian product of derivation is *ingambissima,* "very much O.K.," "fit as a fiddle"; the original expression, *essere in gamba,* literally "to be on one's leg," means to be fit or alert; the preposition, now used as a prefix, is combined with the noun, a superlative suffix is added, and the whole expression turns into an adverb of description.

There is also an opposite process, retrogressive formation, whereby a root is shorn of its prefixes and suffixes and reduced to the status of a different part of speech, as when the French verb *crier* gave rise to the noun *cri,* or when "Canterbury," to which devout Englishmen went on short pilgrimages, gave rise to "canter," or when "withdrawing room" became "drawing room." "Gruntle" from "disgruntle," and "icky" (said to be baby talk for "sticky") follow this model.

Then there is the process known as composition, whereby two existing roots are combined to form a new word which has a meaning different from either of its component parts, like "railroad," or the more recent "rikmobile" of Shanghai, a motorized version of the originally Japanese *jin-rick'sha* ("man vehicle"). The composition process is a very ancient one, being mentioned by the Sanskrit grammarians under various headings with forbidding names, such as *dvandva* and *bahu-vrihi.* It is much favored in German, where such compounds as *Kriegsgefangenenentschädigungsgesetz* ("law for the compensation of war prisoners") are standard. *Halb-starke,* "Half-strong ones," for "juvenile delinquents," is a mild sample; Spanish, with compounds like *correvedile,* "run and go tell it," for "gossip," and *matasiete,* "kill-seven," for "boaster" is a close rival. Even a non-Indo-European language like Finnish, with its word for "world," *maailma,* literally "earth-sky," joins the picture; while languages like Chinese, which, having no prefixes and suffixes, do not admit the process of derivation, go far with composition. English compounds that have drawn fire in the not distant past are "hair-do" and "know-how," but in criticizing these formations it is forgotten that even a word like "kerosene" was originally the compound *keros-elaion,* "wax-oil."

Second only to sheer word creation in potency, and far outstripping it numerically, is the process known as analogy, whereby an originally "incorrect" word or form is coined in imitation of another existing and legitimate form, as when "flang" and "brang" are used as the past forms of "fling" and "bring" because, somewhere in the back of the speaker's consciousness, it is recalled that "ring" has a past "rang" and "sing" has "sang," or when words like "motorcade" and "aquacade" are coined in imitation of "cavalcade." The automobile industry has created an entire series of words coined on the analogy of "automatic"; "narrow-casting," based on "broadcasting," is suggested for pay TV. "General specialist" is more or less jocularly advanced by the medical profession to replace an earlier "general practitioner." "Urbiculturist" was seriously offered by Representative Younger of California to describe those city dwellers who ought to receive government subsidies, as do our agriculturists, otherwise known as farmers. "Telegenic" and "videogenic" attest the power of the *-genic* suffix of "photogenic." The analogic influence of "walkie-talkie" can be discerned in the coinage of "creepy-peepie" to describe a portable TV camera suited to televising battle scenes.

Lastly, in languages like English, which has lost most of its distinctive flexional endings, there is a process known as functional change, whereby a word used as a certain part of speech is, without ado or ceremony, transferred to another function. No better example of this could be adduced than the much-discussed modern use of "contact" as a verb, but the process of functional change has been going on for many centuries, ever since English ceased to be a tongue of complete inflexions and became predominantly a tongue of roots; "box," for instance, which came into English as a noun shortly after the Norman Conquest, began to be used as a verb in the sense of "to fight" in the sixteenth century.

It is perhaps natural that the majority of cases of functional change in English should consist of nouns that get to be used as verbs, because psychologically the object or concept tends to precede the action. "To moonlight," "to reference," "to feature," "to pinpoint," "to headline," "to process," "to service," "to garage," "to audition" are cases in point. But the movement can proceed the other way, witness "a handout" and "a must." Less palatable, for some obscure psychological reason, are prepositional phrases used as adjectives, like "off-the-record comments" and "round-the-clock discussions"; and adjectives turned into nouns: "a higher-up," "young marrieds," "the greats of the musical world." Nouns turned into adjectives, then occasionally turned back into nouns, are almost as bad: "the disadvantaged," "a fun dress" (or party), "a screechy" (sometimes used to describe a type of female singer).

It may be noted in passing that languages that retain flexional endings have little or no possibility of functional change but make up for this deficiency by the derivation and composition processes. Italian, for example, a language that still believes in flexions, has such picturesque formations as *forsennato* ("crazy") from *senno* ("sense"), *sgattaiolare* ("to slink") from *gatto* ("cat"), *scodinzolare* ("to wag one's tail") from *coda* ("tail"); literal translations of these long words would be "out-sensed," "to ex-cat," "to ex-little-tail." Spanish, another flexional language, has a splendid word for "snack" or "bite," *tentempié,* which may be analyzed into "hold-yourself-on-your-feet."

Returning to onomatopoeia used in the sense of an imitative coinage, we find that many words are formed by a process similar to it, which involves the repetition of the original word with a change in the vowel sound or, less often, of the initial consonant. Such are "zig-zag," "tip-top," "flim-flam," "ping-pong," "pell-mell," "boogie-woogie," "walkie-talkie," even "be-bop." At other times there is a process of straight repetition, but in these cases the attempt to imitate a natural sound is more noticeable; "murmur," "cuckoo," Italian *sussurro,* Spanish *cuchicheo,* French *frou-frou* are cases in point.

The connection with an idea only remotely related to a natural sound is sometimes in evidence. In English, for instance, most verbs ending in *-ash* have acquired the connotation of some sort of violent action: "bash," "clash," "crash," "dash," "flash," "hash," "lash," "mash," "splash," "slash," "smash," "thrash." At an earlier period, one Indo-European root gave rise to such diverse English words as "glad," "glass," "gleam," "glisten," "glint," "gloat," "glower," and "glare."

Derivation, retrogressive formation, composition, and analogy often appear in combination. "Iffy," meaning "tentative," "uncertain" (from "if") is easily catalogued as a case of straight derivation. "Ism," a theory, usually of the political, sometimes of the crackpot, variety and "flammable," used to replace "inflammable" because of the confusion caused by the prefix *in-,* are clear-cut retrogressive formations. But what shall one say of Gromyko's "vetophobia," which incorporates both composition and analogy, or of "homestress" and "majorette," formed on the analogy of "seamstress" and "major," with a full-fledged process of derivation?

Many years ago Lewis Carroll jokingly suggested the creation of what he called "portmanteau words," words that would carry two meanings in one suitcase; he offered such creations as "mimsey" ("miserable" plus "flimsy") and "slithy" ("slimy" plus "lithe"). He probably did not expect to be taken up seriously, but words like "brunch" ("breakfast" plus "lunch"), "smog" ("smoke" plus "fog") and, more recently, "motel" ("motor" plus "hotel") show that his suggestion did not fall on deaf ears. What Carroll possibly did not know was that the process he advocated had already been in operation for centuries; "clash" is originally a combination of "clap" and "crash," "flare" of "flame" and "glare," "glimmer" of "gleam" and "shimmer," "smash" of "smack" and "mash." An attempt was even made to coin "upcry" out of "uproar" and "outcry."

Another thing Lewis Carroll could not have expected was the extent to which some of the processes of portmanteauing would snowball (note our own functional changes). "Brunch" was only the first of a long line of creations: "drunch" is Tallulah Bankhead's combination of "drinks" plus "lunch," while "dinter" ("dinner" combined with "interview") was coined by a foreign actress, Miiko Taka, of *Sayonara* fame. "Smog" has given rise to the Los Angeles Air Pollution Control's "smust" ("smog" plus "dust"), quickly followed by such other creations as "smaze" ("smog" and "haze"), "smoud" ("smog" plus "clouds"), "sneet" ("snow" and "sleet"), "snirt" ("snow" combined with "dirt"); there is even a "fozzle," which sometimes is distorted into "foggle," used by C.B.S. weathercasters, which combines "fog" and "drizzle." "Motel," once started on its way, raised an entire family: "airtel" (a Texas institution for the private plane trade); "boatel" (translated by the French into *batotel* with *bateau* replacing "boat"); or "floatel," a waterfront barge with living accommodations. Columnist Phyllis Battelle contributes "foozly" ("foolish" plus "woozy"). Elsewhere we encounter "dipsy" ("tipsy" crossed with "dippy," with just a touch of "dipsomaniac"); Tip-Pack (a European travel agency creation, supplying you with ten dollars in local currency of small denominations, with a guide to tipping customs); "minitour" (a brief tour of a few Paris spots while you are waiting to change planes). The theatrical industry offers you "fantabulous" and "hamateur"; creative California comes up with "slurbs" (defined as "sloppy, slovenly, slipshod, sleazy suburbs"); an enterprising firm devises a "dustuctor," guaranteed to destroy dust; and graduate students of literature, having already blended "irrespective" and "regardless" into "irregardless," now compound the felony with the new vogue of "disirregardless."

Analogy, the process of creation by partial imitation of existing forms, is credited by some linguists with being the most powerful agent in language change. Its operation is evident not merely in the field of vocabulary but also in that of sounds, where "marjarine" is widely used instead of the legitimate "margarine" by mental association with "Marjorie," and in that of morphology, where strong verb forms like "drug," the original past of "drag," are turned into weak ones like "dragged" in imitation of "lag—lagged," "tag—tagged," etc.

The nature of the imitation process in analogy is often easy to determine. "Pea," for example, is known to have been formed from an original collective noun "pease" because the latter was mistaken for a plural. "Shame-faced" was once "shame-fast" ("confirmed in shame"), but changed "fast" to "faced" by reason of a blushing connotation. Historical linguists are fond of telling the story of the medieval extension by analogy of certain suffixes like *-age* and *-ier* in French which gave rise to the family of "voyage," "mirage," "poundage," "garage," and to that of "cavalier"; then, with an English change of spelling, "musketeer" and "carbineer"; ultimately, with an American twist, to "racketeer." They like to expound the *-ana* ("Americana," "Lincolniana," etc.) which was first put in vogue by French scholarly circles of the seventeenth century.

Present-day America is *par excellence* the stamping ground of deliberate analogy. "Electrocute," coined on the analogy of "execute," was one of the first American analogical coinages to draw fire from the purists. "Gerrymander," following the shape of "salamander," was another. We have turned to productive purposes the ending of "cafeteria" to supply us with such terms as "booketeria," a store where college students serve themselves and pay the cashier at the door. We have taken the lowly hamburger, which owes its name to its place of origin (Hamburg in Germany) and was introduced to the United States in 1884, and given it some forty variants. "Litterbug" has been coined on the analogy of "jitterbug"; "contemporama," "cyclorama," "futurama," "motorama" on that of "panorama."

The political scene has yielded such creative combinations as "boondoggle" (this was originally coined by a scoutmaster to describe the elaborate lanyards produced by his troop but was later used against the Roosevelt administration and its made-work policies; lately it has been paraphrased as "moondoggle" by Russell Kirk and applied to the project to reach the moon via twenty billion dollars); "globaloney" (Clare Boothe Luce); "Goldwaterloo" (coined at the end of the 1964 Republican Convention to describe the *débacle* of the liberal-moderate wing of the party); "hatriot" (a left-wing creation dedicated to the John Birch Society—"mediocracy," "idiocracy," and "gliberal" are in the nature of mild retaliation from the right). In Britain, "Belaborites" has been urged for the Conservatives, Loyal Opposition.

The educational world contributes "platitudinarian" and "platedictorian," to which could be added the verb "to cerebrate" and the adjective "intellectuous" (falling a little short of "intellectual" but pretending anyhow; derivative noun: "intellectuosity"). The literary-theatrical field, which gave us "blotterature" four centuries ago ("illiterature" has been suggested as a modern replacement), continues its contribution with "booboisie," "operantics," "huckstetrics," and "grismal." There is also Ed Wynn's "femmedians," *Variety's* "leerics"; from assorted sources come "bi-kiniscope" (originally devised for a Brigitte Bardot picture), "sexterical" (applied by a London paper to Elvis Presley), "orability" (a Marine-devised term for "kissableness"), "videots" and "Televenglish" from the TV division, even "legzotic," devised by a columnist in honor of Marlene Dietrich. The undertaking fraternity offers "cremains" for the mortal spoils of one who has been cremated, and the psychiatrists, with tongue in cheek, present "imaginitis" and "scarecoma," along with "iatrogenic" (or doctor-induced) heart disease and "yoo-yoo" (an ailment defying diagnosis). Their medical and dental colleagues have come up with "canoptic" and "acanoptic" (smoker and nonsmoker), "tooth-doodling" (grinding the teeth, also known as "bruxism"), "videognosis" (a diagnosis based on X rays transmitted to the physician by television). The social sciences offer "econometrician," "psychopantics," "sociopath" (a juvenile delinquent by any other name, especially when he is a repeater); also "autorosis" and "rurbanity," to describe two phases of modern living. The *Aerospace Glossary* published by the U. S. Air Force has, among others, these coinages of very recent vintage: "agravic" (weightless by reason of lack of gravity), "anacoustic zone" (75 miles up, where the air is too thin to transmit sound), "cislunar" (between the earth and the moon), "to destruct" (to destroy, but used only in connection with rockets out of control), "gnotobiotics" (the study of germ-free animals), "infrahuman" (animal used in experiment), "gravipause" (between two fields of gravity), "lox" (liquid oxygen); there is also a "missileer" (based on the analogy of the older "musketeer"), "cannoneer," and a pretty portmanteau word, "rockoon," for a rocket designed for launching from a balloon. A Baltimore physician, in a dictionary of sexology, coins terms from the Greek as follows: "callimelia" (having fine legs), "callicolpia" (having a fine bosom), "callimorphous" (having a fine everything, beautifully shaped), "colpomins" (bosom imitators, vulgarly known as "falsies"). But he turns to Latin for "crurapingia," leg art. In the trades, "generalist" is suggested for "jack of all trades," and "sanitarian" for bus boy. Even the French have coined *burelain* for "office worker," with the first element taken from *bureau* and the suffix from the family of *châtelain* and similar words. Foreigners trying to speak English have innocently bestowed upon us "presentees," coined after "absentees" by a Japanese, and "we are a freedomed people," offered by a Thailander.

The French show occasional flashes of genius in their analogic creations. What could be more picturesque than their description of a topless swimsuit as a *monokini?* (They have other names for it which are not analogic but equally picturesque: "two-pieces-minus-one," "illusion slayer," "demystificator.")

The use of personal and place names as verbs falls under the heading of functional change. The war gave us "to Coventry" (or "coventrize") and "to Quisling." But there are also the very numerous cases where a personal name turns into a common noun, even if still capitalized. Students traveling abroad on government scholarships are said to go on "a Fulbright," since the plan originated with the Senator from Arkansas. The Paris *fiacre,* or horse cab, goes back to the name of a saint much revered in Ireland, St. Fiacre; the original horse-cab stand was located before the hotel that bore his name. But what sounds like a person's name may be misleading for what concerns its etymology. The "roger" much used by the military is simply the word used to represent the letter *r* in spelling out radio communications and stands for "received."

Derivation accounts for numerous formations denoting political shades of opinion—Bilboism, Browderism, McCarthyism—as well as for such coinages as "Zoniac" to denote a resident of the Panama Canal Zone. Analogy plus a sense of humor is responsible for popular coinages of the type of Exurbia and Slobovia.

Coinages of groups of words used in a certain sense give rise to clichés. Among such expressions created by Shakespeare are "tower of strength," "pound of flesh," "made of sterner stuff," "milk of human kindness," "every inch a king," "midsummer madness." More recent cliché coinages are "boom and bust," "loyal opposition," "swing shift," "zoot suit," "sit-down strike," "hope chest" and "whodunit," along with such terms as "overkill" and such analogic usages as that of *-ville* ("Squaresville," "Moneyville") and that of *-wise* ("taxwise," "curriculumwise").

To the question "What proportion of coinages have known

authors, and what proportion are anonymous?" it is difficult to give an answer. Mystery words, in the sense that their origin is unknown, are legion. Words marked in the dictionary as arising in Middle English generally have no known Anglo-Saxon, Scandinavian, Norman-French, Latin, or Greek ancestry. We may, of course, surmise that some of them pertained to the earlier strata of the language and simply failed to be recorded in the documents that have come down to us. "Lad," "lass," "bad," "big," "gloat," "bet" are in this class, together with words of more recent appearance ("job," "blight," "slum," "kibosh"). The best that the dictionary can do with "smooch" is to refer you to a whole series of similar words ("smutch," "smotch," "smudge") and then come to a halt on Middle English *smogen*. But it is remarkable how many words, both living and dead, can be traced back to known creators. From the middle of the fifteenth century we have Reginald Peacock's interesting Anglo-Saxon replacements for Latin and Greek words ("ungothroughsome" for "impassable," "mark word for suchness" for "adjective," "speechcraft" for "grammar"). Later we have strange nonce creations, like Edward Lear's "peterpantheism" and "splendidophoropherostiphongious" (the acme in desirability), or Bulwer Lytton's "amoronthologosphorus," a five-legged animal with three hairs on each leg, possession of any one of which would endow its owner with undying beauty. In very recent times, as against modern mystery words of the type of "gimmick," "gadget," "yammer," "hoagy" (the Philadelphia version of a hero sandwich, which Webster's Third International does not deem worthy of inclusion), we have all sorts of worth-while creations by inventive newspaper columnists ("a statusfying car," "football as a form of wreckreaction," "distinktive ink with a perfume"; "sexgregation" and "sexclusive," suggested as alternatives for racial separation; "sexcretary," "jackassical," and "boloneyize"). It was Chuck Green, a close friend of Damon Runyon, who originated "moolah," Machine-Gun Kelly who first begged the "G-men" (government men) not to shoot, Maury Maverick who insisted that the word he wanted in his article was "urgle," not "gurgle." Gelett Burgess gave us two words that have stuck, "blurb" and "bromide," in the sense of "pacifier." J. Donald Adams, after discussing the various strange terms applied to groups of animals ("gaggle of geese," "clowder of cats," "pride of lions"), goes on to invent a few of his own ("blather of beats," "babel of critics"). Nor can we forget the highly colorful onomatopoetic combination devised by Oliver Wendell Holmes to describe a women's afternoon tea: "giggle-gabble-gobble-git." For my own field, I might suggest "linguacks" and "morphemaniacs."

One magazine writer claims that your choice of words identifies you as to generation and age: if you are addicted to "depot," "jitney," "klaxon," "shirtwaist," "oilskin," "consumption," "muskmelon," "spectacles," "underwear," you are of a dying generation; but if your chosen equivalent terms are "station," "bus," "horn," "blouse," "raincoat," "TB," "cantaloupe," "glasses," "shorts," you belong among those who think young.

Coinage sometimes raises problems among those etymologically inclined. "Bigamy" and "trigamy" appear in Webster's with their legitimate derivatives "bigamist" and "trigamist"; then we find "quadrigamist" but not "quadrigamy." But while having three wives is at least etymologically legal (*tri-* could be a Greek as well as a Latin prefix, to go with the Greek -*gamy*), "bigamy" and "quadrigamy" are definitely Latin-Greek hybrids. Could one venture to suggest "dygamy" and "tetragamy" as "pure" replacements?

"Glossolalia" is the scientific name given to the creation of language by the insane. Often the terms coined by insane persons have a weird and peculiar charm, like *farizitocericia, sirrope, tschario, moemdiana, ariotoebilium, davidiapulom, aprovia, astaerideo, adula,* and *atrobois.* Of late, glossolalia has become increasingly the vogue with certain religious bodies, notably the Pentecostal groups, which attempt to repeat, for "charismatic" purposes, the "speaking in tongues" of the New Testament.

The difference between glossolalia and creative word coinage lies in the fact that the former lacks a recognizable basis of both etymology and meaning. There is, of course, a form of glossolalia which is occasionally used by the sane for very definite purposes. It is known as double talk and is equally meaningless.

— Chapter Nine —

SLANG AND VULGARISMS

All slang is metaphor, and all metaphor is poetry.
— G. K. Chesterton
Lots of people who don't say "ain't" ain't eatin'.
— "Dizzy" Dean

THE term "vernacular" means the current spoken language of a given area, as distinct from the literary language. But the distinction is often extremely difficult to make, since both vernacular and literary language are characterized by social and educational stratification. This has always been true of the vernacular, less so of the literary tongue, which in the past has often tended to be far more conservative than it is today. Conservative or not, the literary language almost always gets around to reflecting the spoken vernacular, though sometimes after a considerable lapse of time. There is a continuous flow from the spoken vernacular to the literary language and another flow, perhaps less conspicuous, from the written to the spoken tongue.

The vernacular is said to be featured by colloquialisms, vulgarisms, substandard forms, and slang. This, of course, is a matter of individual choice and cultural status; also, the literary language of today may be equally so featured, as witnessed by a sporting page, a comic strip, or a whodunit.

Again, the precise distinction between what is a colloquialism, a vulgarism, a substandard form or slang, or a legitimate literary form is not always easy to make. Slang words are subject to precisely the same influences and processes as ordinary language: borrowing from foreign sources (like "crank" and "cranky," which we took from the German *krank*), semantic change (like "bean" used in the sense of "head"), analogy (like "his'n," "our'n," "your'n," formed in imitation of "mine" and "thine," which have a final *n* sound),

181

and downright coinage (like "oomph," legalized by a London court for use as a trade-mark with a decision which said, in part, "It is neither archaic nor poetic, nor is it obsolete").

In all languages and at all times, some slang moves into accepted good usage, though the rate of speed of this movement varies considerably (present-day American English probably achieves the ultimate in swiftness). Shakespeare brought into current good usage such slang terms of his day as "hubbub," "fireworks," "fretful," "to bump," and "to dwindle." One-time slang words which today have full legitimate standing are "strenuous," "spurious," "clumsy," "bogus." "Hectic," always legitimate in the sense of "consumptive," was still slangy thirty years ago in its now-current usage as "wildly busy."

In older editions of *Webster's Dictionary,* there was a New Words Section which included neologisms and slang words concerning the ultimate survival of which there was doubt. Actually, nearly 90 per cent of the new words ultimately became permanent. New words still on probation twenty years ago included such current forms as "cheesecake" (in the sense of feminine shapeliness), "corny" (for unsophisticated), "wolf" (for a rapacious philanderer), "whodunit" (mystery story), as well as "moppet," "gimmick," "snafu," "stooge," and "gremlin." Earlier admissions had been "blimp," "comeback," "getaway," "gun play," "joy ride," "wangle," "strip tease," "zoot suit," "soap opera," "jitterbug," and "juke box." Though they may have originated with an individual or a social class, everyone today understands such expressions as "goof," "in orbit," "make a booboo," "flip one's lid," "knock it off," "leave us go," "on the ball," "play it cool," "bats in the belfry," "behind the eight-ball," "on the beam," "hit the road," "step on it," "mad money," and "I've had it."

Slang is a very ancient phenomenon, extending back into the history of language almost as far as our records can reach. The slang use of the name of a piece of pottery for the head, similar to our "crackpot," has counterparts in many ancient languages: Sanskrit used *kapāla* (literally, "dish"), while the Latin slang use of *testa* ("pot") in the place of the legitimate *caput* ultimately gave rise to the French and Italian legitimate words for "head," *tête* and *testa.*

Plautus, a playwright of ancient Rome, made copious use, in his plays of Roman life, of the underworld slang of the *Suburra,* a quarter of Rome inhabited chiefly by the lower classes. Petronius, the Beau Brummel of Nero's court, has left us an account of a dinner written in the vernacular of his period, with several infiltrations of slang. François Villon was perhaps the first poet to make extensive use of underworld slang in his works, while Bonamy, in his *Réflexions sur la langue latine vulgaire,* first advanced the theory, later accepted by most scholars, that a good deal of information about the rise of the Romance languages was to be gained not from the Latin of Classical literature but from the slang of Plautus, Petronius, Apuleius, and similar "substandard" writers.

Some slang forms are of exalted, even royal, origin. "To sell someone to someone else" in the sense of "to praise" has an exact parallel in Cicero's Latin, when he writes to a friend *"valde te venditavi"* (literally, "I peddled you a lot"). "To get someone's goat" seems to be drawn from French *prendre sa chèvre,* used by Henri Estienne, a great lexicographer and philologist, in 1585. "Ain't" as a substitute for "am not," "are not" was established in current usage by King Charles II.

The word "slang" is said to be derived either from an erroneous past of "sling" or from "slanguage," with the initial *s* coming perhaps from such expressions as "thieves' language." The term was first used in England in the middle of the eighteenth century, but English literature on slang goes back to the sixteenth century and includes a glossary in seven large volumes.

Of some interest is the modern attitude toward slang. The broadminded procedure of our modern lexicographers, who admit slang words to the dictionary on or off probation, is typical. Some specialists go further. A Russian linguistic congress held in Moscow in 1930 defined language purity as a mere fiction, reflecting at best a pedantic attitude, at worst an attitude either aristocratic or chauvinistic. This point of view is shared by some American linguists who declare that "language is what people speak, not what someone thinks they ought to speak." In accordance with this view, there appeared in an English-language booklet prepared by Army linguists for the use of French speakers the phrase: "I laid on the bed." When attention was called to this seeming misprint, it was justified on the ground that "that's the way 90% of the G.I.'s say it."

Slang, of course, includes sounds, grammatical forms, and syntactical constructions as well as mere words and expressions. The points of English grammar over which the greatest controversies have raged are: the use of "I" or "me," "he" or "him," after "it's"; the use of "who" or "whom"

in such expressions as "who(m) did you see?"; "ain't" used
as a substitute for all present negative forms of "to be" and
"to have"; and the use of "shall" and "will" to form the future. Of these, "who" and "whom" lend themselves to the
most picturesque treatments. We find not only "Who do you
want?" but even "Whom are you?" and "Whomever is involved in this prank has a poor sense of humor." The situation is such as to have inspired four lines of exalted verse
from columnist Fletcher Knebel:

> Of all the words of witch's doom
> There's none so bad as which and whom.
> The man who kills both which and whom
> Will be enshrined in our Who's Whom.

Other grammatical points of minor controversy are "different than," "like a cigarette should," "I seen," "you hadn't
ought," "more better," the use of "louses" as a plural for
"louse" (but even its advocates urge that it be restricted
to humans only, with the older "lice" retained for the insect),
the adjectival use of "chicken" ("they are chicken"), the dan-
gling "so far as," with omission of "to be concerned" ("so
far as the new tax laws, we approve of them"). One newspaper correspondent, entering a controversy as to whether
it should be "a number of nurses has donated" or "a number
of nurses have donated," suggests as a way out "a number of
nurses done donated," while the University of South Dakota
reports this statement from one of its coeds: "I came to school
to be went with, but I ain't."

The true stamping ground of slang is vocabulary and
expressions, and while slang may be condemned by purists
and schoolteachers, it should be remembered that it is a
monument to the language's force of growth by creative innovation, a living example of the democratic, normally anonymous process of language change, and the chief means
whereby all the languages spoken today have evolved from
earlier tongues. A great professor of languages at Columbia
University used to argue that Vulgar Latin still lives and
breathes today in the spoken Romance languages. He was fundamentally right. Had it not been for the slangy leaven of
Plautus and Petronius that crept into the Classical tongue of
Cicero and Horace, the works of Dante, Cervantes, and Molière might today appear in majestic Latin instead of in the
graceful, supple tongues that have evolved from it. By the
same token, Shakespeare would have used the Anglo-Saxon

of Bede, Goethe the Old High German of Notker, and Ibsen the Old Norse of the Eddas.

One remarkable characteristic of slang is the creation of a large number of different words for the same thing, like "grouse," "gripe," "squawk," "beef," "bellyache," etc., for "complain"; or "simoleon," "iron man," "smacker," "buck," etc., for "dollar." For "nonsense," we have: "applesauce," "boloney," "banana oil," "bushwah," "eyewash," "hooey," "horsefeathers," "tripe," and some 250 more expressions. An early English traveler to the United States, Sir Richard Burton, delightedly reports an entire series of terms for "whiskey": "tarantula juice," "redeye," "strychnine," "corn juice," "Jersey lightning," "leg-stretcher," and others. He was also struck by "this neck of the woods," "a high old time," "hang out one's shingle," and "liquor up."

Another feature of slang is the extremely large mortality of slang terms in their infancy. For every slang word that survives and becomes a part of the accepted vocabulary, there are dozens, perhaps hundreds, that serve as nonce words, then drop into desuetude. The "kiddo" of the First World War is very little with us today. The Air Force "Roger" of the Second World War has already lost much ground to its older and more seasoned competitor "O.K." The "natch" and "def" of the younger generations are now dropping out of use; so are expressions like "clock the kid" (for "look at me") and "how horrible can you get?" More than half of the French slang, *argot*, and *jobelin* so glibly used by Villon is so thoroughly lost today that French philologists have to guess at the meaning of his words.

One never-ending source of slang, particularly in English, is the clipped word, which seems to stem primarily from the English preference for monosyllables. In many cases ("vet," "doc," "fan" from "fanatic," "mike" from "microphone," "phone" from "telephone") the clipped word is recognized for what it is, and the parent word survives by its side. But often the parent word is all but lost, as in "mutt" from "muttonhead," "bunk" from "buncombe," "bum" from "bummer." Like other slang forms, clipped words may easily acquire respectability and full standing in the dictionary; this has happened to "cab" from "cabriolet," "bus" from "omnibus," "mob" from *mobile vulgus,* "spats" from "spatter-dashes," "fan" from "fanatic." The clipped word may come from the end or the middle of the parent word as well as from the beginning, as shown by "van" from "caravan," "wig" from "periwig," "flu" from "influenza," and "skeet" from "mosquito." Word-clipping occasionally gives rise to bad cases of confusion, as in "gas" from "gasoline," which leaves one in doubt as to whether a liquid or a gaseous fluid is meant.

The British are given to clipping almost as much as we. "Fridge" is their word for "refrigerator," "demob" stands for "demobilization," and "nappies" for a word which is translated by American "diapers."

Flexional languages are less given to word-clipping. An outstanding French example is *Métro* for *"Chemins de fer métropolitains,"* the Paris subway system.

A dictionary of word origins for slang terms is quite as legitimate as, though somewhat more difficult to construct than, an ordinary *Webster's,* and at least as fascinating. There are several in existence, and *American Speech,* a periodical published at Columbia University, makes it a practice to endeavor to trace every neologism to its source as soon as it appears.

A few interesting, though random, slang-word histories are the following:

"Jalopy" (old, battered car) is said to be connected with the French *chaloupe* ("lifeboat"), as well as with "gallop" (there is an alternative form *galopy*) and with aviation (an ancient plane in World War One is said to have been so named).

The use of "grapevine" and "grapevine telegraph" to signify unofficial rumor dates back to the Civil War, the connection being with the many intertwining tendrils of the grapevine.

Many origins are claimed for the use of "doughboy" or "doughfoot" to denote an infantry soldier. One is "adobe," the mud of the Southwest, which the infantry got on its feet. Another is the use of pipe clay for the white trimmings of infantry uniforms, which in the rain used to turn into a dough.

The slang "cop" for "policeman" goes back to an earlier "copper." Policemen were so named because they wore metal helmets, which were made necessary by the fact that bricks often dropped from slum roofs and windows, accidentally or otherwise, upon the minions of the law.

Three versions exist for "goon." One is the Chinese word for "stick"; a second the Hindustani *goonda* ("hooligan"); the third is a cross between "gorilla" and "baboon."

Slang "bambino," "bimbo," and "boloney" are all of Italian origin. The first two mean "child" and were originally applied to "Babe" Ruth. The last comes from the city of Bologna, renowned for its sausage.

While slang words as such find it relatively easy to obtain admission to the dictionary, the same is not always true of combinations of legitimate words in slang connotations. There is nothing in "ulcer" and "gulch," taken separately, which betokens slang; their combination, however, into an expression for "cheap restaurant" is not so easily recorded. "To chew the rag," "to be a shark at," "to sling hash" consist of legitimate words; it is the connotation of the combination taken as a whole that is slangy. The British are at least as adept at this sort of thing as we. They have coined such expressions as "to carry the can" ("to bear the responsibility"), "it's a piece of cake" ("it's a cinch"), "what's it in aid of?" ("what's the purpose behind it?"), "to get a wigging" (or, "to be slated," "to be banged up," roughly the equivalents of our "to get a dressing down," "to be bawled out"), "to write oneself off" ("to kill oneself"). The Canadians have their "rebel picnic" (our "Glorious Fourth"), "unbleached American" (colored person), "improved Britisher" (an Englishman who has resided for some time in the Dominion) and "to have the sun in one's eyes" (to be under the influence of liquor). The New Zealanders have their "to be pie on" ("to be a shark at"), the Australians "to fancy Fannie" ("to play the piano," "to tickle those ivories"), "to sky the wipe" ("throw in the towel"), "to dip south" ("reach for your money"), "blackfellow's gift" ("Indian giver"), and "possum up a gum tree" ("blithe and happy").

There has been a free-and-easy interborrowing of slang among the various sections of the Anglo-Saxon world. Gone are the days when a British audience needed a printed glossary to understand an American underworld play. The Australians have borrowed from us, without change of form or meaning, "scram," "boloney," "okay," "pushover," "says you," "corny," "scanties," "and how." We, on the other hand, have taken from the British Empire terms like "fed up," "swank," and "flapper."

Foreign languages, of course, have their slang terms, many extremely expressive. Italian uses *pappagallo*, "parrot," as the equivalent of our "wolf." A German *twen* is a former teen-ager who still acts like one. Japan, borrowing shamelessly from the western languages, uses the French *avec* ("with") for "date," *pari pari* for "lively party" (this may be a repetition of English "party" or of French *Paris*), *otsumata*, taken purely by ear from "what's the matter," and the loan

translation *wakaru kenji yo* for "I dig you." The Russians
have devised a term *blat* for "graft," or "payola," and use
tolkach, "pestle" or "pounder," for our "five percenter." Their
"yes-man" is an *allilushchik*, or "hallelujah man." They use
the verb "to sit" as a slang euphemism for "to be in jail"
(French uses *être à l'ombre*, "to be in the shade"). The
Russian teen-agers of questionable habits are styled *Stil-
yagi* (influence of the British "Stylists," perhaps, or the other
way round?), who are subdivided by sex: the boy is a
chuvak, the girl a *chuvicha*, names which seem to have no
root in the language unless it be that of Chuvash, one of the
more obscure nationalities in the Soviet Union.

French, with its Parisian background, has perhaps more
pure big-city slang than any other non-English-speaking nation. The older layer includes such terms as "dirty box"
(*sale boîte*) for "awful dump"; "ball of suet" (*boule de
suif*) for "greaseball"; "old nail" or "bathtub" for "jalopy";
"St. Collect's day" for "payday"; "foot wash" for bad coffee;
"to have the cockroach" for "to have the blues." The bill
presented at the end of the meal is called "the sorrowful
one" (*la douloureuse*). *Gratin* is the French equivalent of
"upper crust."

A more recent layer of French *argot* of the printable
variety includes not only such throwbacks to Old French
grammar as *je suis sortant, papa est mourant* ("I am going
out," "papa is dying," appearing in the works of such writers
as Soubiran) but semihistorical expressions like *Farouk* and
demi-Farouk for the old 10,000- and 5,000-franc notes (the
old Egyptian ruler, it seems, threw his money around in
Paris). Side by side with the traditional *casse-croûte* ("crust-
breaker" for "snack") and *bachot* (the student's bachelor's
degree) are up-to-date creations like *moulin à café* ("coffee
mill" for "machine gun"), *à d'autres!* ("to others!," "Tell
it to the Marines!"), *avoir mal aux cheveux* ("to have
a pain in one's hair," "to have a hangover"), *tu me rases*
("you're shaving me" for "you bore me stiff").

Spanish has an expression for "to kid someone" which
literally means "to scalp" (*tomar el pelo a uno*), along with
a "calamity" (*una calamidad*) for a "bore" or pest. Portuguese gives us "big fish" (*peixão*) or "sardine for my cat"
for a shapely girl, "bargain" for "sweetheart," and "how is the
obligation?" for "how is your family?" Italian calls a "sports
fan" *tifoso* (literally, "one suffering from typhus") and
uses *silurare* ("to torpedo") for "to fire from an important
post."

Two subsidiary problems arise in connection with slang.

One is that of foreign influence in its creation. New York slang, which tends to become nationwide, is strongly subjected to such influence, particularly Yiddish. This leads to such creations as "holdupnick" (possibly also "beatnik"), "schmo," "schlup," "schlump," "schnook" (all having, roughly, the meaning of "dope"). Since neither the *-nick*, *-nik* suffix nor the initial group of *sh* (*sch*) plus consonant is native to English, this leads some linguists to postulate the admission to American English of two loan forms, with *-nik* or *-nick* assuming the role of a suffix indicating agent, and *sh-* (or *sch-*) followed by a consonant assuming the role of pejorative prefix indicating contempt.

The other problem is so delicate as to be practically insoluble. At what point does local dialect end and national slang begin? In a more stable, less geographically integrated society than ours the answer would be easy. As matters stand, we find localisms spreading to the point where they become nationwide. Such is the case with the affirmative use of "any more" which originated in the Midwest but has now spread to the East ("It gets so hard to make a living any more"). We suspect that "tail-gaiting" (or is it "tail-gating"?), "drag-racing," "pazazz" began as rank localisms. A recent visit to the Chicago area brought to our notice three colorful expressions that may have reached New York by the time this edition sees the light: "broasted chicken" (a beautiful portmanteau combination of "broiled" and "roasted"), "antsy" ("agitated," "worried," from "to have ants in your pants"), and "got a guy in my trunk" ("the driver behind me follows too closely"). "On safari" (prepared to foot the bill for a lavish evening) and "ham-dogs" (hamburgers in frankfurter shape) are reported from the Boston area; "to flag an exam" ("flunk it with flying colors") from Connecticut; "that's the way the cell grows" ("that's the way the cards are stacked"), "NATO" (anagram for "no action, talk only," used by college girls talking of their dates), "mad-over" (no longer angry but still not made up) are from the East. Brandeis coed dorm decorations, consisting of ribbon from gifts tied in colorful nooses and hung up at the height of the donor, are styled "man snares." Yet some slang terms are locally contradictory: "square," a fighting word in the East, is still a high compliment in the West, like "he'll do to cross the river with"; "raunchy," which means "rotten" in the East, means "good" in the Southwest.

There is a Harlem Negro slang that often spills over into the musical and theatrical world and then turns nationwide. Among terms still largely restricted to Negroes are the now notorious "Mr. Charley" for a white man (this replaces an entire series of older terms, like "ofay," "fay," "paddy," "gravy," "gray"); "ace" for "good friend"; "blow" for "party"; "boos" for "good"; "bust" for "arrest"; "fox" for "girl"; "happy shop" for "liquor store"; "The Man" for "policeman" (interestingly, this term is used in other milieus with different meanings, such as "the government" or "Uncle Sam"); "member" for "Negro"; "mickey mouse" for a "square"; "Ralph Bunche" for "talk your way out of trouble"; "slam" for "jail"; "vine" for "dress swell"; "woof" for "brag"; "woke" for "well posted."

The problem of localism vs. slang arises to an even greater degree in Britain, where there is a London Cockney language that often spills over into general slang. Here we find terms like "lollypop" for "shop," "daisy roots" for "boots" (shoes to Americans), "whistle and flute" for "suit," "needle and pin" for "gin," "pig's ear" for "beer," "Oxford scholar" for "dollar," "storm and strife" for "wife," "Rosy Lee" for "tea." This is, of course, the famous rhyming slang, which partakes of the nature of both cant and jargon. But even using straight prose, we get such terms as "tosser" for "small coin," "twicer" for "double-crosser," "flog" for "pawn," "fluff" for "see," "arf a tick" for "wait a bit," "bogies" for "police," "dekko" for "glance," "shoot the moon" for "make a getaway," "bolo" for "untidy situation," "jam," "fix"; "wallop" for "sell under the counter." Is this local dialect, nationwide slang, underworld cant, or class jargon? Need we decide?

— Chapter Ten —

CANT AND JARGON

> *Saupicquez, fronans des gours arques..*
> *Pour desbouser beaussire dieux,*
> *Allés ailleurs planter vos marques!*
> *Benards, vous estes rouges gueux;*
> *Berart s'en va chez les joncheux*
> *Et babigne qu'il a plongis.*
> *Mes freres, soiez embraieux,*
> *Et gardez des coffres massis!.*
> —François Villon, *Le Jargon et le jobelyn*, 4

> *You yeggs that pull a real good heist*
> *And swipe the moolah from a square,*
> *Watch out for finks that dummy up*
> *Until The Man gets in their hair.*
> (Translation by Mario Pei)

"CANT" is an older term than "slang," but there is a subtle difference between them. The latter is not at all designed to be obscure to the uninitiate, while the former is. It is therefore appropriate to speak of "New York slang" but of "thieves' cant." Concerning cant in his day, William Harrison (1586) wrote: "They haue deuised a language among themselues, which they name Canting, but others pedlers French, a speach compact thirtie yeares since of English, and a great number of od words of their owne deuising, without all order or reason; and yet such is it as none but themselues are able to vnderstand. The first deuiser thereof was hanged by the necke, a just reward no doubt for his deserts, and a common end to all of that profession." Among "the seuerall disorders and degrees amongst our idle vagabonds" listed by Harrison, the following are of note: "rufflers, uprightmen, hookers, priggers or pransers, palliards, fraters, abrams, freshwater mariners, dummerers, drunken tinkers, swadders, baudie baskets, mortes, doxes, delles, kinching cooes."

In addition to slang and cant, there is a third variety of special language, which may be called "jargon" for want of a better name, applied to the special terminology in use in any given walk of life. Every trade, profession, and business has its own special vocabulary, more or less unintelligible to people not in that line, which may run into the hundreds or even thousands of words, expressions, and special meanings, as will be seen later.

The dividing line between slang, cant, and jargon is often difficult to draw. True slang is said to be what is nationwide, or at least generally understood; cant what belongs properly to the underworld and is not understood beyond that comparatively narrow circle; jargon what pertains to a profession or occupation and is not recognized on the outside. A magazine writer trying to establish the distinction and picking his examples from the stage once gave "ham" as an example of true slang and "grip" (for "stagehand") as one of jargon. As for cant, however, it is known that gangster terms, particularly under present circumstances of movies, radio, and comics, have a way of seeping upward and outward into the general slang and even the vernacular. "Jerk" (origin unknown) is an example of this; so are "mugged" in its double sense of "attacked from behind with a strangle-hold" and "photographed by the police"; "mooch" ("to beg" as a verb, "prospect" or "sucker" as a noun); "ice" ("diamonds"); "saw," "double saw," "C" and "grand," for $10, $20, $100, and $1,000, respectively. "Payola" is a term that practically everyone knows.

Criminal terms not so well known on the outside are "mit" ("bookmaker"), "schmier" or "schmear" (variously interpreted as "protection money" or "case of little consequence"), "banker" ("payoff man" of a numbers racket pool), "persuader" ("blackjack" or other weapon), "pie wagon" (police "patrol wagon"), "to sap" ("hit with a blackjack"), "skylarker" ("suspicious character"), "snow-bird" ("drug addict"), "tin" or "potsy" (any badge of office), "to two-finger" ("to pick pockets"), "whiz" (pickpocket job), "scratch" (loose bills), "sneeze" ("arrest"), "snatch" ("payroll"), "kite" (letter to be delivered outside the jail), "breeze" ("jailbreak"), "yellow papers" ("police record"), "quizzer" or "quizmaster" ("District Attorney").

"Snow" for "cocaine," "black stuff" for "opium," "junk" or "foolish powder" for "heroin," "weed tea," "pot," and "balmers" for "marijuana," are much used by dope peddlers. Collectively, any dope is known as "solace." One "cops a bag" ("buys the stuff"), "takes off" ("gets a shot"), goes to a "shooting gallery" (place where they give you injections), or attends a "blast party," where many marijuana smokers get together. A "mule" is a juvenile pusher, who sells the stuff to his own crowd.

Illegal gambling has a terminology of its own. "Box cars" means a pair of sixes if you play dice, long odds in racing ("the horse paid off in box cars"). "Vigorish" (also spelt "viggerish," or cut down to "vig") means the percentage in favor of the gambling house. In the Las Vegas casinos, there is a whole terminology to describe swindlers, who are generically known as "crossroaders." They are further subdivided, according to their specialties, into "handmuckers," "pressers," "pushers," "coolers," and "daubers."

To car thieves, a "stranger" is a car stolen far away from the spot where it is reconditioned and sold, a "blow-in" is a newcomer. "Forgers" are often known as "short-story writers" or "paperhangers." The vocabulary of pickpocketing and con games includes the "cannon" or "shot artist" ("pickpocket"), the "troupe" (team of pickpockets), "to kiss the dog" (face the victim while picking his wallet), "figary" or even "goulash" (a quiet, safe hangout where crooks can meet and plan), "lugger" or "roper" (a "con man"), "mark" or "pigeon" (the "victim" of the con game), "drag" or "pigeon drop" (a pocketbook dropped as bait), "hole" or "snake" ("subway," a promising scene of operations or a means of exiting quickly). The enemy and his accouterments are colorfully described. A "bike" is a "motorcycle cop," a "catch" the detective assigned to the complaint desk; "bag" is "uniform" and "baton" a "night stick." You may be an "outfielder" (a crook that shies away from risky work), but if you are caught anyway you go to "Coney Island" (the thirddegree chamber). If you are lucky, you may be assigned to a "cackle factory" ("mental hospital"). If you are sent to jail instead, you may have to eat such things as "lead pipe" (prison spaghetti), or even "angel cake and wine" (bread and water).

The juvenile gangs have a cant of their own, of which a few terms, like "rumble," have become familiar to the general public. Preliminary to the main attraction are "sounding" (an exchange of dirty looks), "roughing" ("jostling"), "ranking" (taunting the rival gang). Sometimes you "call it on" (hold a prearranged grudge fight, single combat style); more often you "go down" (hold a big rumble), in the course of which you try to "burn," "waste," or "bop" the enemy, even at the cost of using "blades" ("knives") and "pieces" ("guns"). The "clique" or "crew" ("gang"), composed of "down kiddies" ("tough guys"), often has a "schemer" (strategist or military director), who advises them how to "pull a jap" (make a sneak attack) on enemy "turf" ("territory"). In their more peaceful moments, the down kiddies and their "debs" ("girls") may hold a "jump" or "session" ("dance"), even under the watchful eye of a "job man" ("social worker"). But if hostilities break out again, you are free to "shank" your opponents (stab them in the leg).

The British counterparts of our juvenile gangs have evolved a totally different vocabulary. Our "rumble" is their "ding-dong" or "bundle," and to "chiv" is to "knife" somebody. Our "cops" are their "blue-bottles." A "squealer" is a "grasser," a "dope" is either a "Swede" or a "bacon bonce," a "money lender" is a "baron" and a "good pal" is a "china." "Blue eye" is an "apple polisher" or "teacher's pet." "Cigarettes" are "burns" and "matches" are "twigs." To "flog" is to "sell stolen goods," "go spare" is "lose one's temper," "kip" is "take a rest," "skive" is "dodge" (usually the police). "Money" is "lolly" and "bullets" are "candy." Your "necktie" is a "bootlace," your "pants" are "strides," your "clothes" taken collectively are "clobber," your "keys" are "rattlers." Your "nose" is your "hooter" and your "head" is either your "tank" or your "loaf." A native Liverpudlian is a "scouse," and a "girl" is a "bird."

An ancient secret-language device still used by lower-class elements is the combination of meaning and rhyme, as when "moan and wail" are used for "jail," "bees and honey" for "money," "bubble and squeak" for "speak," "gay and frisky" for "whisky," "kick and prance" for "dance." Villon used this device in some of his poems.

In common with ordinary slang, underworld cant has the characteristic of coining or adapting numerous words for the same meaning. A "wallet," for instance, is "poke," "oakus," or "leather," while a "gun" goes by any of these names: "betsy," "roscoe," "iron," "gat," "shooter," "canister," "hardware," "boomstick," "equalizer," "noise."

The case for jargon is more difficult to present. In a sense, all professional terminology, including that of medicine, the law, education, engineering, even business and theology, is jargon, since it offers terms not familiar to the general population. When your physician tells you you are suffering from "bilateral perorbital hematoma" (meaning you have a black eye) or your lawyer speaks of property held in "escrow," when your banker talks of a rise in the "rediscount rate" or your garage man of a blown "gasket," the chances are you won't understand, though all these terms are listed in a comprehensive dictionary. Educators thrive on a diet of "integration," "correlation," and "motivation," while some linguists love mouth-filling terms like "morphophonemic," "sandhi," and "compound juncture." Each occupation and walk of life has its special terminology, a good deal of which has all the earmarks of slang, save for the one feature of being generally understood, a feature which is very often added in due course of time. Terms that were once exclusively nautical, like "even keel," "know the ropes," "give plenty of leeway," "keep a weather eye open" have gotten into everybody's language, though with shifts of meaning from the seafaring originals. So have sporting terms like "to play ball with," "be caught flat-footed," "warm up to," "hit and run." So have labor terms like "lackey," "rat," "check off," "scab," or "fink" (said to come from the Danish word for "finch"), "wildcat strike," "featherbedding," and "graveyard shift."

Some jargon terms are ordinary and matter-of-fact, like the "blooms" and "skelp" used by the steel industry to denote rectangular bars and strips to be bent, or the "breeze" used by coal dealers for small coke, or the "rogues" used by seed growers for plants that revert to earlier types and fail to produce the blossoms expected. Others display imagination, verve, and even poetry, like the musicians' "godbox" for "organ," "licorice stick" for "clarinet," "frisking whiskers" for "warming up." Soda clerks have devised such expressions as "stretch one and paint it red" for "large coke with a cherry," "shake a hula" for "pineapple milk shake," and "ap one" for a "piece of apple pie." The term "nose" is applied by the perfume industry to what the French call a *parfumeur-créateur*, the man whose business it is to devise new blends. The radio has created "hooperating," television has contributed "videogenic." Barbers have their "jistas," customers who want "jista shave."

Several occupational fields have devised complete vocabularies of jargon. Truck drivers have their "pin her ears back" for "glide to a stop." To them a "reckless driver" is a "cowboy," and the road is "dusting." "To swing" means to "cut in sharply," to "put on the air" means to "apply the brakes," to "blow a skin" is to "have a flat tire." Post office workers speak of "red" ("registered mail"), a "bum" ("empty mail sack"), "hash" ("miscellaneous mail"), "nixie" ("undeliverable mail"), a "hypo" ("highway post office"), "killer bars" (the lines in the post-marking stamp).

Railroad men refer to the mail, express, baggage, and

newspapers that travel on a train as "head-end traffic," to a "locomotive" as a "pig," a "refrigerator car" as a "reefer," a "switch" as an "iron," the "conductor" as "brains," a "go-ahead signal" as a "highball," a "railroad yard" as a "garden."

Loggers use "cat" for "tractor," "bull of the woods" and "push" for the "superintendent" and the "foreman," "gut robber" for the "camp cook," "hoosier" for a "greenhorn," "hair-pounder" for a "teamster," and "hayburner" for a "horse." "Payday" to them is "alibi day."

Firemen refer to a "smoky fire" as a "ripe fire." "Apparatus," "spaghetti," "tiller," and "syringe" are, respectively, the "fire truck," the "hose," the "steering wheel," and the "collapsible water tower." The jargon of prizefighters includes such terms as "painter" (a fighter who aims for the face), "bricklayer" (a heavy-fisted character), "cutie" (one who knows all the tricks), "tomato can" (one who is no good), "timber" (one who has been softened up and is about ready for the knockout punch). "Foot-in-the-bucket" is reserved for the handler in the corner.

In the TV world, a "belcher" is a performer who has a frog in his throat, a "billboard" is "sponsor credit," "burp" is an "extraneous noise," "cold" means "drama without music," "cowcatcher" and "hitch-hiker" are used respectively for the commercial before the start of the program and the one at the end, provided the product is not advertised elsewhere in the program. "Crawk" is an "animal imitator," a "fishpole" is a mike at the end of a movable rod, a "woodshed" is a "wearying rehearsal," and a program dealing with antiquity and displaying lots of action is styled a "B.C. Western."

The military profession revels in jargon creations, but the product is, in the nature of things, more transitory than in permanent callings. During the late war, for example, the G.I.s in Italy coined "segnorina," a cross between Italian *signorina* and Spanish *señorita*, to designate a woman of low character, to which the Italians retaliated with *okeyna* (from "O.K.") to indicate a girl who fraternized excessively. Navy men created "sky juice" for "water," "collision mats" for "pancakes," "fuel oil" for "syrup," "gravel" for "sugar," "horizontal duty" for "sleep," and "squack" for "girl." American war prisoners in Germany appropriated "goon" for "German soldiers" and worked out "ferret" for "spy" and "glop" for "food."

Military jargon also suffers from an excess of profanity and obscenity. A lady professor who had undertaken a study of G.I. slang in World War Two finally had to concede that she was handicapped by her sex and sense of decency. "The expressions, the names for food, etc., are so unprintable that my students assure me I can't be told them" was her complaint.

But all army jargon is not that bad. Harmless terms are "slime" for "army food"; "ichiban," a Japanese borrowing, for "A number 1," "the very best"; "Gyrene" for "Marine." There is a Pentagon vocabulary that includes "Chicoms" for "Chinese Communists" and "Chinats" for "Chinese Nationalists," "flap" for a "state of tension." "File 13" or "deep six" means the "wastebasket."

Air Force and rocketry have, of course, their own up-to-date terminology, but some of it goes back to the plane's earlier days. "Baksheesh" is an "easy flying mission," "bandits" are "enemy planes," and "big friends" are the "bombers." Nonflying personnel is variously described as "chairborne troops" and "ground grippers." An "airplane engine" is a "coffee grinder," a "green cadet" is a "dodo," "flak happy" refers to "combat fatigue." "To hang out the laundry" means to "drop paratroops," and the "parachute" is known as "overcoat" or "jump sack," while a "crash helmet" is a "brain bucket." A "junior prom" is a "hot mission," the opposite of "baksheesh." The "control tower" is irreverently known as the "madhouse," the "radio operator" is the "static bender," the "copilot" is a "stooge," a "jet plane" is a "blow torch" (as opposed to the old "propeller plane," a "spam can"), and to "buy a plot" is to undergo a fatal crash. There is a "gaggle of geese," which is a big formation of bombers. The "plane mechanics" are known as "hangar rats." "Plumber," "pussycat," and "pipe jockey" refer, respectively, to a "dumb pilot," a "reluctant pilot," and a "jet pilot." To "take a star" is a pleasant euphemism for "to make errors while in training," and the pilot who makes them is described as a "wobble head." "Unobtainium" is stuff that does not exist or cannot be produced, and "auntie" is the affectionate title bestowed upon an "anti-missile missile." "Burping" is the "intermittent burning of a rocket," and astronauts call the training seat that switches them from an upright to a supine position the "barber chair."

The talk of Broadway and the theatrical world, musicians, jazz, bebop, hep-cats and what have you has several links: to the speech of the Harlem Negroes and the users of Yiddish; to the language of the juveniles, who supply the greats of rock-and-roll, swing, twist, and other assorted gyrations with their most enthusiastic audience; and to the cant of the underworld. It is this jargon, more than any other, that tends to overflow its banks and go to join the eddying current of nationwide slang, carrying great masses of flotsam and jetsam in the shape of disks and recordings, as witnessed by such terms as "for the birds," "in the groove," "for kicks," "crazy" (as a term of approbation), "to dig," "doll," "the end." It is in this field that we find the greatest redundancy of terms for the same object. The "dull person," in all his gradations, may be described not only by the commonplace "schmo" and "square" but also as a "box," "oofus," "zombie," and a dozen other terms, including "lame" (which implies that he is not totally given up for lost). A "girl" may be not only a "broad," "dame," or "chick"; she may also be a "biscuit," "cookie," "vessel," or "rib"; if she sings, she may be a "canary," "chirp," or "thrush"; if she is beautiful, she's "poundcake"; if not too glamorous, she's a "bear," "potato digger," or "frumpy frail"; if too fat, she's "heavy cream"; if she goes out only with musicians, she's a "tone freak."

There is an entire terminology for drinking and its consequences: it starts with "for no" ("free"), "freebie" (a "free loader"), "milk" (a "cocktail"), "grunt" (or "hot," "third rail," or "tab": the "check"); goes on to "glazed" (almost "stoned") and "zonked" (past the stoning stage), and may wind up with "guilty big" ("going to see the psychoanalyst") or even "marble pad" (the "mental hospital").

For actors, there is the new euphemism "Keep in touch with the office," which replaces an earlier "Don't call us, we'll call you," "playster" ("actor"), "mushroomer" (an actor that blossoms forth into big roles), "bellybuster" (a "comedian"), "footlight prancer" (a "showgirl"). For musicians, there is a whole line of instruments and associated terms: "coffin" or "box" ("piano"), "slush pump" ("trombone"), "puffers" ("French horn"), "booms" or "hides" ("drums"), "pipe" ("saxophone"), "whiffer" ("flute"). An "ax" is any musical instrument. "The Man," who in other circumstances may be a policeman or the impersonation of the government, does service also for the "band leader." "Charts" or "maps" are "musical arrangements." A "monkey" is a "music critic."

The jargon of the younger generations might be described as the slang of the future. Fifteen years ago, oldsters were bewildered at hearing from the mouths of their sons and daughters such terms as "his garden is green" or "cut the celery," and they shook their heads because they didn't recall their own youthful equivalents, "he's in the dough" and "shoot the works." Today, both sets of terms are thoroughly outdated and outmoded. The new crop shows "hub cap" (the "big wheel's girl"), "paint happy" (a "showoff"), "warden" (mother, teacher, or school principal), "crocodoll" (a "girl friend"), "pad" ("home"), "prehistorics" ("parents"). Terms of endearment are "smooth potato," "able Grable," "angel cake" or "$C_{12}H_{22}O_{11}$" (the chemical formula for sugar). "Three-D," however, means "dense, dopey, and dumb." School activities include the "corral" ("schoolyard"), "capers" ("tough math problems"), "brain derby" ("exam"), "casbah" ("school lunchroom"), "refreshery" ("the soda fountain"). Other assorted activities include "having a goosh" (the earlier "crush"), "making out" (the earlier "spooning" or "necking"), using "digit dazzle" ("nail polish") and "pucker paint" ("lipstick"), or "hitting the bottle" (this is not as bad as it sounds; it means merely to "bleach your hair"). "TV" is, fittingly, the "idiot box." To "put it down" is to "give it up," "bump gums" is "chew the rag." "What's with you?" has now been transmuted into "What's with it with you?" Other picturesque phrases are "It's many, many funs" (or kicks), "This tears me up" (meaning "I like it"), and "Cast an earball."

There is even an international teen language that has sprung up among the children of our personnel stationed in Europe, typified by *Je suis un jelly-bean. Qu'est-ce que dilly? Comment allez-vous dilly?* (The general meaning of all three expressions is said to be "What's cooking?")

The fate of words and expressions parallels that of human beings. Some rise, others fall; some prosper, others die. It does not behoove us to despise a man by reason of his present lowly estate, because only God knows what potentialities that man may store within himself. Neither is it fitting to scorn words which today are heard only in the slums or within the restricted confines of a trade. Tomorrow those same words may sweep the nation and find their way into the everyday vocabulary of a twenty-first-century Shakespeare.

— Chapter Eleven —

THE ESTHETICS OF LANGUAGE

Prince, give praise to our French ladies
For the sweet sound their speaking carries;
'Twixt Rome and Cadiz many a maid is,
But no good girl's lip out of Paris.
     —François Villon, *"Ballad of the Women*
          of Paris" (Swinburne translation)

THIS chapter deals not with the literary or stylistic beauty of the written language, a topic that properly pertains to literary history and criticism, but rather with a subject generally avoided in language books, mainly because it is reckoned too subjective for scientific investigation. Yet it is a subject that arouses the layman's interest, as witnessed by the frequent repetition of the questions: "Is language (in general) beautiful or ugly?" "Which is the world's most beautiful language?" "What is the most beautiful (or the ugliest) word in the English language?" Those who ask these questions are seldom aware of their implications. What they are asking for is a treatise on the beauty of languages *divorced from their literary output*, and of words *separated from their semantic associations*.

Since the dawn of history, writers, poets, and philosophers have dealt with the topic of the "beauty" of language. The Greeks and Romans held their own languages to be beautiful, but their contempt for other "barbarous" tongues is evidenced not only by occasional slurring allusions but also by the fact that no attempt was made to save them for the benefit of posterity. The Greeks were in touch, throughout their entire history, with numerous tongues of Asia Minor and the eastern Mediterranean basin, of which they might have left us some inkling beyond the rare glosses of their lexicographers. The Romans permitted Etruscan, the tongue of a civilization that had greatly contributed to their own, to go unrecorded, so that today we vainly seek a key to it. It was a matter perhaps of national pride, perhaps of indifference, that the Greeks cared only for Greek and the Romans for Latin and Greek. Allusions to the beauty of the Greek language occur rather frequently in Roman writers, and in the days of the Empire Greek was probably as widespread among cultured Romans as was French in eighteenth- and nineteenth-century Europe.

The early Middle Ages, with their other-worldly preoccupations, cared little for the esthetics of language, which was viewed primarily as a tool for conversion and proselytism. We get an occasional hint that the tongues of the Germanic invaders were considered unlovely, as when an Italian monk ridicules his Ostrogothic colleagues who call loudly for food and drink in their own barbarous jargon, but even here it is difficult to determine whether the antipathy is really directed at the uncouthness of the language or that of its speakers.

It is only with the dawn of the Renaissance that the cult of beauty returns, and with it comes a new reverence for the loveliness of the Classical tongues, together with a series of apologies on the part of authors using the "unlovely" vernaculars, which had already been in spoken use for some centuries, with no appreciable comment.

In the days of Humanism a search for linguistic beauty was undertaken. Greek and Latin words were judged not on the basis of their authenticity but on their supposed esthetic qualities, until the great French philologist Henri Estienne in 1572 finally reminded his fellow scholars that truth is superior even to beauty and that Classical words were not to be accepted or rejected on the ground of their resounding qualities, or use by reputable ancient authors, but on the basis of their objective existence in the ancient languages.

From that point there began a struggle between the defenders of historical truth and the champions of esthetics which still goes on today. The word "Gothic," applied to anything which smacked of the non-Classical Middle Ages, was attached to language as well, and even now Italian refers to an outlandish word as "Ostrogothic."

Nationalism, too, entered the picture, and speakers of languages which had by this time acquired a full-fledged literary tradition undertook to discuss at length the "beauty" of their respective languages. This "beauty" was sometimes confused with expressiveness, effectiveness, clarity, precision, concision, richness of vocabulary, wealth of literary accomplishment;

at other times it was predicated on a more truly linguistic basis, as when the morphological structure or, even more appropriately, the sounds of various languages were compared.

While a full-sized conflict rages today concerning the esthetic merits of the various tongues, internecine warfare is conducted in many corners of the battlefield among the advocates of the relative merits of different dialects of the same tongue, or of correct (*i.e.,* literary) speech and incorrect forms (*i.e.,* slang or colloquial varieties).

The pure linguist normally refuses to take part in such controversies, partly because they lead nowhere, a good many of the assertions made by the contestants being, by their very nature, unprovable; partly because he deems it his task to establish the scientific facts of language, not esthetic theories; partly because the issues involved in such discussions are usually hopelessly mixed, representing a hodgepodge of nationalistic pride, literary evaluation, subjective estimates, and emotional reactions, all of which lie quite outside the domain of science.

There is only one compartment of language concerning which it may be said that there is some justification for an objective esthetic discussion (provided it is granted that there is no inherent antithesis between the two terms "objective" and "esthetic"). This is the field of sounds. Even here, however, we have the injection of factors that are both extraneous and subjective.

Recently a poll was conducted among American and British writers to ascertain which words in the English language were considered the "most beautiful," which the "ugliest." The results of the poll were in part as follows: most beautiful to the Americans are "dawn," "lullaby," "murmuring," "tranquil," "luminous," "golden," "melody"; to the British "carnation," "azure," "moon," "heart," "silence," "shadow," "April." This discrepancy between the two English-speaking countries is *prima facie* evidence of the subjective nature of the choice.

Among the ugliest words selected were "gangrene," "scram," "guzzle," "mange," "swell," "gripe," "spinach," "jazz," and (fittingly) "cacophony." A glance at these partial lists suffices to indicate that the voters were primarily motivated not by the beauty of sound or the esthetic qualities of the words, but by their meaning. Each word was labeled beautiful or ugly in accordance with the associations it contained, not with its melodious features. The sole exception to this general rule is a list once submitted by J. Donald Adams in his Sunday *Times* Book Review column, which included such "ugly" words as "crepuscular," "beautician," and "pulchritudinous" along with "polygamous," "snaggle-toothed," "pneumococcus," "adumbrate," and "pococurante-ism."

The only way of conducting such a poll more or less objectively would have involved using judges who had no idea whatsoever of the meaning of the words, and who would have let themselves be guided in their choices only by the impression made by the sounds upon their ears. Even ordinary cultured foreigners knowing no English would have been unsatisfactory judges, because many of the words have cognates in the principal western tongues and their meaning would have been subject to recognition.

This situation regularly arises in all judgments concerning the beauty of individual words or expressions within a given language when the referees are at all acquainted with the language. It is almost impossible to separate esthetic judgment from semantic associations. Under the circumstances, we are judging not esthetically but semantically or, worse yet, in accordance with prejudice, like the teacher who said that the two most hateful words in the English language were "lousy" and "swell," which were forever cluttering up her pupils' utterances and preventing them from speaking good English. On this point, a newspaper editorial decided that "swell" was a "lousy" word, but "lousy" was "swell."

More objective judgments can perhaps be rendered in the case of foreign tongues, though here again the factors of prejudice, like or dislike for the speakers or their countries, past history, present form of government, or what have you are bound to enter the picture. Familiarity, too, is a factor. A language may sound quite outlandish and uncouth until we begin to learn to speak it and may then unfold previously hidden charms. The tendency on the part of people to lump together all the languages they do not know into a single "foreign" category is well known; Chinese and Japanese are said to sound alike by people who know neither, although no two languages could have a more widely dissimilar sound pattern. Another phase of familiarity that influences our esthetic judgment lies in the fact that speakers of languages like English, which is filled with short, snappy terms, will naturally show partiality toward languages of a similar nature, while speakers of tongues replete with long, rippling, mouth-filling words will like, or at least not mind, similar characteristics in another language.

On the purely objective side, there are a few factors that may be said to contribute to a language's acoustic beauty, and these are for the most part identical with those elements that make for musicality. Languages in which there is an overabundance of involved consonant clusters, or of consonant sounds to the detriment of vowel sounds, are seldom pronounced beautiful. This is because vowels carry musical pitch far better than consonants. Our ear normally recoils from extreme sounds, whether these be of the guttural, palatal, sibilant, or nasal variety. Sounds which are easy for the vocal apparatus to produce, whether or not they appear as phonemes in the language we speak, convey an impression of beauty, though this is to some degree a matter of familiarity. Vowels normally require less juggling with the speech organs than consonants; hence languages rich in vowel sounds are more likely to convey an impression of beauty. There is little to recommend to the esthete in combinations like *sks* in English "asks" or *chtsch* in German *Knechtschaft.*

Purity of vowel sounds constitutes another esthetic factor. The "cardinal" vowel sounds of *a* in "father," *e* in "met," *i* in "machine," *o* in "or," *u* in "rude" may be esthetically more attractive than the *a* of "lame," the *o* of "home," the *u* of "pure," which are diphthongs, or the *u* of "cut," the *i* of "pin," the *a* of "hat," the *o* of "not," which are close-clipped and cannot normally be sustained, or such rounded middle-vowel sounds as French *u* and *eu.* Here we tread on dangerous ground, since it may be argued that preferences among vowel sounds are based largely on the factor of familiarity. At the same time, it is a scientifically established fact that it is impossible to sustain a word like "kiss" on high F for more than five seconds, or to sing a word like "stop" on three beats of slow time plus a retard.

The regular alternation of consonants and vowels has something to do with the esthetic impression. Languages in which a majority of the syllables end in vowels, like Italian, Spanish, or Japanese, normally produce a more pleasing impression on the ear than do those where syllables end for the most part in consonants or consonant clusters.

Languages may also be classified as "clear-cut" or "sloppy," according to their treatment of vowels in unstressed syllables. The clear-cut language gives all its vowels, whether stressed or unstressed, a definite, easily perceptible value. Such tongues as Finnish, Czech, and Italian can be taken down from dictation even if one does not know them thoroughly. This is not at all true of tongues like English,

Russian, or Portuguese, where the unstressed vowels lose their clearness and tend to merge into an indefinite sound. The issue here is of course complicated by the fact that the spelling of these languages has not kept pace with the pronunciation, which was at one time far more clear-cut than it is today.

Intonation, pitch, relative speed of utterance all play a part in the esthetic picture, but here much depends on the individual speaker. It is a commonplace that Italian can sound majestically beautiful when handled by a cultured Central Italian speaker using the appropriate modulations, and ridiculously uncouth when uttered in a shrill, high voice, with a maximum of pitch range, by a Neapolitan *scugnizzo*. The same applies, in somewhat lesser degree, to some of the local intonations of the United States. German can sound lovely in the mouth of an opera singer, unlovely in that of a Bavarian or Swiss peasant.

All of the foregoing classifications, even when based on objective factors, such as the presence or absence of consonant clusters and the relative frequency of vowel sounds, leave the problem of linguistic esthetics largely unsolved. Beauty and its appreciation are things too thoroughly and individualistically subjective for any true scientific evaluation. The sense of beauty is subject to too many factors of habit, education, psychological association, and, in final analysis, the choice of the individual. The application of an esthetic criterion to language, which has objective reality and a practical function, is bound to be not merely unscientific but unsatisfactory. At the most, it can only lead to chauvinistic pronouncements, of which an early one, made in the eighteenth century by the Russian poet-physicist Lomonosov, is given as an example, that the reader may *ab uno discere omnes:*

> Lord of many languages, the Russian tongue is far superior to all those of Europe, not only by the extent of the countries where it is dominant but also by its own comprehensiveness and richness. Charles the Fifth, Emperor of the Holy Roman Empire, said that one ought to speak Spanish to the Deity, French to one's friends, German to one's enemies, and Italian to the fair sex. But had he been acquainted with Russian, he would assuredly have added that one could speak it with each and all; he would have discovered in it the majesty of Spanish, the vivacity of French, the strength

of German, the sweetness of Italian, and, in addition, energetic conciseness in its imagery, together with the richness of Greek and Latin.

An Italian proverb says: "Every bird finds its own nest beautiful." Its closest English counterpart is "Be it ever so humble, there's no place like home." It is well to keep these in mind when we are tempted to make esthetic pronouncements on languages. The speakers of a tongue normally find that tongue beautiful, first because they are thoroughly familiar with its sounds, secondly because it is to them fraught with all sorts and varieties of sentimental associations. The Czech loves his *ř* sound, the Welshman his *ll*, the Hottentot his clicks and grunts, which people with a different language background have extreme difficulty in acquiring. To say that one language is better suited than another for singing, oratorical, literary, or philosophical purposes is legitimate, though with qualifications. To extol a tongue as inherently beautiful, or condemn another as inherently ugly, is unworthy of the enlightened spirit of tolerance that should prevail among civilized men. The function of language is not to be beautiful but to be meaningful; and all languages are equally meaningful to their own speakers.

PART THREE

The Social Function of Language

— Chapter One —

THE INDISPENSABILITY OF LANGUAGE

Language is a city to the building of which every human being brought a stone.

—Emerson

Language most shows a man; speak, that I may see thee!

—Ben Jonson

THE story of language is the story of human civilization. Nowhere is civilization so perfectly mirrored as in speech. If our knowledge of speech, or the speech itself, is not yet perfected, neither is civilization.

Language is forever changing and evolving, as are all human things. Linguistics, the study of the laws governing the evolution of language, becomes socially significant only when it sheds light upon the people who speak languages and their civilization. When this light is properly cast, linguistics ceases to be the dry-as-dust subject that many people have suspected it of being, and becomes as absorbing as the study of mankind itself.

The study of language and languages has been described as fundamentally democratic, in contrast with the study of literature, which is essentially aristocratic. Literature reflects human activity as carried on by the best minds, the intellectual *élite* of the human community. This description is not at all invalidated by pointing to anonymous or so-called "popular" literature. The mere fact that we do not know the name of the author of a literary work does not mean that he was not an individual, and that he did not elaborate, by his own intellectual power, his own masterpiece. "Folk" literature, in the sense that the entire population of a given community collaborated in its production, is a figment of the imagination. At the most, it may be said that an author gathered and expressed the inarticulate thoughts of those around him. But he gave those thoughts his own indelible imprint, and a literary author goes almost as often against the current of his environment as with it.

Language, on the other hand, is something to which everybody contributes by the mere fact that he speaks it. Parents transmit their language peculiarities to their children, teachers to their students, leaders to their followers, members of a social group to one another. Everybody lays his stone in building up the monument that is language. The contribution of the individual, anonymous member of the masses is occasionally a conscious one, far more often unconscious. The most fertile field for the cooperation of the entire community is language, which everyone, with practically no exception, possesses and uses. Therefore the study of language is a social science to the highest degree. Language is the tool and product of all human society.

Language is something more. In spoken or written form, it is the indispensable vehicle of all human knowledge. It is the basic foundation of all human cooperation, without which no civilization is possible. Let us examine these two propositions in detail.

All human records whereby the accumulated experience of the race is transmitted from one individual, one generation, one era, one racial group to another appear in some linguistic form, spoken or written, carved on wood or metal or stone. Even those records which are nonlinguistic in the ordinary sense of the word, artistic, architectural, musical, or even gestural, must be translated into terms of language to be fully understood. In a broader sense, they too form part of language.

But what is even more important, they could never have come into being had language not been there to permit that intelligent, full-fledged cooperation between two or more human beings which is the very wellspring of all human progress and which differentiates the activities of man from those of the animal world.

If people had not been able to communicate with one another, they could not have produced the pyramids of Egypt, the Gothic cathedrals, the cities of the ancient and the modern world. In fact, they could not have produced anything beyond the flint hatchet and the bow and arrow.

If the curse of Babel were to fall upon mankind today, and the mutual understanding that language affords us were to vanish utterly, our great monuments of modern civilization would soon become like the Biblical tower itself and endure in ruins only as a symbol of frustration and defeat.

All our present-day activities are carried on, as they have been carried on for untold centuries, by the grace of and with the help of language, spoken, written, gestural, or symbolic. Only those of us who have found ourselves isolated in the midst of a foreign-speaking community where the spoken and written language was incomprehensible, and even the gestures and symbolic signs differed from our own, can realize the complete bafflement and helplessness that are engendered by the lack of a common denominator of understanding.

Not only is there no walk of civilized life from which language is absent, but all forms of human activity hinge on the use of language taken in its broader sense, as the community of understanding between the producer and the receiver of meaning. "Signifier" and "signified" are terms used in linguistics to denote the cluster of sounds that carries a meaningful message and the burden of the message itself. One is occasionally tempted to shift those definitions to betoken the person, contemporary or dead for thousands of years, who utters a significant statement or carved it on ancient stone, and the person who, through his sensory organs, perceives that statement and accurately translates it into terms of his own consciousness.

Although language is the transmitter of thought, it is not enough to grant it a niche among the humanities and leave it there to serve as a tool of literature and philosophy. Although it has numerous physical manifestations, it is not enough to relegate it among the physical sciences and describe it as a branch of physics, physiology, or anthropology. Although it is one of the most refined products of the mind, it is not enough to view it as a mere psychological activity. Language is the sum of all these things, and something more. It is the conveyor, interpreter, and shaper of man's social doings. It is all-pervasive. It enters into, influences, and is in turn influenced by every form of human activity without exception. Its functions are as numerous as the fields in which human ingenuity operates.

That everything we do and think creates, changes, destroys, or otherwise influences language is self-evident. What is not so obvious, perhaps, is that language in return affects all our actions and thoughts. It has been fully established that a change in language on the part of an individual is attended by corresponding changes in gestures, facial expression, carriage, even humor and taboos. This is readily observable in the case of bilingual speakers when they pass from one language to the other. But this is only one phase, and not the most important, of language's influence upon other activities, paralleling the influences of those activities upon language. To give the full proof of this double relationship would require as many chapters as there are separate fields of endeavor. In the chapters that follow, a mere sampling is offered, but that sampling is fully characteristic of language's role in human affairs. Ancient or novel, material or spiritual, crass or lofty, every form of man's activity calls for a transfer of thoughts, ideas, and meaning, thereby utilizing language; gives rise to a complete terminology, thereby creating language; and is insensibly but powerfully channeled and modified by the pre-existing thought-and-language pattern, thereby submitting to language.

Food and drink, shelter and attire are differentiated and distinguished by descriptive language. Yours is the choice between couscous and smörgåsbord, between kvass and rumgullion, between an atrium and a patio, between a sarong and a toga, but first those objects must be brought to your notice in meaningful terms and translated into terms of your own consciousness. Father and mother and sister and brother and all the complex in-law relationships to which human civilization has given rise become productive of something above and beyond mere animal instincts only when the terms themselves acquire significance, and often the very nature of the relationship is partly based on the conceptual meaning, as when Russian carefully distinguishes between a sister's husband and a wife's brother, or Latin merges nephew and grandson into an identical word.

If the language of the Eskimos has no word for war, it may indicate the absence of that time-worn human institution from that branch of the human family. If Russian relinquishes its word for army and later reintroduces it, the fact may betray a resurgent spirit of militarism.

Abstract political concepts such as parties of the right and of the left reveal trends of thought that hark back to Biblical times and beyond. The division of parties into right and left originated in early European legislative bodies, where the presiding officer, being generally a conservative, would honor his fellow conservatives by seating them at his right and put the liberals at his left; in so doing, he followed the Biblical precedent, where the good are on the right and the bad on the left of God. But the Biblical precedent itself seems to have deeper roots; in most individuals, the right hand is favored by nature, the left disinherited; translated into political terms, this means that the parties representing the privileged classes are naturally the "right-handed," those representing the underprivileged the "left-handed."

The language of the law supplies us with an almost complete history of our legal institutions but at the same time penetrates the spoken tongue of the masses to a degree generally unsuspected. To cite an example: the Latin word for "with," *cum*, survives in Italian and Spanish *con*, but on French soil it was replaced by *apud*, another Latin preposition that had the meaning of "in the presence or company of"; ultimately, this *apud*, combined with *hoc* ("this"), gives rise to the modern French *avec*. The reason for the replacement of *cum* by *apud* was a purely legal one. It was a legal custom among the Franks, if one were accused of a crime, to appear in court *apud* (not merely "with" but, in the precise terminology for which the language of the law has always been noted, "in the presence or company of") a certain number of men of good standing who testified as character witnesses. So great was the force of this legal custom that "in the presence of" ultimately supplanted the ancient "with."

Trade gives rise to complete languages, not only of the pidgin species but of so distinguished and literary a variety as Italian, which, far from being the pure Tuscan that some have claimed, seems to have been in origin a compromise of various local dialects devised by the seafaring men of Pisa and Genoa and Amalfi for purposes of commercial understanding. Money, postage, weights, measures, directions, the calendar, hinge on language and its meaning, as well as on an ancient symbolism which is probably language's older brother.

Art and architecture, music and the dance would lose much of their conceptual force were language not there to sustain it. It is not altogether a coincidence that the speakers of Italian, a tongue of a certain sound pattern, have given the world its best operatic music, while the speakers of English, endowed with a sound pattern of a radically different type, seem almost incapable of producing a satisfactory opera. The concepts of nationalism embodied in national anthems are carried far more on the wings of words than on the wings of music, as evidenced by the fact that some of their tunes were once drinking songs, love ditties, or religious hymns.

Stage, screen, radio, TV, and the press do much to spread language of a certain type, to standardize and normalize the system of utterance and form of expression within a given community. A language's standard pronunciation is most often described as that of the national stage, or that of broadcasters, while the press sets the pace for the national written language. At the same time, stage, screen, radio, television, and press are powerfully acted upon and even transformed in their approach by language itself, as witnessed by the lengths to which they go to gain national and international acceptance based on linguistic comprehension. The sound track is said to be "fostering a new universal English, equally comprehensible in America, Britain, and the Dominions." Actors receive training in this new universal English, as well as in foreign tongues for export films. The amount of foreign-language broadcasting done by our own and foreign television and radio stations for purposes of political and cultural propaganda is enormous.

Sports and games penetrate the language to the same extent that they are penetrated by it. The English tongue is replete with sporting terminology which has overrun its bank ("hit-and-run drivers," "to pinch hit for someone," "to hit below the belt," "to jump the gun," "to be on the inside track," "to be in the chips," "to be behind the eight ball," "it isn't cricket," "according to Hoyle"). "Trump" and "tenace," "pawn" and "checkmate" have international figurative currency. Baseball and its terminology have probably done more to bring the meaning of the American way of life home to the Europeans, Latin Americans, and Japanese than any form of direct cultural propaganda. *Beisbol* and *jonrón* ("home run") are as familiar to the Mexicans as their native *corrida* and *matador,* and Latin-American crowds have learned to cry *"¡Maten al arbitro!"* with the same gusto with which American fans shout, "Kill the umpire!"

Racial intolerance is probably based on the linguistic more than on any other factor. It is no accident that the Greeks coined the term "barbarian" in imitation of the supposed babbling of those whose languages they did not understand, that in many languages the term for "foreigner" coincides with the word that means "dumb" or "silent," and that shameful diseases are frequently given as a qualifying adjective the name of another national group, as when the Renaissance Italians gave "syphilis" the name of *morbus gallicus* or "French disease."

As indicative of the trend of a civilization as the language itself are the taboos, that body of words which may not be uttered, or the list of people who may not be directly addressed. Such taboos lead to circumlocutions, which in turn lead to revolutionary replacements in the vocabulary of the language where they occur.

Names, both personal and of places, are generally history-revealing. Sayings and proverbs give a clear clue to the speakers' mentality and habits. Formulas of politeness and insult often afford a clearer insight into a national psychology than do volumes of historical works.

Ancient civilization had one great form of spiritual activity, religion. Modern civilization has added two more, education and science. In the case of all three the influence of language and upon language is paramount.

The oldest written records of practically every ancient language are religious in nature. With meanings transferred to a thousand other fields, terminology originally religious in nature permeates the vocabulary of every civilized tongue. On the other hand language, more than any other factor, serves as the symbol of religion. Hebrew is the vehicle of Judaism, Latin of Roman Catholicism, King James English of most versions of Protestantism, Greek and Church Slavic of the Eastern Christian Churches, Arabic of Mohammedanism, Sanskrit of Buddhism. Several languages are basically the same, and differ only because in one variant they are spoken or written by speakers of one religious faith, in another version by followers of a different creed. Only a change of wording differentiates certain prayers so that they are recognized as pertaining to one or another branch of a given faith. Under these circumstances, the linguistic form becomes the shibboleth, the distinguishing symbol of religion.

The gigantic and ever-growing vocabulary of science and technology is largely international, as are most scientific and mathematical symbols. If a unified world tongue is ever achieved, it is likely that it will be due to the efforts of scientists and technicians who are irked by time-wasting and confusing language differences. While awaiting that blessed event, science and technology contribute to the fast-expanding vocabularies of all living civilized tongues at a faster rate than all other fields of human endeavor put together.

Education likewise contributes to vocabulary growth and is influenced by it. But education's greatest and noblest contribution to the cause of mutual understanding resides in its attempt to make language, in all its forms and varieties, accessible to all people. The process of education is carried on almost exclusively by means of the spoken and written word. No field of knowledge, with the possible exception of the pictorial and plastic arts, can be efficiently imparted save through the medium of language. In most fields of learning, the language auxiliary is paramount and indispensable.

It is fashionable in certain circles to scoff at language study and to advocate other pursuits, taking language for granted. A moment's reflection will reveal the absurdity of this attitude. In what other pursuits will language and languages not enter as necessary tools of expression and understanding? And if you will scoff at language and languages, how, save in terms of language, will you scoff?

— Chapter Two —

LANGUAGE AND RELIGION

In the beginning was the Word; and the Word was with God; and the Word was God.

—John, 1:1

They shall speak with new tongues.

—Mark, 16:17

IF we were to single out the one sociological factor that has had the deepest influence on the history of language and has in turn been most deeply influenced by language, religion would probably be that factor.

The majority of languages have as their earliest written document a religious text. It might almost be suspected that writing was developed not as an auxiliary to speech but as an aid to religion and a depository of religious tradition.

The Akkadian cuneiform and the Egyptian hieroglyphic inscriptions are overwhelmingly concerned with sacred things (the very word "hieroglyph" means "sacred carving"). The earliest Chinese writings, from about 1500 B.C., deal with the soothsayer's art. The Rig-Vedas and Brahmanas of India are religious hymns and rituals. Hittite records are mostly ritualistic. Avestan, the sacred ancient tongue of Persia, is devoted almost exclusively to the tenets and rituals of Zoroastrianism. The Iguvine Tablets, our most important document of the ancient Umbrian tongue which once vied with Etruscan for the linguistic domination of central Italy, are a detailed description of ritual procedure, while our records of Etruscan itself, insofar as we can decipher them, seem to be predominantly of the same nature.

Nearly all the great religions of the world have either given rise to a language or have carried the obscure dialect that first served them to distant areas and world-wide fame.

The Jewish faith has spread Aramaic and Hebrew, not to mention Yiddish and Sephardi, far beyond the borders of Palestine. Mohammedanism carried not only the Koran but also the once-isolated language of southern Arabia to vast regions of Europe, Asia, Africa, and Oceania; where it influenced, more or less deeply, the native tongues; such languages as Persian, Hindustani, Turkish, Malay, Hausa are replete with Arabic words. Buddhism transferred the sacred writings of Gautama's faith to Tibet, Siam, Indo-China, China, and Japan; today, in the Buddhist temples of Nippon, Sanskrit prayers and the sacred invocation *Om mani padme hum!* ("Hail, Jewel in the Lotus! Amen!") are mumbled by priests who have almost forgotten their meaning.

Christianity found two thoroughly established languages, Latin and Greek, ready to act as its instruments, and it was thanks to Christianity that these two languages survived and spread instead of being submerged by the incoming waves of foreign-speaking barbarians. The conqueror normally imposes his language upon those conquered. Why was the reverse true in the case of the Germanic invaders who overran the Roman Empire? There is only one answer, one so obvious that it is often rejected: as they came into the Empire, the Germanic invaders were converted to Christianity, and the language of western Christendom was Latin. Adoption of the religion carried with it adoption of the language indissolubly bound with that religion.

At a somewhat later period, however, Christianity, having developed a mass appeal that had to be made in their own tongues to peoples living beyond the borders of the former Roman Empire, broke down the Classical system of aristocracy in language whereby only Greek and Latin were considered worthy of study.

The work of missionaries in reducing spoken languages to written forms, giving them dignity, culture, and a literature, began even before the Empire's fall and has continued uninterruptedly since. Many, if not most, of the modern languages of Europe have as their first written document a translation of the Bible made by missionaries. This is true of the first Germanic tongue to boast a literary form, Gothic, which the Bishop Ulfilas introduced to the world in the form of a fourth-century translation of the Bible; of Armenian and Georgian, which first appear in similar form in the fifth century; of Slavic, for which the Bishops Cyril and Methodius, missionaries from Constantinople to the Slavs, devised the Cyrillic alphabet in the ninth century; of Albanian, with its baptismal ritual of 1462; of Finnish, with its 1548 Bible; and of many others.

At the same time, established languages were assisted on the road to standardization and modernization by religious texts. Luther's translation of the Bible in 1531 laid the foundation for the modern German tongue, and the role played by the King James version in fixing the standards of modern literary English is too well-known to bear repetition.

Today, it is thanks largely to the missionaries of the Christian religions that we are acquainted with countless tongues of Africa, Asia, North and South America, Australia, and the Pacific. Long before linguistic scientists and linguistic explorers arose, these missionaries repeated the historical performance of their early predecessors. Arriving on the scene of their religious activities, they at once proceeded to study the native tongues, devise for them written forms, and translate into them the Bible for the use of their converts. Nor is the process limited to the missionaries of the Christian faith. In the eighth century A.D., Buddhist missionaries from India gave the people of Java their first religious-literary document, and in many localities of Asia and Africa the sole written form possessed by the local tongue appears in the Arabic script introduced by Mohammedan missionaries.

There is what may be described as a negative influence, as well as a positive one, that religion exerts on language. A tongue used as the sacred vehicle of a religious faith tends to become petrified and to stifle linguistic development. In medieval Hungary, all writing had to be done in the Latin of the Church; it was an offense occasionally punished by death to use the vernacular in written form. This kept Hungarian for a long time as a series of purely oral dialects and retarded its formation as a national tongue. One of Mustapha Kemal's objections to the Arabic alphabet, which he replaced with Roman characters, was that it had retarded the progress of the Turkish language; his reform entailed not only a change of script but also a purification of the language, which was purged of its Arabic and Persian loan words, many of them religious in origin.

Language, particularly in its written form, is often made the symbol of religious faith, even to the point of becoming a shibboleth. The Serbo-Croatian of Yugoslavia is to all intents and purposes a single spoken tongue. But the Catholic Croats use Roman characters while the Orthodox Serbs use Cyrillic. Railroad stations in Yugoslavia bear the identical names in the two scripts. Hindustani, the leading of India's many tongues, takes two written forms according to whether its speakers are Hindus, in which case they call the language Hindi and use the Devanagari characters of ancient Sanskrit, or Moslems, in which case the tongue is called Urdu and spelled out in flowing Arabic script. In the Romansh-speaking Engadine section of Switzerland are two villages, one Catholic, the other Protestant. They speak the same dialect but spell it differently to accentuate their religious individuality. English speakers are, for the most part, acquainted with those minor differences in the wording of the Lord's Prayer or Apostles' Creed which mark the service as Roman Catholic, Episcopalian, or of other Protestant sects ("Who art in Heaven"—"Which art in Heaven"; "trespasses . . . those who trespass against us"—"debts . . . our debtors"; "the living and the dead"—"the quick and the dead"). The use of "For Thine is the kingdom and the power and the glory" at the close of the Lord's Prayer definitely marks the service as Protestant.

Perhaps the most important historical incident in which language and religion played an interrelated part was Charlemagne's encyclical of 786, ordering the bishops and priests of his realm to use a more grammatically correct Latin in the sermons and scriptural readings of the churches. The result was a *coup de grâce* to the already tottering Vulgar Latin then spoken in France. Deprived of the support of the familiar Church language, now suddenly restored to Classical standards incomprehensible to the masses, the spoken tongue of the entire region was swiftly transformed into Old French. In 813 Charlemagne was forced to recognize the new state of linguistic affairs in his northern French provinces and, reversing his earlier decision, ordered the Church sermons to be delivered in the *lingua romana rustica*, the newly born French language, instead of the *lingua latina*.

The influence of religion upon vocabulary in all civilized languages is immense. To cite examples from English, we have in the first place words that have largely retained their religious meaning, like "temple," "church" and "chapel," "altar" and "shrine," "minster" and "monastery" (originally the same word), "prayer" and "worship," "anoint" and "sacrament," "nun" and "convent," "mass" and "litany," "preach" and "sermon," "cross," "cassock" and "canon," "pilgrim" and "puritan," "heaven," "purgatory" and "hell" (with its Italian variant "inferno"), "mystic" and "ascetic," "apocryphal" and "blasphemy," "divine" and "venerable," "sin" and "salvation," "penance" and "atone."

Then we have words which, though originally religious,

have traveled far afield and acquired the most diversified meanings. "Dogma," "creed," "sect," "schism," "heresy," "orthodox," "infallibility," "bigot," "fanatic," "zeal," "inquisition," "hierarchy," "convert," "council," "mediation," "minister," "mission," "anthem" are perhaps more frequently used in political than in religious parlance; so are many verbs in -*ize*, originally a Christian suffix ("baptize," "christianize," but later also "socialize," "patronize," "Americanize"). "Disciple," "dean," "syllabus," "lecture" are today chiefly educational terms. "Sponsor" and "patron" have gone into the broadcasting industry; "hood" and "cowl" into the automobile; "aisle" into the theater. Words like "box," "stigma," "indulgence," "charm," "faith," "vow," "relic," "voyage," "vigil," "symbol," "image," "dirge," "credence," "confession," "clerk," "scribe," "chapter," "novice" (and its more learned variant "neophyte"), "lay," "confirm," "millennium," "martyr," "hermit," "grace," "enthusiasm," "iconoclast," "carnival," "abyss," "exodus," "genesis," "miracle," "myth," "jealous," "virgin," "demon," "imp," "omen" have passed into fields completely unconnected with religion.

These terms come from all languages and all religions. Side by side with Anglo-Saxon "tithe" and "gospel" we find Latin "sepulcher," "limbo," and "fate"; Greek "apostle," "monk," "prophet," "epistle," "patriarch," "hymn," and "psalm"; Syriac "abbot"; Hebrew "cherub," "rabbi," "sabbath," and "amen." "Kismet," "harem," "Islam," "muezzin," "mufti," "dervish," "mosque," even "hegira," which many New Yorkers formerly used for "moving day," are contributed by the Moslem religion and the Arabic tongue, while "arabesque," the graceful style of architectural decoration consisting of flowing letters from the Arabic alphabet as used in the Koran, which forbids the representation of living beings, comes to us indirectly from the same source. "Juggernaut," "mahatma," "purdah," "karma," "avatar," "nirvana" come from the Hindu faith and Sanskrit. The Book of Common Prayer presents interesting series of double words of which one is in origin Anglo-Saxon, the other Latin-Romance: "to acknowledge and confess," "dissemble nor cloke," "assemble and meet," "pray and beseech," "mortify and kill," "perceive and know," "power and might."

Assorted religious terms include the names of God, such as the *El* of Hebrew and the *Allah* of the Moslems (the latter seems to have once been *Al-ilah,* the name of the Arabian moon god before the rise of Islam); or the *Jahveh-Jehovah* of Hebrew, which may have been derived from the Egyptian *Yauhu,* one of the names of the Apis Bull god.

They include such seldom-heard terms as the *Kagyur* or *Kanjur* of the Tibetan Buddhists, containing the religious teachings of the Buddha as translated from the original Sanskrit and Pali of India, of which only three copies are said to exist in this country.

The history of religious terms is fascinating. In the original Greek, an "angel" is a "messenger," a "devil" a "slanderer," a "priest" an "elder" ("presbyter" is a form closer to the original; the Presbyterian Church was originally governed by elders); "bishop" is an "overseer" ("Episcopal" is the form that comes close to the original; the Episcopal Church is governed by bishops, or overseers). "Synagogue" is a Greek term, denoting originally not a Jewish, but an early Christian assemblage. The Arabic *fakir* means "poor," "beggar"; but the beggar is also a holy man, who performs miraculous stunts and thereby gives rise to our "faker" and "fake." "Pagan" and "heathen" are interchangeable terms, the former from the Latin, denoting one who lives in a *pagus,* or village, the latter from the Anglo-Saxon, denoting one who lives on the heath; Christianity spread first in the large cities, leaving the villages and remote country districts untouched in their ancient beliefs. The Chinese "joss house" is not Chinese at all but Portuguese; the "joss" represents a corruption of Portuguese *Deus* ("God"). The Japanese call "fried shrimp" *tempura;* this is not a Japanese word but borrowed from the religious Latin of the early Portuguese traders, who ate only seafood during the *Quattuor Tempora,* literally, the "Four Times" of the year, or Ember Days.

Latin *gentilis* ("of the same race, nation or people") gives rise to four widely differentiated English words: "Gentile," which carries the Biblical meaning, "genteel," "gentle," and "jaunty." Our "holiday" is in origin a "holy day," the feast of some major Saint. "Tithe" is the Anglo-Saxon word for "tenth" (all people were supposed to contribute one-tenth of their income to the Church); its Latin-Romance counterpart is "dime," from Old French *disme* which goes back to Latin *decima,* the same word that gives us "decimal" and "decimate."

"Church," "basilica," and the *ekklesia* that appears in "ecclesiastical" and in the Romance words for "church" (*église chiesa, iglesia, igreja*) are all of Greek origin: the first is *kyriake,* "pertaining to the Lord"; the second is *basilike,* "pertaining to the king"; the third was in origin an Athenian assembly. "Altar" is from the root of Latin *altus,* "high"; "shrine" is from *scrinium,* "coffer" or "strongbox," where precious relics and writings were kept safe. The word tha gives us "chapel," "chaplain," and "a cappella" originally means a "little cloak" and goes back to the legend of St. Martin of Tours, an officer in the Roman legions; on a cold winter day he cut his cloak in half to share it with a beggar, who turned out to be Christ. A "cardinal" is a "hinge," a "Pope" is a "father," an "apostle" is a "messenger." "Anathema" originally meant not "cursed" but "set aside" as an offering to a god. "Manna" and "Messiah," "Calvary" and "Paschal" are all of Hebrew or Aramaic origin, but while "Messiah" ("anointed") has its loan translation in the Greek "Christ," "Calvary" ("place of skulls") is a loan translation from *Golgotha* or, more precisely, *Gulgolep*.

"Demon" is a Greek word, meaning originally a god or divine being, or "fate"; the "evil spirit" connotation appears first in the New Testament. "Christmas" is "Christ's Mass"; the use of "Mass" for "feast day" is frequent in the older English language, where we find such words as Candlemas and Michaelmas. "Mass" itself comes from the Latin *missa,* the feminine past participle of the verb *mitto,* "to send"; the origin of this use lies in the priest's command to the faithful, *"Ite, missa est."*

One word that still retains its Latin form, though it is now used almost exclusively in a political sense, is "propaganda"; it comes from the Catholic organization known as *Congregatio de Propaganda Fide,* which means "congregation for the propagation of the faith" or, more literally, "the faith to be propagated." "Imprimatur," the term appearing on books that have received the official sanction of the Roman Catholic Church, is straight Latin and means "let it be printed." "Monsignor" is a curious linguistic hybrid, since the *mon* is French while the *signor* is Italian. "Mardi Gras" is French for "fat Tuesday," the adjective referring to the fact that this is the last day on which fat foods (*i.e.,* meat) may be eaten before Lent; its English equivalent is "Shrove Tuesday," in which "shrove" is from the archaic verb "shrive," to confess or absolve, and refers to the custom of going to confess one's sins before Ash Wednesday, on which penance begins.

The influence of religion is felt not merely in language proper but even in significant symbols. The early Christians often used a fish as a symbol, owing to the fact that the letters in the Greek word for "fish" (*ichthys*) were the initials of the words in the expression "Jesus Christ, Son of God, Savior" (*Iesous Christos Theou 'Yios Soter*). The X in Xmas is not irreverent but an abbreviation for "Christ," used in early and medieval Christian documents. The X is not an X at all but the Greek letter *Chi,* transcribed in English as

ch and appearing as the initial letter in the Greek *Christos.*
The X which serves as the mark of the illiterate in place of
a signature is an outgrowth of the sign of the cross, which
early Christians placed beside their signature as an attesta-
tion of good faith.

The interaction of language and religion goes on apace
today. Some years ago, the Salvation Army revealed that its
workers throughout the world were then using no fewer than
81 languages in their work. The number has no doubt increased since then. In the vicinity of Montreal, there is a
town, Sault-St.-Louis, inhabited by some 3,000 Christian Mohawks, whose Catholic services are carried on in their own
ancestral tongue, with *Tekwanoronkwanions* replacing *Ave
Verum, Kwasennaiens* replacing *Adoramus Te,* and *Areriia*
used for *Hallelujah* (in the Mohawk sound scheme, *r* has
to be used to replace *l,* and *i* to replace *u*).

The Reverend Eugene Nida, a Baptist minister and mis-
sionary who is also one of the world's foremost language
scientists, informs us that while portions of the Bible have
been translated into well over 1000 of the world's approximately 3000 tongues, 2000 or so still remain to be covered,
located mainly in New Guinea, Africa, southeast Asia, the
Philippines, and South and Central America. Fortunately,
these languages, numerous as they are, are spoken by less
than 5 per cent of the world's inhabitants.

The lack of certain religious words (or of their distor-
tions) presents a curious anthropological feature. When a
Sioux-language translation of the swearword "damned" was
sought, it was discovered that the tongue of the benighted
Indians was superior to that of the white man in that it
possessed no swearwords of any kind or description.

But the lack of religious terms in certain languages unfortunately involves more than swearwords. In translating
the Bible into the Bulu language of the Cameroons, missionaries found that "straightness" and "kindness" were the closest they could get to "righteousness" and "grace," while
"forgiveness" had to be translated into the Misketo Indian
language of Nicaragua by "taking-a-man's-fault-out-of-our-
hearts" and into Labrador Eskimo by "not-being-able-to-think-
about-it-any-more."

There are numerous other samples of the work in
idiomatic translation that has to be performed by Dr. Nida
and his associates. "They shook their heads" becomes in one
of the languages of the Philippines "Their heads went u

and down," for that is the way these tribesmen show disapproval. "I am sorrowful" comes out in various central African tongues as "My eye is black," "My heart is rotten," "My stomach is heavy," "My liver is sick"; while "He smote his breast" has to be turned into "He beat his head," and "being troubled" appears as "shivering in one's liver." In one of these tongues, "prophet" becomes "God's town crier." Of poetic interest among Dr. Nidas' translations is the Ivory Coast "song in the body" to translate "joy," while at the opposite end of the line are the Panamanian Valiente Indian "What people on the handle told you to do these things?" for "By what authority do you do these things?" (the ruler among these tribes is the person who holds the handle of the hunting knife) and the Mexican Cuicatec translation of "to worship," which is "to wag one's tail before God."

These illustrations may cause us to smile, but they prove two things. The first is that any language can create the necessary machinery for the rendering of a new concept; the second is that when divine grace wishes to find a way to reach men's hearts, it can do so, even by devious ways.

— Chapter Three —

LANGUAGE AND THE FAMILY

Next to God, thy parents.
—William Penn

ALTHOUGH anthropologists are not at all in accord as to the origins and sociological implications of the family group, linguists have long been agreed in recognizing that family relationships and their designations are of paramount importance for linguistic studies. It is only fitting that what seems to be the oldest of social institutions should provide one of the best clues for the grouping and affinities of languages. Names of close family relationship are part and parcel of a language's fundamental stock of words, and while some of them may occasionally be borrowed from another linguistic group, there is a natural reluctance to do so. "Father" and "mother" (or their informal equivalents, "dad," "pop," "mamma," "mom") are among the very first words the child learns. He does not easily give them up. So far as English is concerned, it is significant that "father," "mother," "son," "daughter," "sister," "brother" have come down to us straight from our ancestral Germanic, whereas the more distant "uncle," "aunt," "nephew," "niece," "cousin" and the "grand" of "grandfather" and "grandmother" were borrowed from Norman-French after the linguistic upheaval caused by William the Conqueror.

It is not surprising to find that a word like "mother" is easily identifiable in all the languages of our group as stemming from the same original word. Irish *mathair*, Latin *mater*, Greek *meter*, German *Mutter*, Russian *mat'*, Sanskrit *mata* definitely point to the kinship of those languages with our own.

The same is true, but to a lesser degree, for "father." The difference in degree is perhaps due to the fact that a child in infancy has a closer relationship with its mother than with its father. Nevertheless, the display is impressive: English "father," German *Vater*, Latin *pater*, Greek *pater*, Sanskrit *pita*, Persian *pidar*—even Irish *athair* and Armenian *hayr*—show a common origin.

"Sister" and "brother" are almost as conclusive. English "sister," German *Schwester*, Russian *sestra*, Latin *soror*, Sanskrit *svasr* on the one hand; English "brother," German *Bruder*, Slavic *bratr*, Latin *frater*, Greek *phrater*, Sanskrit *bhrata*, Persian *biradar*, Irish *bhrathair* on the other, are unmistakable. "Daughter" and "son" display a fair degree of unanimity. The former has relatives in German *Tochter*, Russian *doč*, Greek *thygater*, Sanskrit *duhita*, Persian *dukhtar*, Armenian *tovodr*, while the latter finds its counterparts in German *Sohn*, Russian *syn*, and Sanskrit *sunu*.

These fundamental relationships indicate that the basic family unit existed as a well-established institution in Indo-European times. There are enough similarities among the languages of other linguistic groups besides our own to show that the situation was substantially the same in many localities and that the relationships of "father," "mother," "son," "daughter," "sister," "brother" are among the most ancient and stable in human civilization.

But there are startling exceptions. The natives of the South Sea island of Ponape are reported to have five words for "brother" but none for "father." This state of affairs is probably indicative of a matriarchal social structure, widespread among many primitive groups, in which the identity of the father is unimportant. A distant reflection of the more important social position once held by women, even in our own group, is perhaps betokened by the German form *Geschwister*, a collective noun formed on the root of *Schwester*, which includes both brothers and sisters. On the other hand, the lead taken by the male sex in Latin countries is reflected in Spanish *padres* (literally "fathers") used for "parents," by the use of *hermanos* ("brothers") to include both brothers and sisters, and of the masculine plural *niños* ("children") and *hijos* ("sons") to denote children of both sexes.

As a reflection of social custom, it is interesting to notice the various subsidiary concepts which assume importance in connection with names of relationship in different languages. The concept of relative age, for instance, is paramount in the Far East. Chinese, Siamese, Burmese, Tibetan, Japanese, Korean, Malay, and the Tamil and Telugu of southern India all use an entirely different word for "brother" according to whether one means an older or a younger brother. On the other hand, the concept of gender is relatively unimportant in some of these tongues. In Malay, *saudara* is used indifferently for "brother" or "sister," provided it is an older one.

When it comes to more distant degrees of relationship, similarity among languages of the same group is far less in evidence. Also, some languages display a considerable measure of confusion, often coupled with extreme niceties of distinction. Italian lumps together "nephew," "niece," "grandson," and "granddaughter" into a single word, *nipote*, distinguished for gender only by accompanying words, such as articles or adjectives. This confusion in part goes back to Latin, where *nepos* and *neptis*, originally "grandson" and "granddaughter," were extended in Imperial times to cover the additional meanings of "nephew" and "niece." The only explanation that can be vouchsafed for this shift lies in a general spirit of vagueness with regard to the more distant relationships. Another example of this is the Latin-Romance handling of terms meaning "uncle" and "aunt." Latin distinguished between a father's brother (*patruus*) and a mother's brother (*avunculus*), as well as between a mother's sister (*matertera*) and a father's sister (*amita*). In the general linguistic transformation that followed the fall of the Roman Empire, *patruus* and *matertera* were lost; *avunculus* emerged with the meaning of both maternal and paternal uncle, giving rise to French *oncle*, German *Onkel*, and English "uncle"; while *amita*, extended in similar fashion, became *tante*, *Tante*, and "aunt." Why the *mother's* brother, but the *father's* sister, survived in the elimination process has not been satisfactorily explained. Spanish and Italian, incidentally, gave up the entire series of Latin words, replacing them with Greek *theios* (originally "god-given" but already used in Greek with a meaning that covered both *patruus* and *avunculus*), from which they derived *tío* and *zio*.

Strong symbolism appears in some names of family relationship. "Uncle" in many Italian dialects assumes the form "beard" (*barba*). The uncle is the "bearded man," the strong man who protects you if your parents fail you. There is in medieval French and Italian literature a vast array of uncles as natural protectors, which starts with the role of Charlemagne, the uncle of the great epic hero Roland. That the symbolism is one of strength is proved by the fact that the same word for "beard" gives rise in Rumanian to the generic word for "man" or "male" (*barbat*, from Latin *barbatus*, "bearded").

Forms like "grandfather" and "grandmother" appear in

French as well as in English and German, which borrowed them from French. *Magnus,* "great," had previously been applied to *avunculus* in Latin, with the meaning of "grand-uncle." Spanish and Portuguese, however, use words for "grandparents" which originally meant "little ancestor," just as Russian uses for "grandmother" a term that means "little old woman" (*babushka*). Italian uses words of religious origin (*nonno, nonna*), coming from the same root that gives us "nun."

The names of in-law relations display linguistically interesting features. German uses a series of forms (*Schwieger, Schwager, Schwäger*) which are akin to Latin *socer* and *socrus* ("father-in-law," "mother-in-law") and which appear also in Sanskrit, Russian, and other tongues of the Indo-European group. Italian and Spanish generally follow the Latin forms, but Spanish has developed a "political brother" (*hermano político*) for "brother-in-law" which shows the same legalistic line of thought as our own English "in-law." Another Spanish word for "brother-in-law" is *cuñado,* which, like Italian *cognato,* of the same meaning, goes back to Latin *cognatus* which meant "related by blood or birth," an evident semantic shift of major proportions.

French, breaking completely away from the Latin tradition, instituted a series of "beautiful" names for in-laws (*beau-père, belle-soeur, beau-fils,* etc.) which becomes significant when we remember the old English custom of using "fair" in polite address. *Belle-mère* ("beautiful mother") to a mother-in-law is convincing proof that French is *par excellence* a diplomatic language. Side by side with the "beautiful" forms, French has another term for "daughter-in-law," *bru,* which comes from the Germanic and is akin to our own "bride" and German *Braut.*

Affective connotations play a rather large role in the creation of names of relationship. This is well borne out by Italian, where the present-day words for "brother" and "sister" (*fratello, sorella*) were originally affectionate diminutives meaning "little brother," "little sister." Spanish *abuelo,* originally "little ancestor," for "grandfather" and French *petit-fils* ("little son") for "grandson" may be other cases in point. The Russian word for "father," *otyets,* which differs so widely from the general Indo-European pattern of "father" (*pater, pita,* etc.) was originally an affectionate diminutive related to the Gothic *atta.* Both words are probably connected with our own "dad."

Linguistic oddities in names of relationship abound. The Chinese word for "mother," despite the lack of kinship between Chinese and the western tongues, is *ma*. In another totally unrelated language, the Otetela of the Congo, "my father," strangely enough, is *papa;* but here the similarity ceases: "your father" is *sho,* "his father" *shi,* "our father" *shesu.* The Japanese for the speaker's mother is a laugh: *haha.* In the Georgian of the Caucasus, *deda,* although it sounds like "dad," is "mother," while *mama* means "father."

— Chapter Four —

LANGUAGE AND MATERIAL EXISTENCE

With words alone, you don't make the soup.
—Rumanian proverb

MAN'S primary needs are summed up by sociologists in the triad "food, clothing, and shelter." The first is basic, the other two contingent. In some island paradises of the South Seas, man can practically dispense with the latter two. Nowhere can he dispense with food.

Eating is probably the oldest, though not the noblest, of human activities. The interaction of food and language must therefore have taken place at a very early date. From the dark days when human beings ate one another there come down to us certain terms that make us shudder. "Cannibal" is a comparatively modern word, devised by the Spaniards at the time of the discovery of America. Some say it was first applied by Columbus himself in the form *Caríbal* to describe the anthropophagous Carib Indians, and that it was later changed to *Caníbal* by getting confused with Latin *canis* ("dog"). But the ancient Greeks, many centuries earlier, had devised the term *anthropophagoi,* "man-eaters" (Herodotus calls them *androphagoi*), which they applied to a people of Scythia who ate human flesh.

Samoyed is the Russian name of a Siberian tribe, as well as of a breed of dogs. The Russian term means "self-eating" and was first applied when the Russians thought they discovered traces of cannibalism among the Samoyeds. *Nyam-Nyam* is the name of an African tribe, said to have been coined in imitation of the noisy sounds accompanying cannibalistic feasts. "Long pig" is not a western euphemism for a human body roasted on the spit by cannibals but an actual literal translation of *puaka enata,* a widespread Polynesian term from the South Seas Marquesas Islands.

Cannibalism as a deliberate practice is characteristic only of the lowest grades of civilization. At the other end of the line, there is not only refinement in food but also intimate collaboration between food and language in the form of recipes and cookbooks.

The oldest cookbook of which we have a record is a Chinese one that goes back some 4,700 years. It was compiled by the Emperor Shen Nung and elaborated by three great Cantonese chefs. The Chinese are poets as well as cooks. A soup of pigeons' eggs is called "golden moons on a silver sea"; a dish of sharks' fins and eggs bears the title, "10,000 arrows piercing the clouds"; cabbage shoots on crab roe is named "jade growing out of coral," while a dish of pork sausage and chicken is titled "famous scholar's abandon."

The Hindus believed that all foods and forms of cookery were specifically created by the gods, and in the fifth century A.D. all references to food appearing in the Vedas, Upanishads, and other holy books of the Hindus were carefully collected and separately issued by the Brahmin Khema Sharma.

Archestratus of Gela, a friend of Epicurus, composed for the ancient Greeks a work entitled *Heduphagetica* ("Sweet Eating"), which contained the recipes of the Greeks; it was unfortunately lost, but parts of it survive in a Latin translation.

The Roman writer Apicius composed in the third century A.D. a book entitled *De Re Coquinaria* ("About Cooking Matters"), in which the dishes of the fastidious Romans were described. The memory of Lucullus, prince of Roman gourmets, survives in our present-day adjective "lucullan," applied to repasts.

How food can contribute to language growth is spectacularly illustrated by the Romance words for "liver" (French *foie*, Spanish *hígado*, Italian *fegato*, etc.). The ancient Romans were fond of fig-stuffed liver, *iecur ficatum*. As time went on, the Latin word for "liver," *iecur*, disappeared, leaving only the adjective "fig-stuffed" to do service for the noun. It is from *ficatum* alone that the Romance forms are derived.

The fact that in English comparatively few names of foods, particularly among the fruits and vegetables, are of Anglo-Saxon origin is explained on the ground that many of them were discovered or imported only in relatively recent times. Among foods that were unknown in Europe until after the discovery of America are potatoes, maize, tomatoes, chocolate, and cocoa. But even in the matter of meats, which were well-known to our Anglo-Saxon forebears, a noticeable shift of names occurred after the Norman conquest. Gurth, in *Ivanhoe*, remarks that food animals are Anglo-Saxon while alive (ox, calf, swine), but become Norman-French after they are slaughtered (beef, veal, pork). Could this be because meat had largely become the prerogative of the Norman upper classes?

A great many of our common eating terms are borrowed from foreign languages. "Delicatessen" and "ersatz" come to us from the German. The former is "delicacies," borrowed from French *délicatesse,* the latter a term for "substitute" in general, but more particularly applied to foods. The modern Russian equivalent of a German-American delicatessen is a *gastronom,* operated by the government, in which nonrationed foods are sold on an official black market basis; the word, however, is taken from French, in which it means a "gourmet," and ultimately goes back to the Greek for "belly" and "law."

A few terms taken at random from the restaurant list will show our indebtedness to foreign tongues. What some people call "appetizers," on the doubtful theory that they stimulate appetites which as a rule need no stimulus, others call "hors d'oeuvres." This French term literally means "outside of work," referring to the fact that the *hors d'oeuvre* is eaten outside the regular meal. This term calls to mind the "whets" and "whigs" of American Revolutionary days; the former were appetizers, the latter small cakes, though earlier, in England and Scotland, "whig" had meant a cooling drink, usually made from whey. The Italian *antipasto* means "before meal." *Smörgåsbord,* the delectable Swedish tableful of assorted delicacies, has the modest literal meaning of "buttered-bread table." An Italian *minestrone* is "big soup," with reference to the number and variety of the ingredients. Russian *borsch* comes from a root that means "prickle," perhaps a reference to the stimulation of jaded appetites. The exotic East Indian *mulligatawny* is in its native Tamil *milagutannīr,* or "pepper water"; and "curry," also from the Tamil of southern India, is originally *kari.* The naturalized *gumbo* soup comes from the *ngombo* of one of the African Negro tongues of Angola; one of its indispensable ingredients is *okra,* also of African origin. "Goulash" is a Hungarian stew of beef and vegetables flavored with paprika; its native form is *gulyás* or *gulyáshús,* "herdsman's meat." "Chowder" is related not to "chow" but to the French *chaudière,* "cooking pot," which in turn goes back to Latin *caldaria.*

"Biscuit" is half Latin, half French, and means "twice-baked"; in the days of sailing ships it was difficult to keep bread from spoiling, but bakers discovered that if the bread was baked twice it would keep much longer. The German *Zwieback* is a literal translation of the Latin-French *biscuit*, and crackers and hardtack are still called "biscuit" in England. The sandwich owes its name to an earl of Sandwich who, being inordinately fond of card-playing, felt he could not leave the gaming table long enough for a regular meal but munched at slices of beef between two pieces of bread as he played.

National customs and ways of life are often revealed in terms of food and its nomenclature. The French enjoy the well-deserved reputation of being the world's finest cooks, and the term *cuisine française* has spread to all countries of the earth as the synonym of what is best in cookery. What many do not know is that side by side with the *cuisine française* there exists also in France a *cuisine canaille* ("rapscallion cookery") which is in vogue among the lowest classes. The chasm between *cuisine française* and *cuisine canaille* is a reflection of social and economic differences which are fundamental.

The Italians, like most Latin races, are great eaters of bread. Italy's economy does not permit bread to be regarded as a mere accessory of the dinner table, as is the case with us. Accordingly, the Italians have devised the word *companatico*, a convenient generic term meaning "anything that is eaten with bread." Italian also speaks of "earning your bread and wine" where English speaks of "earning your bread and butter." The "staff of life" is, of course, standard in the tongues of the western world. The "bread" root is common to all the Germanic tongues, the *panis* root of Latin to all the Romance languages, while the Slavic tongues use *khleb*, which is etymologically related to our "loaf" (*hlaifs* in ancient Germanic). What we often forget is that the majority of the world does not eat bread. To the rice-eating Japanese, for instance, "bread" is a loan word, *pan*, imported along with the object itself by seventeenth-century Portuguese traders. The Catholic Eskimos have an interesting variation in the Lord's Prayer which runs "Give us this day our daily fish."

There is another Italian staple, called by the generic name of *pasta* ("dough"), whose many ramifications (*spaghetti, macaroni, vermicelli*, etc.) display to a superlative degree the interrelation of language and food. *Spaghetti* is literally "little pieces of cord" and *vermicelli* "little worms." What goes by the name of "spaghetti" in America is "vermicelli" in

Britain, whereas in Italy the two names apply to two different thicknesses of the same basic product. "Spaghetti," "vermicelli," and "macaroni," along with "zucchini," "broccoli," and a few other food names, illustrate the tendency of languages to borrow the name of an object along with the object itself when the latter was previously unknown. They also illustrate another tendency of languages to adapt the borrowed names to their own requirements and notions. In Italian, all these nouns are plural and require plural verbs; in English, we choose to view them as collective singulars and accordingly say, "The spaghetti *is* on the table," which makes Italians laugh, or, worse yet, "The spaghettis are on the table." *Al dente,* in connection with *pasta,* means "to the tooth," "toothsome" and above all "not overdone."

The food *macaroni* seems to have existed as far back as the eighth century, at which time a Greek lexicographer records *makaria* (literally, "blessed") and describes it as "a food made out of dough and sauce." Over five hundred names of different macaroni products have been recorded in Italy. The products themselves are not so numerous, but different regions of Italy use different names for the same product. The only limit to the number of ways of preparing macaroni products is the number of individual Italian localities.

"Chocolate" and "tomato" come to us from the language of the Aztec Indians of Mexico, "potato" and "maize" from the tongues of the North American Indians. The tomato, however, before settling down to its original Aztec name, was known by a variety of picturesque European names, such as "wolf peach" and "love apple"; in Italian it is still called "golden apple" (*pomodoro*); borrowed by Russian in the form *pomidor,* along with originally Aztec *tomatl.* The Europeans at first believed it to be a flower, poisonous if eaten, and used it only for decorative purposes. The potato, for its part, was in disrepute some centuries ago. Some Englishmen who did not fancy potatoes formed a "Society for the Prevention of Unwholesome Diet," but the people of England kept right on eating potatoes. The French *pomme de terre* means "earth apple," and the original German *Erdapfel* is a literal translation of the French. *Kartoffel,* the more common modern German term, has the same origin as French *Tartuffe* and English "truffle"; all these words go back to Latin *terrae tuber,* "a tuber of the earth." But not all the commonest vegetables go back to the discovery of America. Some were well known in remote antiquity (oldest, apparently, is the onion, mentioned in Egyptian inscriptions). *Finocchi* is the

Italian name of a vegetable otherwise known as "fennel" or "anise"; both "fennel" and *finocchi* come from the Latin *foenuculum* ("little hay"). "Celery" gets its name from *selinon,* the Greek word for "parsley"; celery was given as a prize to winners in the ancient Greek sports arenas. Garlic, despite its use by foreigners, is a pure Anglo-Saxon word, originally meaning "spear leek." Its Latin name is *alium,* from which French *ail* is derived. Provence, the southern part of France, has been nicknamed by the French *la terre frottée d'ail* ("the garlic-rubbed land"), by reason of the abundant use of garlic in Provençal cookery.

Tukki is a Hebrew word that appears in the Old Testament with the meaning of "peacock." This seems to have given rise to our "turkey." Hebrew merchants in Europe, to whom Spaniards in America sent the fowl, mistook them for peacocks. The French call a turkey *dinde* or *dindon;* this was originally *d'Inde* ("from India") and shows a misconception as to the bird's original habitat, paralleled by the Italian word for maize, *granturco* ("Turkish grain"). The Turks call the turkey "American bird," which is geographically correct.

That beefsteak and roast beef were originally native English dishes is proved by the forms they assume in the languages that have borrowed them. Portuguese uses *bife* for "beefsteak," taking the whole for a part; French uses *bifteck,* Spanish *bistec,* Italian *bistecca,* Russian *bifshteks,* Japanese *bifuteki. Beefsteak mit Hindernissen* ("with hindrances") is the picturesque German term describing a garnished steak. Roast beef assumes the form *rosbiffe* in Italian and *rosbif* in both French and Spanish.

Among meat dishes we have acquired from abroad in return for our steaks and roast beef may be mentioned *shish-kebab,* a tasty Turkish dish of skewered lamb, which is what the name means. Its Russian-Caucasian variant, *shashlik,* comes from the Turkish *shish* ("spit") and the suffix *-lik.* The *Wiener Schnitzel* is simply a "Vienna slice," a very thin veal cutlet, breaded and fried. *Chop suey,* though not an authentic Chinese dish, has its origin in the Cantonese *chap siu* ("roast pork"). *Sukiyaki,* the Japanese dish consisting of thinly sliced beef plus a mixture of vegetables, stewed together in soy sauce and chicken broth, has the literal meaning of "spade roast"; in accordance with Buddhist practice, if one dares to eat the meat of four-legged animals, the cooking should at least not be done with household utensils and should preferably take place out of doors; an old spade might therefore be used for such cooking. There is a Chinese variant of *sukiyaki* called *da-ban-lo.*

The Spanish *cocido* (or "stew") is perhaps better known by the name of *olla podrida* or the French equivalent *pot pourri*. These terms literally mean "rotten pot," indicating that spoiled meat was used in the Middle Ages, when refrigeration was unknown. The condiments would disguise the flavor. Both *pot pourri* and *olla* have come into English (the latter also under the form *olio*) to indicate a hodgepodge or medley. "Hodgepodge" itself comes from an earlier "hotchpotch" and a still earlier "hotchpot," from the French *hochepot*, a "shaken pot" of many ingredients.

A picturesquely titled Azorean soup which includes among its ingredients wine, sugar, and cinnamon is *sopa de cavalo cansado*, "tired horse soup." But Portuguese speakers are nothing if not poetic in their names for foods; in various dialects the mushroom is called *chapeu de feiticeira*, "witch's hat"; *pão do diabo*, "devil's bread"; *frade*, "friar." Corresponding to the Spanish *paella* (originally from Latin *patella*, "frying pan," but now used to indicate the frying pan's contents, a savory combination of rice and seafood), Portugal uses *caçoila* for the pan, while the Azores use it to signify the stew cooked in the pan.

Cheeses generally take their names from their places of origin. Cheddar cheese, for instance, comes from the English town of Cheddar, which began manufacturing this cheese in the seventeenth century. Limburger is so called because it originated in the Belgian province of Limburg. Parmesan gets its name from the city of Parma, in northern Italy. Some cheeses, however, have more interesting names. Liederkranz means "singing circle" cheese. The *Liederkranz* is a singing society of men of German origin, and members of such societies would normally retire to drink beer and eat cheese after their choral efforts. Camembert was named by Napoleon after the peasant woman who originated the cheese and to whom there is a statue in a market place in Normandy.

As we have already seen, when a nation borrows a dish from another the name generally goes with the dish, enriching the borrower's vocabulary. Wholesale borrowing from English is displayed in the case of Japanese in the case of western foods, drinks, and even tableware. "Butter" is *bata*, "soup" is *soppu*, "chop" is *choppu*, "ham" is *hamu*, "bacon" is *beikon*, "sauce" is *sosu*, "salad" is *sarada*, "cheese" is *chitzu*, "lemon" is *remon*, "dessert" is *dezātō*. *Biru* and *kohi* are the forms taken by "beer" and "coffee," while "knife" is *naifu* and "fork" is *fōku*.

A food-and-language story from the forties serves to prove that food is food, regardless of the language in which it may be clothed. During the filming of a restaurant scene for *Arch of Triumph,* this exotic item on the luncheon menu was spotted by the hungry extras: *"Petite saucisse de Frankfort braisée dans la choucroute à la mode alsacienne."* When the food arrived, they all exclaimed almost in unison: "Hot dogs and sauerkraut!"

Drinking is, in a sense, the acme of social living. Conviviality, the art of "living with" other people, depends to a large degree upon the ability to partake, in moderation, of the heart-warming beverages that a bountiful nature has placed at mankind's disposal.

The Bible describes wine as having been accidentally discovered by Noah and in the same breath issues a warning against the dangers of overindulgence. The New Testament describes the turning of water into wine by Christ at the marriage feast of Cana. Is wine actually the oldest of fermented drinks? Whether it is or not, there is more in the way of linguistic tradition about the juice of the grape than about all other beverages put together.

Vinum, from which practically all modern languages get their word for "wine," appears in Latin but seems to have been borrowed by Latin speakers from Etruscan or, perhaps, from the "Mediterranean" language that preceded the coming of the Indo-Europeans on the shores of the great inland sea.

Famous wines often bear the name of the region to which they are native. Such is the case with the French Champagne, Burgundy, and Bordeaux, the Italian Chianti, the German Rhine wine, and the Hungarian Tokay. Champagne is the name of the famous French wine-growing district whose Latin name was Campania ("land of fields"). "Sherry" is the English form of Spanish *Xerez,* originally produced in a district close to the Portuguese border, called Xerez de la Frontera. Another Spanish wine is called *manzanilla* ("little apple") but is definitely made from the juice of the grape, not the apple. The word *añejo* on a bottle of wine or liquor produced in a Spanish-speaking country means "aged" or "many-yeared"; it comes from *año,* "year." "Port" comes from the name of the Portuguese city of Oporto, which itself means "the port"; according to one etymology, the left side of a ship is called the port side because the red lantern displayed on that side was the color of port wine.

One famous Italian wine bears the Latin name of *Est Est Est* ("It is! It is! It is!"). According to the story, a notable who went on a journey sent an envoy before him to sample the wines of the various localities through which he was to pass, with instructions to write *Est* ("It is!") wherever the wine was good. When the envoy reached Montefiascone (the name of the locality means "big bottle mountain") he found the wine so good that he gave it the medieval equivalent of three stars.

Muscatel comes from the nutmeg or *nux muscata*, which in turn gets its name from Muscat in Arabia. By popular etymology the Italians believe that its name is due to the fact that its sweet flavor draws flies (*mosca* in the Italian for "fly"), so that to them the name means "wine with flies in it." This does not keep them from drinking *moscato*.

Other fermented beverages also have their linguistic tradition. The ancient Celtic name for beer is *cerevigia*, the "drink of Ceres," goddess of grain. French *cervoise*, Spanish *cerveza*, and Italian *cervogia* still bear Ceres' name. Porter beer is so called because at first its chief consumers were porters and other members of the laboring classes, while Lager beer, from the German, is beer that "lies" in storage for some months before being consumed. But the New York Metropolitan Museum of Art has in its possession a Babylonian clay tablet from about 1500 B.C. indicating that a form of beer was consumed in Mesopotamia long before the time of the ancient Celts, let alone the modern Germans. The beverage, made with an ingredient called *bappir* and a mash named *patuti*, was manufactured in breweries called *sabitum*. *Sirde* and *sikaru-kas* were apparently names of ancient brands, and the month in the Babylonian calendar named *iti-manu-ku*, "month for the eating of green malt," appears to indicate some link with our bock beer. "Red beer," "threefold beer," "beer without a head," and "beer from the nether world" seem to have given the Babylonians plenty of variety. *Tebibtu* were the progenitors of our beer bottles, and *kan-kan-nu* were the three-legged stands from which you drank.

Beyond the elemental need of a protection against the outside weather, which our primitive ancestors supplied by wearing the skins of animals they had killed, clothing is largely a matter of deference to social custom. This is to some extent proved by the fact that our "garb" is derived from Italian *garbo*, which in the broadest sense means "social grace." "Costume" and "custom" were also originally the same word, Latin *consuetudo*, meaning "what is customary."

The names of many ancient garments have come down to us, together with their description. The *chiton* or tunic of the ancient Greeks got its name from the Semitic *kuttōneth*. Joseph's "coat of many colors" was a *kuttōneth*. Among the garments mentioned by Homer in his *Iliad* and *Odyssey* are the *peplos* and *himation*. A later Greek garment was the *chlamys*.

A few of our present-day garments derive their names from the languages of the Middle Ages. "Jacket" is derived from the name of a medieval piece of armor, the *jacque*, though it has also been described as going back to the garment worn by the rebel peasants in France's fourteenth-century peasant revolt, *la Jacquerie*, which was named after the derisive designation given the peasants by the nobility, *Jacques Bonhomme* ("James Goodman"), a sort of John Q. Public of the period. The earlier form of "pants" is "pantaloons," so called because they were in vogue among the Venetians, whose patron saint was San Pantaleone. The name of the saint goes back to Greek, in which language it means "all merciful."

Names of materials often come from the cities of the east and west. "Shantung" is the name of a Chinese province. "Madras" and "calico" come from the cities of Madras and Calicut in India. "Cashmere" comes from the name of an Indian state, "muslin" from the city of Mosul in Iraq. "Worsted" comes from the name of the English town (Worstead) where it originated, while "gingham" and "lisle" represent the towns of Guincamp and Lille in France, and "poplin" is *papeline*, or "pertaining to the Pope," because it was first manufactured in Avignon, a Papal seat.

Accessories and their names might lead us too far afield. It is of interest, however, that "lavaliere" comes from the name of Louise de la Vallière, mistress of Louis XIV, and that "umbrella" and "parasol," both from the Italian, indicate the purpose for which the articles are primarily used in Italy, to ward off the sun. The same idea appears in the Spanish *sombrero* ("hat"), from *sombra* ("shade"). French *parapluie* and German *Regenschirm*, on the contrary, are "warders off of rain," which in the northern countries presents more of a problem than the sun.

It is a matter of doubt whether the generic idea of shelter was at first associated with protection from the elements or concealment from one's enemies. The English "house" is related to the verb "to hide"; "hall" comes from an old Teutonic root *helan* ("to conceal"); the Latin *cellarium*, from which we get "cellar," is connected with *celare* ("to hide or conceal"). The caves of our ancient ancestors, the cliff dwell-

ings of southwestern Indian tribes, the villages on stilts in
the middle of lagoons, one of which gave rise to Venice,
hold in common the elements of concealment and defense.
The latter predominates in "garret," which comes from the
Old French *garite* ("watchtower"), which in turn goes back
to a Germanic root found also in "guard" and "garrison";
Spanish *garita* and Italian *garitta* ("sentry box") are the precise etymological equivalents of "garret."

Side by side with the concept of concealment or defense
appears the idea of "dwelling" or "staying," in such widely
scattered forms as the Sioux Indian *ti-pi* (or "tepee"), a verb
form meaning "they dwell," and the French *maison* and
manoir (our "manor"), both derived from the Latin verb
manere ("to remain").

Extraordinary transformations in meaning are in evidence
among names of dwellings. The Latin *casa*, from which
Spanish and Italian derive their general word for "house,"
was in origin a tent, or at the most a hut. "Palace" is
Latin *palatium*, which gets its name from the Palatine hill,
but the hill itself was named after the verb *palari* ("to wander or graze"), the hill having once been a grazing place
for sheep. A return to the primitive is indicated by one of
the Russian derivatives of *palatium palatka*, which means
"tent." *Domus*, the regular Classical Latin word for "house,"
appears in numerous Indo-European languages, including Russian (*dom*). It gives rise to our "domicile" and "dome" and
to the Italian *duomo*, or cathedral, the "house of God."

A castle and a château are both of military origin, coming from *castellum*, a diminutive of the Latin *castra*, which
was a soldier's camp. "Camp" itself, on the other hand, is
originally an open field. Latin *castra* reappears in English
"-cester" and "-chester" and in the Spanish *alcázar*, which
is an arabized version.

"Court" and "yard" have approximately the same original
meaning ("enclosure"), but one is Latin, the other Anglo-
Saxon. "Home" is connected with the "-ham" that appears
as a suffix in many English place names (Birmingham, Gotham, etc.), and with the German *-heim* of Mannheim and
Hildesheim.

Groups of dwellings are indicative of a relatively high order
of civilization. *Villa* was the name originally applied by the
Romans to a country estate. During the early Middle Ages,
many of the old Gallo-Roman cities of France became de-
serted, and the population regrouped itself around the *villa*,
or manor, of a feudal lord who could afford some measure
of protection. As a result of this social-historical change, the

French partly relinquished their old word *cité*, which had already entered English in the form of "city," and *ville* became the general French term for a city or town. *Cité* had arisen from Latin *civitas*, which had rather the meaning of "city-state" than that of "city" pure and simple, for which Latin used *urbs*.

In food, attire, and shelter, we are faced with the lower manifestations of what sociologists call the "ethos," which Aristotle defines as that element of character which determines what man thinks and does, the spirit that actuates manners and customs. It is no more than natural that a people's ethos should be widely reflected in that people's language, and that language, once established, should in turn influence the ethos, setting up what may be styled, in modern parlance, a chain reaction which is to all intents and purposes infinite. There is no doubt that the ethos of the ancient Gauls and Iberians was fundamentally changed when they came in contact with the Romans and their language, or that the ethos of the Anglo-Saxons was radically affected by their contact with the French-speaking Normans, who brought to them new ideas couched in new words.

One important question which the sociologists have not yet attempted to answer is this: Granted the interrelation of ethos and language, which in the past has always been of an incidental and accidental nature, to what extent would it be possible to change the ethos of future generations by a deliberately planned change in their language?

— Chapter Five —

LANGUAGE AND ECONOMIC RELATIONS

Language is a steed that carries one into a far country.
                                              —Arab proverb

TRADE is coeval with civilization. When man first began to expand the field of his activities beyond the narrow confines of the family circle and the hunt for the barest necessities of life, the need for barter and exchange of products began to make itself felt. This must have exerted a powerful influence on the creation and development of language, since bartering, to become effective, needs a means of communication and understanding. Barterable objects require names unless they are directly at hand and can be pointed to; the terms of exchange must be set in some sort of intelligible language; the medium of exchange, to be created and established, requires a measure of acceptance based on mutual understanding. As commerce becomes more complex, specific measures, weights, numbers, dates must be set.

Under the circumstances, it is not surprising that some of the most sought-after products which mark the progress of man from the age of stone to the age of metals appear among the oldest linguistic forms that have come to our knowledge. The term for "iron" is to be found in some of the most ancient languages of which we have a record. Tin and copper, the two metals which in blended form lead to the Bronze Age, are repeatedly mentioned in the Bible and other ancient books. The name of copper comes from the island of Cyprus, where the metal seems to have been first found in abundance. The relentless search for tin led to early exploits in navigation on the part of the Phoenicians, who reached both the Iberian Peninsula and the British Islands, which they called the "Tin Isles," and planted Phoenician-speaking colonies along the shores of the Mediterranean.

243

The repetition of these exploits, in more recent times, by trader-navigators of the modern nations, has by the same process enriched the modern languages with words like "copra," "kapok," "cinchona," "karakul," and "mahogany."

The role of trade in language formation is more generally underestimated than is the role of language as an auxiliary to trade. It is primarily to the desire for trade that we owe the creation of the many pidgin languages that encircle the globe. Malay, the tongue of some 100 million people in Indonesia and nearby regions, is primarily a compromise trade language used by persons who speak various related, but mutually incomprehensible, Malayo-Polynesian tongues. Chinese-English pidgin sprang into existence because of the desire of English-speaking traders to communicate with Chinese-speaking customers in the South China ports. Spreading to the South Sea islands, Chinese-English pidgin turned into Melanesian-English pidgin. The *lingua franca* of the Mediterranean basin in medieval times was essentially a trade language that served as a common means of intercourse for speakers of Italian, French, Spanish, Greek, and Arabic. Some linguists superficially attribute the creation of the literary Italian tongue to Dante. But it is common knowledge that this literary Italian language was in existence and use at least a century before the time of Dante, and it is not unreasonable to suppose that it first arose as a trade language, designed to facilitate commercial exchanges among traders from the great seafaring city-states of Genoa, Venice, Pisa, and Amalfi, whose local speech varieties diverged to the point of mutual incomprehensibility. Today, one of the chief arguments for the use of English as an international language is based on the extensive commercial importance of our language.

But American business houses have learned, often the hard way, that it does not always pay to insist on using English in international trade, with the result that they have founded institutes like the American Institute for Foreign Trade, located at Phoenix, Arizona, where young men are trained for commercial service in the Latin-American countries by learning to read, write, and speak Spanish and Portuguese, with emphasis on colloquial and business terminology.

The foreign languages most extensively used for foreign advertising by American firms are Spanish, Portuguese, French, German, Italian, the Scandinavian tongues, and Dutch. The same is true of banking firms. The Chase Manhattan Bank receives over 50,000 communications a month in foreign languages and has a staff of thirty-five polyglot employees to take care of them. The electrical appliance business goes in also for Russian and Chinese. Most airlines now require their stewardesses to have a fluent knowledge of one or more foreign languages. Our New York department stores find it profitable to employ "personal shoppers" to assist foreign purchasers, and each personal shopper is competent to handle at least one foreign tongue. New York hotels maintain foreign departments with clerks speaking French, German, Spanish, and often several other languages. Even the real estate industry has seen fit to issue leasing guides in a dozen foreign tongues, including Arabic, Hindi, Japanese, and Persian, largely for the benefit of UN personnel.

But foreign languages have also entered on large-scale advertising for home consumption. It was remarked by one agency that this is not at all strange, since there are in the New York area more Italians than in Rome, more Jews than in Israel, more Germans than in any German city with the possible exception of Berlin and Hamburg, more Poles than in any Polish city with the exception of Warsaw and Lodz, and three times as many Puerto Ricans as in San Juan. It is therefore not surprising that we hear on the radio a jingle to the effect that a certain beer *"tiene rico sabor y refresca mejor,"* or see on TV a Chinese plying his chopsticks and telling us that *"La Choy hên hao."*

It is difficult, on the other hand, to judge to what extent this foreign-language advertising is genuinely addressed to the foreign buyer and to what extent it is mere snob appeal, designed to *épater le bourgeois.* This suspicion seems justified when you see a full-column ad in a Poughkeepsie paper completely composed in Italian, plugging for shoes made by *"le famose sorelle Fontana"* of Rome. Are there enough Italian speakers in Poughkeepsie to warrant that ad? And what about the little boy or girl on TV who goes through a complete scene in perfect Spanish, French, or Italian about cleaning his or her teeth with a certain toothpaste? Or the newspaper ad that tells you not to say you can't find it until you have shopped a certain department store and does so in three dozen languages, including modern Hawaiian and beautifully Ciceronian Latin?

Trade terms, as apart from trade names, generally pertain to the field of professional jargon and do not penetrate the everyday language of the multitudes. Such is the case with the "Keno!" used by commodity traders to indicate that corn has reached the limit for one day's decline, or the stock market's "fish-hooking out" (the rise after a depression), "saucering out" (leveling off at the bottom of a bear market), "boiler room" (an office for the sale of questionable securities sold over the phone by high-powered salesmen), "locked in" (term used of customer who has a paper profit but can't sell because of short-term capital gains tax), or even "flat" (said of a security that sells ex-dividend or without accrued interest). In the same class are the "compur," "sonnar," "supermatic," "fresnel," "capacitron," "panatomic," "stereotach," and "chromatoscope" introduced into the language by the photographic industry.

But with trade names it's a different story. Many become generalized, their original connection with a single firm is forgotten, and they come to describe a certain product irrespective of who puts it out. Trade names like "vaseline," "cellophane," "kodak," "orangeade," "flit," "jello," "aspirin," "thermos," "percolator," "dictaphone" have permeated the popular language of America. Some of these popularizations have ludicrous aspects, as when an entire row of children went down in a spelling bee on the simple word "does," which they insisted on spelling *duz*.

A few firms make a brave attempt to save their trade names from this type of vulgarization, others don't seem to care. Among carefully guarded trade names are "Band-aid," "Teletype," and "Coke" (in the sense of "Coca-Cola").

That foreign languages should enter the composition of trade names and trade-marks is, of course, inevitable. This happens not only in the case of exotic perfumes and cosmetics, which receive equally exotic names like "Nuit d'Amour" and "Chen-yu," but also in the case of household products like "Bon Ami" (French for "good friend," though you would never guess it from the pronunciation of its radio boosters), "Sozodont" (Greek for "tooth saver"), "Pepsodent" (half Greek, half Latin, with the meaning of "tooth digestion"), and "Mavis" (Latin for "you prefer").

That our own products, on reaching foreign lands, should receive new names more in accordance with the speakers' mental processes is likewise to be expected. "Coca-Cola" is rendered in Chinese by characters which literally mean "Make Man Mouth Happy."

Extreme care has to be exercised by firms wishing to sell their products abroad under a given trade name, lest the latter resemble in sound or appearance some word that has unpleasant, ridiculous, or obscene connotations in one of the languages of the countries aimed at. The same care must be exercised in connection with any customs or be-

havior that may be included in the advertising. One result
is that many language and area experts find temporary or
permanent employment just checking on trade names and
advertising copy for foreign use. Another is that the suscep-
tibilities and good taste of foreign audiences often get far
more tender care than do those of American consumers. A
harmless example of idiomatic precision is the Pepsi-Cola
slogan, which in German-speaking countries is *Für Leute
von Heute* ("for the people of today"), in Spanish lands
La Bebida de Cordialidad ("the drink of friendship"), becoming where French is spoken *Entre Amis, C'est Pepsi*
("among friends, it's Pepsi"), while in Britain it is "Pepsi
peps you up."

Personal names of inventors and manufacturers lead to
the enrichment of the language not only as nouns but even
as verbs, as proved by "simonize." The personal name process is particularly observable in the case of automobiles.
Fords, Chryslers, Chevrolets, Buicks, Oldsmobiles are all
named after their original designers.

The use of certain words in trade-marks assumes imposing proportions. "Gold," for instance, has been found to appear in no less than 3,800 such trade-marks, "ideal" in
1,000, "star," "sun," and "imperial" in about 800 each, and
"champion" in 600. The recent addition "atomic" appears in
such widely separated products as brake fluid, toy guns, lead
pencils, washing machines, golf balls, and tomatoes. "Easy"
is to be found in the following spellings; *eazy, eezi, eazi, ezey,
e-z, eezy, ezy, easi, ese,* and even *eeez.* Certain suffixes
like *-ex* are very popular in trade-marks, perhaps because of
the "excellent" connotation. "Maltex," "Cutex," "Kleenex,"
"Windex" are only scattered examples. Another widespread
characteristic of trade-marks is the use of what might be
styled phonetic spelling: "Apl-jell," "Bif," "Gro-Master,"
"Handipak."

The use of trade-name abbreviations has led to what almost amounts to a new language. Not only do we have such
terms as C.O.D. and F.O.B., the full form of which no one
ever takes the trouble to use, but trade-mark short cuts like
G.M., M.G.M., Socony, Katy, Nabisco, Sunoco permeate the
language. Other languages are at least as bad in this matter
as is our own. Italy's FIAT stands for "Italian Automobile
Factory, Turin," and Russia's Amtorg for "American Trading Corporation." An abbreviation such as "Coke" for "Coca-
Cola" leads to the displacement of a legitimate word used
in a legitimate function. So does "gas" for "gasoline."

Of special interest among business abbreviations are the

American "Inc." and the British "Ltd." The American idea is that a firm is "incorporated" into a single legal entity, which has the advantage, among others, that none of its members may be individually sued. The British, on the other hand, achieve the same result but express it more forthrightly: the liability of any member of the firm or stockholder is "limited" at law. Long before it was used to denote a stock company, "corporation" had the meaning of a union or guild of artisans and traders constituting practical monopolies in their branches of employment. Such "corporations" existed in thirteenth-century France and lasted until the French Revolution.

In the Romance languages, stock in a concern is translated by the word that means "action" (*action, acción, azione,* etc.), since it authorizes the owner to act. "S.A." ("Society by Actions," share company) is the abbreviation corresponding to our "Inc." or "Ltd." Another Romance-language expression for "corporation" is "anonymous society"; here the "anonymous" means that none of the shareholders' names can be drawn into a lawsuit. Corresponding to English "Co." for "Company" are Spanish *Cía.* (*Compañía*) and French *Cie.* (*Compagnie*).

The creation of a medium of exchange, whether it be the round, flat stones of certain South Sea islands, the cacao bean of the Aztecs, the shell and bead wampum of the North American Indians, the gold and silver of our own civilization in its earlier stages, or the bank notes, checks, and deposit money of modern times, relies upon symbolism. Language is likewise a form of symbolism, and this creates an intimate link between the two. No greater linguistic symbolism could be exhibited than that which characterizes our monetary terms.

To the Germans, money is "gold" (*Geld* is a variant of *Gold*); to the French (*argent*) and the Scots (*siller*), it is "silver"; to the Italians and Spaniards (*danaro, dinero*), it is an old Roman coin, the *denarius.* Our own "money" goes back to the French *monnaie* ("coin"), which in turn goes back to the Latin *moneta,* which also gives us "mint." The temple of Juno Moneta was used as a mint for the coining of money in ancient Rome. *Moneta,* however, has the original meaning of "warner" (from *moneo,* "to warn," "to admonish"). Juno had been given this surname because the sacred geese of her temple once gave warning by their cackling to the Romans that the besieging Gauls were trying to scale the walls by surprise.

"Salary" really means "salt money" and goes back to the Roman custom of paying part of the soldiers' wage in salt, which in turn is an indication of the importance salt had in ancient and medieval life, when it was needed to preserve perishable foods. "Fee," on the other hand, is of Germanic origin and originally meant "sheep" or "cattle," reminding us that before metallic media of exchange commercial transactions took place in terms of cattle, as they still do today among the African natives.

The term *valuta*, frequently used by the European governments and banks in the sense of "foreign exchange," is of Italian origin and means "that which has value." *Valuta pregiata*, or "high-value currency," was used by the Italian Fascist regime to denote such currencies as the dollar and the pound sterling, which were worth while obtaining for international exchanges.

Fiat, from the Latin, means "let it be" or "let it be made." Fiat money is money created by the will of the government, without real backing.

The names of coins and currencies almost invariably tell a story of unfolding civilization. The Biblical "talent" of the New Testament (*talanton* in Greek) is both a coin and a measure. The corresponding Hebrew word of the Old Testament (*kikkār*) is a coin, but its earlier meaning is "loaf"; bread preceded money. Other Biblical coins are the "shekel," sometimes slangily used today, and the "mite" (about one-quarter of a cent but with a vastly greater purchasing power in those days).

The *drachma* and *mna* were among the popular coins of ancient Greece; the former survives in the druggist's "dram." The Romans had the *nummus*, from which we get "numismatics," the lore of coins, and the *solidus*, from which we derive "solid" and the Romance words that mean "hire" or "cent" (French *sou*, Italian *soldo*, Spanish *sueldo*). This word, with a French suffix, ultimately gives us "soldier," a man who fights for pay, a hireling or mercenary.

Among Anglo-Saxon coins we find the *sceatta* ("treasure") and the *styca* ("piece"), from the same Germanic root as German *Stück*. The "sequin" owes its name to the Italian *zecchino*, derived from *zecca* ("mint"), which in turn comes from the Arabic *sikkah* ("die" or "stamp"). The "bezant," a gold coin of the Middle Ages, owes its name to the city of Byzantium, where it was first coined. The "ducat" is named after the Venetian rulers of thirteenth-century Venice, the *Doges* or Dukes (strangely, "ducat" is used in present-day theatrical slang to indicate an admission ticket). The "florin" is named after Florence, the "city of the flower," whose emblem is a lily.

The "pistole" was a gold coin of France and Spain; its connection with "pistol" (the weapon, which was originally the name of a type of dagger) is doubtful; both may go back to the city of Pistoia in Italy. A "doubloon" was a Spanish double pistole, worth about sixteen dollars; early Spanish silver doubloons could be clipped into eight equal parts, each called a *real;* this gave rise to the terms "two bits," "four bits." Another name for doubloons, due to their divisibility into eight parts, was "pieces of eight."

A *grivna* was an ancient Russian silver coin, the equivalent of one pound of silver, in which the *Pravda Russkaya,* the medieval law of Russia, decreed that fines should be paid. Forty *grivni* would pay for a man's life or arm, three for a finger, but twelve for a moustache or beard. In this respect, the Russian custom differed little from that of the early Germanic tribes, with their *weregeld* and *launegeld,* compensation money to be paid after due process of law for taking a man's life.

Piaster and *dinar* are coins used at various times and in various places. The first is from Low Latin *plastra,* "thin sheet of metal," from which we also get the word "plaster"; the latter from *denarius,* which derives its name from *decem,* "ten," because it was worth ten *asses* (not donkeys, but a smaller Roman coin, whose singular form is *as*).

Among our own coins, the "nickel" is named after the metal of which a comparatively small amount enters its composition. The metal itself has a longer German name, *Kupfernickel* ("Old Nick's copper"), given by early miners in Saxony to the metal because it was difficult to smelt and work.

The "dime" is Jefferson's creation. Its name, likewise Jeffersonian, comes from Old French *disme,* which in turn comes from Latin *decima* and means "tenth." The term "uncurrent" is used by our monetary authorities to describe coins that are worn out or twisted.

The "dollar" got its name from the German *Thaler,* short for *Joachimsthaler,* coined from silver mined in Joachimsthal, Bohemia, in 1519. Different values were assigned to the dollar by the various states in 1783, when English pounds, shillings, and pence, French *livres tournois, Louis d'or,* and pistoles, Portuguese Johannes, or "joes," Dutch ducats, guilders, and florins, and even Swedish rix dollars were current. The most plausible account of the origin of the $ sign is that it represents the first and last letters of the Spanish *pesos,* written one over the other.

Spanish has two words for "dollar," beside the borrowed *dólar.* They are *peso* and *duro.* One refers to the weight of a silver dollar, since the original meaning of *peso* is "weight," the other to its consistency (*duro* means "hard," somewhat like the Latin *solidus* at an earlier date). An interesting reflection of western penetration in Japan is given by the two Japanese words for "dollar," *doru* and *dara,* of which the first reflects British, the second American, pronunciation.

Among the currencies of modern states, the French, Belgian, and Swiss *franc* gets its name from the Germanic invaders of ancient Gaul, the Franks. The Italian *lira* is from Latin *libra* ("pound"). Both the *lira* and the pound sterling were originally one pound of silver. Brazil's *cruzeiro* is named for the Southern Cross, Costa Rica's *colón* after Columbus, Panama's *balboa* after the discoverer of the Pacific, Guatemala's *quetzal* after the ancient Mayan god, Peru's *sol* after the sun, Paraguay's *guaraní* after the predominant Indian tribe of the country, the *sucre* of Ecuador after one of the leaders in South America's wars of independence from Spain.

The Russian *ruble* comes from the root of "to cut," and the Russian *kopek,* or, more precisely, *kopeika,* from a root that means "to save," "to heap," "to buy." The Japanese unit of currency is the *yen,* which literally means "circle"; this word was chosen because money is something that should go around in a circle, or circulate. The Japanese *sen,* on the other hand, was chosen because of similarity in sound to the English "cent." Both the *rupee* of India and the *rupiyah* of Indonesia come from a root meaning "silver," while the Indian *lakh* of rupees means a 100,000 unit.

The Haitian monetary unit is called *gourde.* It was inaugurated by Christophe, the Haitian dictator, who cornered all the gourds, which were used for a variety of purposes by all Haitians, and valued them at 20 sous apiece.

Monetary terms often get into the language when you least expect them. When you "don't give a rap" for something, you are referring to an Irish counterfeit halfpenny of the early eighteenth century, which was called "rap." When you "don't give a dam," you are not swearing, but referring to a small coin of India. Not "giving a continental" is, of course, a reference to one of our own early monetary units.

Rio de Janeiro's streetcars are known as *bondes,* which properly means "bonds." A British company founded the Rio streetcar system some sixty-five years ago and issued bonds to finance the enterprise, but the Brazilian public, not accustomed to bonds, thought that was the name for the streetcars and has been calling them "bonds" ever since.

As old as or older than monetary terms are the weights and measures which permit trade to be carried on systematically. "Shekel" and "talent" were originally not monetary units but units of weight.

Many measures owe their names to parts of the body. "Foot" is obvious. In many languages the equivalent of the "inch" is the "thumb." A "cubit" is an elbow, as is also an "ell." "Palm," "arm," and "hand" are used in many countries as units of measure. So is "digit," which is originally "finger." These words change their form according to the language in which they appear. They also do not by any means designate the same amount of length or width in the various tongues.

The names of ancient Egyptian and Akkadian units of length and weight have come down to us. Among them seems to be the "parasang," in which the Greek author of the *Anabasis* measures his distances. From ancient Persian names of units of length we cull *bāzu*, which is definitely an "arm." One ancient Greek unit of length is the *stadion*, from which we get our "stadium." The "league" as a measure of distance comes down from the ancient Gauls, who called it *leuca* or *leuga*. "Mile" comes from the Latin *milia passuum* ("thousands of paces"). The Latin *uncia* gives rise both to our unit of length, the "inch," and to our unit of weight, the "ounce." The original meaning of *uncia* is "one twelfth," of either a pound or a foot. "Carat," the name of the weight unit for jewels, comes from the name of the Mediterranean "carob" tree, the seeds of which are of very uniform weight and were used in ancient times as units of weight. India's poetic basic unit of weight is the *chawal*, described as the "specific gravity of an ideal grain of rice."

France, which today is proud of having conferred the metric system upon the world, had the most complicated assortment of weights and measures before the French Revolution. Many of them, like the *arpent* and the *aune*, went back to the ancient Gauls. While the entire terminology of the metric system (*meter, kilometer, liter, gram*, etc.) is taken from the Greek, it actually came into being only with the Revolution in 1793. It has been estimated that many customers and dollars are lost each year by American exporters because they insist on doing business in "bushels," "feet," and "gallons" instead of using the metric system, which is generally in use throughout the non-English-speaking world. Efforts have recently been made, even in official circles, to make the metric system universal, but the opposition is strong. The American automobile industry, for instance, points out that shifting their measurements from inches and feet to centimeters and meters would involve retooling amounting to a billion dollars.

Many foreign countries also have obsolete or obsolescent measures, some of which have linguistic interest. Prussia and Denmark once used the *morgen* (literally "morning") as a unit of area, while Germany, Austria, and Switzerland used the *Stunde* ("hour") as a unit of distance varying from two to four miles, an hour's walk. The Russian *pud,* which looks somewhat like our "pound," actually represents about 36 pounds. The "seidel" out of which we drink our beer is originally an Austrian liquid measure, something over half a pint.

Among linguistic curios in the field of measures we have the word "quota," which comes from the Latin *quot,* meaning "how many?" The smallest unit of time is the *sigma,* and the smallest unit of space the *micron;* they are symbolized, respectively, by the Greek letters *sigma* and *mu.* "Avoirdupois," the term used for measuring weight, comes from the French and literally means "to have some weight."

Certain time divisions (years, 28-day months, days and nights) are based on natural phenomena. Others (centuries, 30- and 31-day months, weeks, hours, minutes, seconds) are man-made, and may be supposed to have been originally connected with various forms of human activity, particularly of a ritualistic or commercial nature. There is no escaping the fact, however, that both natural and artificial divisions of time became so completely intertwined at a very early period that the distinction between the two departed from the speakers' consciousness before the dawn of civilized records. The Greek *hora,* from which our "hour" is derived, originally meant "season" and probably comes from the same root as our "year." The hours of antiquity were variable in length, with the period from sunup to sundown and from sundown to sunup both divided into twelve equal parts, with the result that the daylight hour was longer in summer and shorter in winter.

Among people of Mongolian stock, months, days, and years are named in accordance with a cycle of twelve animals: rat, bull, tiger, hare, dragon, serpent, horse, goat, ape, cock, dog, and pig. This gives you "the day of the bull in the month of the dragon in the year of the fire-tiger."

The Roman *kalendae* or "Calends" (from which "calendar" is derived) were the first of the month. The Greeks, who reckoned time differently, had no calends; therefore, "to put off until the Greek calends," means to put off indefinitely. The Roman ides (from the verb *iduare*, "to divide") came at the middle of the month, on the thirteenth or fifteenth day. The nones were the ninth day before the ides. In reckoning dates, the Romans would count forward to the next calends, ides, or nones. January twenty-eighth would be to them "the fifth day before the calends of February," since they counted in both the day on which they started and the day on which they finished.

The names of the months cast a good deal of light upon the history of civilization. January is named after Janus, the Roman two-faced god who protected doorways and faced in two directions at once. February takes its name from the feast of Februa or purification, which the Romans held in that month. March, May, and June are named after Mars, Maja, and Juno. July and August, however, desert mythology and take the names of historical characters, Julius Caesar and Augustus, the first Roman emperor. The last four months have simply a numerical significance ("seventh," "eighth," "ninth," "tenth"), but they reveal that the Romans at the very outset of their historical career began their year in March, not in January.

Russian has borrowed the names of the months from the west and has *Yanvar, Febral'*, etc., but Czech still uses the pagan Slavic names: *Leden* ("icy") for January, *Květen* ("blossom") for May, *Srpen* ("sickle") for August, *Listopad* ("leaf falling") for November, etc. A similar system was used by the ancient Germanic tribes. Eginhard, Charlemagne's historian, tells us that the great medieval monarch tried in vain to replace the Roman months with such Germanic forms as *Wintarmanoth* ("winter month") for January, *Hornung* ("horn shedding") for February, *Witumanoth* ("wood month") for September, *Windumemanoth* ("vintage month") for October, thus anticipating by several centuries the abortive attempt of the French Revolution to create descriptive names for the months such as *Brumaire, Nivôse, Germinal,* and *Messidor,* the months of fogs, snows, buds, and golden harvests; but in both instances mythology triumphed over meteorology.

The Greeks and Romans had no clear-cut week until relatively late, but the seven-day week had existed in the East since the days of the Egyptian Pharaohs. When the week was finally introduced to the Graeco-Roman world, it took the customary mythological turn, with the result that, for six of the seven days of the week, Latin and the languages descended from it have the following names: Day of the Moon, Day of Mars, Day of Mercury, Day of Jupiter, Day of Venus, Day of Saturn. The last day, however, is replaced in the modern languages by the Hebrew "Sabbath," which in its original Akkadian form (*shabattu*) meant "day of rest of the heart." "Sunday" in Latin was the "day of the sun," but in the Romance languages it has become the "day of the Lord," from religious Latin *dies dominica*. The Germanic languages have a similar arrangement, with Teutonic gods and goddesses (Wotan, Thor, Freia, etc.) replacing the Roman Olympus. They still retain the sun worship implied in "Sunday," *Sonntag*, etc., which the Romance languages have discarded. Portuguese, an exception among the Romance languages, uses "second day" for Monday, "third day" for Tuesday, etc. Our English system is obviously a combination of the Roman and the Teutonic week.

Economic relations depend on numerals to a greater extent perhaps than on any other factor. It therefore does not surprise linguists to find that numerals are among the oldest and best-defined words indicating connections among the languages of a given family. A word indicative of a given numeral (say "four," or "ten," or "hundred") can usually be traced without difficulty through all or most of the languages of a given group. It is as little subject to borrowing as are names of family relationship.

In the Indo-European tongues, a word like "seven" assumes the form *septem* in Latin, *sieben* in German, *sedm'* in Slavic, *seacht* in Irish, *hepta* in Greek, *haft* in Persian, *sat* in Hindustani. Among the far-flung languages of the Malayo-Polynesian group, "seven" is *fitu* in the Malagasy of Madagascar, *pitu* in Sumatra, *fitu* in Samoa, *whitu* among the Maori of New Zealand, *hitu* in Tahiti, *hiku* in Hawaii. Similarities of this sort leave little doubt about the affiliations of a language.

Occasionally, we get a surprise. Basque, spoken in the Pyrenees, is totally unrelated to its Indo-European Romance neighbors, French and Spanish. As we run through the Basque numerals up to five, we find words that prove this lack of kinship: *bat, bi, hirur, laur, bortz*. Then, at six, we get an unexpected *sei*, obviously borrowed from Spanish *seis*. Slavic Bulgarian has a Greek word, *khiliada*, for "thousand." Ural-Altaic Finnish and Romance Rumanian have both borrowed the Slavic form for "hundred." Why were these numerals singled out for borrowing? In the case of the hundreds and the thousands, it may be claimed that the concept of large numbers is a late one and therefore more likely to be borrowed from people enjoying a higher cultural level. But Basque *sei* must remain among the unsolved riddles of language.

In the language of the Andaman Islands, there are numerals only for one and two. Further numerals up to nine are indicated by raising the required number of fingers, ten by showing both hands with the word "all." No counting is possible beyond ten. Some Australian languages cannot count beyond three; they render "seven" by "pair-pair-pair-one." The Mundurucu Indians of Brazil cannot count beyond five. This would seem to indicate that the numerical concept was far from being, at the outset of civilization, the apparently universal thing it is today. Primitive groups develop their numerals with pain and labor. Many of the numerical concepts which to us are clear and fundamental are to them extremely indefinite. Under the circumstances, it is no wonder that relatively high numerals like a hundred and a thousand could have been borrowed at a time when much of the counting was done on finger tips, and even low numerals, like six, could be borrowed when numerical concepts were still vague.

A similar state of partial confusion is revealed by the form taken by such numerals as eighty in Celtic, French, and even the Ainu of Japanese Hokkaido, "four twenties." French carries it further by having "sixty-ten" for "seventy." Forms like "two-from-twenty," "one-from-twenty" in Latin, and even the "one-and-twenty," "two-and-twenty" which were normal in older English and are still normal in German, or the "four-on-ten" of Russian and Rumanian indicate that insofar as there are basic numerals, they are not likely to reach much beyond ten, the figure that can be counted on the fingers of both hands.

The graphic representation of numerals bears this out. In a system of written numerals like the Roman, the figures, I, II, III, and the earlier IIII stand for an equivalent number of fingers. The numeral V is originally the palm of the hand, with five fingers outstretched, but the three middle ones omitted for the purposes of rapid writing. X stands for two palms, base to base. Our Indo-European forebears, as can be seen, were not too far removed from the savages of the Andaman Islands.

Of interest in the present-day usage of numerals is the conveying of an indefinite concept by assigning to it a specific number value. Italian says "I am going to take two steps" for "I am going to take a little walk," or "There were four cats there" for "There were very few people." We speak of "forty winks" for a short nap. In the Middle East "forty" is a sign of indefinite value, as indicated by the "forty petals" of Greek for a rose, the "forty thieves" of Ali Baba, and the "forty days" and "forty years" of the Bible.

A modern outgrowth of our somewhat monstrous civilization is the development of such figures as "million," "trillion," "quadrillion," etc. They represent astronomical concepts which the human mind, at its present stage of development, is still partly incapable of grasping. A proposal to ban the word "billion" was once made in Congress, on the ground that it is confusing, since some people get "million" and "billion" mixed, that in England "billion" is a "million million," and that people do not get a clear conception of the enormous amount involved. The substitute recommended was "thousand million" for our usage.

The latest addition to our series of complex numerals is "Googol," the figure 1 followed by 100 ciphers. The name was imparted by the very young nephew of a famous mathematician who had run out of -illions and sought inspiration from the mouth of a babe. The process may not be too unlike those which have given us all our other numerals.

— Chapter Six —

LANGUAGE AND POLITICAL INSTITUTIONS

Whatever was required to be done, the Circumlocution Office was beforehand with all the public departments in the art of perceiving—how not to do it.
— Dickens, *Little Dorrit*

AS mankind began to emerge out of primeval darkness, the need for social order began to make itself felt. The individualistic anarchy that had previously prevailed could not be allowed to continue, under penalty of forfeiting progress.

Man's earliest political institutions were interwoven with the patriarchal family system on the one hand, with religion on the other. The *pater familias* was at the same time the officiating high priest of the religious cult and the headman of the clan. It was only by a series of long, often painful steps that the three functions became differentiated. As this process unfolded, political institutions and terminology began to develop.

The family, the clan, the tribe, and the nation differ only in degree. Within the earliest social grouping, fatherhood is implicit in rulership, as indicated by the term "patriarch," whose modern reflections appear in Czarist Russia's "Little Father," India's *bapuji,* applied to Gandhi, and our own "Father of His Country" and "Great White Father." The father, or the member of the community to whom others look up as a father, rules, directs, regulates. In all these words is contained the root of "kingship," one of the most widespread in the Indo-European tongues, which appears in the Sanskrit *rajah,* the Latin *rex,* the Celtic *-rix* of Vercingetorix and Dumnorix, the German *Reich*. Other early political roots are the Greek *archon* ("chief") of "oligarchy," "autarchy," and "patriarch," and *katos* ("power") of "theocracy," "plutocracy," "democracy."

The vocabulary of rulership is as varied as the institution itself. As political institutions change, there is a wholesale shift of words; yet through the kaleidoscopic display, we are somehow always reminded that *plus ça change, plus c'est la même chose.* The *rex* or "ruler" gives way to the republican *consul,* or "adviser," and he in turn to the *imperator* or "commander." Later come the Venetian *doge* ("leader") and the Florentine *podestà* ("power"); still later come the *Duce* and the *Führer* (also "leaders"). Their lieutenants are "patricians," *equites* ("horsemen," men on horseback), "barons" ("heroes," he-men), "counts" (*comites,* or "companions" of the ruler), "dukes" (from the same "leader" root as *Doge* and *Duce*). In Germanic countries they are "thanes," "earls," and "knights," *Fürsts* and *Herzogs,* in Slavic lands *atamans* and *boyars,* in Japan *shoguns* and *taikuns, daimyos* and *samurai,* in Arabic countries *al-quadis* and *al-wazirs.* Their least common denominator is force, which in modern times may be applied by a special political police, whose name may be Gestapo, GPU, Cheka, Urzad Bezpieczenstwa, Ovra, or any of dozens of others.

The true art of politics, based upon the consent of the governed rather than the will of rulers, properly begins, as the word indicates, with the Greek *polis* (or "city-state"). One characteristic of true political institutions as distinguished from earlier government by brute force or traditional authority is the existence of some sort of assemblage in some measure representative of the people and their currents of thought. It is here, perhaps, that mankind has exercised its politico-linguistic genius to the best advantage. The Roman *senatus* was in origin an assemblage of older and more experienced men, as the name implies (the root is *senex,* "old man"). The Greek *gerousia* is precisely the same thing. "Diet" as the name of a legislative assembly comes from the Greek *diaita* ("manner of living"), seemingly crossed with Latin *dies* ("day"). The German *Reichstag* and the Danish *riksdag* also bring in the idea of "day," since they both mean "nation's day." Other Scandinavian assemblies are called *thing,* which is the same word as the English "thing," whose original meaning was "cause" or "judicial assembly." The Russian legislative assembly under the Czars was called the *Duma,* which is the Russian word for "thought" and was possibly meant to imply that legislators should use their heads. *Gikai* is the name of the Japanese Diet, *Cortes* that of the Spanish parliament, while Israel has its

Knesset, Iran its *Majlis,* Ireland its *Oireachtas* (of which the *Dail Eireann* is the lower chamber), and Finland's uni-cameral body is *Eduskunta.* Smaller bodies abound and are a tribute to man's desire to rule himself. India has village parliaments styled *Gaon Sabha,* "Assembly of Adults," which function much like our New England town meetings and formulate policies for the *Gayon Panchayat,* or "Village Re-public." American Samoa had, until recently, a similar in-stitution called *Fono,* with the added feature of a *House of Alii* ("elders," or "lords"), functioning as a senate. Even South Africa has its native *Bungas,* semiofficial deliberative bodies for the African population, with the right to pass on its petitions to the regular South African parliament.

The real essence of democratic politics is the tolerated presence of an opposition, the existence of parties advocating different principles or methods of government. It was in the Greek city-states, Republican Rome, and the free cities of medieval Europe that political activities and the language of politics, in the modern sense of the word, began. Here also is where the interaction of language and politics is most fully displayed, for while politics contributes to language a complete terminology of its field, language reacts by becom-ing the standard-bearer and slogan spreader of political ideals. Such words as "president," "legislature," "session," "motion," "amendment" have their history (most of them originated with the French Revolution), but are relatively colorless. But expressions like "obscurantist," *Lebensraum,* "Bolshevik," "gerrymander," "New Deal," "Dixiecrat," "fili-buster," "white supremacy," "people's democracy" are replete with semantic and emotional force. Wise political leaders know not only how to coin them but also how to exploit them. Language has hidden powers to stimulate political ac-tion, as proved by such slogans as "Workers of the world, unite! You have nothing to lose but your chains!" or Musso-lini's *"A chi l'Italia? A noi!"* ("To whom does Italy belong? To us!") or Hitler's *"Ein Reich, ein Volk, ein Führer!"* ("One nation, one people, one leader!") which was perhaps plagiarized from the motto of the French Vendean counter-revolutionists of the late eighteenth century, *"Une foi, une loi, un roi!"* ("One faith, one law, one king!").

Of all historical movements, the French Revolution was probably the most productive in political catchwords, but the Russian revolutionary leaders were steeped in the lore of the earlier upheaval, and they used its terminology abundantly. "Counterrevolution," "reaction," "speculation," "ship of state," "deviation" are terms common to both revolutions. The excessive use of certain prefixes, such as *ultra-*, *anti-*, *archi-*, *de-* and *ex-*, was characteristic of both French and Russian revolutionary writers. The Russians go so far as to speak of the "ex-letters of the alphabet," those letters which were discarded by the Soviet reform of Russian spelling.

It frequently happens that disparaging political terms backfire and come to be adopted and sloganized by their intended butts. When Louis XIV was still a minor, the parliamentary faction opposed to Cardinal Mazarin's regency was accused by one of the Cardinal's followers of behaving like little boys with slings, who fling their stones at passersby but run when a police officer appears. The simile was picked up by its victims and hurled back into the teeth of the Mazarin faction in the form of the Frondist movement (*fronde* is the French word for "sling"). A few decades later, the term *sans-culottes* ("breechless") was derisively coined by the French nobility to describe the revolutionary rabble, who wore long pants instead of the tight breeches characteristic of the aristocrats; the term met with an enthusiastic reception by its recipients and was duly sloganized. So was *descamisados* ("shirtless ones") in certain Spanish-speaking countries (Evita Perón used to address her husband's followers as "My shirtless ones"). In the course of our own political history, the term "locofoco," previously used of a self-igniting match, was disparagingly applied to the Equal Rights party of 1835, which almost rode to power on it. Shortly before the Second World War, *Camelots du roi* ("king's street hawkers") was scornfully applied to the French royalists and gratefully accepted by them.

Many party names are self-devised or self-inflicted. Ireland's opposition party is the *Clann an Poblachta,* vying with the *Fianna Fail* ("soldiers of Ireland") for the political control of Erin. Israel has its *Mapai* opposition. France has developed a *Force Ouvrière,* or *Troisième Force,* composed of union workers who oppose Communist domination of labor politics. Brazil, under Vargas, had a party picturesquely designated as *Queremistas* or "we-want-ists," the have-nots who opposed the haves, the *Granfinos* or landed aristocrats. Even in Franco Spain the old Carlists, a party of the extreme traditional right, has re-formed under the new name of *Falcondistas,* followers of Manuel Fal Conde, to oppose the Falangists.

In addition to deliberate semantic reversals, the language of politics has others which are at least in part accidental. Our original Republican Party turned into a Democratic Party in 1835, then found itself opposed in 1854 by a new

Republican Party which had borrowed its former name. Other American parties now forgotten include the Particularists, or States Righters, of 1784, the Hunkers, Barn Burners, Dough Faces, Nullifiers, and Know Nothings. "Communism," "Socialism," and "Nihilism" were all terms that arose during the French Revolution, but with other meanings. A Communist was at first defined as "a partisan of the sharing of the public wealth," while the Socialists were described as the "allies of the Royalists"; as for a Nihilist, he was "a profiteer who believes in nothing" or a "man who had been despoiled by the *Sans-culottes* and has nothing."

The use of other languages than the national one in partisan politics is a phenomenon of rare occurrence save in countries like our own, where the foreign element is numerous. A political adage holds that a successful New York mayor must, among other things, be able to say "hello" in eight languages. La Guardia could do even better, making acceptable speeches in French, Spanish, Yiddish, Italian, and Serbo-Croatian, while O'Dwyer was a fluent speaker of Spanish, which he learned in his younger days when he was studying for the priesthood in Salamanca. In a Connecticut campaign, one candidate of Italian ancestry who could speak no Italian found himself hard pressed by his rival, the scion of an old Massachusetts Bay family, who made campaign speeches to the Italian-born voters in flawless and fluent Italian.

The law, that body of conventions whereby men are governed or govern themselves, would at first glance seem to be an outgrowth of present-day political activity; actually, it antedates modern politics by many centuries. The language of the law is frequently referred to (often in disparaging fashion), but the interplay of law and language is seldom noticed.

The oldest legal code, antedating that of Hammurabi by at least one and a half centuries, was brought up to light not long ago in Iraq. Its language is Sumerian, its script cuneiform. The king who promulgated it was Lipit-Ishtar, and its provisions do not differ too widely from those of our present-day legal codes. The language of the law vies in antiquity with that of religion, with which it is often inextricably intermingled.

It is, of course, generally known that, while our legal institutions go back to the days of the Anglo-Saxons, our legal terminology is almost evenly divided between Latin and Norman-French. Expressions beginning with *sub, per,* and *pro* (*sub judice, subpoena, per capita, per se, pro forma, pro tempore*), our writs of *certiorari, mandamus, habeas corpus,* and *venire* (the last with its hybrid derivative *veniremen,* men who are summoned to "come" and serve as jurors), expressions like *sine die, bona fide, prima facie, nolo contendere,* even words that have become quite popular, like *alias* and *alibi,* are pure Latin.

The Norman-French portion of our legal language includes such terms as change of "venue," court of "oyer" and "terminer," "escheat" and "escrow," "grand" and "petty jury," "mayhem" (from which the more popular "maim" is derived). "Digamy" and "bigamy" are among the few Greek terms used at law (the first means remarriage after the death of a spouse or a legal divorce).

The action of the law upon language is well illustrated by the fortunes of the Latin suffix *-aticum,* which under the Frankish Merovingian kings was especially applied to describe forms of taxation (*pontaticum,* a bridge toll; *portaticum,* a harbor or transportation tax; even *rotaticum,* a tax on the wheels of vehicles). This legal suffix in course of time became the French *-age* and, becoming applied to various activities only remotely or not at all connected with legal taxes, appears today in such words as "message," "voyage," "frontage," "acreage," "coinage," "carnage," "sabotage," and "espionage." The Isle of Sark, being very traditional, still conserves a form of taxation called "poulage," consisting of a chicken for every house chimney, payable by the householder to the island's *Seigneur* or *Dame.*

The legal documents of the Merovingian period also show a misuse of certain Latin verb tenses which consist of shifting the tense backward in time: "Let this have been done" for "Let this be done"; "It seemed proper to us to have decreed" instead of "to decree." That this usage has its roots in the well-known legalistic desire to mark something as completed and definitely settled seems beyond doubt.

It is no doubt a desire for precision on the part of those who deal with the law that has led to the creation of the linguistic form variously known as "Washington Choctaw," "officialese," and "Gobbledigook." The first term is inexact, because the British, too, are afflicted with a disease which they describe as "the King's Gobbledigook." The motivating principle behind Gobbledigook is "never say in one short word what can be said in three long ones." Samples of this strange lingo are "thirty-six calendar months" for "three years," "in short supply" for "scarce," "operation of considerable magnitude" for "big job," "implement" for "use," "aperture" for "hole." Random samples of specialized Gobbledigook include the title of a Senate-House Economic Subcommittee report, "Causes underlying the continuing long-term experience of low income encountered by a significant portion of the population," or what a layman might call "Causes of poverty"; the USIA's use of "illustrated continuity" for comic book; the Pentagon's pronouncement that "it is not contemplated that the enforcement procedures would apply retroactively to anyone not now participating"; the Air Force Secretary's "threshold of negotiation," further described as "stop the war at the lowest point of intensity on favorable terms" (in layman's language, "quit while you're ahead").

That Gobbledigook is not a disease confined to government circles is shown by a reviewer's protest about the use in social science popularizations of such terms as "normative," "determinance," "sympathetic issue-orientation," "confident-competent syndrome," and by an educational report on the "Effects on non-target classmates of the deviant student's power and response to a teacher-exerted technique," meaning "How the punishment of an errant student affects the rest of the class."

Side by side with the language of national politics, which appears in separate national editions, there is also what may be described as the universal tongue of international politics, or diplomacy. As so frequently happens in the case of political words, the respectable term "diplomacy" itself has a derogatory origin, having been created out of an earlier French *diplôme*, which means an ancient document of an official nature, something rather musty.

Like our legal language, the tongue of diplomacy is almost evenly divided between Latin and French. The former language gives us *casus belli* (or *foederis*), *ante* and *post bellum, status quo* (which a United Nations wag humorously defined as "the mess we're in"), *modus vivendi, persona grata* or *non grata, de facto* and *de jure*, and at least one expression that has penetrated the general language of the community, "ultimatum." French is responsible for *entente cordiale, acte authentique, aide mémoire, note verbale, fait accompli, raison d'état, coup d'état* (or *de main*), and *démarche*, the last term being variously defined as "step," "offer," "suggestion," "proposal," "protest," "remonstrance," "request," "overture," "warning," or "threat."

The use of languages in international dealings is intimately connected with political history and is, to a large degree, a reflection of that history. Whereas down to the end of the sixteenth century international business was generally carried on in Latin, from the seventeenth century on French became the tongue of diplomacy *par excellence*. Lovers of the French language ascribe this fact to the clarity and precision of the tongue (but see *démarche*, above); others to the military and political predominance that France gained in continental Europe during the course of two centuries. It is an interesting fact that while French was the only language used at the Congress of Vienna in 1815, both French and English were used at the Versailles Conference after the First World War, and Spanish, Russian, and Chinese were added to the list for UN proceedings. But despite the presence of five official languages, directional signs at UN headquarters appear only in English and French. Perhaps the chief merit of UN's multilingualism is to point out the need for a single international medium of linguistic exchange.

National and international politics and the changing fortunes of languages and the nations that speak them are often reflected in postage stamps. The political history of Spain in recent years, for instance, is condensed in that country's postage: Spanish stamps of the monarchy used to bear the inscription *España*; under the Republic, they bore the title *República Española*; under Franco, they were for a time labeled *Estado Español*, to indicate the overweening concept of the totalitarian state. They have now gone back to the original *España*.

The language of stamps may serve the purpose of arousing patriotism, like the inscription *Jai Hind*, "Long live India," on some Indian stamps, or the Hungarian *Talpra, Magyar, hi a haza*, "On your feet, Hungarian, the fatherland is calling." It may serve the purpose of commemoration, like Denmark's *Verdens Postforeningen* and Turkey's *Evrensel Posta Birligi*, to recall the founding of the Universal Postal Union. It may serve the purpose of confusion, like the Hindi *sarkari* ("official"), superimposed on stamps of various Indian states, which led collectors to think the states had merged. It may even serve the purpose of poetry, like Uruguay's beautiful *Un gran amor es el alma misma de quien ama*, "A great love is the very soul of the one who loves."

— Chapter Seven —

LANGUAGE AND SUPERSTITION

The superstition in which we were brought up never loses its power over us, even after we understand it.
—Lessing

Supernatural is the laziest word in the vocabulary of ignorance. Nothing is supernatural, because nothing can transcend the laws of nature.
—Louis K. Anspacher

THE interaction of superstition and language begins in the dawn of prehistory, with the elemental beliefs and taboos of primitive peoples. Anthropologists have remarked upon the striking similarity, among many and scattered races, of the "taboo" idea, the mixture of prohibition, sacredness, danger, and pollution attendant upon the performance of certain acts and the utterance of certain words. This combination is to be noted in such widely diverging families as the Polynesian and Melanesian with their *tabu* and *tambu,* the Javanese with their *pantang,* the Dakota Indians of North America with their *wakan,* the Greeks and Romans with their *hagos* and *sacer.*

In the realm of language, the ritualistic or superstitious taboo involves words that may not be spoken, ideas that may not be expressed save by circumlocution. This leads in turn to the coining of new words and the creation of new ideas, sometimes to a more or less complete change in language.

In many South Sea islands the names of the dead may not be mentioned, and words they have been in the habit of using also become *tabu.* This means word replacement and, eventually, a new vocabulary. In other islands, the chief has the power to change words and to reserve certain words for his own exclusive use.

Among the Zulus of South Africa a wife may not use the words appearing in the names of her in-laws. The result is a series of circumlocutions to replace such words as "bull," "cow," "lion," which often appear in personal names. Ultimately the women of the village find themselves using a language largely consisting of such replacements, while the men, to whom no name is taboo, continue using the original terms. A similar situation appears among the Caribs of South America: the men, when on the warpath, use words which are unknown to the women. In Sierra Leone, on the West African Coast, there existed until recently a numerous and powerful secret society of men, the *Purrah*, whose members had developed, along with a ritual, a secret tongue quite unknown to the women.

In ancient Rome, the *flamen dialis* (high priest of Jupiter) was hedged in with linguistic restrictions: he could not touch or name, under penalty of dire consequences to the entire people, such things as a goat, a dog, raw meat, beans, or ivy.

The Japanese avoid the use of the verb *kiru* ("to cut") at a party, lest it turn into a brawl, and of the verb *kaeru* ("to return") at a wedding, lest it lead to the "return" of the bride (divorce). They also avoid the word for "four" (*shi*) because another word similarly pronounced means "death." Since Japanese has two sets of numerals, it is easy enough to replace *shi* with *yottsu*.

Spaniards avoid the use of the word *culebra* (*"serpent"*) because of a superstition that if they mention it they will see it appear. Old Italian *colubro* has disappeared from use for the same reason. Naturally enough, other words for "snake" have crept in.

Among the Chinese, it is taboo for a son to use in writing the second character of his father's given name, or for a subject to use the second character of his sovereign's name.

In many ancient religions, knowledge of a man's true name was supposed to give power over that person. Some African tribes believe they can injure an enemy by beating a tree over which his name has been uttered.

The Hebrew prohibition of using the name of Jehovah, or Jahweh, led to its replacement by *Adonai* and *Elohim*. In medieval Hebrew Cabalistic lore, a *ba'al šém* ("master of the name") was one who knew the secret vowels of the word "Jehovah," which knowledge gave him enormous magical powers. The belief in this case was that the ability to call upon a supernatural being by his true name gave power over that being. Among the ancient Egyptians, the name of a person was believed to be endowed with separate existence.

A change of names is supposed to be attended by a change of personality, and this lies at the root of the new names given those who enter certain monastic orders as well as Popes on their accession. The Egyptian Pharaohs likewise assumed a "Horus name" at their coronation.

Variations of the name theme appear in the attempt to appease the supernatural being by the substitution of similar-sounding words ("egad" for "by God"; "zounds" for "by His wounds"; *parbleu* for *par Dieu*); in the avoidance by the Euphrates Arabs of all words beginning with the first letter of Satan's name; in the use of a euphemistic name for beings that can do harm. The Greeks called the Furies *Eumenides* ("kindly"). The "good people" (or "good folk") and "little people" of the Celts are another example, and they are accompanied by the English "brownies" and the Spanish *estantigua*, or "ancient host." It is even supposed that our English "bear" (originally "bruin," "the brown one") came into being to replace a more offensive word that appears in Latin, *ursus* ("the harmer," "the bruiser"). Such circumlocutions as "Old Nick," "Old Harry," "Auld Clootie," and proverbs like: "Speak of the devil and you'll see him appear" bear witness to the power believed to lie in names.

Italian developed a remarkable straddle word in *diamine*, used approximately like English "heck," which is itself a modification of "hell." *Diamine* is a cross between *diavolo* ("devil") and *domine* ("Lord"), calling upon both and neither at the same time.

Taboos are not limited to names alone. Numbers are also affected. The Koreans try to avoid their word for "four," *sa*, because it also means "death"; also "fourteen," *ship-sa*, or "ten deaths." The Italians, who go by lottery numbers from one to ninety, each of which has a special symbolism that serves well when it comes to playing your dreams on the state lottery, avoid not only thirteen ("the devil") but also seven and seventeen ("misfortune" or "mishap"). Our own feeling about thirteen, especially when joined with Friday, has added another to the long list of phobias; *treiskaidekaphobia*, or "fear of the number thirteen" (some of the other phobias are the well-known *claustro-, acro-,* and *agora-*, fear of being closed in, of heights, of open spaces, respectively; less known are *ailurophobia*, "fear of cats," *iatrophobia*, "fear of doctors," *nucleomitotophobia*, "fear of atomic bombs," *mageiricophobia*, "fear of having to cook," and, recalling FDR, *phobophobia*, "fear of fear itself").

Our own linguistic taboos, created by prudishness, which is a form of social superstition, consist of the "four-letter words," to which others are occasionally added, according to the status of the speaker. "Hell," and "damn" have been officially banned from TV. We frankly do not know about "bitch" (in use since Middle English as applied to a woman), its modern American derivative "bitchy" (widely used in respectable feminine circles), or that other derivative, "S.O.B.," for which the archaic "whoreson" is suggested as an elegant replacement. The campaign against "bad" words is world-wide, as evidenced by the provision against obscene language in Article 74 of the U.S.S.R. legislative code, which links the use of such language to "hooliganism" and makes it liable to punishment.

It is a curious fact that there are commonly used words of obscene origin which no one worries about (among them are "orchid," "dainty," "pencil," perhaps also "smock" and "hymn") and for which no euphemism has ever been sought.

The field of modern euphemisms is, of course, immense. A few stray samples of it are the use of "mortician" for "undertaker," "passing away" for "death," "lubritorium" for "greasing station," "Salisbury steak" for "hamburger," "colored person" for "Negro," "stomach" for "belly."

Some of our own euphemisms in the labor and employment field are eye openers. Among those reported are "guidance workers" (for Milwaukee "bill collectors"); "clothing refreshers" (for San Francisco "washwomen"); "sanitarians" (for "bus boys"); "utensil maintenance men" (for "dishwashers"); "animal control wardens" (for "dog-catchers").

The essential characteristic of euphemisms, whether arising from superstition or from other social reasons, is that in due course of time they lose their euphemistic character, assume the full, stark significance and connotations of the original word they have displaced, become taboo, and ultimately have to be replaced by new euphemisms.

"Pregnant," replaced at one time by "in an interesting condition" (this idiom still appears in Italian, *in istato interessante*), went on to "expectant" or "anticipating"; "heir-conditioned" and "lady in waiting" are the most recent replacements. Nether garments have gone through a variety of phases: "unmentionables," "inexpressibles," "unspeakables," "sit-upons," "unutterables." Legs have been known as "benders" and "limbs." Another portion of the anatomy has gone through "bottom," "fanny," and *derrière*. A prostitute, once known as a "doxy," "lie-by," "lie-beside," went on to "harlot" (originally used for men jesters, then for dancing girls and actresses), then, through dozens of other transformations, to the demure "streetwalker."

The lengths to which languages will go to create euphemisms for "toilet" are amusing. We have our "rest room," "men's" or "ladies' room," "comfort station." The British prefer "powder room," "convenience," "cloakroom" (which can fool you if you are looking for what we call the checkroom), and even "loo," which seems to stem from "Waterloo." In South Africa they call it "P.K.," an abbreviation for the Kaffir *picanin kyah,* "little house." German has *Abort* ("away place"); French uses an English abbreviation, W.C.; Spanish and Italian use words which mean "retreat"; Russian *ubornaya* means "adornment place," as our own "toilet" once did. "Toilet" is itself a euphemism, however, the original meaning of the word being "little cloth."

The Portuguese never refer to cancer by its real name but replace it with a euphemism, "the little beast, God forbid" (*o bicho, salvo seja*). The name of the devil, which our own not too remote ancestors replaced with "deuce" and "dickens," is in Portuguese replaced by a word similar in sound to *diabo: nabo,* which actually means "turnip."

The French, ever linguistically creative, have a term *chevaliers d'industrie,* "knights of industry," for "confidence men." A "strip-teaser" is to them *effeuilleuse,* "one who takes off the leaves," like a tree in the fall. The Italians describe a "taxpayer" as a *contribuente,* or "contributor," and our "capacity to pay" is described as *capacità contributiva,* or "contributing capacity" (it is not recorded whether this makes the Italians feel better than we do when income tax time rolls around).

In addition to the taboos and euphemisms, both of which are essentially founded on superstition, ignorance, prudishness, and other ancestral traits which the human race, even in its most civilized segments, has far from given up, languages abound in words whose origin or development may be traced back to superstition.

How widespread in ancient times was the belief that death or injury could be caused simply by looking at a person is indicated by the fact that in Italian "evil eye" contracted into a single word, *malocchio.* The disease referred to in medieval English as "the King's evil" was so called because of the belief that only a king's touch could cure it. Even so harmless a plant name as "witch hazel" is based on the belief that the shrub's twigs could be used as divining rods.

In the case of some words, the connection with an original superstitious belief has become so obscured that only etymologists are aware of it: "jovial," "saturnine," "mercurial," "martial," for instance, are in origin superstition words, based on the belief that people showing those qualities were under the influence of Jupiter, Saturn, Mercury, or Mars.

Words whose superstitious origin is easily traced abound in all languages, and English has borrowed most of them. *Poltergeist* and *Walpurgisnacht* come to us from the German. The former, literally a "racketing spirit," is a ghost that produces active physical manifestations, even to the point of killing animals or human beings. The latter is the feast of St. Walpurgis, a female saint said to have converted the Saxons to Christianity; on this feast, the German superstition has it that the witches hold a spectacular Sabbath.

A "ghoul" (from the Arabic) is a demon who robs graves and feeds on corpses. Also from the Arabic comes *jinni,* a supernatural being subject to magic control. The word has gotten crossed with Latin *genius* which had, among other meanings, that of "attendant spirit," and the result of the crossing is "genie."

A "vampire" (from the Hungarian, but said to have originated in Slavic) is the reanimated body of a dead person that comes back to suck the blood of the living. The vampire legend flourishes in the Balkans.

The "werewolf" is a man capable of assuming the form of a wolf. The *were* comes from an Anglo-Saxon word akin to Latin *vir* ("man"). The quality of being a werewolf, however, takes its name from the Greek, with the order reversed: "lycanthropy" (*lykos,* "wolf"; *anthropos,* "man"). Italian and French take the "man" part of their expressions for "werewolf" from Germanic, indicating that the legend probably originated in the northern countries. French has *loup-garou,* in which *garou* comes from the same source as our *were,* while Italian has *lupo mannaro,* in which the *mannaro* seems to be from the German *Mann* or *Männer.*

In Celtic lore, a "banshee" is a supernatural visitor who gives warning to a family of an approaching death by means of a loud wail. The name comes from the Gaelic *bean* ("woman") and *sith* ("fairy"). The "leprechaun," defined as a pigmy sprite that carries money and guards treasures, has a name that comes from the Old Irish *luchorpan* ("small body").

"Incubus" and "succubus" (from the Latin) are demons

supposed to lie upon or beneath persons in their sleep. "Nightmare" has the same general idea.

The "Abominable Snow Man" of Tibet is only one of a series. In the Sudan, there is the legend of a huge man-shaped creature covered with red hair and lacking in joints, which is known as a *waab*. Further south in Africa there is an *agogwe*, four feet tall, walking upright, and covered with russet fur.

The term "voodoo" is said to come from Vaudois, or Waldensian, in its medieval meaning of "heretic." The Waldensians in the Middle Ages were unjustly accused of practicing black magic.

One or two superstitious beliefs in connection with language in general reveal the intimate tie between the two. The North American Indians attached a sacred value to the spoken word; a Navajo account of creation begins: "Therefore I must tell the truth. I hold my word tight to my breast." The Chinese attach a similar superstitious value to the written word, to such an extent that it is a fairly common practice in China for a written prescription to be stewed in a pot along with the ingredients it prescribes.

— Chapter Eight —

LANGUAGE AND INTOLERANCE

Without reprieve, adjudged to death
For want of well pronouncing shibboleth.

—Milton

We have room but for one Language here and that is
the English language, for we intend to see that the cru-
cible turns our people out as Americans of American
nationality and not as dwellers in a polyglot boarding-
house.

—Theodore Roosevelt

HUMAN institutions are as good or as bad as the people who create and use them. Language, intrinsically useful, may also serve to create and foster intolerance and hatred and to diffuse these wretched human qualities by acting as their vehicle. In the latter capacity, the effectiveness of language is more subtle and destructive than in the former, because the intolerance that language serves may be social, religious, racial, and national as well as purely linguistic.

Linguistic intolerance is manifested in the aversion to other languages than one's own. As a student of linguistic sociology puts it, "To the naïve monoglot, objects and ideas are identical with and inseparable from the particular words used to describe them in the one language he knows; hence he is inclined to consider speakers of other languages as something less than human, or at least foreign and hostile to the world of his own experience."

Examples of this unhappy state of mind could be multiplied *ad infinitum.* Beginning with the *barbaroi* (or "babblers") of the ancient Greeks, a term that included all those who spoke anything but the Greek tongue, we encounter such far-flung instances as the *Nemets* ("unspeaking," "mute,"

273

"dumb") conferred by the Slavs upon their German neighbors, the appellations "southern barbarians" and "miserable ones" bestowed by the Chinese upon the Miao and Moso tribes of south China, the name "wild men" given by the Celebes islanders to the Ninchassa whose language they cannot understand. "Circassian" is claimed to be from a Tatar word, *chertkess,* whose original meaning is "robber."

Conversely, many races bestow upon themselves the name of "persons" or "speakers." The Chanktu of Siberia, the Lolos or Ne-su of China, the Tule Indians of Panama, even the Germans, whose *Deutsch* comes from an earlier *tiutisk* ("pertaining to the people"), bear national names which in their own respective languages mean "men," "we men," "persons," "people," while Slovaks and Slovenes have names proudly derived from *slovo* ("word"), which mark them as "speakers," in contradistinction to the Germans, who to them are "mute."

Pride in language is probably the most distinctive mark of national intolerance. A Russian child's history of the late war says in part: "Russians will not tolerate that Russian 'bread' be called *Brot.* We breathe freely if we hear our own language. We write, we think in Russian." How all this is reconciled with the workers' international is a mystery. Perhaps it is merely added proof of something long known, that class hatred and national intolerance can perfectly well live side by side and intermingle, though in theory they should be mutually exclusive.

We are far from being sinless in the matter of linguistic nationalism, which with us ranges all the way from exalted English-speaking Unions to the lowly, "Aw, let 'em speak English!" of G.I.s confronted with the reality of foreign languages. But we need not feel too ashamed. There is probably no national group on earth that does not deem its language the best, not to say the only possible form of human expression. The French generally consider *la belle langue française* as the only one worthy of serious study. Cultured Italians think their language is the only one fit for singing. The Spanish-speaking lands, which relinquished their political unity long ago, are still bound together by a shadowy something of a linguistic nature, very farfetchedly epitomized by what to us is Columbus Day and to them *El Día de la Raza* ("the day of the race"). Actually, Spanish speakers are of all races under the sun, but they forget racial background in linguistic unity and have devised the term *Hispano* which means not "Spanish" (*español*) but pertaining to the great Spanish-speaking group.

The manifestations of linguistic nationalism are almost too

numerous to catalogue. There are the linguistic purity movements, usually initiated by the linguistically uninitiated, but which all too frequently bear linguistic fruit. Iran wants to "purify" the Persian language of Turkish and Arabic words, while Turkey wants to throw out Persian words. Even the Russians have been trying to replace *éclair* and *parfait* with native words, while the Norwegians, who once used Danish as their literary language, not content with having created what they call Neo-Norwegian, are even toying with the idea of changing their country's name from Norge to Noreg in order to remove themselves farther from Danish influence.

Then we have the drive on behalf of the national tongue, conducted against local dialects on the one hand and minority languages on the other. Mussolini, in one of his campaigns for national unity, abolished all Italian regional societies, thinking he could thus get the Italians to relinquish their dialects and use the national language instead. The Republican Spanish government permitted the teaching of Catalan and Basque in the schools of those regions, but the Franco government does not. France, which is usually ultra-liberal in most matters, nevertheless forbids the teaching of Breton in the schools of Brittany; even letters addressed in Breton are returned to the sender by the French postal authorities with the inscription: *"Adresse en breton interdite"* ("Address in Breton forbidden"). One of the most intolerant linguistic insults on record is the admonition "Speak white!" occasionally used by Canadian English speakers to their French-speaking fellow nationals.

This attitude is traditional and goes back to the wave of nationalism that was a by-product of the French Revolution. In 1790, the first decrees of the French Revolutionary government were translated into the minority languages of France (Provençal, Breton, Basque, Catalan, German, Italian, etc.) and the use of these languages was encouraged, but later this policy was reversed with the statement: "French will become the universal language, since it is the language of liberty. Meanwhile, let it become the language of all Frenchmen."

At a much earlier date, the rising spirit of nationalism born of the Hundred Years' War is given as a possible reason for the shift from French to English in the official proceedings of the English Parliament. In 1345 the chronicles of London were still kept in Norman-French, but in 1363 Parliament was opened in English, and the same Parliament immediately proceeded to forbid the use of French in the courts.

The story of linguistic nationalism in Russia is an absorbing one. Under the Czars, the minority languages (Polish, Lettish, Lithuanian, Finnish, etc.) were mercilessly repressed. Under the Soviets, the opposite has taken place. Stalin repeatedly urged the encouragement and use of minority languages which extend beyond the Soviet borders, for propaganda purposes in the adjoining countries, following in this matter the precedent of French revolutionary leaders who urged the encouragement of German in Alsace so that the Germans beyond the border could be reached and won over. But wherever the use of such languages threatens to lead to a resurgence of nationalism or irredentism, the offending language is straightway chastised. At the same time that the learning of English is pushed in the Soviet Union itself, the European satellites are urged to make Russian the primary foreign language in their educational systems.

Also, there is the pride in the national language *vis-à-vis* other national tongues. This has led Mexico to forbid all advertising and store signs in foreign tongues, especially English. It leads Brazilian businessmen occasionally to tear up letters innocently addressed to them in Spanish by American correspondents who think "Latin America" and "Spanish America" are synonymous. It even leads the Gaelic Youth Movement of Scotland to forbid the use of English at its summer camps.

But since the language is the paramount symbol of nationality, it is not surprising that an official prohibition to use a language has often been the prime cause of its survival. Irish Gaelic, Welsh, Catalan, Basque, Breton, Lithuanian, possibly even Polish might have succumbed to the pressure of the dominant language of their respective areas had not linguistic persecution bolstered them up. In India, Pakistan, and Ceylon, attempts to make Hindi, Urdu, and Singhalese, respectively, the sole national language have run into determined opposition on the part of other language groups, notably the speakers of Bengali and Tamil. In the South Tyrol or Alto Adige section of northern Italy, there has been going on, ever since the end of the First World War, a cultural struggle for supremacy between German and Italian speakers. Even in the newly created nations of Africa, which generally use the languages of the old colonial powers, English or French, as their official tongues, there are movements for linguistic separatism. But there is also resistance to such movements. Both Kenya and Tanganyika rejected proposals to make Swahili their official tongue instead of English. India, while trying to implant Hindi as a national tongue, carefully safeguards its English. In Ireland, to the question "Who wants Gaelic taught exclusively in the schools?" one wag replied, "Those who have no children."

Next to flags and languages, it is national anthems and patriotic songs that best serve the purposes of nationalistic intolerance. But it is not a piece of music that conveys intolerant or bloodthirsty sentiments, any more than it is a colored piece of bunting. It is the language of a song that is responsible for whatever hatred may be engendered by it. *"La Marseillaise,"* which speaks of "an impure blood watering our furrows," is in itself a beautiful piece of music. The *"Horst Wessel Lied"* of the Nazis and the *"Giovinezza"* of the Fascists had tunes which were once harmless popular songs. Our own "Star-Spangled Banner," with its screaming shells and bursting rockets, was at one time the British drinking song "Anacreon in Heaven." In *"Deutschland über Alles"* and "Britannia Rule the Waves" the titles speak for themselves. In contrast to these inflammatory pieces, there are other patriotic songs and anthems, like "America the Beautiful" or Czechoslovakia's "Where Is My Home?," which proclaim merely the beauty and peace of the national fatherland and are no more the vehicles of intolerance than "Away Back Home in Indiana" or "My Old Kentucky Home."

National slogans often accompany hymns and anthems. Many are purely religious or philosophical, like our own "In God We Trust" and "E Pluribus Unum" (the latter, in fact, is almost literally copied by Indonesia's *Bhinneka Tunggal Ika,* "Many Remain One," while for the former a good parallel is India's *Sayameva Jayate,* "Truth Alone Triumphs"). Nations that have recent recollections of fighting for their statehood often record the fact in a slogan; Indonesia's *Merdeka* and Kenya's *Uhuru* both mean "freedom," while Ireland's *An Poblacht Abu* is "Up the Republic!" Some slogans are ephemeral, describing a situation which is purely temporary, like Yemen's "Free Yemen Fights for God, Imam, and Country against Imperialistic Egyptian Aggression," which appears on Yemenite stamps. It remained for a South African nationalistic organization, the Afrikaaner Broederbond, to develop a slogan that was linguistic as well as political: *Een volk, een land, een taal,* "One people, one land, one language."

From linguistic intolerance we go by easy stages to national intolerance pure and simple, where language serves merely as a means of expression. But it is a powerful medium, creating entire frames of mind by the use of a few well-placed words, which in themselves often convey no derogatory significance whatsoever. "Polack" and "Bohunk" were until recently, and possibly still are, fighting words in some parts of the United States. Yet the first is nothing but an approximation, closer than "Pole" or "Polish," to the name the Poles give themselves, while the latter seems to be nothing but a telescoped "Bohemian-Hungarian." Some offensive national appellations are, etymologically, a glorification of their recipients, like "wop," an English corruption of the Neapolitan dialect *guappo* ("tough guy"), which in turn comes from Spanish *guapo* ("brave" or "handsome"). Terms that acquire a disparaging connotation lead to strange euphemisms. The Romance languages try to avoid both "Jew" and "Hebrew" by having recourse to a third term, in itself neither more nor less legitimate than the other two, "Israelite"; this is even now kept carefully separate from "Israeli," which is restricted in meaning to "citizen of the state of Israel," not "person of the Jewish faith" in general. In America we wavered for a time between "colored" and "negro" and finally compromised by capitalizing the latter.

National names sometimes give rise to unpleasant secondary meanings. The "Welsh" which is rejected by the Welsh themselves (who prefer their ancient name *Cymry*) has unjustly given rise to the verb "to welsh" on an obligation; "Dutch treat," "Dutch uncle," and "Dutch courage" convey the extremely erroneous impression that the Dutch are ungenerous, overly severe, or addicted to alcohol when battle impends. What we know as a "confidence game" is called in France and Italy "American theft" or "American swindle." The Italians insinuate by the use of a national name that the French originated venereal disease, while the French blame it on the English. We even have "German" measles. The Japanese call the bedbug "Nanking insect," implying that it came to them from the Chinese. In German, "Russian" is synonymous with "barbarous," while "English education" means to the Germans education of the flogging type. Other random samples of this frame of mind are the Italian *portoghesismo*, "Portuguesism," for "gate crashing" or "free loading," the Sicilian *parolacce turche*, "bad Turkish words," for any sort of jargon (this probably goes back to the Saracen occupation of Sicily, with normal confusion between Arabic and Turkish), the ancient Latin *punica fides,* "Carthaginian trustworthiness" (the Roman point of view about the reliability of their opponents roughly paralleled our own opinion of how far you can trust the Communists), and a modern Esperanto expression, *estas volapukaĝo,* "It's Volapük," which parallels our own "It's Greek to me" and points to the fact that you can have linguistic intolerance even among the speakers of constructed languages; as against all this, we can think of only one flattering expression for another group, the Argentine *palabra inglesa,* "English word," meaning a promise you can rely upon.

All these attempts to throw the blame for general human failings on members of other national groups are characteristic of "xenophobia" ("hatred," or better yet, "fear of foreigners"), a word which ought to teach those who practice it a lesson. The Greek *xenos,* while it means a "foreigner," also means "friend" or "guest"; the ancient Greeks had the institution of "guest friendship," whereby two dwellers of different cities would shelter and entertain each other when either went to the other's town. Another expression for unbridled nationalism is "chauvinism," built upon the name of Chauvin, a noncommissioned officer in Napoleon's army who scorned everything non-French.

Racial discrimination, as distinguished from national or religious intolerance, is a relatively modern phenomenon. In the Middle Ages, the Jews were persecuted not as members of an alien racial group but because they would not accept the Christian Messiah. Converted Jews, like the Marranos of Spain, were closely watched for religious relapses but were otherwise admitted to the privileges of the Christian community. Slaves in the seething Mediterranean were indifferently black or white (Cervantes was once a galley slave), and Negroes could rise to high estate in white countries, as evidenced by the story of Othello, the "Moor of Venice." Even national intolerance, as distinguished from mere local antipathy, was not much in evidence. People killed one another enthusiastically and often, by virtue of their being subjects of different liege lords, or because they were citizens of rival city-states like Florence and Pisa, but seldom by reason of the fact that they were Spaniards, Frenchmen, Englishmen, or Italians.

It took modern times, with the nationalistic spirit fostered by the French Revolution and Napoleon, to give us true national hatreds. As for racial antipathies founded on a pseudoscientific basis, they are still more recent. The well-known theory of a superior "Nordic" or "Aryan" race, blond, tall, and long-skulled, the members of which, coming down from the region of the Baltic, conquered and intermingled with dark, short, broad-skulled races (called Alpine and

Mediterranean), was first advanced in the last century by a Frenchman, Gobineau, and restated at the beginning of this century by an American, Madison Grant. According to these racial theorists, whatever greatness exists in the nations of southern Europe, both ancient and modern, whatever contribution to civilization was made by the Greeks, Romans, Hebrews, medieval Frenchmen and Spaniards and Renaissance Italians, was due solely to the Nordic admixture.

Attempts have frequently been made to link this hypothetical Nordic race with the languages of the Indo-European group. Indo-European, in its original, unknown form was according to this theory the language of the original Nordics. Being the conquering race, they imposed their tongue upon the populations with which they came in contact. Here and there, a group of the subjugated races would escape both the conquerors and their language. Such would be, for instance, the Basques of the Pyrenees, speaking a mysterious tongue totally unrelated to Indo-European French and Spanish and thought to be a survival of a once much more widespread Iberian language extending over most of southern Europe; or the Dravidian tongues of southern India, the only part of the great peninsula to which the Indo-European conquerors did not penetrate.

The two hypotheses of an Aryan race and an original Indo-European language were later fused together by propagandists desirous of proving, for political purposes, that the nations in which both the Nordic type and the Indo-European language predominate, such as Germany, are worthy of ruling the earth, while nations in which a non-Nordic racial type is combined with a non-Indo-European language are definitely inferior.

This reasoning is, of course, utterly fallacious. So-called racial traits such as fairness or swarthiness of skin, color of hair and eyes, even length or broadness of skull, appear in hopelessly mixed proportions in all present-day white races, as is natural when we consider the process of intermingling that occurred in prehistoric and historic times, while language is easily discarded and acquired in the course of one or two generations. There is nothing in the human vocal apparatus that renders individuals more partial to one type of language than to another. A Chinese child brought up in a New York school environment will speak exactly the same brand of English as is spoken around him, and if he does not acquire Chinese at home he finds its later acquisition just as difficult as any white child. American-born Jews or Negroes, given the right kind of environment and education, will speak not only English but perfect, flawless, cultivated English. American Indians in Mexico, whose ancestral tongues were Nahuatl and Mayan, speak perfect Spanish today.

All this leads us to the conclusion that language is never necessarily an index of race or nationality. Nationality, in turn, does not historically seem to be an index of superiority. The only superiority that the intelligent man can admit is that which is conferred by individual and national contributions to the world's civilization and progress, and to the general human happiness.

Nevertheless, there is an entire vocabulary of racial intolerance. South African *apartheid,* or racial segregation, calls for three divisions: "European" (this includes not only the descendants of the original Boer or English settlers but also any white immigrant, from whatever country); "colored" (reserved for East Indians and other Orientals); and "native" (all blacks; a black African from beyond the South African borders receives a description that is a logical contradiction: he is called a "foreign native"). The term "Negro" is very seldom used, and the distinction made in segregated places is not, as in our South, "white" vs. "colored" but *blankes vs. nie blankes* or "white," "nonwhite" (the latter takes in both "native" and "colored"). There is abundant evidence that the "natives" resent both the term "native" (which would be logical as applied to them but could equally well be applied to African-born whites or "coloreds") and "Kaffir," which is a name bestowed upon the Bantu tribes by the Arabs and means "infidel" or "heathen." Interestingly, there is similar resentment against the term "native" on the part of the New Zealand Maori.

In the United States, outside of what happens in the South, there are delicate racial nomenclature problems in other areas. The Puerto Ricans, who are numerous in New York and other eastern seaboard cities, object to "Porto Rican" but they object even more to the separate racial classification that used to be made of them by New York authorities, who subdivided individuals into "black" (or "Negro"), "white," and "Puerto Rican." Since Puerto Rican racial complexity runs all the way from "white" to "black," their protests were deemed justified and the "Puerto Rican" classification was quietly dropped. In the Southwest, especially in New Mexico, the descendants of the early Spanish settlers describe themselves as *Nativos* and the Anglo-Saxon relative newcomers as *Anglos.* This seems to bother no one and the *Anglos* have even devised an affectionate term for the *Nativos: Hermanitos,* or "Little Brothers."

The connection of language with religious intolerance is subtler in nature. Religion normally discriminates between true and false believers but also leaves the door open for the latter to enter the fold. Hence the distinction between faithful and infidels, elect and reprobates, is at most a temporary one. Medieval literature offers interesting examples of certain choice adjectives ("felon," for instance, from which the legal language derives "felony") invariably coupled with "pagan," "Jew," or "Saracen." But the authors seem almost ready to remove the offensive qualifier if the "felon" will only recant and accept the true faith. How the language of religious intolerance can penetrate the popular tongue, however, is shown by such words as "patter" or "hoax." The former is an abridgement of *Pater Noster*, the Latin version of "Our Father" in the Lord's Prayer; the latter comes from the lengthier "hocus pocus," whose full form is "hocus pocus filiocus," a parody of the Catholic ceremony of the Mass, in which the priest supposedly pronounces the Latin words *Hoc est Corpus Filii,* "This is the body of the Son." Other expressions of religious antipathy are illustrated by "Papist," "scarlet woman," "black Protestant," the *giaour* ("infidel dog") bestowed by Moslems upon all nonbelievers in the Koran, the *goy* used by some Jews to describe non-Jews, and the "Judas" and "Christ killer" applied to Jews in some European countries.

The vocabulary of social intolerance is the vocabulary of class distinction: the "helots" of ancient Sparta, the "plebeians" of Rome, the *eta* or "outcasts" of Japan, the *pariah* or "untouchables" of India. (For the last-named, there was until recently an entire set of terms: "depressed classes," "exterior casts," *ezhavas, panchamas,* "outcastes," until Gandhi, in his infinite love for all men, devised for them the beautiful *harijans,* "Children of God.") On the other side of the railroad track were the Brahmans, the patricians, the *tai kun* or "great leaders" (from which our "tycoon" is derived). In nineteenth-century Russia, under the Czars, Classical scholars were not allowed to use the word *demos* ("people") or to say that Roman emperors were killed, but only that they "perished," while expressions like "forces of nature" and "movement of minds" were deleted by the censors. But the vocabulary of class intolerance can work both ways, as shown by the terms of opprobrium heaped upon aristocrats, plutocrats, bourgeoisie, and even kulaks by French and Russian revolutionary writers or, to take an example from our own history, by the contemptuous term "codfish aristocracy" bestowed after the American Revolution upon those New England families that showed continued leanings toward the British Crown.

Names of groups devoted to violent, or at least strongly nationalistic, action have always been with us. They range all the way from the purely political to the purely military, with perhaps a touch of the criminal injected. The Middle Ages gave us the "Assassins" (*hashishin*, "hashish eaters"), fanatic Moslems who, under the influence of the drug, fought the Crusaders with commando tactics. Reconstruction days gave us the Ku Klux Klan. The early twentieth century gave us the *chorniya sotnya*, or "Black Hundred," Czarist extremist groups that fought the terrorists and organized pogroms. More recent history has witnessed Ireland's I.R.A. and Israel's *Irgun Zvai Leumi*, Kenya's Mau Mau or "Hidden Ones," The Filipino *Hukbalahaps*, the *Khaksars* or "Children of the Dust" and *Rashtriya Swayam Sevak Sangh* or National Volunteer Corps of India, Morocco's *Istiqlal*, and Indo-China's Viet Minh and Viet Cong. The ideologies may vary, but the least common denominator is violence.

Whether national, racial, religious, or social, intolerance pushed to its logical conclusion has only one outcome: war, which may be of the national kind, like the wars waged by Louis XIV and Napoleon; of the racial sort, like wars of colonial conquest and the Hitlerian invasions; of the religious variety, like the *Jihad* or "holy war" of the Moslems and the Crusades of the Christians; or of the class species, like the French and Russian Revolutions. In war, language is an important auxiliary. As a rule, the importance of a knowledge of foreign languages is fully realized only in the course of an international conflict, when it becomes vital to understand and be understood by one's enemies and allies. Civilian institutions of learning may discard languages from their curriculum as unimportant to the fuller life of the individual, but military and naval academies never follow that idiotic lead. During the last war, the importance of foreign languages was so thoroughly demonstrated that the civilian institutions, it is hoped, will never repeat their prewar errors.

Language, however, is also abundantly used and misused for propaganda purposes, both at home and abroad. When it is deemed expedient to persuade the enemy to surrender, propaganda is blared at him in his own tongue. The "war of nerves" is something of which we have an early example in a Sumerian poem of five thousand years ago, relating how a king, by a series of alternating promises, cajolements, and threats, convinced an enemy city that it was best to submit without fighting.

The charge may be leveled at language that it serves an evil cause when it acts as an auxiliary to intolerance, discrimination, and hatred and lends itself to the deadly ends of warfare and bloodshed. But language, like science, is in itself impersonal. Its true social function, like that of the airplane or atomic energy, is to aid man, not destroy him. Language merely enables man to collaborate with his fellow man. It is man himself who must bear the blame for language's misuse if this exalted function is turned to purposes of violence and destruction.

— Chapter Nine —

LANGUAGE AND LITERATURE

Language is as much an art and as sure a refuge as painting or music or literature.
—Jane Ellen Harrison

IT is unfortunately fashionable in a few linguistic circles to regard literature as something set apart from language, to play up the spoken popular tongue to the detriment of the written literary language, and to view as "language" *par excellence* that form of speech which is most out of accord with the literary tradition—colloquialisms, vulgarisms, and slang. That this attitude is a reaction against an earlier point of view which regarded literature and its language with undue veneration is beside the point.

Language and literature are fundamentally one. Speech gives rise to writing, granted. But once writing has come into being, the written form begins to affect the spoken tongue, stabilize it, mold it, change it, give it a more esthetically pleasing form, endow it with a richer vocabulary.

Attention has been focused upon the fact that the literary language exerts a restraining, conservative influence upon speech. This is largely true and, to the extent that it is true, is also desirable. Were the spoken language not so restrained, it would change at too rapid a rate. Permanent records of civilization's evolution could be kept only with the greatest of difficulty, while mutual comprehension between different areas and different periods would grow even more complex than it is.

Literature serves primarily an esthetic purpose. On the other hand, what is too often forgotten is that literature is linguistically as well as esthetically creative. The "poet" is, in accordance with the original Greek *poietes*, a "maker" or "creator"; an "author," from the Latin *auctor*, which goes back to the verb *augeo* ("to increase"), is an "augmenter" or "producer." The poet and the writer, in their quest for beauty, devise new literary forms, which seep down from above into the popular language. The literary or "learned" expressions that have penetrated the spoken vernacular are legion.

A careful distinction is made by linguists between words of "popular" and words of "learned" origin. The theory is that the first existed at all times in the tongue of the masses and developed in full accord with all the tendencies of popular speech, while the latter were the special prerogative of a small intellectual *élite,* who kept them from changing their form or who lifted them bodily at a comparatively late date out of Latin and Greek lexicons. This is true in part, but only in part. The earliest documents, literary and otherwise, of every modern tongue swarm with words which one would have to call learned from their form, yet their nature and use indicate clearly that these words were not only understood but actively used by the entire population. Under the circumstances, the distinction between "popular" and "learned" words loses much of its rigidity.

Again, it is too often forgotten that the use of many words, expressions, and clichés has its definitely known origin in a specific work of literature. This is "poetic" in the etymological sense of the word. Once, in a financial column describing the state of the stock market, there appeared, untranslated, a famous line from François Villon: *"Mais où sont les neiges d'antan?"* The financial editor, astonishingly, chose to use a highly poetic expression in a highly prosaic article addressed to people interested in profits and losses.

"The snows of yesteryear" is only one of many expressions that have found their way into popular speech. If we were to restrict ourselves to a single facet of the manifold contribution made by literature to language, the names of literary characters that have become household words, with very specific meanings, what a word list we would have! Spenser's Braggadocio; Shakespeare's Shylock, Hamlet, and Romeo; Dickens' Scrooge; Defoe's Man Friday could perhaps head the list, with Galahad and Lochinvar, Mrs. Malaprop, Pollyanna and Babbitt thrown in for good measure. French has Molière's Tartuffe, used as a synonym for "hypocrite," along with Chantecler and Cyrano, while Rabelaisian and Pantagruelian have spread abroad. Spanish gives us Don Juan and Quixote, from whom we even draw an adjective, "quixotic." In Italy, Perpetua, Don Abbondio's servant maid in Manzoni's *Promessi Sposi,* is synonymous with "serving-woman" in general, and Figaro, from *The Barber of Seville*, is a generic term for "barber"; Pulcinella and Arlecchino (Punch and Harlequin of the *Commedia dell'Arte*) are both used with the derisive meaning of "clown," and anti-Fascist Italians often described Mussolini's antics as *pulcinellate*. It is perhaps not too generally known that "eternal feminine" comes to us from Goethe's *Faust* (*Ewig-Weibliche*), and that the very vulgar American "blood and guts" is a paraphrase of an earlier Bismarckian *Blut und Eisen* ("blood and iron"), which in turn goes back to a literary *Blut und Boden* ("blood and soil").

Literary place names, too, have become common words. "Olympia," "Utopia," "Eldorado," and "Shangri-la" are not merely imaginary but literary.

Literary authors have with their very own names given rise to common adjectives. The Marquis de Sade, a French writer of tales of depraved cruelty, is responsible for "sadism" and "sadistic"; L. von Sacher Masoch, an Austrian novelist, for "masochism"; Machiavelli, an Italian writer on political affairs, for "machiavellian."

Classical mythology, which is, after all, a form of literature, has given the language such figures of speech as "a Hercules," "a Venus," "an Adonis." "Herculean," "hermetic," "jovial," "martial," "mercurial," "saturnine," "nemesis," "panic," "protean," "titanic," "volcano," and even the prosaic "vulcanize" are all mythological in origin. So are "cereal," "music," "dragon," and such names of months as January, March, May. From the works of Homer we get "odyssey," "mentor," and "stentorian." Even the ancient Greek philosophical writers survive in popular expressions like "platonic," "epicurean," and "stoic." Scandinavian mythology accounts for the names of four of our days of the week, Tuesday, Wednesday, Thursday, Friday, all named after gods and goddesses of the Germanic Olympus.

"Jeopardy" comes to us from an Old French literary term, *jeu parti*, meaning literally "split game," a poetic composition in which two parties, usually a man and a woman, argue alternately; the outcome of the discussion is in doubt till the end, whence "to be in jeopardy." "Farce" and "farcical" come from the medieval French literary *comédies farcies*, or "stuffed comedies," the stuffing of which was done with highly spiced ingredients. "Vaudeville" has its origin in Olivier Basselin's fifteenth-century skits presented in the town of Vire, later confused with *ville* ("city"). "Robot" (from Czech *robota*, "word") is a word coined by Karel Čapek, a

Czech playwright, in his play *R.U.R. Exposé* is a French press term.

But all this, one may argue, is highfalutin language, consisting of creations of the literary tongue which remain largely in the literary tongue or, at the most, reach only the spoken tongue of the more educated classes. Let us then take the reverse of the medal. Why is present-day English becoming more and more monosyllabic? Why are longer words being replaced by shorter ones? Why do we generally use such terms as "drive," "plea," "crash," "probe," "flay," "blast," and "oust" for "offensive," "appeal," "collision," "investigation," "denounce," "attack," and "evict" which were so current in the speech of an earlier generation? Only because of their widespread use in newspaper headlines, which seek to compress concepts into the smallest possible space so that the printed letter may be bigger. Newspapers are the popular literature of our day. It is they who set the pace for the spoken tongue, repeating the creative experience of the more ancient writers with household-term characters like Caspar Milquetoast and John Q. Public (the latter copied even by the Russians in their *Ivan K. Publika* and the Uruguayans in their *Juan Pueblo*).

That established literary forms give rise to official national languages when conditions are favorable is known. Whatever predominance the Tuscan dialect holds in the standard Italian of today is due to the fact that three great literary geniuses, Dante, Petrarch, and Boccaccio, were Tuscans. Despite the fact that Italian poetic works of note had previously appeared elsewhere, notably at the court of Frederick II of Sicily, the accident of Tuscan birth and environment of the "Big Three" of Italian literature leads many to this day to make the exaggerated assertion that "Italian" is synonymous with "Tuscan."

In medieval France, the Picard dialect of the north was a literary medium of expression at least as important as the Francien which was the dialect of the Paris court. Despite Francien's obvious political advantage, the standard French language hesitated for a long time between the two dialects, and many Picard forms have entered standard French. Even more have entered standard English, because at the time when French words were pouring into English the conflict between the two great northern French dialects was still in progress.

The international benefits that accrue to a language by reason of literary merits are often considerable. Arabic is indisputably the religious tongue of the Moslem world, but

Persian may be said to be its poetic language, by reason of its large and beautiful literary output; for literary purposes, Persian is studied in India, Turkey, Soviet Asia, even in China and Indonesia. The spreading of French as a cultural language, first in the twelfth and thirteenth centuries, later in the seventeenth and eighteenth, was due in part to political and military factors but also to the imposing literary production of France in those two periods. During the intervening centuries, Italian, a language that had little in the way of political or military backing, exerted a powerful influence over European culture, primarily by reason of its literary qualities. We may admire the Greeks for their philosophy and the Romans for their genius of military and political organization, but it is chiefly for their literature that their languages are studied today.

— Chapter Ten —

LANGUAGE AND SCIENCE

Science and art belong to the whole world, and before them vanish the barriers of nationality.

—Goethe

TO say that there is a close interrelation between language and science because the former is the vehicle of scientific thought and discovery while the latter makes vast and ever new contributions to language seems almost trite. Yet science could make no progress were it not for the great linguistic medium which enables scientists all over the world to communicate to one another the findings that result from their constant research. At the same time, it has been estimated that fully one half of the vocabulary of all civilized languages consists of scientific and technical terms, a great many of which are thoroughly international.

There is a third field of collaboration between mankind's oldest communications auxiliary and mankind's comparatively novel achievement. Science has recently cast a new light upon the nature and functioning of language, at least for what concerns language's mechanical side, the production, transmission, and reception of sound. Inventions like the telephone, phonograph, and radio are the chief devices for the artificial conveying of the human voice, but scientists, diligently laboring upon those appliances, have come forth with revolutionary discoveries concerning man's own production and reception apparatus. The Bell Telephone Laboratories have opened their research facilities to linguistic investigators, and the collaboration of descriptive linguists and telephone technicians has proved of untold benefit to both. To mention only one result of this cooperation, there has been devised a visual language for the deaf, whereby phonetic graphs are flashed on a screen by the use of the cathode-ray tube, with sounds electrically resolved into pitch, loudness, and time. On the screen, a word like "we" looks like a tree bending in a high wind, slanting to the right; "sure" is like a diving airplane; the sound of laughter resembles a row of feathers. This device is useful in teaching those born deaf to speak, and also gives linguists a perfect insight into various phonetic differences concerning which doubts had previously existed.

Attacking the problem of communications from other angles, scientists have been able to create, at least in experimental form, a "speech writer," which is a typewriter operated by the human voice. For instructional purposes in the teaching of foreign languages, there is a "pronunciary," which projects written words on a screen and at the same time gives the corresponding sounds through a loudspeaker.

The X ray, laryngoscope, and bronchoscope, once used exclusively by physicians for the diagnosing of certain diseases, are now also used by linguists for the purpose of determining exactly how language sounds are produced by the human vocal apparatus. A Braille shorthand machine enables the blind to take rapid dictation. The Filene Finlay Translator, consisting of an individual lightweight radio receiving set equipped with earphones and an aerial imbedded in the shoulder straps, permits the system of simultaneous translating used in some of the UN proceedings. A variant of this appliance is a portable translating machine, only eighteen pounds in weight, devised by a Frenchman for business conversations among persons speaking different languages; as one person speaks, the translator gives a simultaneous translation which is the only thing heard by his interlocutor. The soundscriber, wire and tape recorder, and mirrorphone have taken their place side by side with the earlier phonograph record for foreign language instruction and speech correction and are gradually being adopted by the more progressive schools of language. Machine translation, while still far from achieving perfection, has advanced to the stage where fairly complex messages can be handled with relative ease. Other computers have proved of great value in documentary research and word counts. It is no wonder that linguists look upon scientists and technicians as their most valuable allies and miss no occasion to express their gratitude for the assistance they receive.

In return, language does all it can to further the advances of science by placing all its semantic resources at science's disposal, for the dissemination of accurate information among both scientists and laymen. The language of science is truly international, because all languages have unlocked the treasure chests of their vocabularies to science. Greek, which supplies large segments of our conversational and literary tongue, is also responsible for about half of our total scientific vocabulary, as is appropriate for the tongue of Hippocrates and Galen. Words like "gastrogue" and "plasmagene" in nutrition; "psychosomatic," "somatopsychic" (this is where the body influences the mind), "mania," and "phobia" in medical psychology; "plankton" and "hydroponic" in biology; "therapy," "antibiotic," "gerontology," and "periston" in medicine; "erythrosuchus" and "pterodactyl" in paleontology; "hypergolic" in jet propulsion; "isotope" and "betatron" in atomic research come straight from Greek. "Atom" itself is the Greek *atomos* or "indivisible," a term first applied by James Dalton, who developed the atomic theory in 1808. Generic scientific suffixes come from Greek, like the *-atrics* used to denote a branch of the medical science ("geriatrics," the study of the diseases of old age; "pediatrics," the diseases of children) or the *-itis* ("appendicitis") used generally to describe an acute, inflamed condition, or the *-osis* ("acidosis") that usually denotes a more chronic state of affairs.

Latin, the tongue of medieval medicine, is still with us to the extent that *U. S. Pharmacopoeia*, the official American druggists' handbook, lists all drugs under their Latin as well as their English names. The scientific names of plants ("Ranunculus," the Persian buttercup), animals ("Felis leo, fam. Leonidae"), parts of the body ("sternum," "femur," "capillaries") are more often Latin than Greek. Terms like "deflagration" ("incomplete explosion"), "supersonic" ("surpassing the speed of sound"), "cumulus" (a type of cloud-formation), "artifact" (an archaeological term denoting what is made by the hand of man) and expressions like the medical "post mortem" and the homeopathic *Similia similibus curantur* ("Like is cured with like") are Latin in origin. So are "radio" and "video."

Arabic, the tongue of medieval culture, gives us astronomical terms like "zenith" and "nadir," mathematical words like "algebra" and "cipher," chemical expressions like "alcohol," "alkali," "alchemy," and "chemistry" itself. Modern German offers terms like "ohm" (from the name of a German physicist) and "graupel," the official scientific name of the granular snow that is not quite sleet. French gives us "moraine," "ampere" and its derivatives, "nicotine" (named after Jean Nicot, French ambassador to Portugal, who first popularized tobacco in France by sending tobacco seeds to Catherine de

Médicis). From Italian we have "influenza," "pellagra," "malaria," and numerous common nouns and adjectives coined from the names of Italian scientists ("volt," "Fallopian," "Malpighian"). From Japanese come *migozai*, the name of a drug that improves night vision, and *tsunami*, the scientific name of an ocean wave arising from a submarine earthquake, often incorrectly called "tidal wave." Chinese contributes "typhoon" or "great wind," and even the languages of the West Indian natives assist science with "hurricane."

Our own native English comes to the fore with "watt" and "farad" (derived from the names of Watt and Faraday, English physicists), "chain reaction," "ramjet" and "turbofan," "white sound" (the mixture of sound waves of all lengths), "radar" (an abbreviation for "radio detection and ranging"), "teleran" ("television radar air navigation"), "loran" ("long-range aid to navigation"), and the now very popular "feedback."

Linguistic hybrids in the scientific field abound, as witnessed by "succulometer" (Latin "juice," Greek "measure"), "criminogenetics" (Latin "crime," Greek "origin"), "dehydrofreezing" (Latin "from," Greek "water," English "freezing"), even "drunkmeter"; other linguistic curios are the "monoethanolaminedinitrocyclohexylphenolate," which is death to moths, the "pneumonoultramicroscopicsilicovolcanokoniosis," said to be the longest word in the English language, which describes an occupational disease of miners, and the "humuhumunukunukuapuaa," which is the native but also the scientific name of the Hawaiian "triggerfish," a little creature considerably shorter than its appellation.

It is an interesting fact that various fields of science show a leaning in their terminology toward one or another of the great source languages. The nuclear vocabulary, for instance, is very largely Greek: "proton," "electron," "positron," "pion," "pi-meson," "muon," "mu-meson," "neutrino," "beta rays." Space terminology also leans largely to Greek but with a heavy Anglo-Saxon admixture: "synergic ascent," "aeroembolism," "aerothermodynamic border," "anacoustic zone," "braking ellipses." On the other hand, mathematics, in its handling of very large and very small numbers, has found it expedient to use a series of Classical prefixes: "mega" for a million, "giga" for a trillion, "tetra" for a quadrillion, "nano" for a billionth, and "pico" for a trillionth. Thus, 1,000,000,-000 volts is a "gigavolt," and a billionth of a second is a "nanosecond." Some jocular use is made of these scientific prefixes by their users, as when they refer to the cost of an operation in terms of "megabucks."

As for the use of languages by scientists, several interesting facts are in evidence. Before the First World War, German was by far the most widespread scientific tongue, with French a somewhat distant second and English a remote third. Other languages, notably Dutch, were in fairly frequent use (Dutch was for a time the only scientific language to penetrate Japan). The great development of the last three decades has been the gradual ascent of English and Russian. In 1918 English already accounted for 45 per cent of all chemical papers published, Russian for less than 1 per cent; in 1940, English still led with 35 per cent, while Russian had risen to 14 per cent. In 1937, over 200 chemical journals (7.3 per cent of all such published in the world) were published in the Soviet Union; since then, Russian publications have outstripped both German and French. At latest count, the Soviet Union publishes over 300 journals and some 30,000 books a year on science and technology, exclusive of the fields of biology, medicine, and agriculture.

Japanese scientists, who had traditionally used German as a medical language (Japanese, it seems, lacks the scope to convey the precise meaning of many scientific terms), are now replacing it with English, while in America some teachers of technical subjects suggest that Russian replace German in our high schools and colleges because of the rapid advances made by the Soviet Union in technology (but, by recent figures, less than 2 per cent of our scientists had any knowledge of Russian). The *Surgery Journal* publishes abstracts of new surgical techniques in French, Spanish, Italian, and Russian. Spanish and Portuguese are becoming increasingly important in the medical field, the former particularly because of the publications of the Mexican Institute of Tropical Diseases, the latter because of extensive research and experimentation conducted in Brazil with antitoxins for snake and insect bites. *Excerpta Medica,* a leading medical journal published in Holland, appears in English.

Along with this jockeying for position on the part of the leading modern languages, there is an interesting resurgence of ancient ones. At the All-India University of Alwar, modern engineering, medicine, and other technological subjects are taught in ancient Sanskrit.

To the scientific and technical worker more than nearly anyone else, linguistic comprehension shorn of linguistic difficulties is important. It is therefore not surprising that scientists and technicians are often to be found in the forefront of the movement in favor of an international language, or at least of some form of simplification of the existing tongues. A bacteriologist recounts listening to lectures in which the speaker "mouthed the ten-syllable term 'desoxyribonucleic acid' [a chemical constituent of nuclei cells] from five to twenty-five times," and wonders why it could not be shortened to "dorna," in the same way that "sulfanilamide" was reduced to "sulfa," or "alphanaphthylthiourea," a rat destroyer, was cut down to "antu."

Still another linguistic movement is discernible among scientists, one that is, in a sense, quite the antithesis of the movement toward internationalization of terminology. This consists in giving scientific concepts their short, terse Anglo-Saxon names, wherever these exist, in the place of the lengthier Greek and Latin words. My physician thinks he is impressing me when he tells me I am suffering from "torticollis" and that he is going to give me a "febrifuge." He forgets that in my mother tongue *torcicollo* is the popular term for "stiff neck" and *febbrifugo* means, in the language of the masses, anything that will put fever to flight (aspirin, for instance). But not many of his patients enjoy the advantage of a double linguistic background.

Regardless of the direction which our scientific and technical terminology will ultimately take, toward internationalism, simplification, or even greater nationalism, one thing is certain. Science will continue to enrich language, in the same fashion and to the same extent that it will continue to enrich the daily lives of each and every one of us.

— Chapter Eleven —

LANGUAGE, EDUCATION, AND LITERACY

The pen is the tongue of the mind.
—Cervantes

"Understandest thou what thou readest?"
"How can I, except some man should guide me?"
—Acts, 8:30–31

EDUCATION, the process of training the individual for his environment, consists of a great deal more than language. Yet it is too often forgotten that language is the medium whereby that training is overwhelmingly imparted. Scientific definitions, historical and geographical accounts, sociological and economic descriptions, mathematical principles, manual handicraft directions all come in linguistic form. Aside from all this, a large percentage of the educational process deals with language itself—the national language as a means of self-expression and understanding, foreign languages as a means of international communication or for cultural values. Of primary interest is the imparting of language as a natural medium of communication with one's fellow man.

The spoken language of the community is normally acquired by the individual, at least in rudimentary fashion and for basic purposes, without the need of deliberate outside intervention. Children pick up language at their mother's knee and improve upon it as they go along by the natural process of observation and imitation of their elders. There is no human community so primitive that it does not possess a spoken tongue. In many illiterate communities, a considerable measure of mass culture is achieved by means of oral tradition. It is supposed, though not proved, that extensive literary accounts like those of the *Iliad* and *Odyssey* were transmitted by word of mouth for numerous generations before they were finally committed to writing. In many countries where illiteracy prevails, there are to be found highly intelligent individuals who achieve oral poetic composition of a relatively high order.

But the arts of civilization demand something more. They require that civilization's records be kept in permanent, accessible form and that all members of the community, or at least the majority, have access to them. The democratic processes, wherein human beings collaborate in making their own choice of political institutions and leadership, are particularly exacting in this respect. Man as a political animal must have recourse to much and varied information which is available to him only in that incarnate, petrified form of speech called writing. Hence the need for mass literacy becomes imperative. If it goes unheeded, man sinks back quickly into an obsolete and inferior form of civilization.

The history of literacy coincides to a considerable degree with the history of civilization. Great and flourishing civilizations have existed in the past with a minimum of popular literacy, but that was only because the burden of those civilizations was carried on the shoulders of that small fraction of the population which was literate. The illiterates were slaves, serfs, peasants, people who fulfilled in their respective civilizations the functions that are today assigned to machines. As the machine liberated man from these functions, the slaves and serfs became human beings in the full sense of the term; and as human beings they demanded and received human prerogatives, not the least important of which was the right to know how to read and write.

It is far from a coincidence, today as in the past, that the nations that enjoy high standards of literacy also lead in material progress and living standards. These are based upon the full, intelligent collaboration of the entire community, unlike the more aristocratic esthetic and cultural values which are based upon the personal achievement of the individual. It is only when we realize this fact that we begin to reconcile the apparent contradiction of nations like Italy and Spain, whose cultural output has been and is extremely high but whose living standards and economic progress have been until recently relatively low. A Carlo Levi and a Blasco Ibáñez can aristocratically lift themselves far above the environment described in their own works, but Eboli and *La Bodega* remain to drag down the average man. Eventually, they will drag down the Levis and Ibáñezes if the situation is not corrected. Correction consists of social improvement, which is invariably followed by economic improvement. The first and most essential step in social improvement is literacy.

Literacy is at the vanguard of education, which in turn is the spearhead of all social progress. Recognition of this essential fact came late. To our own shame it must be admitted that our American Constitution, an admirable political document in all other respects, makes no mention of the educational process. In this one matter our Founding Fathers failed to display the prescience that characterized most of their thinking. They did not see beyond their own times, and the educational standards of their times were substantially what they had been for tens of centuries before them. The educational process was something left to individual or, at most, to institutional initiative. We do not have precise statistics concerning the literacy of the ancient and medieval empires, but it is surmised that the state of affairs in ancient Greece, the Roman Empire, the realm of Charlemagne, the kingdoms and republics of the Middle Ages and Renaissance did not materially differ from the state of affairs we find toward the end of the eighteenth century, when no more than 20 per cent of the population was literate.

The spreading of literacy and education in the civilized nations of the west is predominantly a nineteenth-century phenomenon. In our own land, a population that was barely 20 per cent literate at the time of the Revolution was still only 40 per cent literate in 1840. Today, we still have some 10 million "functionally" illiterate adults in our midst, almost equally divided among native whites, native Negroes, and foreign-born. In view of the determined, relentless onslaughts that are being made against this surviving citadel of ignorance by national and state governments as well as numerous private agencies, it is to be hoped that by the end of the twentieth century American illiteracy will be a thing of the past.

Literacy figures, like population figures, are forever shifting, fortunately upward. The present-day literacy average for Europe is about 90 per cent, slightly lower than our own. Among highest-literacy countries (99–100 per cent) are Denmark, Sweden, Switzerland, England, Germany, Austria, Norway, and Finland. Low literacy (75 per cent or less) is reported from Spain, Greece, Portugal, Rumania, Yugoslavia, Albania, and Malta. Iceland has practically 100 per cent literacy, an enviable record. Russia was about 80 per cent illiterate under the Czars. Today, the Soviets claim close to 100 per cent literacy. Yugoslavia claims to have taught 500,000 of its people how to read and write since the end of the war and has initiated a program designed to wipe out illiteracy altogether in the 1960s. Italy's experience closely parallels our own. From 20 per cent literacy at the dawn of the nineteenth century, she gradually crept up to 52 per cent by 1900 and stands at about 80 per cent today. Just as our own illiteracy is largely concentrated in certain sections, so Italy's illiterates reach 40 per cent and over in regions like Sicily, Sardinia, and the heel and toe of the Italian boot.

Illiteracy in Latin America is still more rampant. Puerto Rico, when it first became a part of the United States, had a high level of 77 per cent; today, this has been reduced to less than 25 per cent. Mexico has over 48 per cent illiteracy, a reflection of the average national income of 100 dollars a year. The Mexican way of disposing of illiteracy is "each one teach one"; every person between the ages of eighteen and sixty who knows how to read and write is required to take under his wing an illiterate between the ages of six and forty and instruct him. Brazil's illiteracy reaches the high figure of over 50 per cent. It is estimated that in Brazil's richest and most populous state, São Paulo, almost 40 per cent of the 15 million inhabitants are illiterate. But Brazil is launching a strenuous campaign to eradicate its illiteracy, with the adoption of the "each one teach one" system of the Mexicans.

The illiteracy of Asia is quite high (about 75 per cent for the entire continent), although in one country, Japan, fully 99½ per cent of the people are at least partly able to read and write. In China illiterates number close to 300 million, or about 40 per cent of her population. In Indonesia, the Republican government claims that since its advent and strenuous literacy campaign the number of literate persons has risen from 7 to over 20 per cent.

India's literacy average is about 20 per cent, or 100 million out of nearly 500 million. But the last ten years have seen an average growth of over half a million adult literates a year, along with a comforting situation for what concerns the younger generations. Because of the complicated syllabic scripts of many of the Indian languages, about half of those attending school relapse into illiteracy soon after they leave, and to combat this phenomenon members of the American Board of Foreign Missions have been devising simpler alphabetic scripts for those languages. Burma, Malaya, Thailand, Korea, Ceylon, do not go beyond 30 per cent literacy, Iran and Iraq 20 per cent. Turkey, despite the adoption of the Roman alphabet, still has only about 35 per cent literacy, or some 10 million out of 20 million Turks.

Africa has equally low literacy averages. Only Algeria, Kenya, Tunisia, Uganda, and the Union of South Africa attain the maximum percentages of 10 to 20 per cent literacy among their native populations. The percentage of literates is almost negligible in many West African states. Despite this fact, there are in Africa over one hundred newspapers and periodicals published in native languages, with the Swahili of East Africa and the Zulu of South Africa in the lead. A single Nigerian weekly bears articles in English, Ga, Fanti, Ewe, Kru, Ibo, Yoruba, Hausa, Ijaw, Benin, Sobo, Jekri, and Efik.

Even the islands of the Far Pacific are making strenuous attempts to end illiteracy. Instruction in the written form of pidgin English is given by missionaries. In a monthly magazine, *Frend Belong Mi*, that has been published for the natives of New Guinea since 1935, everything, including the fiction and crossword puzzles, is in pidgin.

Just as religion took the lead in conserving and spreading linguistic culture after the fall of the Roman Empire, so today it joins the governments in the great world-wide battle against illiteracy and ignorance. Missionaries have reduced to writing innumerable oral languages of the far corners of the earth. A mere glance at the American Bible Society's *Book of a Thousand Tongues* reveals the marvelous work that has been done by the representatives of the various Christian faiths in creating, perfecting, and imparting written forms of primitive languages to their speakers.

The picture of the world's struggle against illiteracy and ignorance would be incomplete without a reference to the Braille system, devised by a nineteenth-century Frenchman, Louis Braille, which by a series of dots and dashes perceptible to the touch enables the blind to "read" and "write." The story of the application of the Braille code to the world's various languages is a romance in itself; its latest chapter is the development of a uniform code for the major languages of India, which will permit the blind of that vast area to become literate.

Unlike most of the issues that confront the world today, literacy is one that finds all nations united and anxious to cooperate. The crusade against ignorance is being waged by the human race as a whole, without any perceptible Iron Curtain to separate the east from the west. If anything, there is a noble, generous rivalry in the struggle to free mankind from the fetters of ignorance which are forged by illiteracy. The aspects of this common campaign inspire the world's educators to hope that, despite all the distressing political omens that beset our generation, the torch of enlightenment may yet show the way to a better life for those who will follow us.

— Chapter Twelve —

LANGUAGE AND PSYCHOLOGY

Smells, colors, and sounds are in direct correspondence.
—Baudelaire

Proverbs are the wisdom of peoples.
—Italian proverb

ONE of the most fascinating and mysterious areas of language is its connection with the mental processes both of the individual and the social group. Among the branches of science that deal with this relationship are two that go by the names of "psycholinguistics" and "metalinguistics." The former treats such topics as aphasia (the loss of the power of speech due to causes that are not perceptibly physiological), glossolalia (forms of speech devised by the insane), and the thought-and-language processes of infants. Metalinguistics, first propounded by Benjamin Lee Whorf, may be presented in oversimplified form as a theory to the effect that the type of language customarily used by the individual affects his type of thinking; for instance, that the reason why westerners have a clear sense of time distinctions, as embodied in train schedules, time clocks, and due dates for payments, is that the western languages have specific time distinctions built into their verbal systems, while the speakers of some American Indian languages in which the verb is timeless shrug their shoulders at the idea of doing things on time. It might be objected that the reverse is true: the language develops clearcut time distinctions, with present, past, future, pluperfect, and future perfect tenses, to keep pace with the needs, customs, and institutions of its speakers.

A study was recently undertaken at the University of California to determine why certain Indian tribes of the Northwest know the pathological phenomenon of stammering while other groups of Indians do not, and it was established that among the stammering tribes there is strong emphasis on competitive aspects, both in social life and in ceremonial ritual. But the conclusions are still tentative.

The number of unsolved problems in the field of linguistic psychology is tremendous. Why is there such a widespread tendency to lump together all those who do not speak our language, and to minimize the differences between languages we do not know, or know only imperfectly, like Chinese and Japanese, or Slavic and Hungarian? Before we ascribe this tendency to mere ignorance of the facts, let us recall that there is an equally widespread tendency to identify with objective reality a series of sounds or words with which we are familiar. Margaret Mead brings out the contrast between the normal American way of presenting the name of an object to a child or to a foreign learner ("This is a hat") and what goes on among certain New Guinea tribes ("We call this a hat"). The American fashion of presenting the object and its name immediately sets up an inherent link between the object and its English name, with all other links excluded; the method of the supposedly backward Papuans leaves room for other possible ways of linguistically describing the same object and makes it psychologically possible for the child in later life to accept *chapeau, Hut, sombrero* as equivalent terms.

Another mental tendency of the same general type is the one observed among the speakers of many languages to equate the word with the deed. Once the thing is stated to have happened or be happening ("The Arab nation has begun to restore its former glory"), it is psychologically considered as having happened, with the equally psychological corollary that nothing more need be done about it. This time the word is equated with an action or process rather than with an object. The result is different, but we again have the phenomenon of the spoken word being paired off with reality.

It is a moot question to what extent the formal differences of various languages are indicative of the mentality of their speakers. It is a commonplace that each language is a law unto itself as to what distinctions are important enough to call for a specific language signal. But what are the further implications? Reversing Whorf's theory, is it significant, and of what, that Japanese seldom deems it necessary to specify *who* performs the action denoted by the verb, while to western speakers the concept of "subject" is all-important? The Japanese verb, as normally used, does not express "I am going," "you are going," "he is going," but simply "there is a going";

on the other hand, the very form of "there is a going" that the speaker uses will normally imply greater politeness or greater familiarity on his part toward the person addressed. Does this in turn imply that the Japanese are less interested in personality and more polite than we are? Or is the distinction something that merely happened by chance and has no particular significance?

Cases of this kind could be multiplied. Why do we not think it is important to distinguish between "we" that includes the person to whom we are speaking and "we" that excludes him? Many languages distinguish carefully between the two. Why does Hungarian feel that it is unnecessary to distinguish between "he," "she," and "it," using a single pronoun for all three, which to us is highly confusing, until we stop to realize that we do exactly the same thing in the plural, using "they" for males, females, or objects, whereas the Romance languages, having only two grammatical genders, distinguish between a masculine "they" and a feminine "they"? Again, does the fact that when there is a conflict of genders it is regularly resolved in favor of the masculine mean that the male has a psychological advantage among speakers of Romance languages? If "they" are all females, in French you use *elles;* but if "they" are all males, or of mixed genders, you use the masculine *ils.* In Spanish, *mis hijos* (masculine) can mean not only "my sons" but "my sons and daughters," and if you speak of parents, you use *padres,* literally "fathers." Even Italian, which has a separate word for each "parent," *genitore* in the masculine, *genitrice* in the feminine, uses the masculine *genitori* in the plural.

In the matter of number, does the fact that we, having leveled down all second person pronouns to a single "you," nevertheless create dialectal plurals of the type of "youse," "you-all," "you 'uns," indicate that we desperately feel the need of a psychological distinction of number? Is there significance, along lines of mental precision for what concerns space, in the fact that Spanish makes a threefold distinction for its demonstratives (*este libro,* "this book" near me, *ese libro,* "that book" near you, *aquel libro,* "that book" far removed from both of us); that English, having once had the same threefold distinction, has now settled for a twofold one ("this," "that," with "yon" thrown into the discard); while French, having had a twofold distinction in its older period (*cist, cil*), has now given up all spatial distinction, save exceptionally (*ce livre* normally does service for both "this book" and "that book," and only if a distinction between the two must be made is *-ci* or *-là* appended to *ce livre*)?

In the matter of words, attention has repeatedly been called to the fact that certain languages have created or developed single words which other languages can express only by means of word groups; Spanish *prendas*, for example, means "articles of clothing"; English could use "garments," but the connotation is not precisely the same. Even more clear-cut is the German *Geschwister*, which English can render only by "brothers and sisters," and which, unlike the Romance *padras* and *hijos*, is built on the feminine *Schwester*, not on the masculine *Bruder*.

Why are certain groups of words arranged in different sequences by different languages? "Romeo and Juliet" regularly appear in Italian as *Giulietta e Romeo*, and if one were to try to explain this on the ground that the Italians are more considerate of the fair sex, he would be immediately contradicted by other similar couples, such as *Paolo e Francesca*, or *Dante e Beatrice*, where the man comes first. Why does English regularly say "black and white" while Spanish just as regularly uses *blanco y negro?* Alphabetic sequence might explain it, as witnessed by Italian's *bianco, rosso, e verde* ("white, red, and green"), which does not range the colors in the order they appear on the Italian flag; but the explanation falls apart in the face of France's *le rouge et le noir*, and our own "red, white, and blue."

Why is a certain constellation viewed by the speakers of some languages (Greek, Latin, English, Finnish, Iroquois) as a "Great Bear" but by others as a chariot (Scandinavian "Thor's Chariot," Celtic "King Arthur's Chariot") and by still others as a funeral procession (Arabic *Banāt an-Na'ash*, "the coffin women attendants")?

Is there a link between sound and meaning? Or, more precisely, does the sound of a word in a strange language offer a clue to the meaning? In a Harvard experiment, eighty students with no knowledge of Chinese were given the words *ch'ing* and *ch'ung*, one of which means "heavy," the other "light." Seventy-four guessed correctly that *ch'ing* is "light" and *ch'ung* is "heavy." There was only a 60 per cent score in the interpretation of pairs of words one of which means "beautiful" or "beauty," the other "ugliness" or "ugly" (Chinese *mei—ch'ou*, Czech *krása—ošklivost*, Hindi *khubsurst—badsurat*). Was it the "heaviness" of the vowel sound in *ch'ung* as against the "lightness" of the *i* in *ch'ing* that led to the impressive score in the first test? The "pretty" sound of *mei* and *krása* as against the inherent "ugliness" of *ch'ou* and *ošklivost?* To this reader at least, *badsurat* sounds prettier than *khubsurst*.

There is the interesting phenomenon of colored hearing, described by Jakobson, with vowel sounds generally impressing the subjects as "chromatic" and consonant sounds as "grayish." But this writer can go much farther; in his childhood, he "saw" the Italian vowel sounds as endowed with specific colors: *a* was white, *e* green, *i* red, *o* blue, and *u* black.

But color symbolism has a far greater linguistic import. Explaining this away on purely "idomatic" grounds is begging the question. Why are we "blue" when depressed? Why "yellow" when cowardly? Why "red" when radically inclined? To French speakers, "to be blue" is to be amazed. To Italian and German speakers, you are yellow with envy or jealousy, not with fear. To Russian speakers, red is the color of beauty, and both "red" and "beautiful" stem from the same Slavic root. White may be the color of innocence to us, but to the Russians and Koreans it is the color of death and mourning. In the Russian civil war, the "Reds" enjoyed a tremendous psychological advantage over the "White" armies of Denikin and Kolchak. Where an English speaker is "in the red," his Italian counterpart is "in the green." The French "blue story" is a tall story, or a fairy tale; the French "green reply" is a tart reply. The Italian "blue voice" is a crooning voice. The Russian "black laborer" is a manual laborer, not at all a Negro. The American "blue Monday," which is washday or hangover day, is in German an extended week end, a holiday Monday.

We have a "yellow" press. The French call a whodunit a "black" novel, the Italians a "yellow" novel. We are immersed in a "brown study," the Italians in "gray thoughts." We have our "green thumb." To the Sardinians, "green words" are magic words, spells and incantations. "Green language" to the French is slang or argot. "Green wine" to the Portuguese is new wine, and our "cold war" is the "white war" of the French.

Politically, we have our "black Republicans," but the term is usually applied in disparagement by their opponents. Medieval Italy had its "Whites" and "Blacks" (otherwise known as Guelphs and Ghibellines). Uruguay has its *Blancos y Colorados* ("Whites and Reds"), and a Mexican state at one time called its local liberals "Greens" and its conservatives "Reds."

Terms like our "pink of condition," "blue funk," "red tape," "white feather," "red herring," even "blackmail," would be quite meaningless if translated into other languages.

More startling yet are differences in coloration where physical objects are involved. "Red" cabbage to us is "blue" cabbage to the Germans, "black" cabbage to the Italians. To the latter, the yolk of an egg can be, indifferently, the "yellow" or the "red" of the egg, and red wine can perfectly well be "black" wine. To some African tribes, half that portion of the spectrum which we describe as "blue" is "black."

It is often claimed that proverbs and sayings are indicative of national psychology. But the imagery of such sayings is more often than not international, even though the words may differ. The Russian "What is healthy to a Russian is death to a German," coined centuries before Stalingrad, is simply our "One man's meat is another man's poison." Whether we use our own "Too many cooks spoil the broth," or the Italian "With so many roosters crowing, the sun never comes up," or the Japanese "Too many boatmen run the boat up to the top of a mountain," or the Persian "Two captains sink the ship," or the Russian "With seven nurses, the child goes blind," the basic idea is the same. Spanish says: "If the pitcher hits the rock or the rock hits the pitcher, it's too bad for the pitcher"; Chinese says: "Don't set out unarmed to fight a tiger"; one of our Southland proverbs runs: "The worm is wrong when it argues with the hen." The idea that you should not pit yourself against superior forces is the same. Even ancient Sumerian had: "Do not say to the god of the underworld: 'I want to live.' "

Yet some proverbs seem to show individualistic traits, with perhaps a touch of that elusive element, national psychology. Here are a few from the Russian to press the point:

"The Russian is strong on three foundations: maybe, never mind, somehow." "If you drink, you die; if you don't drink, you die; so you'd better drink." "Those who know a lot are our friends; those who know too much are our enemies." "Eternal peace lasts only till the first fight." "The harm we do others we easily forget."

Italian shows its individuality by giving old bromides new twists: "Slow but sure—and you never get there"; "Silence is assent—but if you keep your mouth shut, you're not saying anything." Korean has: "Everyone meets his enemy on a narrow bridge." Chinese has: "A hundred listenings is not equal to one seeing."

Obviously, far more evidence will have to be accumulated before a link between language and national psychology can be firmly established.

PART FOUR

The Modern Spoken Tongues

— Chapter One —

THE GEOGRAPHY OF LANGUAGE

Therefore is the name of it called Babel; because the Lord did there confound the language of all the earth.
—Genesis 11:9

The man who knows no foreign language knows nothing of his mother tongue.

—Goethe

THE world's population of nearly three billion people is scattered, in very uneven fashion, over practically all of the earth's land surface. The world's languages are still more unevenly distributed.

It has been estimated by French and American linguists, working separately, that the world's peoples speak 2,796 different tongues, exclusive of minor dialects, the number of which has never been satisfactorily determined. Making allowance for differences of interpretation as to what constitutes a language and what measures up as a dialect, we may set the total number of languages at somewhere below 3,000. If the speakers were equally apportioned among the languages, each language would have nearly one million speakers.

Obviously, this proportion does not hold. English is spoken by practically all of the United States' 190 million inhabitants, to which are added the 100 million native English speakers of the British Commonwealth of Nations. We have heard of "50 million Frenchmen" (actually, the number is 45 million) who speak French. There is a Latin-American world to the south of us, with a population slightly surpassing our own total of 190 million, and even if from that total we subtract the 75 million Portuguese speakers of Brazil, Spanish is left in linguistic control of some 130 million Western Hemisphere people. The population of the Soviet Union passes the 230-million mark; not all of them speak Russian but at least three-quarters of them do. China's inhabitants are estimated at over 700 million, and nearly all of them use one or another dialect of Chinese.

If some languages have 50, 100, 200, or 700 million speakers, others must have far less than the one million to which the share-and-share-alike plan would entitle them. As a matter of fact, over 1200 of our 2,796 languages are spoken by American Indian tribes, most of which number only a few thousand or even a few hundred people. Some 700 more are used by African Negro groups, many of which are quite small. Five hundred more belong to the natives of Australia, Tasmania, New Guinea, and the islands of the Pacific. Hundreds of others are spoken by small Asiatic groups.

There are in existence only thirteen languages with 50 million or more speakers. They are, in order of numerical importance, Chinese, English, Hindustani, Russian, Spanish, German, Japanese, Arabic, Bengali, Portuguese, Malay, French, and Italian. The roughly approximate figures, which include non-native as well as native speakers, are as follows:

Chinese	700,000,000	Arabic	90,000,000
English	350,000,000	Bengali	90,000,000
Hindustani	200,000,000	Portuguese	85,000,000
Russian	200,000,000	Malay (Indonesian)	80,000,000
Spanish	160,000,000	French	80,000,000
German	100,000,000	Italian	65,000,000
Japanese	100,000,000		

The distribution of these languages varies widely. Among the Asiatic tongues, Chinese is largely limited to China and Manchuria. Hindustani and Bengali have little currency outside their native India. Japanese is the tongue of the islands of Japan and enjoys some currency in Korea and nearby sections of the Asiatic mainland. Malay is spoken in Indonesia and Malaya and is understood as far as the Philippines. Arabic enjoys a tremendous sweep of territory, extending across Africa north of the Tropic of Cancer from Casablanca to Cairo and beyond, into Israel, Syria, Iraq, and Arabia, and is widely understood wherever the Moslem religion reaches; but it is almost everywhere mingled with other languages of non-Arabic though kindred stock (Berber, Cushitic, Hebrew, etc.).

English, as a native or colonial tongue, covers one fifth of the earth's land surface. It holds almost undisputed sway over the United States, the British Isles, Canada, Australia, New Zealand, and portions of Africa, and is current in all British and American possessions and former possessions. There are over 200 million English speakers in the Western Hemisphere; over 60 million in Europe; over 25 million in Asia; over 5 million in Africa; and over 13 million in Oceania, including Australia and New Zealand. Five million people on the European continent speak English in addition to their own native tongues.

Russian holds control over one sixth of the earth's land surface, being the predominant language or, as the Soviets put it, the "binding tongue" of the far-flung Soviet Union. But little more than half of the Union's 230 million inhabitants use Russian as their native tongue. The rest speak 145 different languages, including the Ukrainian of southern Russia, the Georgian of Stalin, and a host of Turkic tongues.

Spanish appears in its Spanish homeland, the Canary Islands, and the Spanish colonies, but less than one fourth of its speakers are located there. The other three fourths are in the Western Hemisphere, where Spanish is second only to English, covering Mexico, Central America, Cuba, Puerto Rico, the Dominican Republic, and all of South America with the exception of Brazil and the Guianas.

Portuguese is the tongue of Brazil, a country larger than the continental United States, as well as of Portugal and the Portuguese colonies in Africa, Asia, and the Pacific. The Azores, Madeira, and Cape Verde Islands speak Portuguese.

German is largely restricted to Europe. There it is spoken not only by the populations of Germany, Austria, and most of Switzerland but also by some 20 million continental Europeans in neighboring central European countries—Czechoslovakia, Poland, the Netherlands, Hungary, Yugoslavia, Sweden, etc.

French is the language of France, part of Switzerland and Belgium, the former Belgian Congo and the French Union (the latter, which includes what the French call *la France d'Outre-mer,* or "Overseas France," has an area several times that of France and a population almost double that of the mother country), as well as of Haiti and the Province of Quebec in the Western Hemisphere. It is widely used as a cultural tongue in Europe, Asia, Africa, and Latin America. Over 5 million Europeans outside of French-speaking countries speak French in addition to their own tongues.

Italian, the language of Italy and one of the Swiss cantons, is current in the former Italian colonies (Eritrea, Somaliland, Libya, and Cirenaica) and is used by Italian emigrant groups numbering some 10 million, located mostly in various Mediterranean countries, the United States, Argentina, Brazil, Uruguay, and Chile.

Germanic languages, including English, German, Dutch, and the Scandinavian tongues (Swedish, Norwegian, Danish, and Icelandic) number well over 400 million speakers. The total for the Romance languages (French, Spanish, Portuguese, Italian, Rumanian) is close to 400 million. The Slavic tongues, of which Russian is the most important, run well beyond the 260 million mark, with Russian accounting for over 130 million, Polish and Ukrainian for 40 million each, Czech and Slovak for about 14 million, Serbo-Croatian for approximately the same number, and Bulgarian for 8 million.

India's 480 million inhabitants speak thirty-three major tongues, along with a host of minor languages and dialects. Hindustani, with its 180 million, and Bengali, with 90 million, are the leading languages of India.

The "National Tongue" of China, based on the North Mandarin dialect, is spoken by about two thirds of China's 700 million. The remainder speak various dialects, like the Cantonese most frequently heard in the United States.

Ural-Altaic is the name given to a group of languages which cover a wide territorial extent in northern and central Asia but whose speakers do not exceed 100 million. These Asiatic tongues have several spearheads in Europe, Finnish, Hungarian, and Turkish among them.

The Malayo-Polynesian languages, of which Malay, one of the leading thirteen, is a sample, range from Madagascar off the east African coast, across the Indian and Pacific oceans, to Easter Island, off the western coast of South America. They embrace Malaysia, Indonesia, the Philippines, the islands of Melanesia, Micronesia and Polynesia, New Zealand, and Hawaii, with about 130 million speakers.

It is a curious fact that Hindustani and Russian, though numerically they rank third and fourth, outstripping German and Spanish, are not the leading languages of their respective continents. Hindustani is outnumbered by Chinese, the most widely spoken tongue of Asia, while Russian speakers are divided between Europe and Asia, so that Russian is outnumbered in Europe by German's 100 million speakers, who form a European plurality. English leads in North America and Oceania, Spanish in Central and South America, while Arabic holds the palm for Africa.

The overwhelming majority of our own population of 190 million speaks English. There are about 26 million people here, however, whose mother tongue is not English. German accounts for some 5 million, Italian for 4, Polish and Spanish for 3 each, Yiddish for 2, Russian and French for 1½ each, Swedish for 1, while Norwegian, Czech, and Ukrainian approach the 1-million mark. Almost 1 million French speakers, immigrants from Canada's Quebec Province or their descendants, inhabit our New England states; over 1 million Spanish speakers live in our southwestern states (Spanish is co-official with English in New Mexico); at least 1 million, mostly Puerto Ricans, in New York's metropolitan area; ¼ million Portuguese speakers live in California and Massachusetts.

— Chapter Two —

KING'S ENGLISH AND AMERICAN LANGUAGE

In richness, good sense, and terse convenience, no other of the living languages may be put beside English.
— Jakob Grimm

ENGLISH is the language that has enjoyed by far the fastest growth within recent times: four centuries ago, it was outstripped by French, German, Spanish, and Italian; today, it has almost as many speakers as the four put together. After Chinese, English has the world's largest speaking population —some 300 million; or, to put it another way, one person out of every ten in the world. In addition, it gives access to colonial or former colonial populations numbering 500 million more. It is the native or official language of countries covering one fifth of the earth's land surface, outstripping its nearest competitor for area, Russian, by several thousands of square miles and having the further advantage of being widely distributed over the globe, instead of being concentrated in one land mass.

English is at present the most widely studied language in countries where it is not native, being the favored foreign language in the higher educational curriculum of such widely scattered nations as Russia, Japan, and Turkey. It is conspicuously the language of trade and business transactions and bids fair to become a tongue of common intercourse in many parts of the world. Three fourths of the world's mail is written in English. Over half of the world's newspapers are printed in English. English is the language of over three fifths of the world's radio stations. It has a literature as flourishing as any, and has recently become one of the leading tongues of international scholarship and scientific research. More than half of the world's scientific and technical periodicals are printed entirely or partly in English.

In addition, English is a language of widespread international intercourse among speakers of other tongues. The Communist propaganda that is beamed by both Red Russia and Red China to the new countries of Asia and Africa is largely broadcast in English, so that it may reach the top intellectual layers of those countries. When twenty-nine African and Asian nations held a conference at Bandoeng in 1955, English was the official language of the gathering. The official text of a cultural treaty between Egypt and Indonesia is the English text. A Ceylonese mission to the U.S.S.R. is greeted by Soviet officials in English. Our USIA, with its four hundred centers and libraries scattered throughout the world, spreads the cult of English. So does the British Institute, with its English-language schools.

All these features make modern English a language similar in scope to the Latin of ancient times—a mighty imperial tongue, and the chief and most formidable contender among the languages aspiring to the honor of becoming the world tongue of the future.

Historically, English belongs to the West Germanic branch of Indo-European, having developed from the Anglo-Saxon of the invaders from the continental North Sea coast who wrested control of Britain from its Romanized Celtic inhabitants in the sixth and seventh centuries of our era. More than nearly any other tongue, however, English has displayed remarkable powers of adaptation and assimilation, absorbing so many and such varied elements of vocabulary and syntax from diverse sources (notably Norman-French, Latin, and Greek) that today it would be a definite misstatement to pronounce it a Germanic language pure and simple.

While accepting these large foreign contributions, English has revealed, in the course of its history, astounding capacities for growth from within, the ability to coin, combine, create, and simplify to the point where its vocabulary has become the richest on earth and one of the most precise and expressive.

At the same time, English has shown, in common with many other Indo-European languages but to a greater degree than most, the tendency to evolve from the original Indo-European structure. The latter was highly synthetic, expressing many concepts by means of a single lengthy word consisting of a root and its associated prefixes and suffixes. English, in its historical development, tends toward an analytical state, wherein the same multitude of concepts is expressed by numerous short words, loosely held together by syntactical devices. It is a normal experience for high school students who translate from Latin into English to discover that, while their translation usually contains about the same number of lines as the original, the number of words is double that of the Latin passage.

Some linguists choose to view this process as a simplification of the language, something almost deliberately designed to make the language easier to its speakers and learners. That this is not altogether or necessarily true is indicated by the crazy quilt of verb-and-preposition combinations which have been pointed out elsewhere, expressions like "go through with," "put up with," "get away with," which must be separately learned as idioms and correctly arranged. The difficulties of our analytical language stand out in full only when one undertakes, as this writer once did, to compose a grammar of English for the use of speakers of a more synthetic tongue. It is then, and only then, that constructions which we have taken for granted all our lives rise to smite us between the eyes and to convince us that the foreigner who wants to learn to speak English with something more than vaudeville-immigrant correctness and fluency must labor at least as hard and as long as the American student who struggles through lists of French or Spanish conjugational endings.

One of the greatest structural merits of the modern English tongue (though it is not altogether an unmixed blessing) lies in the numerous parts of speech that have become invariable in form. The learner of English is faced with a single form of the definite article ("the") and of the adjective ("large"), a double form of the indefinite article ("a" or "an") which, however, alternate euphoniously, in accordance with the initial sound of the word that follows, not with the gender of the noun). The distinctions of our demonstrative pronouns apply only to number ("this," "these"). Personal, possessive, relative, and interrogative pronouns show few complexities of gender, number, or case ("I," "me," "we," "us"; "my," "mine"; "who," "whom"). The noun has discarded all case endings save for a genitive ("boy's"), and the plural of the noun, with a few exceptions ("men," "oxen," "children," "feet," "deer," etc.), is formed by the addition of an -s or -es.

At this point, however, we encounter an important stumbling block. The so-called -s of the plural sounds like an -s only when it follows unvoiced consonants ("books," "trips," "goats"); after voiced consonants, liquids, nasals, and vowels

it sounds like a -z ("eggs," "ribs," "goads," "tears," "boys").
Additional complications are offered by special spellings
("lady," "ladies") and by shifts in the consonant of the
root ("loaf," "loaves").

The English verb is, at first glance, a mechanism of extreme simplicity. Weak verbs have only four forms ("love,"
"loves," "loving," "loved"); strong verbs have five ("write,"
"writes," "wrote," "writing," "written"). All other verb forms
are produced by combining some of these forms with various
personal pronouns ("I," "you," "he," "they") and with auxiliaries ("has," "had," "am," "was," "shall," "should," "will,"
"would," "may," "might," etc.). This, according to some
linguists, is a vast improvement over such synthetic forms as
Latin *amabo* ("I shall love") or Spanish *quisieran* ("they
might want"). In reality, there are as many possibilities of
confusion and error in one system as in the other, nor is
memorizing English auxiliaries and their functions easier than
memorizing straight verb forms with endings.

In addition, the same pronunciation difficulties that appear
in the plural of nouns also appear in the -s and -ed forms of
verbs. The -s is an -s only after unvoiced consonants
("speaks," "wants"), but becomes a -z after voiced consonants
liquids, nasals and vowels ("bids," "calls," "has," "owes").
The -ed has an e which is sometimes pronounced ("wanted"),
sometimes silent ("called"). The -d is pronounced like a -t
after unvoiced consonants ("laughed," "asked"). The past of
strong verbs is unpredictable, save to Germanic scholars (why
"sing," "sang," "ring," "rang," but "cling," "clung," and
"bring," "brought"?). So is the past participle ("take,"
"taken," but "speak," "spoken"). Add to this our use of "do"
as an interrogative and negative auxiliary ("does he go?," "he
did not go"), which does not apply to the verb "to be" and
may or may not apply to the verb "to have" ("has he?,"
"does he have?"), and it will be seen that the English verb is
not so simple as it looks.

It is often remarked that, in spite of all these difficulties,
foreigners manage to make themselves understood. This, of
course, is true of any language. An English speaker using
the wrong case of a Russian noun, or the wrong form of a
French verb, has as much chance of being understood (and
ridiculed) as a Slav who says, "Please, I want not go," or a
Frenchman who says. "I am een America seence two weeks."

English spelling, as has been frequently pointed out by
G. B. Shaw, Senator Robert Owen, and others, is a monument to traditionalism so weird as to be practically incredi-

ble. We have only five written vowels but at least thirteen vowel sounds, plus some thirty vowel combinations, or diphthongs, many of which are represented by simple vowels in writing (our so-called "long" vowels, *a*, *i*, *o*, and *u*, are all phonetically combinations of two vowel sounds). A group like *ou* appears with a different phonetic value in each of these words: "house," "cough," "cousin," "through," "furlough," "could." Words like "Polish" and "polish" are distinguished in writing only by the capital. Shaw is said to be responsible for the statement that "fish" could be spelled "ghoti" by using the *gh* of "enough," the *o* of "women" and the *ti* of "nation."

It is conceivable that a foreigner, with the aid of a good grammatical introduction to pronunciation and a few short lessons from a teacher, could learn to speak acceptable Spanish, Italian, Russian, German, Portuguese, even French. This is not true of English, where every word is a law unto itself. There are no English rules of pronunciation, in the same sense that there are Spanish, Italian, German, even French rules. If the learner proceeds from the written to the spoken language, as foreigners usually do, he must learn the pronunciation of each word, separately and painfully. If he begins with the spoken tongue and passes on to the written, as is the case with our own school children, then he must learn to spell. The process of learning to spell is an endless one, continuing through elementary school, high school, and college, and often not quite completed by the time the English-speaking student emerges with a university degree. In this one respect, English is a tongue of infinite difficulty, far harder than any of its kindred Indo-European languages. Indeed, the only comparison possible is with languages like Chinese and Japanese, where the ideogram for each word must be individually learned. Whether we realize it or not (and we are quick to realize it when we hark back to the spelling bees of our school days), every English word is at least in part an ideogram, with the pronunciation offering some clue, but never a complete key, to the spelling.

Yet despite these glaring disadvantages, English manages to hold most of the ground it has gained and to make additional progress. This has been due in large measure to the colonizing habits of English speakers, who have spread their language from the British Isles to the far corners of the earth. Obviously, this tremendous sweep of territory and population could not have been achieved without a considerable degree of dialectalization and the creation of diverging forms of English speech. Linguists often express surprise that the divergences among the various speech forms of the Anglo-Saxon world are as relatively slight as is actually the case.

The main varieties of English speech (each, of course, subdivided into local subvarieties) are the British, with its numerous and widely diverging dialects; the American, with its three main subdivisions (Eastern, Southern, and the General American); the Canadian, which tends to approach the American; the Australian and New Zealand, which in part coincide; and the South African. In addition, we have numerous pidginized forms of English, in which the influence of one or more other languages is distinctly perceptible.

If we first consider English as it appears today on its original home heath, we find, in addition to the local dialects, which are numerous and varied, a national standard known as the "King's English" which is generally used by the more educated classes of Britain and is spoken by B.B.C. announcers and broadcasters. It is distinguished from American English primarily by its enunciation, which is more clipped, incisive, and staccato, and by its greater modulation of tone and rise and fall in pitch.

This *koine* of Britain is not to be confused with the Oxford accent, with which it coincides only in part. The latter is not at all the Oxfordshire dialect but a cultivated language that grew up around the university and did not become current in England till the beginning of the nineteenth century. Both King's English and Oxford English come closer to cultured Londonese (not Cockney, however) than to any other local English dialect.

Nearly all Britishers approve of the King's English. Oxford English does not meet with such unanimous approval, as witnessed by the description given of it by a Scottish philologist, who calls it "artificial, slovenly, difficult for foreigners to acquire, and inharmonious." It is still less popular abroad; a Russian linguistic congress in 1930 defined Oxford English as "an aristocratic tongue purposely fostered by the highest British governing and land-owning classes in order to maintain their icy and lofty exclusiveness"; at the same congress the charge was made that the swallowing of final sounds characteristic of Oxford English was deliberately designed to make the language difficult for others to speak. It is difficult in an appraisal of this sort to separate what is purely linguistic from what is political, but the fact remains that whenever the speech of Britain comes in for ridicule from American sources, it is invariably the excesses of the Oxford language that supply most of the ammunition.

Differences in pronunciation between British English and American English are numerous, though nearly all of the British peculiarities have their counterpart in one section or another of the United States. King's English gives a broad *ah* sound to words like "bath" and "dance," but so do several New England varieties. This pronunciation, incidentally, is a comparatively recent innovation and is said to have come from a stage affectation originally introduced by the actor David Garrick in the eighteenth century. The "flat" sound of General American "bath" and "dance" antedates it. The sound given by most Englishmen to words containing so-called "short *o*" ("pot," "lot") comes close to the French open *o* of *notre,* while the General American sound is more like a shortening of the *a* of "father." Long *o* (as in "bone") is a diphthong in both languages, but in English pronunciation the sound comes close to *ou* of General American "house." Final consonants are far more explosive in British than in American English. The sound of long *i* for long *a* ("lidy" for "lady") and the dropping of initial *h* ("an 'orrible 'eadache") are characteristic of lower-class London Cockney.

Differences in the pronunciation of individual words are quite numerous. In a *Dictionary of English Pronunciation with American Variants,* 28 per cent of the words show different pronunciations. The British Army pronounces "lieutenant" "leftenant," though a pronunciation similar to ours is used for the rank in the British Navy. "Shedule" and "figger" are the British pronunciations of "schedule" and "figure." Place names like Leicester, Harwich, Auchinleck, St. Osyth, St. Olav, Marjoribanks are pronounced by the British "Lester," "Harridge," "Afleck," "Toosey," "Tooley," "Marchbanks." (Our Wooster is believed to be an attempt to give a phonetic spelling to the British Worcester.) Words with *er* followed by a consonant ("clerk," "Derby") are pronounced as though they had *ar.*

Many words are differently stressed. The British stress "*ne*cessary, "*pri*marily," and "*ga*rage" on the first syllable, but "pa*pa*" and "mam*ma*" on the last. "Speci*a*lity," with stress on the *a,* is the British version of "specialty." "Labo*ra*-tory" in Britain is stressed on the second, not on the first syllable, "fin*an*cier" on the second, not on the last.

Among differences of spelling usage, the following are worthy of note: the British spelling for nouns ending in *-or* is usually with *-our* ("honour," "labour," "flavour," "neighbour"; of special interest is the notation on some British films: "Colour by Technicolor"); *x* instead of *ct* appears in words like "connexion," "inflexion"; nouns in -*ense* normally take -*ence* in Britain ("offence," "defence," "licence"; the legal document used for the wedding of Queen Elizabeth is entitled "Licence for Marriage"). Many suffixes which in American written usage have a single *l* appear with double *l* in British ("traveller," "libellous"). A few words are used, both in spoken and written form, with what to us would be an archaic spelling and pronunciation ("whilst," "amongst"). Many individual words show spelling differences: "gaol," "kerb," "tyre," "programme," "grey," "cheque," "jewellery" instead of "jail," "curb," "tire," "program," "gray," "check," "jewelry."

There are variations in verb forms and subtle distinctions of usage. The British tend to avoid such Americanisms as "dove," "gotten," "proven," "stricken" for "dived," "got," "proved," "struck." The use of "do" with "have" is generally restricted by them to permanent states ("Does he have blue eyes?" but not "Do you have that book?"). Prepositions are differently used. The Britisher fills "up" (not "out") a coupon or form; he caters "for," not "to," someone; he lives "in," not "on," a certain street, and travels "in," not "on," a train, which is supposed to run "to," not "on," time. He sells "by," not "at," retail, has a lease "of," not "on," life, provided he can get "through," not "by," and that is all there is "about," not "to," it. Take such a simple thing as the directions for a dehydrated soup: "Mix the content [not "contents"] of this packet [not "package"] with a little cold water; bring to the [not "a"] boil; add small pieces of grilled [not "toasted"] bread." Though they have adopted a good many Americanisms, there is still opposition to "teacher guidance," "language usage," "neighborhood projects," "consumer spending," "aim to provide," "I charge that he did it," "to turn down," "to pass up," "to let up," "to slip up."

Vocabulary and semantic differences between British and American usage are sufficiently numerous to have warranted the compilation of many lengthy glossaries, some of book length. In Britain, our "information bureau" is an "inquiry office," a "ticket agent" is a "booking clerk" (pronounced *clark;* this term, by the way, is not applied in Britain to a salesperson but only to a "black-coated"—not "white collar" —office worker). "Railroad tracks" are "metals" or "lines," a "freight car" is a "goods waggon," and "transportation of freight" is the "carriage of goods." A "subway" is our "underpass," "underground" being our "subway." (This not only can be confusing but can lead to ludicrous replies, as when a Londoner in New York inquired how he could "get to the

underground" and was irreverently told, "Drop dead!")
"Cheesecloth" is "butter muslin"; a "chicken yard" is a "fowl
run"; our "sneakers" are "plimsoles" or "sand shoes," with
the corollary that our "slippers" are their "shoes" and our
"shoes" their "boots." Our "kindergarten" is their "infants'
school," our "rummage sale" their "jumble sale," our "book-
mobile" their "caravan library," our "clipping bureau" their
"press cutting agency," our "landslide" their "landslip," our
"cockroach," or its nearest British equivalent, their "black
beetle." "Wireless" is, of course, our "radio," and "telly" our
"TV."

Shop names and shop signs differ. Our "clothing store,"
"poultry shop," "tobacco shop," "vegetable store," "candy
shop," "drug store," "movie house" become in Britain "haber-
dashers," "poulterer," "tobacconist," "greengrocer," "sweets
shop," "chemist's," "cinema." "Fishmonger" and "ironmonger"
are our "fish store" and "hardware store." The sign on a
British shop may read: "Post Office, Stationery, Readings,
Cosmetics, Dispensing." The third and fifth terms mean that
they sell books, magazines, and newspapers as well as ice
cream and soft drinks.

"Dessert" in Britain means "fruit," and you must use
"sweet" if you want a dessert, while if you ask for "biscuits"
you will get crackers; "scones" (pronounced *scawns*) are the
nearest British equivalent of our "biscuits." "Apartment" in
Britain means a single room; for the American apartment,
one should use "flat" or "rooms," while an "apartment house"
is a "block of flats." To an English bride, a "can opener" is
a "tin-opener," a "pancake turner" is an "egg-scoop," and an
"egg beater" an "egg-whisk." An American worker's "pay
envelope" is a British worker's "pay-packet." A "mist" in
Britain is a "light fog," not a "drizzle" as it is in America.
Bewildering to an American when it comes from a British
telephone operator is the expression "You're through," which
means not "You're finished" but "You're connected."

Three areas of speech can get to be particularly confusing:
legal and official terminology, the language of automobiles
and driving, and colloquialisms. For the first, the British
politician "stands for," does not "run for," office. A witness,
who really stands in Britain when he "takes the stand," is
told to "stand down," not "step down," when his testimony
is finished. The court audience is told to "be upstanding"
when the judge comes in. A British police report will state
that a woman victim was "interfered with," not "molested"
(both expressions, of course, are rank euphemisms). In Britain you have "barristers-at-law" and "solicitors," not "at-

torneys-at-law" and "counsel." An estate pays "death duties," not "inheritance tax." There are regulations against "gaming and wagering," not "gambling." You are sold "assurance," not "insurance." You do not buy on the "installment plan" but on "HP" ("hire purchase"). A letter is "posted," not "mailed," and the answer may be "reply-paid," not "post-paid." A British "redcap" is a "military policeman," not a porter, and their "Blue Cross" is for animals only. To "vote down" is used, but one wonders whether Britain would accept President Johnson's "vote up." Our "newscaster" is B.B.C.'s "news-reader."

The difference in automobile terminology is so extensive as to constitute practically a different language. Our "sedan" is their "saloon," our "station wagon" their "utility car," our "dump truck" their "tipping lorry," our "convertible" their "drophead," our "trailer" their "caravan." There is almost no coincidence in the names of car parts. Our "hood" is a "bonnet," our "fender" a "mudguard wing," our "trunk compartment" a "boot," our "defroster" a "demister," our "bumpers" are "buffers" or "overriders," our "windshield" a "windscreen," our "crankcase" a "sump," our "transmission" a "gearbox," our "muffler" a "silencer," our "shock absorbers" "dampers," our "choke" a "strangler," our "glove compartment" a "cubby locker," our "dashboard" a "fascia," our "horn" a "hooter," our "directional signal" is a "trafficator," even our "wrench" turns into a "spanner." The "highway" is a "carriageway," the "shoulder" is a "verge" or "verge on heath," a "private road" is "unadopted land," a "detour" is a "diversion," "curves" are "bends," a "traffic circle" is a "roundabout" or "circus," an "overpass" is a "flyover." "Loose chippings" is our "fallen rock," "double banking" is "double parking," a "zebra crossing" is a "pedestrian's right of way," and "precedence" a "motorist's right of way." "Road up" means "the road is under repairs," "left coming" means "merging traffic from the left." "Topping off" is "filling your battery" (which is more often styled "accumulator"), and "dipping your lamps" is "dimming your headlights." The "near" side of the car is the "left" side, the "off" side is the "right." A "road hog" goes by a picturesque name: "Crown stroller."

Without going into downright slang, the colloquial language can be fully as colloquial in Britain as in America. Anthony Eden doesn't mind saying that "there ain't too much to worry about," and Viscount Montgomery says that people who do certain things are "crackers," which means "crazy" (this is a multivalued word, however, for "cracker" can also mean a "doll").

The difference between the English of Britain and that of America was first noted around the middle of the eighteenth century, and the first statement concerning the "language of the United States" appears in 1778. By the beginning of the nineteenth century, British writers complained that the language of the former American colonies was as far removed from English as Italian is from Latin. Their chief criticisms of American pronunciation were the same then as they are today: American pronunciation is said to be monotonous or "flat" and extremely nasal. By the middle of the nineteenth century, Englishmen who got as far west as the Ohio valley were struck by the "barbarity of the English language as spoken in America," and Dickens, in 1842, voiced a bitter complaint about the American use of the word "fix," which another English visitor of the period defined as having as many possible meanings as any word in Chinese. "Notify" and "fellow countryman" had previously been among the very first Americanisms to draw British fire. American writers of the period hotly retorted that American English was less corrupt than British English, and from the standpoint of historical phonology they seemed justified in their assertion. Numerous attempts were made at this period, both in the state legislatures and in Congress, to declare officially that the name of the language spoken in the United States was the "American language," and there are even unproved stories to the effect that after the Revolution certain members of Congress advocated that English be altogether discarded and replaced by Hebrew or Greek as the official language of the United States. As late as 1920, an attempt was made to coin the term "Unitedstatish" to describe the language of the American Union. Today, about half the students in linguistics classes who are polled as to their native tongue reply "American" rather than "English."

G. B. Shaw used to claim that "England and America are two countries separated by the same language," while a contemporary American writer says that interpreters are far more needed between ourselves and the British than between either one and the French or Germans, but such statements are humorously and paradoxically advanced, even if they are aided and abetted by continental Europeans who hang out such signs as "English spoken here—American understood" or who offer to teach English in three months or American in two months. That the British themselves are not above such low humor is evidenced by the following sign noted on a London theater marquee: "New sensational American Western film—English subtitles."

The fact of the matter is, however, that the two languages have in recent times been drawing closer and closer, by reason especially of the radio and spoken film, and of the numerous American soldiers stationed in Britain, which bring the spoken-language peculiarities of one section of the Anglo-Saxon world to the other. British terms and pronunciations which fifty years ago would not have been understood in America are now commonplace, and vice versa. To cite only two examples, we have taken from the colloquial of Britain "to take a dim view" of something, and "to have had it." On the other hand, British youngsters back from an extended stay in the United States fill the British atmosphere with such expressions as "Hi ya, Pop!" and "buddy," and their elders have to re-train them to speak English.

As for the linguistic background of American English, many (generally unsuccessful) attempts have been made to link it with the tongues of origin of non-English speakers. It has been repeatedly pointed out that in the eighteenth century a knowledge of Dutch was almost indispensable in New York, while one third of the population of Pennsylvania was German-speaking, and Franklin was afraid they might make German the official language of the Commonwealth; that in various localities in New York State records were kept in Dutch for seventy-five years after the Revolution, while French was almost as current as English in the South during the eighteenth century. Many early records of Virginia and Maryland were kept in French, and Charleston had an English and a French theater, while in eighteenth-century Philadelphia the French schools outnumbered the English, and the *Courrier de l'Amérique* was the favorite morning newspaper.

Actually, however, there is no perceptible influence from Dutch, French, or German in the speech sounds of American English, save insofar as German has given rise to a new mixed language like Pennsylvania Dutch. The influence of the African Negro languages of the original slaves on the sound pattern of our Southern speakers is likewise unproved. Those who are too ready to admit foreign influence in the American sound pattern should also recall that 80 per cent of the present white population of the United States has English as its mother tongue. On the other hand, loan words from the immigrant languages are numerous, and they are favored by the fact that American English seems to have a greater tendency to admit such words than British English.

The tongues of the other British Commonwealth lands show a great deal of variety, but rather in vocabulary and expressions than in sounds or grammatical constructions. Very generally speaking, the sounds of Australian, New Zealand, and South African English are closer to the British standard, those of Canadian English to the American standard. Australian English is distinguished by a certain number of words borrowed from the native Australian tongues, while New Zealand English has drawn upon the Polynesian Maori of the original inhabitants. South African English has both Zulu and Dutch (or, more precisely, Afrikaans) words and expressions. A "kiwi," for instance, is a New Zealand G.I. (the kiwi is a wingless bird native only to New Zealand), while a "springbok" is a South African G.I. (the springbok is the Dutch name of a South African gazelle). *Kapai!* (a word borrowed from the language of the Maori natives) is New Zealand slang for "Attaboy!" *Inkoos* or *inkosi* is the Zulu word for "chief" and is used even by white South Africans with the meaning of "thanks" for a favor received. "The river is down" in South Africa means "there is a flood"; also, you "trek" at "schimmel day" instead of "setting out" at "dawn," while "mealy-meal" is the name of the popular South African ground maize. "Cooee!," a native Australian call, is the Australian "yoohoo!" Other picturesque expressions of South African English are "shebeen" for "speakeasy" (this seems to be due to Irish influence), "blerry" for "no good," *ou* for "man," "donner" for "to beat up," "lekker" for "nice," "strandloper" for "beachcomber"; in some of these the influence of Afrikaans is visible.

Expressions derived from the local background parallel our own. "Big scrub" and "great outback" are the Australian equivalents of our "great prairie" and "great plains." "Black-fellow's gift" is the Australian counterpart of "Indian giver." "Wurley" and "humpy" are the Australian equivalents of "wigwam" and "tepee." Just as American place names often come from the Indian languages, Australian place names are frequently of native origin, like Woogarora and Marangaroo.

Canadianisms which have no counterpart in the United States or Britain are comparatively rare. One of them, in addition to those listed under *Slang,* is "the Gridiron" for "Old Glory"; another is "toadskin" for "dollar bill." A third is "to stand sam" for "to treat" someone to something (Australia uses "to shout" in the same meaning). Canadians with a French language background often use loan translations such as "I am unbuttoned" for "I have been found out" and "another pair of shoes" for "a horse of a different color."

Semantic shifts in words which lie on the borderline between legitimate and slang vocabulary are frequent. In both Australia and New Zealand, "graft" means "hard work"; "chewing the rag" means not to chatter away but to "brood" over something; to "snowdrop" is to "swipe."

The dialect of Australia, which is particularly original and picturesque, has been the subject of numerous articles and books. The Australians call Italians "Dingbats," Englishmen "Pommies," Scotsmen "Geordies," and New Zealanders "Enzedders" (the last comes from the initials N.Z., the last letter of the alphabet being called "zed" in all parts of the British Empire, something that enabled immigration officials to distinguish between authentic Americans and authentic Canadians during the war).

In Australia, you don't "smooch a jane," you "smooge a sheila"; you don't get "plastered," but "shikkered"; you don't "borrow dough from a sidekick," but "bot some oscar from your cobber." Australian has borrowed heavily from American English, though giving it its own twist. Our "bonanza" has become "bonzer," "sockdolager" has turned into "sollicker," "whole caboodle" has become "whole caboose," "give it a twirl" has turned into "give it a burl," "whiz" has become "swiz," "wade into someone" is now "weigh into someone."

One interesting variety of English that came to light when the population had to be evacuated by reason of a volcanic eruption was that of Tristan da Cunha, an isolated island settled by a few Englishmen in 1816. British linguists who investigated the language of the refugees discovered such interesting archaisms as "arth" and "sarch" for "earth" and "search," "hother" for "other," and "wery wiolent" for "very violent."

More than any other world language, English has given rise to pidginized versions. The basis of a pidgin language is what the scientists call "hypocorism" and the layman "baby talk." It stems from the erroneous belief that it is easier for a baby or an untutored native to learn to speak if the language is "simplified." The simplification often takes the form of grammatical incorrectness, such as saying, and

teaching the baby to say, "Him see?" for "Does he see?"
Other features are the creation of words and suffixes, like
"snookums," "baby-ums," etc. Modern psychology shows
us that hypocorism is not only unnecessary but definitely
harmful, and that a young child may be taught to speak a
language as correctly as a university professor.

Pidgin is in the nature of baby talk imparted by and to
adults. Its use arose in the seventeenth century in the sea-
ports of southern China, where British traders sought a
compromise language between their own and the Chinese of
the natives. The observation having been made that Chinese
syntax was of the "simplified" or isolating type, the compromise hit upon was to use, for the most part, English words,
but with native syntactical arrangement and concessions to
native pronunciation. The word "pidgin" itself is the Cantonese corruption of English "business."

From the trade ports of China, the use of pidgin spread
southward to the islands of Melanesia, giving rise to the
pidgin *par excellence*, Melanesian pidgin English. The old
Chinese sentence pattern, however, generally continued to
be adhered to.

The total number of people using some form or other
of pidgin English is estimated at about thirty million. Most
of them are located on the China coast, the South Sea
islands, Australia, Malaya, and the west coast of Africa.
The territorial extent of pidgin English may be judged from
the fact that during the war the Japanese issued leaflets in
pidgin for use in the islands they had conquered.

Pidgin is anything but a unified speech, though there is a
certain measure of standardization. In addition to the
original Chinese-English pidgin, there is the Melanesian
variety, current in the Solomon, Fiji, and New Hebrides
islands; a variety used in New Guinea; one used by the
Blackfellows of Australia; a *bêche-de-mer* or "Sandalwood
English," that appears in Tahiti, Samoa, and other islands
of Polynesia; a West African pidgin spoken along the
African coast from Nigeria to Southwest Africa; a Kitchen
Kaffir used in the Union of South Africa and Rhodesia; an
Anglo-Indian or "Hobson-jobson," used in India; a Ningre-
Tongo or Jew-Tongo used by descendants of slaves along the
Surinam coast in Dutch Guiana; even a Chinook jargon,
formerly current in our north-western states; and a Negro-
American pidgin called Gullah, once spoken along the South
Carolina coast, which is now all but extinct. To this list
may perhaps be added Pochismo, a pidgin that has grown up
in Mexico along the American border and is extensively

used by our border patrols in their dealings with Mexican immigrants (the name comes from *pocho*, "discolored").

A few samples of the type of expression appearing in these various compromise languages may be of interest. In Chinese pidgin, "chin-chin" is "worship," "chop-chop" is "quickly," and "have-got-wata-top-side" is "crazy." In Melanesian pidgin, "kai-kai" is "to eat," "kinkenau" is "to steal." "Shoot 'im kai-kai" means "serve the dinner"; "capsize 'im coffee along cup" is "pour the coffee."

The pidgin of the West African coast presents such phenomena as "no humbug me" for "don't bother me," "wait small" for "wait a minute," "no more chop palaver" for "he's dead." There is a commonly used "dash" for "to tip" which seems to go back to Portuguese *deixar*, "to leave." "Jagwah," from the name of the Jaguar car, means "terrific."

The pidgins of southwest Asia have developed the noun "incharge," which seems to have originated in Pakistan and means "head man." There is a tendency to pluralize nouns normally used in the singular, such as "normal wears and tears," and even "newses," and to use "can" in the sense of "yes."

Pidgin (English or otherwise) is on the one hand a marker of man's inefficiency and erroneous thinking, on the other a monument to human ingenuity. It displays the multiplicity of wrong roads which the human mind occasionally takes, but also the relentless will of man to create understanding under the most difficult of circumstances. The fact that English, more than any other tongue, has given rise to pidgin forms is a tribute to the mighty force of expansion of the English language.

A tongue which in the brief space of four centuries has multiplied its speaking population 5000 per cent, and which, in addition to its own 300 million speakers, has some 30 million persons using it in pidgin form, is a tongue that has proved its practical importance. Whether this is such as to entitle it to make the winning bid for the post of the universal language of the future is something yet to be determined.

The projection of the English language into the future is perhaps an idle speculation. The present trend of the language seems to point in the direction of greater unification and standardization, brought about by improved systems of communication and education and by a tendency toward centralization, even of a political variety, on the part of its numerous and far-flung speakers. This, however, is coupled with a rapid rate of change and accretion, both by native coinage and by foreign importation.

Granted a continuation of present historical conditions, the English language of two hundred years hence will be likely to represent a merger of British and American phonetic habits, with comparatively little in the way of morphological or syntactical innovations, but with a turn-over in vocabulary and semantics that would make it difficult, not to say incomprehensible, to the English speaker of today.

— Chapter Three —

SCANDINAVIAN, DUTCH, AND GERMAN

I have shown that the German language needs reforming.
—Mark Twain, *"The Awful German Language"*

GERMAN, Dutch, Swedish, Danish, Norwegian, and Icelandic fill out the official national roster of the Germanic family of languages. Minor members, sometimes classed as languages, sometimes as variants or dialects, are the Flemish of Belgium, the Frisian of the Dutch and German North Sea coast, the Afrikaans of South Africa, the Yiddish of the northern or Ashkenazic Jews, the Schweizer-Deutsch of Switzerland, the Pennsylvania Dutch of the United States.

Before the outbreak of the Second World War, German was spoken by over 80 million people in the Reich, Austria, Switzerland, and regions like the Sudetenland of Czechoslovakia, the Polish Corridor and the Free State of Danzig, Danish Slesvig, French Alsace-Lorraine, Belgian Eupen and Malmédy, Luxembourg, even the Saratov region of Russia. It was widely used as a secondary cultural and business language throughout central Europe, including the Netherlands, the Scandinavian and Baltic countries, Poland, Czechoslovakia, Hungary, and Yugoslavia. In addition, it was spoken by several millions of German immigrants and their descendants in North and South America, particularly the United States, the Brazilian states of São Paulo and Rio Grande do Sul, Argentina, and Chile. It is probably no exaggeration to say that well over 100 million people can still be reached with it.

Dutch, with its Belgian variant, Flemish, and its South African variant, Afrikaans, is spoken by some 17 million people in the Netherlands and Belgium and by perhaps 3 million in the Union of South Africa, who are descendants of the original Boer settlers from Holland. The former Dutch colonial empire, now constituting the Republic of Indonesia, with close to 100 million people, is still to some extent subject to Dutch linguistic influence.

The Scandinavian languages, Swedish, Danish, Norwegian, and Icelandic, have approximately 9 million, 5 million, 4 million and 200,000 speakers, respectively. Faroese, the tongue of the Faroe Islands, is a cross between Danish and Icelandic. It may be mentioned at this point that, while Finland has enjoyed close political relations with Sweden in the past, and while Swedish is still extensively spoken along the Finnish coast, the Finnish language is definitely not a Scandinavian tongue or, for that matter, an Indo-European one.

German and Dutch belong, like English, to the West Germanic branch, while the Scandinavian tongues are of the North Germanic variety. A third Germanic branch, the Eastern, was represented by ancient Gothic, which has become extinct.

Historically, the Germanic languages appear comparatively late on the world's scene, but this is due merely to the absence of written records, not to the fact that a Proto-Germanic tongue was not spoken contemporaneously with Sanskrit, Greek, and Latin. The fourth century A.D. Gothic translation of the Bible by Bishop Ulfilas is the earliest satisfactory record of a Germanic tongue. Some Runic inscriptions found in Norway and Denmark may go back to the third or even the first century A.D., but of this there is no sure proof.

Among early Germanic (or Teutonic) languages are Old Saxon, of which we have a ninth-century literary monument, the *Heliand* or "Savior"; Old Franconian, from which Dutch stems; Old High German, the ancestor of modern German; and Anglo-Saxon, from which modern English is derived. All of these tongues begin to appear in satisfactory recorded form between the seventh and the ninth century A.D. Scandinavian records, save for Runic inscriptions, do not begin till the eleventh or twelfth century.

Beginning with the eighth century, the history of the various Germanic languages, including English, can be traced with fair accuracy. At the time of their first recorded appearance, the Germanic languages had already distinguished themselves from the other Indo-European tongues by a shift in certain consonant sounds, whereby an Indo-European *d* became *t*, *t* became *th*, *p* became *f*, *k* became *h*, etc. This is well exemplified by words like English "tooth" and "foot," which appear in Latin, Greek, and Sanskrit as *dent-*, *odont-*, *dant-*, and *ped-*, *pod-*, *pad-*, respectively. A second characteristic of the Germanic languages is a tendency to umlaut, which may be described as the fronting of a back vowel in the root of a word by reason of anticipation of a front vowel in the ending; this is exemplified by German *Satz*, plural *Sätze*, or Danish *Fod*, plural *Födder*, in which the *a* or *o* of the root becomes *ä* and *ö* because the speaker unconsciously prepares for the more frontal position of the *e* of the plural ending; English "foot—feet" and "mouse—mice" show the identical phenomenon but with the added feature that the vowel sound of the ending, after having caused the change in the vowel of the root, dropped out. A third characteristic of Germanic languages is the division of verbs into two classes: weak, forming the past and past participle by means of an ending (like English "love," "loved," "loved") and strong, where the past and past participle show a change of the vowel of the root (like English "sing," "sang," "sung").

One of the main distinctions between the Scandinavian and the West Germanic members of the family is that the former have developed a postposed definite article, so that an expression like "the boy" appears as "boy-the." Another is the Scandinavian formation of the passive of verbs by the addition of *-s*, or the change of an *-r* ending of the active to an *-s*. In Swedish, for instance, *jag kallar* is "I call," *jag kallas* "I am called." English, Dutch, and German, on the other hand, use an auxiliary to form the passive ("to be" in English, "to become" in German and Dutch). Since it has been determined that this *-s* of the Scandinavian passive is in origin a reflexive pronoun, like "self" of English or *se* of Latin, the question rises whether it betokens a special connection with Slavic, which likewise forms its passive by means of an invariable reflexive pronoun. The link, on the other hand, may be with the old Indo-European middle voice, showing the subject acting on or for himself.

There is also a decided vocabulary difference between North and West Germanic. English generally uses words which have a cognate in German and Dutch (our "great," for example, coincides with Dutch *groot* and German *gross*, not with Scandinavian *stor*); but since the Danish occupation of parts of England brought many Scandinavian words into Anglo-Saxon, we find occasional coincidences with Scandinavian (our "die," for instance, is the Scandinavian *dö*; Dutch *sterven* and German *sterben* have a cognate in English "starve," but the latter has acquired the special connotation of "to die by inanition").

Within the West Germanic branch there occurred about the eighth century A.D. a further differentiation between Low and High German. The West Germanic dialects of the south, particularly in the Alpine region, underwent a second consonant shift whereby in certain positions *d* became *t*, *th* became *t*, *t* became *ss* or *z*, *p* became *f* or *pf*, *k* became *ch*, etc. English and Dutch, which were originally Low German dialects of the North Sea coast, did not participate in this change, but High German, which eventually gave rise to standard modern German, did. The result is that today English and Dutch have *d* in "cold" and *koud*, "good" and *goed*, but German *kalt* and *gut* show *t*; English "two" and "water," Dutch *twee* and *water* have *t*, but German *zwei* and *Wasser* have *z* and *ss*; English "break" and Dutch *breken* have *k*, but German *brechen* has *ch*; English "lope" and Dutch *loopen* (or *lopen*) have *p*, but German *laufen* has *f*. English "dapper," with *d* and *p*, is German *tapfer*, with *t* and *pf*. The second sound shift sets German apart from the other Germanic languages to such an extent that a Scandinavian word often seems more similar to English than the historically more closely related German word.

Among the Scandinavian languages, special mention must be made of Icelandic for its archaism. All other Germanic languages give evidence of a trend away from the old Indo-European synthetic structure and toward analysis. Icelandic, however, has been described as a linguistic living fossil, displaying the same structure that appeared in the days of the Vikings. The four cases of the ancient Germanic languages (nominative, genitive, dative, and accusative) are still very much alive in Icelandic. The noun is fully declined, and so is the suffixed article. A sample of this plethoric declension is the following: *heimur-inn* ("the world"—subject); *heims-ins* ("of the world"); *heimi-num* ("to the world"); *heim-inn* ("the world"—object); *heimar-nir* ("the worlds"—subject); *heima-nna* ("of the worlds"); *heimu-nun* ("to the worlds"); *heima-na* ("the worlds"—object). Adjectives and most pronouns are fully declined. A trace of the dual number appears in the personal pronoun: *vid* ("we two"); *vjer* ("we"—more than two). Verbs carry a full set of conjugational endings. The verb "to have" in the present runs as follows: *hefi*, *hefir*, *hefir*, *höfum*, *hafid*, *hafa*.

By way of contrast, the other three Scandinavian languages have a simplified system of noun declension, wherein there is only one form for the singular and one for the plural, plus a genitive or possessive universally formed by the addition of

-s. A distinction is made between nouns which are neuter and those which are "gender" (*i.e.,* masculine, feminine, or common), but this distinction appears only in the article and occasionally in the adjectives that accompany the noun (*gosse-n,* "the boy," but *arbete-t,* "the word"). Characteristic of Swedish and Norwegian is the use of a double article when an adjective precedes the noun (*den stygga gosse-n,* literally, "the bad boy-the"). In spoken Swedish, Norwegian, and Danish, verbs are simplified to a point that outstrips English: a single form means "am," "is," "are"; another single form takes care of "was" and "were."

Modern Swedish, Norwegian, and Danish are fairly close, and the speaker of one of these tongues can generally manage to understand the others. Danish was at one time the official and literary language of Norway, but popular spoken Norwegian always diverged from the Danish literary standard. Present-day literary Norwegian is largely based upon the popular spoken tongue, or *Landsmål,* and the spelling has discarded certain Danish characters and replaced them with Swedish orthographies. The difference between the older Book Language, used by Ibsen, and the modern Combined Norwegian may be illustrated by the phrase "I have eaten": *Jeg har spist* vs. *Eg har ete.*

Despite the fact that there is more difference between two so-called dialects of Italian, like Sicilian and Piedmontese, than between any two of the three main Scandinavian languages, the Scandinavians are quite touchy about the individuality of their languages. It will not do to tell a Norwegian that he is speaking a variant of Danish, or vice versa. This writer at one time erroneously used a Danish orthography in a Norwegian sentence, and a Norwegian correspondent indignantly wrote back: "That spelling is Danish, and the Danes can keep it!"

Of particular interest to English speakers are the numerous words that have come into the Scottish dialect from Scandinavian. Bobbie Burns' "braw" and "bairn," to take only two examples, are directly traceable to Scandinavian *bra* and *barn.* Other Scandinavian words, like "skoal," "ski," "slalom," "saga," "Edda," "geyser," "smörgåsbord," have recently gained full citizenship in the English language, just as other Scandinavian words which gave us "sick," "die," and "them" did over a thousand years ago.

Dutch, English's closest kin among the national tongues, is a language replete with guttural sounds and misleading spellings. The letter *g* normally indicates a rasping guttural in

Dutch (*goed* is pronounced "khood") and the combination *sch* denotes not the *sh* sound of English but an *s* quickly followed by a guttural fricative; that is why Dutch names in America, spelled with *sch*, like Schuyler, Schuylkill, Schermerhorn, are pronounced with a *sk* sound. Written double vowels (as in *raad, heet, groot*) do not indicate length but only sound quality. A diphthong like *ui*, which is claimed to have given rise to our Brooklyn "boid" for "bird," actually represents a sound closer to the *ou* of "house" as spoken in Virginia (a more precise counterpart is the *eui* of French *deuil*). Grammatically speaking, Dutch has simplified itself almost to the same point as English, at least in its spoken variety. Only a trace of the possessive in -*s* remains (*de dochter van de vader* is more common than *de vaders dochter*). The indirect object is generally expressed, as in English, by its position before the direct object (*ik heb Oom Jan een brief geschreven*, "I have written Uncle John a letter"). The plural ending is -*en*, less frequently -*s*. Adjectives and pronouns present few difficulties, and verb conjugation strongly resembles English, save that there is normally an -*en* in the plural forms. But Afrikaans, the South African variant spoken by the Boers, dispenses even with these endings and has a single form that is used straight through the tense, being differentiated only by the subject pronoun. It is from Afrikaans rather than from Dutch proper that we get words like "boss," "spoor," "trek," and "veld." Dutch, on the other hand, gives us "slaw," "spa," "blunderbuss," and the *vrijbuiter* or "freebooter" that turns into "filibuster."

Official written Dutch, which stems from the fifteenth-century Flemish of Belgian Flanders and Brabant, rather than from the spoken form of the provinces that today constitute Holland, is much more conservative, retaining even a semblance of a four-case declension. Differences between the written and spoken form are especially striking in vocabulary, the formal expressions of the written tongue often being jocularly referred to as *stadhuiswoorden*, or "city hall words."

German, as the language of a great and populous nation, is naturally divided into numerous dialects, some of which, particularly in the coastal area, have a sound scheme that approaches that of English and Dutch (in Hamburg, for instance, *stehen* and *sprechen* are pronounced with the *s* sound of English instead of the *sh* sound which is normal in German for *s* before *t* or *p*). Austria, Bavaria, Switzerland have very well-defined High German dialects, and a few

Swiss nationalists even advocate the rejection of standard German as the official tongue of the German-speaking cantons of the country, and the adoption in its place of the local *Schwyzer-Tütsch.*

Among the variants of German is Yiddish, which goes back to the German Jewish communities of the Middle Ages and has been generally adopted by the northern European Jews as a language of common intercourse. It is written with a modified Hebrew alphabet and has borrowed from both Hebrew and various European languages outside of German, but it is still fundamentally a strongly conservative Renaissance German. In the Jewish communities in America it has been largely interlarded with English words and has at the same time made numerous contributions to the American vocabulary (*kibitzer* is one of our acquisitions from this source).

Printed German normally makes use of the Black Letter alphabet, which at one time was current in England as well and which occasionally still appears in Scandinavian writings of the past centuries. The use of the angular German hand-script, on the other hand, is more limited. Among spelling peculiarities, German is in the habit of capitalizing all nouns, both proper and common, and in this is accompanied by Danish.

The sounds of spoken German present relatively few difficulties to the English speaker (Mark Twain, in one of his writings, humorously undertakes to prove that any American can speak German if he wants to). One of the few phonetic stumbling blocks is the *ch* combination, which is a rasping guttural if it follows a back vowel, a hissing palatal if it follows a front vowel or a consonant. The Germans conveniently label these sounds the *ach-Laut* and the *ich-Laut,* these names giving even a reasonable clue as to the position in which each of them occurs. Yiddish, which broke away from German at a time when only the *ach-Laut* existed in all positions, still has the rasping guttural instead of the hissing palatal in words like *ich.*

The German grammatical scheme retains the four official Germanic cases (nominative, genitive, dative, accusative), but the distinction among them appears rather in the article than in the noun. A sample of the German declensional scheme is a noun like *der Bruder* ("the brother"), which is used as the subject; "of the brother" is *des Bruders;* "to the brother" *dem Bruder;* "the brother," as the object of the verb, *den Bruder.* In the plural, "the brothers" used as subject is *die Brüder;* "of the brothers" *der Brüder;* "to the brothers"

den Brüdern; "the brothers," used as object, *die Brüder,*
like the nominative, but distinguished by position after the
verb or some other syntactical device. Only the genitive singular and the dative plural have endings that differ from the
general singular and the general plural forms.

German gender is largely unpredictable. Typical of this
unpredictability are the names of three common table tools:
"the spoon" is *der Löffel,* masculine; "the fork" is *die
Gabel,* feminine; "the knife" is *das Messer,* neuter. One cannot even rely on the general linguistic rule that nouns
indicating males are masculine and those indicating females
feminine, since the diminutive endings *-chen* and *-lein* turn
any noun to which they are attached into a neuter, with the
result that *Mädchen* ("girl"; the English cognate is "maiden")
and *Fräulein* ("miss," a diminutive of *Frau,* "woman") are
declined and treated as neuter nouns. Certain suffixes carry
with them a certain gender; *-heit, -schaft, -ung,* for example,
form abstract nouns which are feminine, while *-tum* forms
neuter abstracts. But here another difficulty rises to plague the
English learner. The English cognates of *-heit, -schaft, -ung,*
and *-tum* are respectively *-hood, -ship, -ing,* and *-dom,* but
their application almost never corresponds. *Freiheit* is English
"freedom," not "freehood"; *Knechtschaft* is not "knightship"
or even "knighthood," but "slavery"; *Altertum* is not a nonexistent "olderdom," but "antiquity." Perhaps it is English
that is at fault for using so many borrowed words and suffixes
from non-Germanic sources; at all events, the process of
literal etymological translation of two parts of a compound
word almost invariably leads to disaster.

The German adjective declension is a difficult matter. The
attributive adjective takes a "strong" ending that bears indication of gender, number, and case, provided it is not itself
preceded by an article or some similar word that bears such an
ending. If the preceding article, possessive or demonstrative,
bears an ending indicative of gender, number, and case, then
the adjective takes a "weak" ending (*-e* or *-en*). Lastly, if the
adjective is used after the verb "to be," it takes no ending
whatsoever. This means that in an expression like "a good
man" (*ein guter Mann*), since *ein* bears no inflectional ending,
the adjective *gut* must take on the *-er* suffix indicative of
nominative case, masculine gender, singular number. But in
der gute Mann ("the good man"), where the article *der* bears
the significant *-er* ending, the adjective can take a subordinate position and assume a noncommittal ending like *-e.* In
der Mann ist gut ("the man is good"), where the adjective
follows the verb "to be," no ending whatsoever is used. A

certain lesser degree of this complication appears also in the Scandinavian languages and in Dutch; English is the only Germanic language that has had the courage to make the adjective altogether and under all circumstances invariable.

The German verb bears a full set of personal endings but also requires the use of a subject pronoun. In addition to this, many strong verbs effect a change of root vowel in the second and third persons singular of the present (*ich sehe,* "I see," but *du siehst,* "you see," *er sieht,* "he sees"). In addition to the two original Germanic tenses, present and past, German, like English, Scandinavian, and Dutch, has developed a full system of compound tenses formed by means of auxiliaries. The future and conditional are both formed with *werden* ("to become"), and, since this verb is also used as an auxiliary to form the passive voice, one must carefully note whether it is followed by the infinitive or by the past participle. In the former case, it is a future or conditional active form; in the latter, a present or past passive form: *ich werde rufen* (literally "I become to call") is "I shall call," but *ich werde gerufen* (literally "I become called") is "I am called."

Perhaps the most distressing feature of German to an English learner is its word order. If the subject does not begin the sentence, it normally follows the verb ("On Monday went we home"). A past participle is normally separated from its auxiliary by the object and adverbial modifiers ("I have a letter early written"). In a dependent clause, the verb usually appears at the end ("I know not, where you this book bought have"). An infinitive is normally separated from its governing verb and placed at the end of the sentence ("Shall we now home go?"). All of these syntactical traits, and others as well, have been properly and repeatedly satirized by English humorists, but to no visible avail.

Grimm's laws of sound correspondences and the etymological connections between English and German are occasionally of use in the study of the German language, but they are just as often misleading. *Langsam* is etymologically "longsome" but means "slow"; *unter* may be "under" but it is also "among"; *überall* looks like "overall" but really means "everywhere"; *bald* looks like "bold" but means "soon." Similar confusing etymologies appear in the other Germanic languages which have retained a higher proportion of the old Germanic vocabulary than English has.

Yet the intimate relationship among the various Germanic tongues cannot be denied. An expression like "good morning" is *guten Morgen* in German, *goeden morgen* in Dutch, *god morgon* in Swedish, *god morgen* in Norwegian and Danish.

"Give me" is *gib' mir, geef mij, giv mig, gi meg.* When we compare these extremely common expressions with their Romance or Slavic equivalents, we see why English is classified as a Germanic tongue and why learning to speak English is generally easier for a Norwegian than for a Pole or a Spaniard.

— Chapter Four —

THE ROMANCE TONGUES

*I love the language, that soft bastard Latin,
Which melts like kisses from a female mouth.*
—Byron, "Beppo"

THE name "Romance" comes from the Latin expression *romanice loqui* ("to speak in Roman fashion"). All other meanings of "romance," it is well to note, are derived from this original use.

Preoccupation with descent from the Romans was the primary consideration of Latin speakers in the dark days after the fall of the Roman Empire. A term, "Romania," was coined in the fifth century to denote those regions of the former empire where the language of the Romans continued to be spoken. This term was later appropriated by the Rumanians as a name for their own land. The province of Romagna in Italy is the same word, differently treated. The first reference to a Romance language, appearing in Charlemagne's proclamation of 813, describes it as *lingua romana rustica* ("rustic Roman tongue"). The medieval Spanish word *romance*, used to describe the new language of Spain, and the Old French verb *enromancer* ("to put into Romance," "to translate into the vernacular"—whence comes the use of "romance" as a tale of fiction, unworthy of Latin and composed in the tongue of everyday speech) are further demonstrations of this nostalgia for Rome on the part of those who still spoke the language of Rome.

The national Romance languages of today are five in number: French, Spanish, Italian, Portuguese, and Rumanian. To these may be added several non-national forms which are nevertheless usually classed as languages (Provençal, Catalan, Sardinian, Rhaeto-Romansh, Dalmatian), plus a very large number of dialects.

Had the course of history run differently, it is likely that we would have today three additional Romance tongues, one in North Africa, another in Britain, a third in the western part of the Balkans. Under the Empire, Latin flourished as a popular spoken tongue in the lands that today constitute Morocco, Algeria, Tunisia, and Libya, while the colonies first planted on British soil by Julius Caesar succeeded to a considerable degree in romanizing the Celtic-speaking Britons. But the great Moslem sweep of the seventh and eighth centuries of our era erased Latin from Africa and implanted the Koran's Arabic, while the Anglo-Saxon invasions stripped the romanized Celts of Britain of their Latin veneer. In like manner, the Latin of Illyricum, on the eastern coast of the Adriatic, was obliterated by the great Magyar and Slav infiltrations of the centuries that followed the Empire's downfall, separating the future Rumanians of Dacia from their Italian kinsmen. But the Vulgar Latin of Illyricum, developing into a Dalmatian form of Romance, survived for a long time in cities like Ragusa, Spalato, and Trau on the coast of Dalmatia; and in one of the Adriatic islands, Veglia, a form of Dalmatian Romance continued to be spoken until the end of the nineteenth century.

Despite these staggering losses, the Roman world survived and after a time began to march on to new conquests, particularly in the Western Hemisphere. Today, about 400 million people speak Romance languages, which constitute, after the Germanic group, the largest subdivision of Indo-European.

French is spoken by some 70 million people in France, Belgium, and western Switzerland, the Canadian provinces of Quebec and Ontario, and the Republic of Haiti. The former French Union and associated states, comprising part of North and West Africa, Madagascar, South Vietnam, French Guiana, and numerous Pacific and Antillean islands, has a population of over 80 million, of which perhaps one fourth can be reached with French. In addition, French is one of the great world languages of common intercourse, second only to English in that function. In Europe over 5 million people outside of the countries to which French is native speak the language. It is current in Asia and the Near East, in Central and South America, where the majority of educated people have learned it, even in North America, where it is one of the leading high school and college languages.

Spanish is the tongue of about 30 million people in Spain and the Spanish African colonies. It is also the tongue of some 130 million inhabitants of the Western Hemisphere. All of South America, outside of Brazil and the Guianas, all of

Central America, Mexico, and the two Caribbean islands of Cuba and Puerto Rico, as well as the Republic of Santo Domingo, speak Spanish, which is widely spoken and studied in the United States as well.

Portuguese is the language of the 9 million inhabitants of Portugal and the official tongue of the two Portuguese African colonies of Mozambique and Angola. It is also the tongue of Brazil, which contains over half of South America's 160 million inhabitants.

Italian, spoken by 50 million people in Italy, is the language of large emigrant communities in North and South America and in the Mediterranean area. It is also, in superlative measure, the language of music.

Rumanian, with about 20 million speakers, most of whom are located on Rumanian soil, is the smallest of the national Romance languages and one of the most interesting to linguists, since it represents a special development of Latin uninfluenced by the currents that were common to the four contiguous Romance lands of the west.

The non-national Romance tongues and the dialects of the major tongues present the most diversified and picturesque aspect. The Provençal of southern France was a highly polished literary tongue in the Middle Ages, until the Albigensian Crusade. The lyric form of modern poetry, the love sonnet, the *contrasto* of Italy, and the *jeu parti* of France all had their inception in the rich and beautiful literature of eleventh- and twelfth-century Provence. Today Provençal is only a series of local dialects and *patois,* which Mistral in the nineteenth century vainly attempted to restore to literary form.

The Catalan spoken in Spanish Catalonia and the adjoining French region of Roussillon, as well as in Valencia, Andorra, and the Balearic Islands, managed on the contrary to retain its literary form throughout the centuries. The Spaniards would like to classify it as a Spanish dialect, the French as an offshoot of Provençal, but the Catalans proudly cling to their linguistic individuality. Even today the *jocs florals de la llengua catalana* ("floral games of the Catalan tongue," a literary and poetic contest in which writers and poets vie for prizes) are held by Catalans in exile from their native land.

The two dialects of central and southern Sardinia, Logu-dorese and Campidanese, are so completely different from Italian and come so close to the Latin of Classical times that many Romance linguists consider them the most archaic and conservative of all the Romance species. Logudorese, in particular, still keeps the Latin vowels unchanged and retains before front vowels the Latin guttural sounds which became palatals in practically all other Romance areas. "Pear" is still *pira* in Logudorese, as it was in the lower-class Latin of Cicero's days (Spanish and Italian have changed it to *pera*, French to *poire*); "hundred" is *kentu* (Latin *centum*, with *c* pronounced as *k;* French *cent,* Spanish *ciento,* Italian *cento* retained the *c* spelling, but the sound today is *s, th,* or *ch*). The insular, comparatively remote position of Sardinia is supposed to account for this extraordinary conservatism.

The Rhaetian varieties of the Alpine region are also known by the names of Romansh, Rhaeto-Romansh and Ladin. On Swiss soil, Rhaetian is spoken in the Engadine (in Graubün-den) by less than 100,000 people; on Italian soil, it appears in some isolated valleys to the east and west of the river Adige and in the great plain of Friuli, northeast of Venice, and Italian speakers of Rhaetian number well over half a million. Many Italians choose to consider Rhaetian as an outgrowth of the North Italian dialects, and in protest against this point of view the Swiss government some years ago made the Engadine variety of Rhaetian a fourth national language of Switzerland, where three tongues, German, French, and Italian, were already official.

Within the national languages themselves, strong dialectal divergences are to be noted. In the Middle Ages, Francien, the dialect of the Paris region from which the literary French language ultimately stemmed, was under severe competition from the local dialects of Picardy, Normandy, Lorraine, and southern Belgium. Many of the French forms that came into England with the Norman conquest are Norman-Picard rather than Francien.

Spanish, in addition to its medieval dialects, Leonese, Aragonese, and Mozarabic, which were largely crowded out by Castilian, has an Andalusian form which gave rise to most of the Spanish-American varieties; an Asturian dialect, spoken in the north; and an infinity of minor local peculiarities. One interesting offshoot of Spanish is the Ladino (not to be confused with the Ladin of the Rhaetian areas) spoken by the descendants of the Spanish Jews who were forced to leave Spain in the fifteenth century and who settled in various localities along the Mediterranean basin, par-

ticularly around Monastir and Salonika in the Balkans, forming the so-called Sephardic or southern Jewish communities.
Ladino is a strongly conservative fifteenth-century Spanish
interlarded with words borrowed from Greek, Turkish, Arabic, and other Mediterranean tongues and written, like Yiddish, with a modified Hebrew alphabet.

Galicia, in the northwestern corner of the Iberian Peninsula, belongs politically to Spain but linguistically to Portugal. Indeed, the Galician of the Middle Ages, which had a
flourishing literature even before Castilian, was in large part
responsible for the growth of Portuguese. Many local divergences appear on Portuguese soil, but among the most
striking varieties of Portuguese are the ones which appear in
the Azores and the numerous local dialects of Brazil.

Italian has a Gallo-Italian series of dialects, covering the
northwestern part of the peninsula and displaying strong
affinities with French and Provençal; a Venetian group; a
mass of central dialects, including the literary Tuscan, the
dialect of Rome and the native speech of Corsica; a southern
brand of which Neapolitan is perhaps the most representative member; and a Calabrian-Sicilian variety spoken in the
extreme south and on the island of Sicily. The range of
variety of the Italian dialects is amazing; a form like "to
comb," which in standard Italian is *pettinare* (from Latin
pectinare), becomes *pittinari* in Sicily and *pnär* in Bologna.

Rumanian, outside of minor localisms appearing in the
provinces of Moldavia, Walachia, Bessarabia, Bucovina,
Transylvania, etc., has produced two offshoots which diverge
considerably from the mother tongue, one spoken in southern
Macedonia, the other in Istria, near the Italian-Yugoslav
border.

The Romance languages differ phonetically more than they
do structurally. Written Portuguese, Spanish, and Italian are
to a large degree mutually comprehensible; but while a
Spaniard and an Italian can manage to understand each
other, a Spaniard and a Portuguese will encounter difficulties, and an Italian and a Portuguese will have still greater
trouble. French is phonetically in a class by itself and cannot
be understood without special study by the speakers of any
other Romance language, while Rumanian, which would not
present insurmountable phonetic difficulties to Italian or
Spanish speakers, is structurally out of their reach.

On the grammatical side, all of the Romance languages
have given up the neuter gender, absorbing Latin neuter
nouns into the masculine or feminine category; this means

that a pencil is referred to as "he," a pen as "she." All, with the exception of Rumanian, have "simplified" their noun morphology to a point that outstrips even English. No trace of the Latin case system survives; a single form for the singular and one for the plural are general. The majority of masculine nouns end in -o in Spanish, Portuguese, and Italian, in a consonant in French. Feminine nouns generally end in -a in the first three languages, in -e in French. In addition, Spanish, Portuguese, and Italian have a number of nouns of either gender which end in consonants or in -e. Spanish, Portuguese, and French generally form the plural by adding -s, Italian by changing -o to -i, -a to -e, -e to i.

All the Romance languages have developed a definite article out of the Latin demonstrative pronoun *ille,* but while the western languages place the article before the noun, Rumanian attaches it to the noun; thus "the wolf," which in Classical Latin was simply *lupus,* became in Vulgar Latin *ille lupus* or *lupus ille,* and is today *le loup* in French, *el lobo* in Spanish, *o lobo* in Portuguese, *il lupo* in Italian, but *lupul* in Rumanian.

Adjectives agree in gender and number with the noun they modify in all the Romance languages. This does not mean that the adjective and the noun will necessarily have identical endings, since the noun may be of the -o class and the adjective of the -e class, or vice versa.

Verbs, unlike nouns, have undergone considerable change but no appreciable process of simplification. Indeed, a Romance conjugational scheme is even more complex than a Latin one, having a greater number of tenses and forms.

The syntax of Romance is to a considerable degree unified. This is due partly to kinship of origin but also to the fact that at all periods of their history the four western Romance tongues were in constant contact, borrowing from and imitating one another. The same may be said of their vocabularies, particularly in the more learned and literary division. It would be difficult to say which of the Romance languages was the greatest giver or which the greatest receiver in this historical interchange. Italian borrowings from French go back to the days of Pepin's war against the Longobards and Charlemagne's Kingdom of Italy, while the Provençal influence is particularly strong in the *dolce stil nuovo,* the earliest current of courtly Italian literature. French and Provençal influence likewise made itself felt in Spanish and Portuguese as early as the eleventh and twelfth centuries, when the pilgrim routes across the Pyrenees led devout Frenchmen to the shrine of Santiago de Compostela in northwestern Spain and the French monks of Cluny set up their monasteries in that northern band of provinces which was free from the Moors. The Italian Renaissance contributed very heavily to the formation of French and Spanish culture in the fourteenth, fifteenth, and sixteenth centuries, while the French and Spanish occupations of parts of the Italian peninsula aided in the formation of the modern Italian language to the same extent that they hindered the cause of Italian political unity. Spanish world predominance immediately after the discovery of the New World led to the spreading of all sorts of new words and concepts in the sister Romance languages. In the days of Louis XIV, the French Revolution, and Napoleon, French military, political, and cultural preponderance left its mark on all the other Romance languages. The Romance peoples have at all times been keen students and admirers of one another's literature and culture. All this has meant that any innovation in the syntactical or lexical field occurring in one of the Romance tongues stood an excellent chance of being appropriated and copied by the others. "Romania" still exists today, and it is no accident that American universities and even high schools ordinarily institute departments of Romance languages rather than separate divisions of French, Spanish, and Italian.

Among the individual Romance languages, French is distinguished by reason of its phonetic pattern, the comparatively large divergence between its spoken and written form, and its deliberately sought lucidity of style and regularity of syntactical arrangement. It is the last-named qualities that make French an ideal language both for the compilation of diplomatic, legal, and business documents, in which precision is of the essence, and for literary composition in prose form. When it comes to poetic form, French is less fortunate, the modern language having largely lost the element of stressful rhythm that characterized the medieval tongue. Modern French poetry possesses neither the device of quantity (the regular alternation of long and short syllables so typical of the Classical languages), nor the more modern accentual effect of languages like English, German, Spanish, and Italian, whereby poetic rhythm depends upon the regular alternation of stressed and unstressed syllables. Instead, French poetry is scanned merely by the number of syllables to the line. In the course of its historical development, French has partly lost in rhythmical quality what it has gained in symmetrical regularity, just as French grammar has lost in syntactical elasticity what it has gained in precision. All this, of course, does not mean that there is not a rhythm, and an extremely pleasing one, in the speech of a cultivated French speaker.

The sound pattern of spoken French is dominated by the middle rounded vowels (French *u* and *eu*, as in *lune*, *feu*, *peur*) and the full-bodied nasals (as heard in *blanc*, *vin*, *bon*, *un*), both of which recur with striking frequency in French speech. There is a theory among some linguists to the effect that these two series of sounds, whereby French sharply differentiates itself from most other Romance varieties, is due to the original Celtic speech habits of the pre-Roman Gauls. This point is the subject of much controversy, and it is hardly worth while to discuss it here. Another distinctive French sound is the *r grasseyé*, or uvular *r*, typical of Parisian but not current throughout all of France. French phonology is further distinguished by the relative tenseness of the vocal organs in speech and by the clearly explosive quality imparted to final consonant sounds. For the latter phenomenon, a point worth remembering is that French imparts to the *final* consonant of a breath group the same force of utterance that English imparts to an *initial* consonant. In English "pat," we give special force of utterance to the initial *p*, which is accompanied by a slight puff of breath, while the final *t* is restrained and unaccompanied by a breath explosion; in French *patte*, it is just the reverse: the *p* is lightly pronounced while the *t* sound which ends the word is distinctly audible and accompanied by the breath puff.

French (and, to a much lesser degree, the other Romance languages) is characterized by a tendency to link together the final consonant sound of one word and the initial vowel sound of the next. A phrase like *les grands hommes avaient annoncé* ("the great men had announced") sounds in speech like *lé grã zom za vé ta nõ sé*. This feature imparts to the Romance languages in general and to French in particular a syllabic rhythm of the consonant-vowel variety which is altogether at variance with the Germanic rhythm wherein most syllables end in consonants. It also tends to rob the individual word of its phonetic individuality within the spoken sentence and to make the sentence or phrase, rather than the word, the unit of understanding to the listener.

French spelling is highly traditional, though not to the same degree as English. This means that many letters representing sounds that the spoken tongue has not pronounced for centuries continue to be written. In *ils tiennent* ("they hold"), for example, the final *-s* of *ils* and the final *-ent* of *tiennent* are silent, though they were at one time pronounced. There are numerous minor irregularities of spelling and pronunciation, representing exceptions to rules which are of themselves quite involved. In *cuiller* ("spoon"), for instance, the book rule would indicate a silent *r* and a closed *e* when actually the *e* is open and the *r* pronounced; in *aiguille* ("needle"), the *u,* which is normally silent in the *gui* group, is pronounced; in *second,* the *c* is, very exceptionally, sounded like a *g.*

It has already been stated that, whereas written French regularly forms noun plurals by adding *-s,* this *-s* is generally silent, so that the true spoken-language distinction between singular and plural is normally made in the article (*la femme,* "the woman," is distinguished from *les femmes,* "the women," only by the vowel sound in *les* which differs from that of *la*).

The French verb, like the Romance verb in general, has a complex conjugation. The past tenses are particularly numerous. There is an imperfect, used in Romance to denote what was happening or used to happen, in contrast with a past definite which tells what happened, but which spoken French (though not the other Romance tongues) generally avoids in favor of a past indefinite, denoting what happened or has happened. The French (and generally the Romance) future and conditional were in origin compound analytical forms, consisting of the present or past of "to have" plus the infinitive, but at a very early date these forms were telescoped together, producing new synthetic forms the analytical origin of which has long since been forgotten by all but linguistic experts. The French passive is formed by means of the verb "to be" and the past participle, as it is in the other Romance languages, but there is widespread avoidance of these forms, which in French are often replaced by *on* with the active (*on parle français ici,* literally "man speaks French here," instead of *le français est parlé ici,* "French is spoken here"). Four subjunctive tenses, mostly restricted in use to certain types of subordinate clauses, complete the French (and generally the Romance) verb picture, but in French two of these tenses are widely avoided in the spoken tongue while in the other languages they are abundantly, even enthusiastically, used.

The French vocabulary of everyday usage is predominantly of Latin origin, though French has perhaps a slightly larger proportion of Germanic words than its sister tongues, along with a number of Celtic words inherited from the Gauls which the other languages lack. It has been pointed out, with some justification, that French and Italian seem to share those vocabulary innovations which probably arose from the large-city slang of the Roman Empire, while the lateral areas, Spain, Portugal, and Rumania, display a more conservative and Classical Latin vocabulary. French and Italian, for instance, share the slang innovation of using *diurnus,* which was originally an adjective meaning "daily," for "day" (French *jour,* Italian *giorno*), while the other languages use the more Classical *dies* (Spanish *día,* Portuguese *dia,* Rumanian *zi*). But Italian also has *di,* as did Old French (it appears in the modern French names of the days of the week: *lundi, mardi,* etc.). It is possible that the use of some of the reputed archaisms and innovations is rather the result of a later choice.

Spanish, in comparison with French, is a language of relatively simple sounds, few spelling-pronunciation difficulties, and a grammatical pattern which was deliberately regularized by the Spanish Academy. This makes Spanish an ideal beginner's language. It is only after a year or so of study that the true difficulties of Spanish begin to become apparent, and they are mostly of a syntactical type. Spanish word order, particularly in literary works, is loose, elastic, and often arbitrary, whereas the word order of French, bound into a syntactical strait jacket by the French Academicians, is a model of clarity. Teachers of Spanish often have to warn their second- and third-year students that in translating a Spanish sentence into English the first thing to do is to go on a fishing expedition for the subject, which may be found anywhere, even at the very end of the sentence.

There are only two or three Spanish sounds which do not have reasonably approximate facsimiles in English, the *j* (or *g* before *e* and *i*), which is pronounced like a strongly aspirated *h,* and the trilled *r* and *rr,* which call for an exercise of the tongue. Spanish spelling, once you have learned a few elementary rules, fits the pronunciation perfectly. The accented syllable is clearly indicated. The elementary grammatical structure is, if anything, simpler than that of French. In French, as in German and Italian, some active but intransitive verbs are conjugated with "to be," but in Spanish, as in English, all active verbs are conjugated with "to have." The personal endings of the various tenses are quite distinct, permitting one to omit the subject pronoun. A few complexities are offered by the presence of two verbs that mean "to be" and two that mean "to have," but the choice is regulated by very simple rules. The varieties of pronunciation and vocabulary appearing in the Spanish-speaking countries of the Western Hemisphere are not so great but that an intelligent person who has studied the official Castilian cannot become accustomed in two weeks to whichever one he may be exposed to. The basic Spanish vocabulary is essentially Latin, with a certain proportion of borrowings from Basque, Arabic, and Germanic. Words ending in *-arro, -orro, -urro*, as well as words like *izquierdo* ("left"), *manteca* ("grease"), *vega* ("plain") are of Basque origin, while Arabic words are very often identified by their *al* prefix.

Portuguese presents a phonology which is second only to French in complexity. Vowels have open or closed sounds when stressed and are frequently reduced to an indefinite value when unstressed. Portuguese has nasal vowel sounds which in some ways resemble those of French. The palatal sounds indicated by English *sh* or the *s* of "measure," which are never heard in modern Spanish, are frequent in Portuguese. The spelling of Portuguese is of the constantly changing variety. Every few years, Portuguese and Brazilian academicians go into a huddle over the matter of spelling and emerge with a number of reforms, which in theory are applicable to both countries but in practice often show a considerable time lag in one or the other. The result is somewhat confusing and reminds one of the fluctuating status of the official Norwegian language, which has undergone at least four noteworthy revisions within the last century. Upon completing, with the help of a distinguished Portuguese colleague, a brief outline of the Portuguese language some years ago, I flattered myself that I had used the very latest official orthography, in accordance with the rules established by mutual agreement between the two Portuguese-speaking countries in 1943. Just as the book was going to press, my good Portuguese mentor rushed up breathlessly to inform me that the rules had been changed once more, and were we still in time to catch the edition and bring it up to date?

Both in structure and in vocabulary, Portuguese shows strong traces of archaism. Whereas in the other Romance languages the future and conditional have been telescoped into an indivisible whole, in Portuguese it is still possible to break them up into their original component parts, the infinite and the verb "to have" (*chamarei*, "I shall call," but *chamá-lo-ei*, "I shall call him," etymologically "to call-him-I have"). Portuguese retains a future and future perfect subjunctive, which Spanish once had but has long since discarded. Portuguese has a personalized infinitive (*parti depois de terem falado*, "I left after they had spoken," literally "I left after to-have-they spoken"). Object pronouns, which in medieval French, Spanish, and Italian could not be placed before the verb at the very beginning of the sentence, still must follow that archaic rule in Portuguese (Spanish *le hablo*, Italian *gli parlo*, but Portuguese *falo-lhe*, "I speak to him").

The Portuguese vocabulary is generally close to that of Spanish, but there are occasional striking differences. "Window" is *ventana* in Spanish but *janela* in Portuguese, "to dine" is *comer* in Spanish but *jantar* in Portuguese. The story goes that a Portuguese professor, incensed at the constant reiteration of an American colleague that anyone who knows Spanish can read Portuguese, composed a letter in which not one of the words was identifiable to his Spanish-speaking friend, with the exception of a few pronouns and prepositions. The Brazilians in particular are very touchy about being linguistically lumped with their Spanish-speaking neighbors and haughtily inform Americans who try to use Spanish with them that they would rather converse in English.

Italian is a tongue of smooth sounds and comparatively easy spelling. Of particular interest in Italian phonology is the very frequent occurrence of double consonants. These become easy to pronounce when one remembers that what is orthographically a double consonant (like *tt* in *fatto*) is phonetically simply the holding of the breath for a fraction of a second before one releases the consonant sound. One grave stumbling block in Italian pronunciation is the fact that the learner has no clear-cut indication, as he has in Spanish, of the syllable on which the accent falls. The result is constant mispronunciation of Italian words and names by Americans who think all Italian words are stressed on the next to the last syllable. During the war, American newscasters insisted on pronouncing as "Ra*pi*do" the name of an Italian river that should be pronounced "*Ra*pido." In like manner, Judge "Pe*co*ra's" name becomes "Pe*co*ra," "Es*po*sito" becomes "Espo*si*to," etc.

The fact that Italian uses vocalic endings for practically all its words and seldom has difficult consonant clusters within a word renders the language ideal for singing purposes and for certain types of declamation. But all is not gold that glitters; a word like *sdraiarsi* ("to lie down") presents its own peculiar difficulties to an English speaker.

Italian syntax outstrips Spanish in possessing a certain quality of looseness which, while it makes for elasticity and expressiveness, is often bewildering to the learner. In French, for example, "I don't think that he will come" is *je ne crois pas qu'il vienne,* with an obligatory subjunctive in the subordinate clause. In Italian one has the choice between *non credo che venga,* with the subjunctive, and *non credo che verrà,* with the future indicative. But there is just a trifling shade of difference between the two expressions, perceptible only to a native. The rules for the agreement of the past participle in French are quite arbitrary, even unreasonable, but definitely fixed. In Italian the same rules are delightfully vague. Save in one special connection, the participle may or may not agree with the direct object, as the speaker or writer sees fit. Here again the native lets himself be guided by his instinctive senses of fitness, but the foreign learner does not have this linguistic intuition at his disposal.

The Italian vocabulary is perhaps more predominantly Latin than those of the other Romance languages, but Italians are often amazed when one points out to them the relatively large proportion of Germanic words which were brought in by the Ostrogoths and Longobards and which have become as thoroughly naturalized in Italian as our own Norman-French importations in English. It used to be a joke among linguists that the Fascist government tried to make the Italians give up *hotel,* which though it has a French appearance is of Latin origin, in favor of *albergo,* which sounds quite Italian but is of Germanic origin; and this not in the name of the Rome-Berlin axis, which had not yet been created, but in the name of the "purity" of the Italian language!

Despite these borrowings, Italian remains amazingly close to the ancestral tongue, particularly in its learned and literary vocabulary. The story is told of an Italian high school student who, having been assigned to compose a Latin poem, appeared the next day in class and read off some lines of verse which caused the class to titter and the professor to remark caustically: "Perhaps you forgot that the assignment was for a piece of *Latin* poetry?" "My verses *are* Latin, sir!" replied the student in an aggrieved tone. After a careful rereading, the professor was forced to apologize. The verses were perfectly good Latin and, at the same time, perfectly good Italian. This had been achieved by a carefully restricted use of only those Latin forms which have a one hundred per cent correspondence in Italian, of which there are several. Lest my readers think the story is made up, here is the poem:

> *Te saluto, alma Dea, Dea generosa,*
> *O gloria nostra, o veneta regina!*
> *In procelloso turbine funesto*

> *Tu regnasti serena; mille membra*
> *Intrepida prostrasti in pugna acerba;*
> *Per te miser non fui, per te non gemo,*
> *Vivo in pace per te. Regna, o beata!*
> *Regna in prospera sorte, in pompa augusta,*
> *In perpetuo splendore, in aurea sede!*
> *Tu serena, tu placida, tu pia,*
> *Tu benigna, me salva, ama, conserva!*

Last among the Romance languages in speaking population, but most individual in development, is Rumanian. Its
only difficult sound is the one represented by *â* or *î*, a
guttural *i* sound for which the closest English approximation
is the *y* of "rhythm." Rumanian has a postposed article
and a double case, nominative-accusative and genitive-dative.
Cal is a "horse," *calul* is "the horse" (subject or object),
calului is "of" or "to the horse"; *calul vecinului* is "the horse
of the neighbor." Rumanian likewise is distinguished from
the other Romance languages by the use of the adjective
without an ending as an adverb (the other Romance languages use *-ment* or *-mente* as an adverbial suffix). The
Rumanian future is formed not, as in the other tongues, by
telescoping the infinitive into the verb "to have" but by using
"to want" with the infinitive after it (*voi cântă*, literally
"I want to sing," "I shall sing").

The Rumanian language has been subjected in the course
of its historical development to strong Slavic influences,
deriving partly from geographical proximity, partly from
the fact that the Rumanians adopted the eastern, not the
western, brand of Christianity. The earliest Rumanian texts
(fifteenth century) that have come down to us are written
in Cyrillic characters. The Rumanian vocabulary is replete
with Slavic infiltrations, but these have for the most part
Latin synonyms. "Time," for example, can be expressed either
by the originally Latin *timp* or by the originally Slavic
vreme. As the Rumanians say:

> *Mult e dulce si frumoasa*
> *Limba, ce vorbim.*

> (Very sweet and beautiful is
> The language that we speak.)

Multum est dulcis sic formosa lingua quam verbamus
would be the equivalent in the Vulgar Latin of Dacia. What-

ever the Slavic infiltrations may be, Rumanian is a worthy Latin sister of the Romance languages of the west.

The same type of fundamental unity that underlies the Germanic tongues also characterizes Latin and Romance. "Good bread" is *bonus panis* in Latin, *bon pain* in French, *buen pan* in Spanish, *buon pane* in Italian, *bom pão* in Portuguese, *bun pâine* in Rumanian. "One thousand" is *mille* in Latin, French, and Italian, *mil* in Spanish and Portuguese, *mie* in Rumanian.

The spoken language of Rome lives on, not only in the foreign tongues which, like English, have adopted it in part and adapted it to their modern needs but also in its numerous and picturesquely diversified direct descendants. While our civilization endures, it will never die.

— Chapter Five —

THE SLAVIC LANGUAGES

The Russian is strong on three foundations: "perhaps," "never mind," and "somehow."
                                                    —Russian proverb

THE Slavic languages comprise a speaking population of about 270 million, of whom almost three-fourths are concentrated on Soviet soil. Speakers of "Great Russian" number some 130 million, Ukrainian speakers some 40 million, and White Russian speakers about 10 million.

Outside the Soviet Union, Polish speakers number almost 40 million, speakers of Czech and Slovak about 14 million. Approximately 14 million of Yugoslavia's 18 million inhabitants use Serbo-Croatian, and nearly 2 million more Slovenian, while Bulgarian is the language of about 8 million people. A small group of about 150,000 spoke Wendish, or Lusatian, in the region of Cottbus and Bautzen in east central Germany, but they were entirely surrounded by German speakers, and it is reported that not many survived Hitler's persecutions.

In comparison with the Germanic and Romance tongues, the Slavic languages present a conservative, archaic aspect, close to what seems to have been the original Indo-European state of affairs. There is a considerable spread between Gothic, earliest of the Germanic tongues on record, and modern English or German, or between Latin and modern French or Spanish. There is no such divergence between the modern tongues of the Slavic group and the earliest of their number, the so-called Old Church Slavonic or Old Bulgarian of the ninth century, concerning the original location of whose speakers there is some difference of opinion, some linguists holding that this tongue was spoken in Macedonia, others placing it as far north as Moravia in Czechoslovakia.

The process of transition from a synthetic to an analytical structure, so apparent in the other two great western groups of Indo-European, is largely nonexistent in Slavic.

The phonology and structure of the Slavic languages will become apparent as we discuss the various languages of the family, notably Russian. Suffice it here to say that, with the single exception of modern Bulgarian, the Slavic languages retain a full inflectional morphology for nouns, adjectives, and pronouns, with seven of the eight original Indo-European cases (nominative, genitive, dative, accusative, vocative, instrumental, and locative), while the verb system retains the ancient aspects, perfective and imperfective, one indicating an action as carried through, completed, or instantaneous, the other showing the action as occurring continuously or repeatedly.

The Slavic languages possess a wealth of consonant sounds, including a full series of palatals (*ch, j, sh, zh,* etc.). One of the main points of difference among them is the place of the stress. Polish invariably stresses the next to the last syllable of the word, Czech and Slovak the initial, Serbo-Croatian usually the initial, while in Russian, Ukrainian, and Bulgarian the place of the accent is unpredictable. Czech and Slovak distinguish carefully between long and short vowels, while the other languages make no such careful distinction; in Russian and Ukrainian, however, the stressed vowel is often prolonged, while unstressed vowels tend to become indistinct in pronunciation. Polish keeps two nasal vowels, somewhat similar in sound to French *on* and *in,* which Old Church Slavonic also had but which the other languages have turned into simple vowels or diphthongs.

The Slavic peoples who received Christianity directly or indirectly from Byzantium (Russians, Ukrainians, Serbs, Bulgars) adopted the Cyrillic alphabet, while those who became Roman Catholics (Poles, Czechs, Slovaks, Croats, Slovenes) use the Roman characters. This gives the Slavic languages a diversity in written appearance which does not correspond to their comparative closeness in spoken form. A Czech, a Pole, a Russian, and a Serb, each speaking his own tongue, manage to achieve a measure of mutual understanding which could never be duplicated by an Englishman, a German, a Hollander, and a Swede or by a Frenchman, a Spaniard, a Portuguese, and a Rumanian. "Good evening" is *dobry vyecher* in Russian, *dobry wieczór* in Polish, *dobrý večer* in Czech, *dobra večer* in Serbo-Croatian and Bulgarian. "Land" and "sea" are *zemlya* and *morye* in Russian, *ziemia* and *morze* in Polish, *země* and *more* in Czech, *zemlja* and *more* in Serbo-Croatian, *zemya* and *more* in Bulgarian. The identical word, *sto,* does service for "hundred" in all five languages.

Official Russian or "Great Russian" (in contradistinction to "Little Russian," or Ukrainian), accounting for about half of all Slavic speakers, is also the predominant tongue of the Soviet Union, a country which has achieved a dominant, though not predominant, position in world affairs. This present role of the Soviet Union has had as a by-product in America a widespread interest in the Russian language, a tongue that is strangely beautiful, piquantly intricate, and that now challenges the primacy of long-established tongues like German and French.

It must, however, be remembered that out of the Soviet Union's estimated 230 million inhabitants, only a little more than half use Russian as their native tongue. The rest speak at least 145 different languages, including closely related Slavic tongues like Ukrainian, White Russian, and Polish; more distantly related Baltic tongues like Lithuanian and Lettish; distant Indo-European relatives like Armenian and the Moldavian variety of Rumanian; Caucasian languages like Georgian, Circassian, Lezghian, and Avar; and an infinity of Ural-Altaic languages such as Finnish, with the closely related Karelian and Estonian, Lapp, Cheremiss, Votyak, Ostyak, Tatar, Kirghiz, Turkoman, Uzbek, Kalmuk, Buriat, Tungus, and Samoyed; even languages concerning whose affiliations practically nothing is known, like Yukaghir. Each of the sixteen Soviet Republics has its own language, which is semiofficial, while the term *sovyetsky* ("pertaining to the Soviet Union") is not interchangeable with *russky* ("Russian") and is never applied to the language.

The Soviet government does not compel its 230 million citizens to speak Russian but on the contrary encourages and helps them to speak, read, and write their 145 major and minor tongues, even devising some fifty alphabets for language groups that previously had no written language. This policy of linguistic and cultural liberalism of the Soviet rulers reminds us that Leibniz, at the end of the seventeenth century, urged Peter the Great to do what the Soviets did later—order studies to be made of the languages of the Russian Empire, reduce these languages to writing, and make dictionaries for them.

In the course of the last century and a half, the originally scanty populations of Asiatic Russia, largely nomadic and speaking languages of the Turkic stock, have been joined by millions of Russian speakers from Europe who have given their own distinctive tone to the new civilization that is springing up in northern Asia. The spreading of the Russian tongue into Siberia, even under the Czars, had generally followed the course of the Trans-Siberian Railway, with larger groupings along the intersecting courses of the three great rivers, Lena, Ob, and Yenisei, as well as in the extreme east, in the region of Vladivostok, and this movement continued and expanded in recent years.

Furthermore, despite the lack of linguistic compulsion, some 50 million inhabitants of the Soviet Union were estimated to have learned Russian between 1926 and 1960. Russian is described as the "binding tongue" of the Soviet Union, and it is doubtful if any of the Union's inhabitants fail to realize that it is the language that pays dividends in terms of political and economic preferment.

To a person with English language habits, Russian is difficult, but not insurmountably so. What the Tatars and Kalmuks and Kazakhs and Uzbeks can do, Americans and Englishmen can do.

The first obstacle, and the one that often terrifies beginners, is the Russian system of writing, a sensible and fairly phonetic one, but one that differs from ours. It fascinated me when I used to collect stamps as a boy. Some of the letters were (or seemed to be) exactly like ours; others were peculiarly different. Later I learned that alphabet and its history: how two Greek bishops, Cyril and Methodius, left the city of Constantinople in the ninth century to bring Christianity to the heathen Slavs, who had not yet developed a satisfactory system of writing, and painstakingly constructed an alphabet for them at the same time that they taught them the Gospel.

Today the Russian thirty-two-letter alphabet is practically the same as the one devised by the bishops. Fittingly, it is called Cyrillic, after one of its inventors. It serves a population of nearly 180 million Russians, Ukrainians, and White Russians on Soviet soil, and with minor variations is used by the Serbs and Bulgars.

In the Russian variety of the Cyrillic alphabet, a few characters have the same form and approximately the same value as in our own: *A, E, K, M, O, T*. Others are misleading: *B* is not *b*, but *v*, *H* is not *h*, but *n*, *P* is not *p*, but *r*, *C* is not *c*, but *s*, *X* is not *x*, but *kh*. Once the alphabet hurdle is taken, the real difficulties begin. The Russian vocabulary is predominantly Slavic, which means that it is related, but not too closely, to the three great language groups that go to make up our English vocabulary: the Germanic, the Latin-Romance, and the Greek. To cite a few examples of this kinship: the Russian word for "house," *dom*, is easily recognizable as akin to the Latin *domus*, from which we have gotten *"dome"* and *"domicile."* The Russian verb "to give," *dat'*, is the Latin *dare;* the Russian verb "to see," *vidyet'*, is the Latin *videre*. *Moloko* is our "milk," *lyubov'* our "love," *dyen'* our "day," and *noch*, our "night"; *novy* is the Latin *novus* and the English "new." *Solntse* is "sun," *luna* is "moon," and *mysh* is "mouse."

Nowhere does the relationship stand out more clearly than in nouns of relationship. *Mat'*, which changes to *mater-* in most case forms, is common to English "mother," Latin *mater*, and Greek *meter*. *Brat* (once *bratr*) is "brother"; *sestra* is "sister"; *syn* is "son"; *doch'* (*docher-* in most case forms) is "daughter."

More numerous than most people think are the Russian words already familiar to Americans. Everyone knows *vodka* (a diminutive form of *voda*, "water," which gives the potent drink the literal translation of "little water"); *tovarishch* (freely translated as "comrade" but originally "merchant's apprentice" or "junior salesman," derived from an originally Turkish word *tovar*, meaning "goods" or "merchandise"; the original Turkish form has reference to cattle; *tovarishch* was at first viewed with suspicion by the Russian peasants, and they frequently prefixed *gospodin*, "Mr.," making a "Mr. Comrade" out of the combination); *Kremlin* (from the root *kreml'*, "citadel" or "fortress"); *Soviet* (the Russian word for "council"); *kulak* (literally "fist," applied to well-to-do Russian peasants prior to the collectivization of Soviet agriculture). Then there is the *-grad* or *-gorod* that ends many Russian place names and means "city" or "town." The *bolsh* part of Bolshevist is "big"; the Bolshevists were so named because they claimed to constitute the majority of the Socialist Party ("Maximalist" is the literal Latin translation of *Bolshevik*).

Russian has been a great borrower of words from the western languages, Latin, Greek, French, German, and English. Here is a series of borrowed words which, while differing slightly in pronunciation, are spelled like their English counterparts: *agent, angel, bank, diplomat, flag, front, general, motor, park, pastor, pilot, port, poet, professor, tank*. In spite of the very slight modification in spelling, the following are easily identified: *avtobus, avtomobil, appetit, aktsent, arest, armiya, atmosfera, arifmetika, allo!, aeroplan, bagazh, bandazh, bifshteks, chek, fotograf, garazh, kalendar', kapital, kanal, klub, klass, klimat, kharakter, lampa, limon, menyu, metall, metod, mekhanik, natura, nerv, pasport, president, produkt, restoran, piknik, salat, sekretar, sigara, soldat, telefon, tabak, taksi, teatr, vazelin, zhelatin, zhurnal.*

Some words take a little longer to fathom, chiefly by reason of spelling complications: *byulleten'* ("bulletin"), *gospital'* ("hospital"), *koketka* ("coquette"), *inzhenyer* ("engineer"), *obyekt* ("object"), *pochta* ("mail," "post"), *reportyor* ("reporter"), *sakhar* ("sugar"), *sup* ("soup"), *shofyor* ("chauffeur").

Russian pronunciation is complicated to an American ear. In addition to a wealth of palatal sounds which recur frequently (*sh, zh, ch, shch, ty, dy, ly, ny*), there is a tough guttural *i* sound, best produced by shaping the lips for *ee*, then trying to say *oo*. There are also difficult consonant combinations, like *vstr, vstv, zdr* (try, for example, to pronounce *zdravstvuytye*, which is the common form of greeting, and which the Russians themselves often cut down to *zdrastye*). There are prepositions consisting of a single consonant (*v*, "in"; *k*, "toward"; *s*, "with"); the trick here is to link them with the following word, as in *v ogorodye* ("in the garden"); but sometimes the next word begins with an unvoiced consonant, in which case *v* becomes *f* in pronunciation (*v ponyedyelnik*, "on Monday"). In spite of all this, Russian miraculously succeeds in sounding beautiful, with strange words like *ptitsa* and *skazka*, which seem to be taken out of fairy tales.

Here are a few expressions that are frequently used in ordinary intercourse. The stressed syllable is here indicated by small capitals. Russian, which does not have a fixed place for the stress, like Czech or Polish, gives absolutely no indication in written form of the syllable that is to be stressed.

DA—yes

NYET—no

*spa*SIBO (or *blagoda*RYU)—thank you

*po*ZHAL*sta*—please, don't mention it

KTO?—who?

CHTO?—what?

GDYE?—where?

ZDYES'—here

TAM—there

*pri*YAT*no*—glad to meet you

*do svi*DAN*ya*—good-bye

SKOL'*ko?*—how much?

ZAV*tra*—tomorrow

*sye*VOD*nya*—today

*vche*RA—yesterday
ETo—this
DAY*tye mnye*—give me
*izvi*NI*tye*—pardon me
KAK *vy pozhi*VA*yetye?*—how are you?
*ochen' khoro*SHO—very well
*poni*MA*yetye li vy?*—do you understand?
YA *nye poni*MA*yu*—I don't understand
YA *nye* ZNA*yu*—I don't know
*govo*RI*tye li vy po-an*GLI*sky?*—do you speak English?
*govo*RI*tye* MYED*lyennyeye*—speak more slowly

While learning phrases, one should not forget *nichevo*, which is to the Russian what a shrug of the shoulder is to a Frenchman: "don't know," "can't help it," "nothing to be done about it."

Many Russian expressions are picturesque when literally translated: "railroad" is "iron road"; "fountain pen" is "self-writing pen" or "eternal pen"; and (though we of the capitalist countries are supposed to be the rugged individualists) "to learn" is "to teach oneself."

There are picturesque sentences, too. When someone thanks you, you may reply: "Not for that!" You don't say, "I have a book," but "There is by me a book." Instead of: "How old are you?" you ask: "How much to you of years?" Some Russian sentences are telegraphic in style: "You here long?" does service for "How long have you been here?"

In spots, the Russian mind runs in different channels from ours. The same word is used, as it was once in English, for "moon" and "month." A single word is used for "Sunday" and "resurrection." You cannot say: "It's raining," "It's snowing"; what you say is: "Rain comes," "Snow comes." You may say: "I'm hungry" (though the more common expression is: "To me wants itself to eat"), but not "I'm thirsty" or "I'm sleepy"; it is: "I want to drink," "I want to sleep."

Like many Americans, Russians have three names. The middle name, however, is what the ancients called a patronymic—a designation of one's father. Thus, Ivan Nikolayevich Kerensky means John, son of Nicholas, Kerensky. Both patronymic and family name change according to the sex of the owner. Ivan Nikolayevich Kerensky's sister would be Nadyezhda (or Tatyana, or Yekaterina) Nikolayevna Kerenskaya. The common family-name ending *-off* (*-ov*), *-eff* (*-ev*) becomes *-ova, -eva* in the feminine.

There are words in Russian for "Sir" or "Mr.," "Madam,"

"Mrs.," "Miss," but the Soviets prefer the use of "comrade" (*tovarishch*), "citizen" (*grazhdanin*), and "citizeness" (*grazhdanka*), except for foreigners.

Russians have a sense of humor and a sense of poetry and display both in everyday conversation. One frequent reply to "How are things?" rhymes with the question and means "as nice as soot is white."

Russian grammar is quite involved for an English-speaking learner, though probably no more so than the grammar of Latin.

There are no articles, definite or indefinite, in Russian. *Zhena* means "wife," "a wife," "the wife." That is why Russians and others Slavs take such picturesque liberties with our "an," "a," and "the." There are three genders, masculine, feminine, and neuter, but inanimate objects do not necessarily belong to the neuter gender. On the other hand, the ending of a noun generally gives some clue to the gender. Consonant endings are mostly masculine, *-a* endings feminine, and *-e* or *-o* endings neuter.

Russian has six cases (nominative, genitive, dative, accusative, instrumental, locative), with an occasional extra vocative form. This means a continual shift of endings, as indicated by the following phrases: *ofitser zdyes'* ("the officer [is] here"); *kaska ofitsera* ("the helmet of the officer"); *daytye pis'mo ofitseru* ("give the letter to the officer"); *ya vizhu ofitsera* ("I see the officer"); *ya byl s ofitserom* ("I was with the officer"); *ya govoryu ob ofitserye* ("I am speaking about the officer"). This process is repeated in the plural, with a different set of endings; and when one considers that there are several distinct declensional types of masculine nouns, of feminine nouns, and of neuter nouns, one readily perceives the strain on the learner's memory, if the learning is done out of a textbook.

Adjectives also have case forms and case endings which differ from those of the nouns. The adjective used after the verb "to be" is given a special distinctive form which, while it appears in only one case, the nominative, nevertheless changes for gender and number. Even numerals are declined. An additional complication affecting the numerals is that you say "one house," but "two," "three," or "four" "of house," then, from five on, "of houses."

In the verb scheme, Russian leaves out the present of "to be" but not the past or future. *Ya ofitser* means "I (am) an officer," but "I was" and "I shall be" are translated (*byl, budu*). There are only three tenses, present, past, and future, but verbs usually go in pairs, one imperfective (like *pisat'*, denoting the action as habitual or repeated: "I was writing," "I used to write," "I shall be writing," "I write habitually or repeatedly"), the other perfective (like *napisat'*, denoting the action as occurring once and then being over: "I wrote," "I shall write").

The reason for this seemingly complicated structure is that Russian, like Latin and Greek and, to a lesser degree, German, is simply more conservative of the old Indo-European structure than are tongues like English, French, or Spanish. But just as French and Spanish were once Latin, so English was at one time Anglo-Saxon, with a structure similar to that of modern Russian. It is a case of one brother letting his beard grow while the other shaves it off.

Anyone having the patience to study Russian will have many rewards at his disposal: in the first place, a tongue current over one sixth of the earth's land surface, serving, directly or indirectly, a Eurasiatic population of over 200 million; secondly, the vehicle of one of the world's richest and most beautiful literatures; thirdly, the key to a new culture and system of life with which we must either fight for survival or learn to live side by side; fourthly, a thoroughly modern insight into the ancient structure of all the languages of our great Indo-European family—Sanskrit, Latin, Greek, Anglo-Saxon, Germanic, Celtic; lastly, an excellent introduction to all the languages of the Slavic group of Indo-European, and a rapid means of communication with their speakers.

Just how close is the relationship between Russian and the other Slavic tongues can be gauged by comparing the one with the others.

Ukrainian and White Russian are close enough to Great Russian to be described as variants of the latter. Together, the three Russian languages are sometimes said to form the eastern branch of Slavic.

Polish, Czech, Slovak, and Wendish are classified together in a northwestern group. All use the Roman alphabet, but since the twenty-six bare letters of this are quite insufficient to represent the Slavic sounds, many diacritic marks were evolved to distinguish between two or more phonetic values of the same letter. Polish, in addition, evolved consonant combinations some of which look quite strange, though the sounds they represent are not unpronounceable.

Polish places hooks under *a* and *e* to represent the nasal values of *o* and *e*, which it alone retains among the Slavic tongues. Accents and dots over consonants like *c, n, s, z* indicate palatalized pronunciations. A bar through an *l* shows the lateral sound of *l* in "milk," while if the *l* does not have the bar, the sound comes closer to *lli* of "million." Combinations like *cz, dź, sz, rz, szcz* indicate sounds similar to English *ch, j, sh, zh, shch. W* is sounded as *v*.

The Polish system of noun, adjective, and pronoun declension and verb conjugation is quite close to the Russian, and many endings are almost identical. The Polish system of penultimate accentuation confers upon the language a majestic, flowing rhythm which distinguishes it on the one hand from Russian, with its heavy stress and slurred unaccented vowels, on the other from Czech, with its staccato, machine-gun-like initial accent.

Czech prefers in the matter of orthography a series of hooks over certain consonants (*c, d, n, r, s, t, z*) to indicate palatalized pronunciation. One of the toughest sounds in any language to a person who does not grow up with it is the *r* with a hook over it, which indicates a blending of the trilled *r* of Spanish or Italian with the *s* of "measure," pronounced simultaneously. Written accents over Czech vowels indicate not stress, which is always initial, but length, and it is perfectly possible in Czech to have in the same word a short accented and a long unaccented vowel (in *dobry,* for instance, the *o* is stressed but short, the *ý* unstressed but long); this makes Czech an ideal living language in which to study the same phenomenon occurring in Classical languages like Greek and Latin. In structure, Czech greatly resembles Russian and Polish, and many of the case and verb endings are almost identical.

Slovak may be described as a variant of Czech, or perhaps to an even greater degree as a bridge between Czech and Polish. Because of its central position among the Slavic tongues, Slovak has at times been advocated as a mediating language, or tongue of common intercourse among all Slavs. The point is well taken, for it is closer than Czech to the South Slavic languages, and close enough to the East Slavic tongues, particularly Ukrainian, to serve as an intermediary.

Serbo-Croatian, Slovenian, and Bulgarian are often classified as South Slavic tongues, in opposition to the eastern (Russo-Ukrainian) and to the northwestern (Polish-Czech) divisions. This classification is perhaps more geographical than linguistic, because while Serbo-Croatian and Slovenian follow the general Slavic pattern, Bulgarian displays such radical structural differences as to warrant a separate classification for itself.

Serbian and Croatian are the same language, with minor dialectal differences. The main point of divergence between them is the writing, Serbian using the Cyrillic, Croatian the Roman alphabet. Serbo-Croatian is more musical than the other Slavic languages, having preserved in certain words traces of the ancient Indo-European musical pitch accent. Its system of inflections parallels to a considerable degree that of the languages already described. Slovenian may be called a variant of Serbo-Croatian.

Bulgarian, however, differs widely from all other Slav tongues in two important particulars. It has a fully developed definite article, which the others lack, and which is post-posed, like the definite article of Scandinavian and Rumanian; and it has reduced the numerous case forms of Slavic to a single case. This means that while Russian and Bulgarian both use *selo* for "village," Russian will say *selo* for "the village," but Bulgarian will say *selo-to*. On the other hand, Russian will decline *selo* in six cases, while Bulgarian will express case relations by means of position and preposi-tions, like English.

Many theories have been advanced for the structural di-versity between Bulgarian and the other Slavic tongues. One is to the effect that the Bulgars were not originally Slavs but speakers of a Turkic language who adopted Slavic speech and found the Slavic cases too complicated for use. This hardly seems a satisfactory explanation, as the Turkic lan-guages use plenty of inflectional endings—more, in fact, than Slavic itself. For the use of the postposed article, it has been suggested that proximity to Rumanian may be responsible. But Bulgarian uses as an article the word which in other Slavic languages is a demonstrative pronoun, meaning "this" or "that." Had the use of the article been borrowed from Rumanian, it is possible that the Rumanian form itself would have been borrowed. Other linguists suggest that it may have been Rumanian that borrowed the postposed article from Bulgarian. If Scandinavia were territorially contiguous with Rumania and Bulgaria, instead of being separated by broad expanses of languages that do not use a postposed article, our linguists would undoubtedly claim an influence from the Scandinavian languages upon the Balkan ones, or vice versa. The real fact of the matter seems to be that languages often develop parallel traits in phonology, morphology, and syntax without the necessity of a direct influence by one upon the other. It is quite possible that the Bulgarian reduction of the Slavic cases to a single form paralleling the experience of the western Romance languages is another case of this stray similarity, and that the Bulgars are as much Slavs as any of the other Slavic nations. The occasional traces of ancient case forms, particularly the vocative, appearing in modern Bulgarian, and the fact that old Church Slavic was probably spoken in what is today in great part Bulgarian territory, would seem to bear out this view.

The Slavic picture would hardly be complete without a reference to the tongues of the Baltic group, which are often linked with the Slavic in a Balto-Slavic subdivision of Indo-European. Today only two Baltic tongues remain, Lithuanian and Lettish, and together they reach barely 5 million speakers. During the Middle Ages there was also an Old Prussian tongue, but its speakers were practically exterminated by the Teutonic Knights (some, however, survived until the end of the seventeenth century). Lithuanian enjoys the distinction of being described by linguists as the modern tongue which comes closest to the original Indo-European of all the modern languages of the group. It retains practically all of the Indo-European inflections, and a measure of the old Indo-European pitch accent.

It is a fact, though not perhaps as universally known as it might be, that speakers of Balto-Slavic languages and their descendants are quite numerous in the United States and Canada. It has been estimated by reliable sources that no less than 3 million Polish speakers and their descendants are located on U. S. soil, along with 1½ million original speakers of Czech and Slovak, as many of Russian, 1 million of Ukrainian, and close to ½ million each of Yugoslav and Lithuanian. These original Slavic speakers, while mostly concentrated in the mining and industrial districts of Pennsylvania, Ohio, Illinois, and Michigan, are to be found today in practically every state in the Union. Their attachment to their mother tongues is attested by the large number of parochial elementary schools in which these tongues, particularly Polish, are taught.

— Chapter Six —

OTHER INDO-EUROPEAN LANGUAGES

"But, for my own part, it was Greek to me."
—Shakespeare, *Julius Caesar*

THE three great branches of Indo-European (Germanic, Romance, Balto-Slavic) have at least five existing relatives, of which one, Indo-Iranian, is as numerically extensive as they. The other four (Greek, Albanian, Celtic, Armenian) are today quite insignificant as to number of speakers, but two of them have in past centuries exerted a decisive influence over the destinies of western culture.

Greek is today the tongue of perhaps 10 million speakers, located in Greece, the islands of the Aegean, southern Albania and Yugoslavia, southwestern Bulgaria, and European and Asiatic Turkey, as well as on the islands of Cyprus and Crete. It was at one time the tongue of common intercourse of the central and eastern Mediterranean, most of Asia Minor, and parts of Egypt, the language of the old Greek city-states whose colonies ranged from Spain and southern Gaul, Sicily and the coast of Italy, to the shores of the Black Sea and beyond. Greek was the first of the western Indo-European tongues to become the vehicle of a distinctive civilization which endures to this day. It was the language of philosophy, of poetry, of literature, of rhetoric, of science when the other tongues of the west, Germanic, Slavic, even Latin, were unwritten dialects. It was the Greek form of the alphabet, brought originally from Phoenicia, that gave rise to the Etruscan and Roman alphabets, whence all our western scripts are derived. As the direct ancestor of the Cyrillic alphabet, the Greek form of writing also gave rise to the written characters of the eastern Slavs.

Greek was the one foreign tongue the Romans respected. Ruthless as they were with all other foreign languages, at no time did they attempt to supplant Greek where they found it. As a result, Greek and Latin lived in a state of symbiosis under the late Republic and the early Empire, with Greek used as a popular language in most of the eastern provinces. When the seat of the Empire was transferred from Rome to Byzantium, the official language of the eastern Empire was Greek, and while the Roman Empire of the West fell in the fifth century, the Byzantine Empire continued to exist until the fall of Constantinople to the Turks in the middle of the fifteenth century.

The transformations that have occurred in the Greek language from about 800 B.C., when it first appeared in the Homeric poems, to the present day, are astoundingly slight, particularly in the written form of the language. Greek high school students today can read the *Iliad* and *Odyssey* without much difficulty.

The Greek of antiquity was a language of many dialects—Attic, Doric, Ionian, Aeolian, etc. While these did not differ too greatly, and there was undoubtedly a community of understanding among their speakers, some of the ancient dialectal forms show striking individual traits. By the time Greece came in contact with Rome, Greek speakers had developed a *koine,* or tongue of common intercourse, which did service for all of them, and the ancient dialects gradually dropped into disuse. Only one, the Laconian of Sparta, survives to the present day in the form of the modern Tsaconian. The *koine* alone served the medieval Byzantine Empire.

Between the schism that separated the eastern and western churches and the fall of Constantinople to the Turks in 1453, the study of Greek in western Europe, which had flourished when Roman power was at its peak, declined to the point where the famous saying "It's Greek to me" came into being (actually, the expression seems to be a translation of a phrase with which western monks annotated Greek passages in their religious manuscripts: *Graecum est, non legitur,* "It is Greek, it is not read"; but at the outset this phrasing seems to have referred to the possibility of heretical statements in the Greek texts rather than to difficulty with the language).

The taking of Constantinople saw the downfall of Greek on its own ancient territory, since it was replaced by Turkish in the Balkans and Asia Minor and became thenceforth merely the tongue of a peasant population in the Greek peninsula and adjoining islands; at the same time, this event marked also the resurgence of Greek in the west. Brought to Italy by Byzantine refugee scholars, the Greek language and Greek literature aroused a new interest in the lands of the Renaissance, and the west was suddenly reminded of the tremendous debt it owed Greece. Greek became once more the great language of scholarship, even while it was declining into an almost illiterate tongue on its home soil. For the last four and a half centuries, Greek has again been contributing mightily to the languages of the civilized western world, supplying them with terms of learning, science, technology, and all the myriad activities in which the Greeks once showed the way.

After the liberation of Greece from Turkish rule in the early nineteenth century, the spoken Greek tongue regained a small measure of its former splendor. The modern official Greek language, called Romaic (a reminder of the Roman Empire of the East), has two forms: one, used in literary composition, called *katharevusa*, which is very close to the ancient tongue of Homer and Aristotle; the other, a popular spoken tongue, called *demotike*, which has borrowed considerably from foreign sources, particularly Turkish, and shows a certain measure of simplification of some of the old grammatical forms.

Yet in both the present-day Greek languages, literary and popular, there is an undercurrent of archaism which is most noticeable in the vocabulary. The spoken Greek tongue is replete with words which we use in the more cultured portion of our own vocabulary. The modern Greek word for "army," *stratevma*, comes from the same root that gives us "strategy." "I count" in modern Greek is *arithmo;* the link with "arithmetic" is clear. "Bad" is *kakos,* and "sound" is *phone,* which makes the origin and meaning of "cacophony" quite comprehensible. *Psyche* is "soul" or "mind," and *soma* is "body," and "psychosomatic" medicine is thereby defined.

The Greek alphabet is still precisely the same as it was in the days of Demosthenes, and our Greek-letter fraternities have made us partly familiar with it. "Beta" and "gamma" rays, the "delta" at the mouth of a river, the "iota" which indicates a minute quantity, the "pi" of mathematics, expressions like "from alpha to omega" have also acquainted us with the names of the letters.

The phonology of Greek has changed somewhat from the days of old, but to a lesser degree, perhaps, than the phonology of the Romance languages from Latin. The letter *beta* is no longer pronounced as *b,* but as *v,* so likewise the ancient *upsilon* in diphthongs, so that the *autos* from which the front part of our "automobile" is derived is today sounded *avtos* or *aftos* on Greek soil. Many vowels and diphthongs have altered their values. The ancient accentuation of Greek, which contained elements of musical pitch, has turned into an accent of stress. The old rough breathing which we still pronounce as *h* has become silent, so that while we pronounce "hypnotism," a modern Greek pronouncing *hypnos* ("sleep") will say *ypnos.*

Ancient Greek differed from Latin in possessing a definite article, and modern Greek still has it. *Anthropos* is "man," but "the man" is *o anthropos.* The ancient Greek cases (nominative, genitive, dative, accusative, vocative) still exist, but there is a tendency in the spoken tongue to discard the dative to mark the indirect object and use instead the accusative with *eis,* "to," "into."

The Greek verb still has all the complexities of person, number, tense, voice, and mood that appeared in the older language, with new ramifications brought about by the use of analytical compounds (similar to the English "I have brought") which did not succeed in displacing the old synthetic forms but only in making a place for themselves by their side. In ancient Greek, for example, a form like "I shall loose" was expressed simply by *lyso;* today one may use *lyso, tha lyso,* or *tha lyo,* all with different shades of meaning. Modern Greek has, however, discarded the old dual number.

A few samples of the spoken Greek tongue of today will make clear the intimate bond that exists between it and our own language in its more cultured reaches. "Thank you very much" is *evcharisto para poly,* where the first word, "I thank," gives us the key to "eucharistic," *para* ("by") is the preposition that appears in such English compounds as "paranoic," and *poly* ("much," "many") supplies us with the prefix of "polytheism," "polyglot," etc. "I am thirsty" is *dipso,* which appears in our "dipsomaniac." "Do you speak Greek?" is *omileite Ellenika,* where the first word reminds us of the religious "homily" (merely a "talk"; "sermon" is its precise Latin counterpart). "Very little" is *poly oligon,* and we recognize the second word in "oligarchy," the rule of the few. "So long" is freely translated by an expression that sounds like *yasoo,* but which in full written form appears as *hygeia sou* ("health to you"); needless to say, *hygeia* gives us "hygiene."

Xenophon Zolotas, governor of the Bank of Greece, recently gave a graphic demonstration of the infiltration of his language into ours. After discoursing of "numismatic plethora," otherwise known as inflation, he added: "With enthusiasm we dialogue and synagonize at the synods of our didymous organizations in which polymorphous economic ideas and dogmas are analyzed and synthetized." The ten non-Greek words will be easily spotted.

The Albanians are often closely linked with the Greeks, but the main bond is geographical rather than racial or linguistic. The best hypothesis concerning the racial stock of the Albanians is that they are the descendants of the ancient Illyrians who once occupied the entire eastern coast of the Adriatic and formed the bands of Liburnian pirates who on one occasion held even Julius Caesar for ransom. Linguistically, Albanian was at one time thought to be a dialect of Greek, but it is today regarded as a separate branch of Indo-European, with plenty of words borrowed from Greek, Latin, Slavic, and Turkish. The first known written document of the language is a baptismal ritual of the year 1462. There are today perhaps 3 million speakers of Albanian, which has two principal dialects, Gheg, spoken in the north, and Tosk in the south.

The Albanians use the Roman alphabet, with an unusual value given to some letters. *Q,* for instance, represents approximately the sound of *cky* in "stockyard." It is estimated that at least 60 per cent of the Albanian vocabulary is borrowed from its neighbors. Words like *ar, ergjënt, qen, kupë* ("gold," "silver," "dog," "cup") come from Latin or Romance; *keq* ("bad") is from Greek *kakos; mish* and *trup* ("meat" and "body") are from Slavic; *fildxhán* ("glass") is from Turkish.

The Celtic languages are remarkable in that their speakers were once far more numerous than they are today. Celtic groups ranged from Asia Minor and ancient Sarmatia on the east to Britain and Portugal on the west. Most of ancient Gaul, the British Isles, Germany as far east as the Elbe, the great Po Valley of northern Italy, a large part of the valley of the Danube were at one time solid Celtic-speaking territories.

Yielding gradually to Roman conquerors, the Celts were for the most part absorbed and latinized, and the most extensive of their languages, Gaulish, disappeared altogether. The two surviving branches are almost entirely located on British soil. Welsh and Cornish are the descendants of the language of the Britons who succumbed to Caesar and later were forced back into the mountain fastnesses of the west by new Anglo-Saxon invaders. "Welsh," incidentally, is an English name which the Welsh do not fancy; they call themselves Cymri. The Gaelic originally spoken in Ireland was brought to Scotland by a series of conquering expeditions that overwhelmed the ancient Picts and mingled with them. The Breton of France is the descendant of Welsh, brought to the Roman province of Armorica (present-day Brittany) in the fifth and sixth centuries by fugitives from Britain. Welsh, Breton, and Cornish together form the Brythonic branch of Celtic, while the Gaelic of Ireland and Scotland and the Manx of the Isle of Man constitute the Goidelic branch. The name "Erse," applied by the English to the Gaelic of Ireland, is as little favored by the inhabitants of Eire as "Welsh" is by the Cymri.

There is a curious parallelism between the two branches of Celtic (Brythonic and Goidelic) and the two branches of Italic (Osco-Umbrian and Latin). Brythonic and Osco-Umbrian both turn Indo-European labialized gutturals, like *qu*, into labials (*p*), while Goidelic and Latin retain the guttural, so that *quinque* ("five") of Latin is *cuig* in Irish, but *pump* in Welsh and *pumpe* in Oscan. This has given rise to some rather far-fetched theories concerning an original Italo-Celtic unit, a hypothetical subgroup of Indo-European, which later split into separate Italic and Celtic branches.

Today, Irish is the official tongue of Eire, most of whose inhabitants prefer to speak English, with or without a brogue (recent figures for the 3 million people of Eire are to the effect that 2,900,000 of them can speak English, but only about 1 million can speak Irish). Scots Gaelic is used by perhaps 100,000 Highlanders. Welsh is the language of about 1 million people in Wales, most of whom use English as well, and Breton of as many more people in Brittany, who for the most part also speak French. The number of people speaking Manx and Cornish is negligible, and most linguists set down the latter as a dead tongue.

In all of the Celtic languages complicated phonological phenomena appear, particularly in connection with initial consonants, which change in accordance with the final sound of the preceding word, so that a form like Breton *kalon* ("heart") may appear as *halon* or *galon*. In Irish and Scots Gaelic the spelling is antiquated and no longer represents the modern pronunciation (for instance, Irish *mo mháthair*, "my mother," is pronounced *mo vaher*). Welsh and Breton are far more modern in this respect and use a fairly phonetic spelling, provided one remembers that in Welsh *w* and *y* are full vowels (as in *Bryn Mawr*, pronounced *Breen Ma-oor*, or, better yet, in *rhy ddrwg*, "too bad!" pronounced *ree dhroog*). The Welsh *ll*, as in the proper name Llewellyn, is pronounced as an *l* unaccompanied by vibration of the vocal cords, with the tongue cupped and retracted so that its tip touches the middle of the palate.

All other Celtic languages use the Roman alphabet, but Irish still makes use of the beautiful and distinctive "Irish hand" said to have been introduced from Gaul by St. Patrick and continued uninterruptedly since the sixth century.

Irish still retains four cases (nominative, genitive, dative, and vocative), while Welsh and Breton have given up their ancient case system.

The Indo-European nature of the Celtic languages and their relationship to other branches of the family can be easily gathered from a few examples. "Arm," which is *brachium* in Latin, giving rise to such forms as *bras, brazo, braccio* in the Romance languages, is *brac* in Irish, *braich* in Welsh, *bréac'h* in Breton. "Friend" is *cara, câr, kâr* in the three main Celtic languages, and seems connected with Latin *carus,* French *cher,* Italian and Spanish *caro,* "dear." The *novem* of Latin (our own "nine") is *naoi, nāw, naô.* "Eighty" is "four-twenties" in the Celtic languages, as in French *(quatre-vingts),* which may have borrowed it from them.

English is indebted to the Celtic tongues for many of its most picturesque words. "Bard," "leprechaun" and "banshee," "blarney" and "shillelagh," "colleen," "mavourneen," and "macushla" come from Irish, as does "whiskey," the "water of life." From Highland Scots come words like "slogan" and "clan"; the *Dhu* which adorns the name of Roderick in "The Lady of the Lake" is Gaelic for "black." Welsh has contributed "eisteddfod" and "Lloyd." "Druid" seems to hark back to ancient Gaulish. The archaeological "dolmen" (a large unhewn stone resting on two other stones, probably designed for sacrificial purposes) is from the Breton *dol* ("table"), while "cromlech," another term for the same object, is Welsh *crom* ("bent") and *llec* ("flat stone"); the objects seem to come from the prehistoric inhabitants of Europe, but the names were imparted by the Indo-European Celts. The ancient Gauls contributed numerous words to the vocabulary of their Roman conquerors. The Latin *camisia* which turned into the French and English "chemise," the Vulgar Latin *pettia* that ultimately became "piece," possibly even the slangy *caballus* that supplied the Romance languages with their words for "horse" and English speakers with derivatives like "cavalier," "cavalcade," and "chivalry," were among these contributions.

Armenian, the smallest and most downtrodden member of the Indo-European family, is spoken in the eastern section of

Turkey and the southwest of European Russia, in the Black Sea area, around Lake Van and the Mount Ararat of Biblical fame. Less than 4 million of its speakers have survived Turkish and Kurdish massacres and persecutions. Byron pronounced Armenian "a rich language which would amply repay anyone the trouble of learning it." It is written with an alphabet of thirty-eight letters, introduced about A.D. 400 by St. Mesrop.

The border between Turkey and Iran marks the beginning of one of the most extensive of the Indo-European branches. Beginning with seminomadic Kurdish, which straddles the frontier regions of Turkey, Iran, and Iraq, this great group sweeps eastward across Iran, Afghanistan, Baluchistan, and northern India to the borders of Burma. Its speakers number nearly 500 million, including about two thirds of India's teeming population of 470 million, most of Pakistan's 100 million, the 17 million inhabitants of Afghanistan, Iran's 22 million, and about half of the 11 million people of the great island of Ceylon.

Modern Persian, the chief Iranian representative of the great Indo-Iranian group, uses the word *Iranī* to refer to people, places, and institutions, but retains the old *Farsī* ("Persian") when speaking of the country's language and literature. Both of these have a long and glorious history, beginning with the Old Persian inscriptions of Cyrus, Darius, and Artaxerxes, who built a mighty empire at the expense of the Babylonians and Assyrians, and continuing with Avestan, the sacred tongue of Zoroaster or Zarathustra, who taught the Persians fire worship and the principle of everlasting struggle between the forces of good (*Ahura-mazda* or *Ormazd*) and those of evil (*Angra-manyu* or *Ahriman*). Under the Seleucid and Sassanidan kings, the Persians, now renamed Parthians, fought a long and partly successful struggle against the Romans, but in the seventh century A.D. they succumbed to the Moslems from Arabia. Fire worship was replaced by the Koran (the Parsees of India are the fire-worshiping refugees who found flight to be a third alternative between the Koran and the sword), and the Persian language, until then fully Indo-European, became a conglomeration of Arabic loan words, which were later carried by the Moguls to India and became part and parcel of the Urdu variant of Hindustani used by Indian Moslems.

The Persian language of today bears little resemblance to the ancient tongue of Xerxes or that of the Zend-Avesta. Noun declension and verb conjugation have been simplified to almost the same extent as in English. The language is now written in flowing Arabic characters, to which slight modifications and additions have been made to conform to the rich Persian phonology. The spoken tongue is a majestic, sonorous one, replete with impressive long vowels, and well fitted to serve as the vehicle of such poetry as that of Omar Khayyam, Firdausi, and Hafiz.

Across the mountain barrier from Persia lies the fabulous land of Hind, itself a Persian, not an Indian, word. In this vast subcontinent, races, languages, and religions intermingle in an inextricable, overlapping maze. The people who share the same faith seldom share the same tongue, or vice versa. Some seventeen major Indo-Iranian languages appear, along with sixteen major non-Indo-European languages of the Dravidian stock, as well as myriads of minor tongues, dialects, and languages of other, obscure families. The Dravidian languages are for the most part concentrated in the Deccan, or southern part of the Indian peninsula, while the Indo-Iranian languages appear in the north. The situation is curiously reversed in the adjoining island of Ceylon, where the northern portion speaks Dravidian Tamil, while the south uses Singhalese, an Indo-Iranian tongue.

Out of a total population of 580 million for the three countries, at least 400 million speak Indo-Iranian languages, while over 120 million use Dravidian tongues. Of the former, about 200 million can be reached with Hindustani, by far the leading language of India, which bids fair to become the Indian *koine*. But Hindustani is broken into two variants, Hindi, used by people of Hindu religion, and Urdu, spoken by Moslems and the official language of West Pakistan. The former is written in the ancient, monumental Devanagari characters inherited from Sanskrit, the latter in the Arabic alphabet imported by the Moslem Mogul conquerors. Hindi conserves the old Sanskrit words, Urdu replaces many of them with Arabic and Persian loan forms. "Death," for example, is expressed in Hindi by *mrityu*, obviously related to Latin *morte(m)*, from which our "mortal" is derived, but in Urdu the current word is the Arabic *mawt*. "Foot" in Hindi is *panw*, from Sanskrit *pādah*, related to Latin *pede* (*m*) and Greek *pod(a)*, even to our own "foot," but in Urdu the Arabic *qadam* is used. Of course Hindi and Urdu speakers can understand each other, but they both take pride in showing their religious affiliations by the use of specific words.

Hindustani and its related Indo-Iranian tongues (Bengali, with 70 million speakers, Marathi, Punjabi, Rajasthani, etc.) go back to ancient Sanskrit, earliest of the Indo-European languages to appear in recorded form. The antiquated form of Sanskrit in which the Vedic hymns were composed may go back as far as 2000 B.C. or thereabouts, antedating Latin, Greek, and Avestan by many centuries. It is a hieratic, symmetrical, highly inflected tongue, singularly fitted for precise priestly rituals, and displays the original Indo-European structure better than any other known tongue, with the possible exception of Lithuanian. The accent is one of musical pitch. There are in Sanskrit clearly defined vowel quantities and a division of consonants into aspirated and nonaspirated (*p* as in "upper" and *ph* as in "uphill"; *g* as in "go" and *gh* as in "hoghouse," etc.). The cases are eight in number, and prepositions are altogether dispensed with, though the equivalents of the prepositions of other Indo-European languages often appear as verb prefixes. In addition to singular and plural, there is a full-fledged dual number for nouns, pronouns, adjectives, and verbs. The latter have abundant complications of tense, mood, voice, and aspect.

From Vedic Sanskrit, the language proceeded to Classical Sanskrit, then to the Prakrits, or popular vernaculars. In an ancient Indian play, the kings, princes, and priests use Sanskrit, while the lower characters speak the Prakrits, in accordance with their station in life. Through several intermediate stages, the present-day vernaculars of northern India were developed, Hindustani among them.

The structural changes from Sanskrit to Hindustani are striking. The dual number and the ancient case endings have entirely disappeared, and the latter have been replaced by an entirely new and unrelated set, which works for both singular and plural, the plural suffix being inserted between the root and the case ending. Verbs which in Sanskrit appear in a variety of conjugational schemes are reduced in Hindustani to a single, very simple conjugation, with relatively few tenses and a standardized syntax. The process of simplification has gone on apace in the eastern as in the western portion of the Indo-European domain.

An increasingly large number of words and terms have come to us of late from the languages of India. *Maharajah* is Sanskrit for "great king"; the *maha* is cognate to Latin *magnus* ("great") and appears also in *mahatma* ("great-souled"; *atman*, "soul," corresponds to Latin *animus*); the *raj* root corresponds to Latin *rego*, whence our "regal," "royal," etc. *Raj*, without further qualification, was formerly used in India to describe the British rule, and *svaraj* is "self-rule," or independence, which India now enjoys. Among the titles of India's princes are *ranee* ("queen," closely allied to Latin *regina), begum* (also reserved for ladies), *rawal, raikwar, nizam, khan,* and *nawab,* from which we get "nabob," though the original meaning is not a man of immense wealth but a deputy or viceroy.

The Hindu *swami* refers either to a prince or a teacher. *Guru* is more specifically a teacher or professor. *Pundit,* from Sanskrit *pandita* ("gatherer," "one who keeps up"), is also a learned man, particularly a Brahman versed in Hindu lore. *Babu* is a native who serves as a clerk and knows how to read and write, especially English. A *yogi* is a follower of the *yōga* philosophy, which in Sanskrit literally means "union" (with the Godhead). *Khaki,* the color of many western uniforms, is Hindustani for "dust-colored" but comes originally from Persian *khāk* ("dust"). The slogan of present-day Hindustan is *"Jai Hind!"* ("Live India!"), with *jai* from the Sanskrit; that of Pakistan is *"Pakistan zindabad!"* ("Pakistan forever!"), with both Urdu words derived from Persian. Just as Gandhi's title was the Sanskrit *mahatma,* that of Mohammed Ali Jinnah was the Arabic *qaid-e-azam* ("great leader"). From the tongues of India come "pajama" and "sari," "curry" and "chutney," "swastika" and "thug."

The present tendency is for Hindustani to impose itself as the common language of both Hindustan and Pakistan. In so doing, it must overcome lesser languages which have formidable speaking populations: the Indo-Iranian Bengali of the Bengal and Calcutta regions, with 90 million; the closely related Bihari of the northeast, with 35 million; the Marathi, Punjabi, and Rajasthani of the northwest, with a combined speaking population of over 70 million; the Dravidian tongues of the south, Tamil, Telugu, Canarese, Malayalam, with 15 to 40 million speakers each.

The process is on its way, but it is slow and fraught with difficulties. Words embodying the technical civilization of the twentieth century have to be created or adapted to make Hindi and Urdu usable languages for modern states. Nearly 100,000 have already been supplied for Hindi by a special commission of linguistic scholars. Some have been taken over as loan words from English, others ingeniously compounded from Sanskrit roots; but it is estimated that at least 300,000 more are needed before Hindi can take its place as a language of science and technology by the side of the western tongues.

The worst language problem facing not only India but Pakistan and Ceylon as well, however, is that of linguistic nationalism. Small but bloody wars rage from time to time in all three countries on the language issue, often overshadowing that other great controversy of the Indian subcontinent, religion. Typical in recent times have been the language war in western India between speakers of Mahrati (or Maharashtri) and those of Gujarati; the East Pakistan rebellion against Urdu on behalf of the local Bengali, which led to the establishment of the latter language as co-official with the first; the struggle in Ceylon between speakers of Singhalese and of Tamil.

The beneficiary of this internecine strife is no doubt English, which is spoken by less than 5 per cent of the total population of the three nations but still manages to maintain its position as the "binding tongue" of all three, since it is the educated top layer of the population that speaks it. Native speakers of English number about 2 million in India, ½ million in Pakistan, perhaps 100,000 in Ceylon, but at least 25 million out of total combined populations of nearly 600 million handle English reasonably well.

As time goes on, the duel between Hindi-Urdu, the language of a one-third plurality, and English, the Commonwealth tongue which is also a key to the outside world, will continue to unfold. Hindi-Urdu has numbers on its side, coupled with nationalism and anticolonialism. English has its practical world position and its neutral status among the tongues of the subcontinent. It is perhaps too early to predict the outcome.

— Chapter Seven —

POSSIBLE RELATIVES OF
INDO-EUROPEAN

And the whole earth was of one language, and of one speech.
—Genesis, 11:1

PERENNIALLY the question comes up: "If there was original unity among such widely diversified tongues as English, Russian, Greek, Armenian, and Hindustani, what is there to belie the possibility that at a much remoter epoch all of the world's languages may have sprung from one common stock? May not the Biblical account of Babel's Tower of Confusion be figuratively, even if not literally, true?"

There is really nothing to belie this *possibility*. But whereas among the languages labeled "Indo-European" the kinship is demonstrable and demonstrated, there is little or nothing to go on when we come to linking such groups as Indo-European and Malayo-Polynesian, or Chinese and Hottentot.

A few daring linguists, like the Italian Trombetti, have strenuously asserted the thesis of the "monogenesis," or single common origin, of all the world's tongues. But their demonstration has been based primarily on elements of vocabulary, individual words, where chance resemblances may occur in accordance with the statistical laws of probability. Just as, if you deal a sufficient number of bridge hands, the identical thirteen-card combination will recur after a few thousand deals, so two languages may independently, and by pure hazard, have the same or a closely similar combination of sounds for the same or a similar meaning in one word out of a few thousands. Italian *donna* and Japanese *onna* sound alike and both mean "woman," yet we surmise that they are quite unrelated, and while we cannot trace the Japanese word to an earlier form, we can press the Italian word back to its original Latin form *domina,* at which point its similarity to the Japanese word becomes far less marked.

Other linguists, basing themselves upon a combination of geographical, historical, and linguistic data, have approached the problem from a different angle, endeavoring to set forth a kinship between groups of languages geographically contiguous and which have had some bearing upon one another's historical development. The two language groups geographically and historically closest to the Indo-European family are the Semito-Hamitic and the Ural-Altaic. After investigating the structure, geographical location, and known history of these two groups we shall be in a better position to pronounce on the question of their relationship to Indo-European.

The Semitic tongues are so called because they are supposed to have originated with the descendants of Shem after the Tower of Babel episode. Ham's descendants are supposed to have given rise to the Hamitic tongues. Japhet, Noah's third son, is responsible for the "Japhetic," or European tongues, though the term "Japhetic" has also been applied to a hypothetical language group including Iberian, Caucasian, Sumerian, Etruscan, and other "Mediterranean" tongues.

Because of the Biblical account of the Tower of Babel and the confusion of tongues, we have "babble" from the Akkadian *bab-ilu,* which really means "the gate of the god." The fact that there is a Hebrew verb *bālal,* "to confuse, confound, mix," is perhaps in part responsible for the tradition.

The Semito-Hamitic tongues, spoken today by approximately 125 million people, cover the Arabian peninsula, Iraq, Syria, Israel and Jordan, northern Africa from Egypt to Morocco, and from the Mediterranean to the Tropic of Cancer, Ethiopia, Eritrea, and Somaliland.

In ancient times, the Semitic branch included Akkadian (the tongue of Babylon and Assyria), Canaanite, Moabite, Phoenician (with its variant Punic, spoken by the Carthaginians), Hebrew, Aramaic or Syriac, and the early Arabic of the Arabian peninsula. The Hamitic branch, which in those days dominated all of North Africa, included the ancient Egyptian of the hieroglyphic inscriptions as well as the Libyco-Berber tongues of North Africa that still exist today.

In the Ethiopian region, Semitic and Hamitic are intermingled. The Cushitic tongues of Ethiopia (Galla, Somali, etc.) are of the Hamitic variety, while the Semitic Amharic and Tigré spoken by the dominant race seem to have been imported from Arabia across the Red Sea.

Within historical times, many of the ancient Semitic languages disappeared, but Hebrew, Arabic, and Syriac lived on. The first tongue, expelled from its Palestinian homeland after the destruction of Jerusalem by Titus and Vespasian, existed somewhat precariously for centuries as a semiliturgical tongue used by the Jewish communities of Europe and North Africa, but has recently made a triumphal re-entry into Palestine, where it is now the official national tongue of the state of Israel and its rapidly growing population.

Syriac (the ancient Aramaic of the Bible and the language spoken by Christ) is still used today by perhaps 200,000 people, mostly Christians who live among the Arabic-speaking Moslem populations of Syria, Lebanon, Jordan, and Iraq.

Arabic, once the isolated language of the Arabian peninsula, served as the vehicle for the conquering religion of Mohammed and spread like wildfire across North Africa in the seventh century, supplanting the African Latin which at an earlier period had replaced Carthage's Punic. It made its influence powerfully felt in southern Europe, particularly Spain and Sicily, where many words and place names are of Arabic origin. It gave rise to Maltese, a somewhat hybrid mixture of Arabic and Italian. Moving northward and eastward, it extended as a spoken popular tongue into the countries of the Near East and influenced Turkish, Persian, Hindustani, even the Malay of southeastern Asia and Indonesia. Wherever the Moslem religion reaches, in the Balkans, in central Asia, western China, India, Indonesia, the Philippines, central and east Africa, there the Arabic tongue appears as a religious language, fulfilling approximately the same function among Moslems of many races and tongues that Latin fulfills wherever the Roman Catholic faith extends. While the actual number of Arabic speakers is probably about 90 million, it is no exaggeration to say that Arabic influences, both linguistically and psychologically, hundreds of millions.

The chief tongues of Ethiopia, Amharic and the closely allied Tigriña and Tigré, have a speaking population of perhaps 8 million out of Ethiopia's 22 million inhabitants (the remainder use languages of the Hamitic-Cushitic branch, chief among them Galla and Somali).

Among the Hamitic languages interest attaches particularly to ancient Egyptian because of its function, through tens of centuries, as the vehicle of one of the greatest ancient civilizations. Its use began to decline with the Roman conquest of Egypt, and it became practically extinct after the Moslem invasion. Its most direct modern descendant is Coptic, still used as a liturgical language by Christian groups in parts of modern Egypt, Ethiopia, and the Sudan. The Libyco-Berber dialects (Kabyle, Shilh, Tuareg, etc.) still endure in North Africa, side by side with Arabic, while the Galla and Somali of Ethiopia and Somaliland eke out a somewhat precarious existence in East Africa.

The main structural characteristic of the Semito-Hamitic family is the word root consisting of three consonants, with shifting vowels that carry auxiliary meanings, performing the same function as the endings of Indo-European. To exemplify: the Arabic root that conveys the general ideal of "writing" is K-T-B. Vowels placed at the beginning and end, or between the consonants, give this root all the needed accessory notions. *Kataba* is "he had written"; *kutiba,* "it has been written"; *yaktuba,* "he will write"; *yuktabu,* "it will be written"; *'aktaba,* "he has made someone write"; *kitābun,* "writing" or "book"; *kātibun,* "writer"; *katbun,* "act of writing."

This characteristic mode of flexion is sometimes compared to the Indo-European ablaut system, as exemplified by English "sing," "sang," "sung," "song." But the Indo-European ablaut is generally traceable to the place of the accent in the original parent language, with a vowel assuming different grades according as it was originally stressed, had the stress on the syllable preceding it, or on the syllable following it. The vowel changes in the Semitic root, on the other hand, do not seem to have anything to do with the accent. Furthermore, the normal three-consonant Semitic roots are not paralleled by Indo-European roots, which display a varying number of consonants.

There is, in addition, a distressing lack of similarity between Indo-European and Semito-Hamitic words of what might be described as the fundamental kind. Corresponding to the "brother," "sister," "father," "mother" roots of Indo-European we find in Arabic *akh, ukht, ab,* and *umm.* For the "tooth" root of Indo-European, Arabic has *sinn.* The "one," "three," and "ten" roots have as their counterparts *ahad, thalāth,* and *'asr,* respectively. Worse yet, no system of regular phonetic correspondences can be found between Indo-European and Semitic similar to those which govern the various branches of Indo-European, permitting one to predict that a word with *p* and *d* in Latin will, under given conditions, appear in English with *f* and *t.* Under the circumstances, such chance resemblances as Hebrew *eretz,* English "earth," or Arabic *saba'a,* Latin *septem* lose much of their value.

The two languages of the Semito-Hamitic group which have

most influenced the tongues of the west are undoubtedly Arabic and Hebrew, the former of the southern, the latter of the northern, Semitic branch. From the standpoint of early Semitic, Arabic is quite conservative, Hebrew extremely innovating, as befits a language that was situated at the Palestinian world crossroad. Yet the two languages are still quite close to each other, as much so as Spanish and Italian, and a measure of mutual comprehensibility between their speakers exists. "Great," which is *kibīr* in Egyptian Arabic, is *kabbīr* in Hebrew. "Eye" is *'ayn* in Arabic, *'ayin* in Hebrew; "death" is *mawt* in Arabic, *māvet* in Hebrew. The common form of greeting, "Peace to you!," is *assalamu aleykum* in Arabic, *shalom alekhem* in Hebrew.

Arabic preserves many of the emphatic consonants of early Semitic which Hebrew has lost or merged, and while spoken Arabic produces the impression of being extremely harsh and guttural, Hebrew is comparatively soft and flowing. Both languages have a powerful, majestic rhythm.

Classical Arabic is a unified and highly conservative language and is used throughout the entire Arabic world for written-language purposes. Spoken Arabic, as a tongue which has been in constant use for many centuries over an extended area, has broken up into numerous dialects, of which the principal ones are the Moroccan, the Algerian-Tunisian-Libyan, the Egyptian, the Syro-Palestinian, the Iraqī, and the peninsular Arabian. Hebrew, on the other hand, ceased to be a popular spoken tongue some centuries before the time of Christ, surviving as a cultured and liturgical language during the centuries of the dispersion, and this has kept it fairly unified. Minor differences of pronunciation appear in the Hebrew of the Ashkenazic or northern European Jews and of the Sephardic Jews of southern Europe and the Mediterranean basin. In the resurrected national Hebrew of Israel these differences have been merged, with Sephardic pronunciation generally getting the upper hand.

In modern spoken Arabic, as in the Romance languages, there are only two genders, masculine and feminine, and the gender distinction is made not only in nouns, adjectives, and pronouns but even in verb forms. The dual number still survives in modern Arabic, particularly for things that come in pairs, like hands, feet, and eyes. While feminine nouns generally form the plural by a change of suffix, most masculine nouns form their plural by a change of internal vowels which is reminiscent of English "foot—feet"; "book" is *kitāb* but "books" is *kutub;* "dog" is *kalb* but "dogs" is *kilāb*. Classical

Arabic had three cases (nominative, genitive, and accusative), but modern Arabic has merged them into one form.

The definite article *al* (or *il* in some spoken dialects, notably the Egyptian) is invariable, like English "the," but the *-l* is assimilated to many following consonants, so that *il sā'a* ("the watch"), becomes *is sā'a*. Possession is indicated by simply placing the possessor after the thing possessed; "the man's house" is *bēt ir rāgil,* literally, "house the man." Adjectives follow nouns and agree with them in number and gender.

The Arabic verb, like the Germanic, has two true tenses: a present, which also serves for the future, and a past. More precisely, the present is an imperfective form, indicating action not completed, while the past is a perfective, denoting completed action, which is reminiscent of the aspects of Slavic verbs. Object pronouns are added on to the verb, which reminds one of what used to happen in the old Romance languages and still happens generally in Romance with imperative and other forms of the verb.

These and other syntactical points of contact between Semitic and various branches of Indo-European cannot here be discussed in detail, but the possibility that the two families had, if not a common origin, at least a definite historical influence upon each other cannot *a priori* be discarded.

The words that have come into English from Arabic, generally through the intermediation of Spanish, Italian, or French, are numerous and varied. "Algebra," "alcohol," "alchemy" (whence "chemistry"), "alkali," "cipher," "zero," "zenith," "nadir" are indications of the progress made by the Arabs in the sciences, particularly mathematics and astronomy, at a period when Europe's cultural standards had lagged behind. Our "magazine" is the Arabic *al-makhsan,* more faithfully transcribed by the Spanish *almacén.* "Dragoman," the Near Eastern term for guide or interpreter, comes from Arabic *tarjuman,* the root being *tarjama* ("interpret"); the word was borrowed at a very early date by the Crusaders, as evidenced by thirteenth-century French *drogueman.* "Minaret" comes from Arabic *manārat* ("lamp" or "lighthouse"), based on the root *nār* ("to shine"); the lighthouse at Alexandria was taken as a model for this feature of Moslem religious architecture. "Assassin" is the Arabic *hashishin* or "hashish eaters," a sect of fanatics who killed Crusaders by treacherous attacks.

As for Israeli Hebrew, the charge that its revival and use as a twentieth-century vernacular tends to impede Israel in developing a modern state does not seem to be borne out by the linguistic facts. The language shows great powers of adaptation to modern conditions. "Eyeglasses" are *mishkafaim*, formed on the root of *shakaf* ("to watch attentively"); a newspaper is *itton*, from the root of *et* ("time"); *otzer*, the ancient word for "sterility," is used for "curfew." Translated words from the western languages are many: *iparon*, "pencil" (from the Hebrew *ōfereth*, "lead") is reminiscent of German *Bleistift; tappūakh-adāmāh*, "potatoes" (literally, "apples of the earth") is built on the model of French *pommes de terre;* coffee with milk or cream is *kafe hafukh*, (literally "overturned coffee," on the model of the Viennese *ein Verkehrter*). Loan words from the European tongues abound (*flartet*, "to flirt," *mbalef*, "to bluff," *talfen*, "to telephone"); so do loan translations (*gan yeladim*, for instance, is an exact translation of *Kindergarten*, and *mchonat ktiva*, "typewriter," translates the French *machine à écrire*).

A few words of Yiddish, the fifteenth-century German adopted by the modern Jews in the course of their European wanderings, have penetrated the language of Israel, among them *kumsitz* ("come and sit"), the name of the favorite communal pastime, sitting on the lawn and conversing in the cool of the evening, and *ayzin* (German *Eisen*, "iron"), used slangily for "strength." But, generally speaking, the use of Yiddish is frowned upon in the Hebrew Israeli community, where only Hebrew is officially recognized.

Numerous words have of late come from Israel to join the ranks of those that had already acquired English naturalization, like the older "seraph," "cherub," and "cabalistic" and the more recent "Yeshiva" ("academy") and "Hadassah" (literally "myrtle," the name of a Jewish American women's organization). Among the newcomers are *sabra* (native-born Palestinian Jew, as distinguished from newly arrived immigrants); *Yishuv* ("Jewish community"); *kibbutz* (communal farm, or training camp for those going to Palestine); *Hati kwah* ("The Hope," which is the name of the Israeli national anthem). The *ha-* appearing at the beginning of many Hebrew words is the definite article "the."

An Amharic contribution to our vocabulary is the official title of the Ethiopian monarch, *Negus neghesti*, or "King of Kings." Little has come to us from the tongues of the Hamitic branch, if we except the title "Pharaoh" ("great house" in ancient Egyptian), the names of the Egyptian gods (Amun-Ra, Isis, Osiris, Horus, etc.), and terms current among Egyptologists, like *ka* (the double of the individual supposed to linger in the burial place), *ankh* (the looped cross, symbol of life), etc.

The question of the kinship between Indo-European and Semito-Hamitic must for the present remain in abeyance. Arabic, most extensive among the modern languages of the Semito-Hamitic group, bids fair to continue its influential world role, while Hebrew, in its revivified and rapidly expanding modern form, appears to be scheduled for a rosy future.

The Ural-Altaic tongues cover a sweep of territory even broader than the Semito-Hamitic. From Lapland, Finland, and Estonia in northern Europe, Hungary in the Danubian valley, and European Turkey in the Balkans, they skip over wide expanses of Indo-European territory to attain extensive continuity in their true homeland, the boundless plains of northern and central Asia. Eastern European Russia, Siberia, Turkestan, Turkey, Mongolia, Manchuria constitute the major portion of the gigantic playground of these languages. But despite this vast territorial range, the speakers of these tongues are relatively few, perhaps 100 million at the most.

Their possible relationship to Indo-European is complicated by another and more intimate issue, their relationship to one another. Many linguists reject the thesis of Ural-Altaic unity and prefer to classify these languages into two separate and unrelated families: the Uralic, or Finno-Ugric, including Finnish, Estonian, Lapp, Hungarian, and some of the Siberian languages, like Ostyak and Samoyed; and the Altaic or Turkic, including Turkish, the tongues of the Tatars, Turkomans, and Kirghiz, the Mongol of the Kalmuks and Buriats, and the Manchu and Tungus of the Far East.

Those linguists who believe in Ural-Altaic unity predicate their belief upon structural similarities. Those who disbelieve it point to the lack of vocabulary resemblances or phonetic correspondences between the two divisions. As for connection with Indo-European, that is fully as difficult to prove as is the relationship between the latter and the Semito-Hamitic group.

Generally speaking, both the Uralic and the Altaic languages show a structure which the older generation of linguists described as "agglutinative." This means that the process of adding suffixes to roots, which appears in Indo-European, is carried on to a far greater degree, suffix upon suffix being attached to the root to convey a variety of meanings. In Turkish, for instance, *sev* is the root conveying the general meaning of "love"; *sev-mek* is "to love"; *sev-dir-mek* "to cause one to love"; *sev-me-mek* "not to love"; *sev-il-eme-mek* "to be impossible to be loved"; *sev-il-dir-eme-mek* "to be impossible to be made to be loved."

Nouns in the Ural-Altaic languages take on a variety of suffixes covering all possible case endings and prepositional constructions of Indo-European; but, whereas in Indo-European the case ending has no separate existence, in Ural-Altaic the postposition is an independent word; also, Indo-European has entirely different sets of case endings for the singular and for the plural, while Ural-Altaic uses the same postpositions for both numbers, inserting the plural suffix between the root and the case suffix. Hungarian, for instance, has *a ház-ban,* "in the house"; *a ház-ak-ban,* "in the houses."

A second general characteristic of these languages is the principle of vowel harmony. If the root has a front vowel (such as *i* or *e*), the suffix must have a similar vowel, while if the root has a back vowel (like *a, o,* or *u*), the suffix must have one too.

A third general feature of the Ural-Altaic tongues is the total absence of the concept of grammatical gender. Nouns are not divided into masculine, feminine, and neuter, and consequently there is never any agreement for gender. This absence of grammatical gender is carried to the point where "he," "she," and "it" are expressed by the same word.

Japanese shares some of these features, notably the absence of gender and the system of postpositions to express case relations, and this led many early linguists to affiliate Japanese with Ural-Altaic in one great "Scythian" or "Turanian" family. Modern linguists are much more skeptical on this point.

When it comes to vocabulary resemblances or a system of phonetic correspondences, such as we find in Indo-European or in Semito-Hamitic, Ural-Altaic unity (let alone connection with Indo-European) leaves much to be desired. It is easy to link the vocabularies of contiguous tongues, like Finnish, Estonian, and Lapp, and it is possible to trace, with considerable difficulty, some relationship of these tongues with Hungarian. It is likewise possible to link Turkish with most of the Soviet Asiatic tongues, even with Mongol and Manchu. But the vocabulary links between the Uralic and the Altaic languages are extremely tenuous and doubtful. This may be due to the fact that in the case of populations whose literary records appear at a relatively late date, and which were for a long time largely nomadic, vocabulary changes and innovations occurred to a far greater degree than with the comparatively stable Indo-European and Semito-Hamitic speakers, whose linguistic history we can trace back to a much earlier period.

How relatively recent is the appearance of the Ural-Altaic languages may be gauged from the known history of the three chief European components of the group. A few Hungarian words appear in documents of other languages as far back as the ninth century A.D., but the first full-fledged document of the tongue is a thirteenth-century funeral oration; in the Middle Ages the use of Hungarian as a written language was generally forbidden under severe penalties. For Finnish, our earliest record is a Bible translation of the year 1548, and the *Kalevala,* the great epic poem of Finland, was not collated from oral sources until the nineteenth century. Turkish first appears in sparse inscriptions of the eighth century of our era, but in the eleventh century a Turkish-Arabic dictionary was composed. The Asiatic languages of the family are even more recent so far as written records are concerned, Mongol first appearing in the thirteenth century and Manchu even later.

In written appearance, Finnish is distinguished by the use of double vowels (*aa, ii, oo,* etc.) which indicate length; double consonants also appear, but many other languages have them; there is in Finnish perhaps the greatest correspondence between spoken sound and written symbol that has been achieved by any tongue. Hungarian likewise uses double consonants but indicates length of vowels by a written accent mark over the vowel to be designated as long, as does its close Slavic neighbor, Czech. Turkish, which discarded the Arabic alphabet in favor of the Roman under the guidance of Kemal Atatürk in 1928, represents the *j* of "John" by *c,* the *ch* of "church" by *ç,* the *s* of "measure" by *j,* the *sh* of "she" by *ş.* An *i* with a dot represents the *i* sound of "machine," but if the dot is absent the sound approximates that of *y* in "rhythm."

When one recalls the broad areas of similarity appearing among the Indo-European or the Semito-Hamitic languages, the lack of such similarity in the Ural-Altaic tongues is distressing. "Yes" is *kyllä* in Finnish, *igen* in Hungarian, *evet* in Turkish; "no" is *ei, nem, hayir,* respectively. But when one considers that, despite proved original kinship, "good morning" in English is *bonjour* in French, *dobry dyen'* in Russian, *kalimera* in Greek, one can perhaps agree with those who hold that time and separation can lead to infinite divergence among languages of the same stock.

Few words have come to us from Finnish; *sauna,* or

steambath, is one. A sample of Hungarian contributions to our vocabulary is "goulash" (*gulyás* or *gulyáshús*, "herdsman's meat") and *csárdás* (the name of a national dance). "Hussar" may come from Hungarian *húsz* ("twenty"—a member of a twenty-man platoon); one item of the hussar's uniform, the "shako," comes from Hungarian *csákó*; another, the "dolman," is from Turkish *dolaman*. "Coach" goes back to *Kocs,* the name of a Hungarian town where the vehicle seems to have originated. "Janissary" (from *yeni-cheri,* "new soldier"), "uhlan" (*oghlan,* "youth"), "tulip" (*tülbend,* "turban") are among the words that come to us from Turkish.

In the world of today, which seems directed toward ever larger political groupings, with cultural predominance exerted by those languages which combine factors of political, economic, military, and population preponderance, the future of Finnish, with its 5 million speakers (perhaps 8 million if one adds the nearby and closely related Estonian, Livonian, Lapp, and Mordvin), Hungarian, with 10 or 12 million at the most, and Turkish, with perhaps 30 million, does not appear too bright. Yet these languages are the vehicles of rich and individualistic cultures which the world can ill afford to lose.

— Chapter Eight —

THE FAR EASTERN TONGUES

One picture is worth many thousands of words.
                                        —Chinese proverb

THE Far East is a vast linguistic world in its own right, with tongues as varied and picturesque as are their speakers, and distributed among several of the world's important language families.

Outstanding among these languages, by reason of the numbers and accomplishments of their speakers, are Chinese and Japanese, the former a member of the great Sino-Tibetan group, which includes also Burmese, Thai (or Siamese), and Tibetan; the latter unaffiliated, save for a possible but doubtful connection with Korean.

Many believe that there is an intimate connection between Chinese and Japanese, but this opinion is completely erroneous. The only link between the two tongues lies in the fact that they use the same system of writing and that Japanese has borrowed heavily from Chinese, in the same fashion that Germanic English borrowed from Romance Norman-French. Otherwise, no two tongues could be more dissimilar in structure and basic vocabulary.

The Sino-Tibetan language family comprises about 760 million speakers, of whom approximately 700 million are Chinese. The characteristics shared by these languages are monosyllabism, the complete lack of any system of inflection or grammatical endings, and the use of tone, or pitch, to convey semantic differences between words otherwise similarly pronounced.

Chinese is not only the greatest but also the earliest of these languages to appear in recorded form. Its documents reach back to at least 1500 B.C., making it coeval with Sanskrit and not too far removed from Akkadian and ancient

Egyptian. Tibetan, Burmese, and Thai are relative new-comers to the field of recorded languages, going back to the ninth, eleventh, and thirteenth centuries of our era, respectively.

The great Chinese literary records (the so-called Classics, often attributed to Confucius) go back to the sixth century B.C. Lao-tze, the founder of Taoism, is said to have written one century earlier, and Mencius one century later. This chronology places the golden era of Chinese literature and philosophy at approximately the same period as that of Greek, giving the east and the west an equal share in the founding of the great modern civilizations.

There are in China some 700 million people, more than three times as many as in the United States. Of these, over 500 million speak variants of Mandarin, the dialect of north China and the former Imperial Court of Peking, which has more recently been rebaptized *Kuo-yü* or "National Tongue." (Mandarin is not a Chinese but an originally Sanskrit word, *mantrin*, "counselor," blended with Portuguese *mandar*, "to command," so that a Mandarin came to mean "leader" or "boss.") The remaining 200 million speak widely diverging dialects, the major of which are Cantonese, the Wu of Shanghai, and the Min of Fukien.

When it comes to writing, all of China, regardless of spoken dialects, uses a common language which in its more literary reaches is known as *Wên-li*, or "elegance of composition." This is possible because the Chinese characters have little or no connection with sounds but rather symbolize ideas and concepts. The word for "man" is variously pronounced *jên, nyin, lên, nên, yên* in different spoken dialects, but the written symbol is the same. Comparison lies with such western written-language symbols as "$5," "lb.," or "$H_2O$," which each western language pronounces differently but which convey the same meaning to all.

There is a Chinese tradition to the effect that an early emperor, about 2200 B.C., first conceived of a system of straight and broken lines to replace the knotted cords that had previously conveyed simple messages, and that the system was later improved by a sage, who was inspired by the marks of birds' claws in the sand to devise hundreds of additional characters. But it seems more likely that the earliest characters were pictures pure and simple: a circle with a dot in the center to represent "sun," a crescent to indicate "moon," a torso with two legs to convey the idea of "man," etc. Then, with the passing of time and the growth of ideas, some of these characters were combined to convey new meanings. Many of these combinations are self-evident even today: the symbol for "light," for instance, is the combination of "sun" and "moon"; the "tree" symbol repeated twice is "forest"; the "sun" over the "horizon" is "dawn"; "mouth" plus "bird" gives "song." The symbol for "words" is "mouth" with "steam" issuing from it, which is somewhat reminiscent of our "hot air." "Woman" plus "broom" equals "housewife," and "woman" under "roof" equals "peace," but lest anyone acquire too exalted an idea of what the "woman" symbol means to the Chinese, it may be pointed out that "two women" equals "quarrel," "three women" equals "gossip" or "intrigue," and that the "woman" symbol enters into the characters for "jealous," "treacherous," "false," and "uncanny." The "man" character is said to enter into 600 combinations, and the "tree" character into 900.

The person who looks at written Chinese for the first time is bewildered by the maze of characters and wonders what sort of I.Q. a literate Chinese must have, to remember all of them. Actually, the situation is not quite so bad as it seems. The radicals, or primary characters, are only 214 in number, and it is simply a matter of combining them into compound characters, of which the Chinese dictionaries list some forty thousand, but with only four thousand to eight thousand in general use. To make things still easier, compound characters often consist of two parts, of which one conveys the general idea, the other gives a clue to the pronunciation. For example, there is a character for "horse" (pronounced *ma* in Mandarin) which originally was a real picture of a horse, with a plainly discernible head, neck, tail, and four legs. The spoken word for "mother," by a strange coincidence, is also *ma,* but pronounced in a different key from the *ma* that means "horse." The written symbol for "mother" is a combination of the "woman" symbol and the "horse" symbol, the former indicating that the word has something to do with the feminine sex, the latter informing the reader that the word is to be pronounced somewhat like the word for "horse."

The actual number of one-syllable combinations permissible in standard Chinese is 434. How, then, can we reach the enormous total of forty thousand "word ideas" appearing in Chinese dictionaries, or even the four to eight thousand in common use?

In the first place, there is nothing in Chinese, as there is nothing in English, to prevent two words with entirely different meanings from being pronounced alike and written differently. Just as in English we have "waist" and "waste";

"meat," "meet," and "mete"; "right," "write," "rite," and "wright," so the Chinese have long lists of words sounding exactly alike but represented by different symbols. In actual speech, they are distinguished by the way they are used in the sentence, just as the English words are.

Secondly, there is nothing in Chinese to prevent combinations of two or more one-syllable words into compounds like our "railroad" or "foxhole," where the compound carries a very special meaning not exactly contained in either of the two component parts. Our compound words are often picturesque, and the Chinese are no less so: "cream," for instance, is "milk-skin"; "lantern" is "lamp-cage"; "strait" is "sea-waist"; "parent" is "father-mother," "God" is "upper-ruler." The generic compound of "clothing" is *i-shang*, where *i* means "upper clothing," *shang* "lower clothing"; "coat-pants," as it were. Often Chinese uses a compound where we would be satisfied with just one of the two components: "way-path" for "way," "look-see" for "see," "bright-intelligence" for "genius" or "talent," "bright-clear" for "understand," "lightning-message" for "telegram." Often two words that have the same meaning are combined: *huan-hsi* or *hsi-huan* ("joy-joy") for "pleasure"; *jen-shih*, "know-know," for "knowledge." Occasionally, Chinese compounds can get to be complete definitions, "crisis," for example, is "danger-opportunity," while "virtue" is "faith-piety-temperance-justice." The rendering of foreign words in Chinese often leads to compounds of interesting meaning. "Martini," for instance, may be rendered by *ma-t'i-ni*, with the literal meaning of "horse kick you."

There is a third resource at the disposal of the Chinese which has no exact counterpart in English. If one is given the name "George" to pronounce, he will utter it noncommittally, on an even tone; if he is calling the man in to dinner from the fields, he will shout: "Geo-orge, where are you?," first dropping the voice a trifle, then giving the name a definite upward lilt as he comes to the end of it; if he is deploring something George did, he will say reproachfully: "Geo-orge, how could you?," but this time the voice will drop as he comes to the end of the name; lastly, if there is a sudden knock on the door, and George is being expected, one may ask quickly before unlatching: "George?," with a quick rise of the voice. All these different tones of the voice, which we use to indicate varieties of emotion, or under special circumstances, are used by the Chinese to convey different meanings of one and the same combination of sounds. The *ma* that means "mother" and the *ma* that means "horse" are distinguished in speech by being pronounced in two different tones, while if we use the other two tones for *ma* we get "flax" and an interrogative participle somewhat similar to our "huh?"

This matter of the tones of the voice used not to indicate feeling or stress but to convey different meanings is the hardest thing about Chinese for a foreigner. It is easy enough to remember the correct tone when you are handling a single word, but when you have a six- or ten-word sentence, and each of the words is to be "toned," you run into difficulties. There is a probably untrue story from Burma (Burmese uses tones like Chinese) to the effect that an American soldier stationed there wanted to buy a native coat but got a caged tiger instead because he said *hsu* in the wrong tone. It is, however, a standard and true joke in linguistic circles that in one Burmese dialect our old friend *ma* pronounced in five different tones spells out the sentence: "Help the horse; a mad dog comes!"

History informs us that the Chinese were not always aware of the fact that they were using tones. When the theory was first advanced by some Chinese scholars, about A.D. 500, many high-placed Chinese were skeptical. The Emperor Wu Ti, one of the unbelievers, summoned the sage Shên Yo. "Come, tell me," he said. "What are these four tones?" "They are . . ." replied the sage, and then he used four words, each clearly exemplifying a different tone; but the four words, freely translated, meant: "Whatever Your Majesty pleases to make them." The ingenious example was too much for his Majesty, who thenceforth became a firm believer in the existence of tones.

One man who had spent many years in China told me that he had never bothered to learn tones. He had made use instead of another typical Chinese-language device, the addition of a classifying or explanatory word. We can say in English: "This is a lovely ash" or "This is a lovely ash tree." "Ash," of course, should be enough, but "tree" classifies "ash" and removes all possibility of misunderstanding; "ash" is now placed in the "tree" class beyond the shadow of a doubt and cannot be confused with the "ash" from a cigarette. Chinese has dozens of similar words, which serve to explain other words and make their meaning absolutely clear. There is one, for instance, that is applied to round objects, like rings and coins; another works for small things, like pearls and grains of rice. The "head" in "fifty head of cattle" has been described as the perfect English counterpart of a Chinese classifier. The classifiers very frequently appear in pidgin

English, originally a compromise between English vocabulary and Chinese syntax.

Chinese grammar is distinguished by its lack of morphology (that is, inflectional endings) and its almost complete reliance upon syntax, or word order. The majority of Chinese words cannot be classified as nouns, verbs, adjectives, and adverbs. They are roots and can be made to serve any function for which there is a call. *Ta,* for instance, conveys the "large" or "great" idea. It can be used as an adjective to mean "great," as an adverb to mean "greatly," as a verb to mean "enlarge." The "up" root can mean "upper," "up," "to climb." This means, however, that position is everything in the life of the Chinese sentence. A word used as the subject normally comes before the word used as the verb, with the object following. "I see he" and "he see I" are perfect renderings of Chinese sentences, since Chinese does not even make the distinction of subject or object form in the pronoun which English still makes (separate forms do, however, appear in the classical Confucian texts). Words used as verbs have none of the distinctions appearing in English: "he writes," "I wrote," "you will write," "they have written." What we get instead is "he this day write," "I past day write," "you next day write," "they write finish." There are no genders, no endings, no cases, no declensions or conjugations—only individual words. Chinese, generally, does not even take the trouble to indicate singular or plural; all its nouns are like our "sheep" and "deer" (you can, of course, say "one sheep," "two sheep," "many sheep").

The intricacies of Chinese syntax, style, and imagery are perhaps best illustrated by a few examples. Where we would describe an orator as "silver-tongued," Chinese says "gold mouth jade words"; the warning posted in the vicinity of railroad tracks, which in an English-speaking country would run "Trains—Danger," is expressed in Chinese by "small heart fire car." For our "bon voyage" to one departing, Chinese says: "one road tranquil quiet," while if one wishes to express regret over the fact that he has not seen another person for some time, the proper expression is "one day not see like three autumns." The state of the weather is often picturesquely described by the peculiar combinations "one coat day," "two coat day" and so on up to seven or even nine coats, to indicate varying degrees of temperature.

Two very common Chinese expressions are *ding hao,* which does service for "O.K.," "all right," and *mei yu pan fa,* "nothing can be done," which is as fully effective in denoting frustration or helplessness as the Frenchman's shrug of the shoulders or the Russian's *nichevo*.

The fact that Chinese writing has little phonetic value deprives spoken Chinese of the visual support and stabilizing influence that western tongues normally derive from their written counterparts. To this difficulty is added the faulty transcription of Chinese sounds which is in general use, under the name of Wade, its deviser. In accordance with this system, *p, t, k* are used to render sounds which come closer to English initial *b, d, g*, while *p', t', k'* render sounds similar to those of English initial *p, t, k;* the same holds true for *ch* and *ch', ts* and *ts'*, with the result that a name is commonly spelt *Chiang* when it is more properly pronounced *Jiang*, while the name of the Chinese language, *Kuo-yü* in spelling, is better pronounced *Guo-yü*. Many vowel sounds are dull and indefinite and variously pronounced by different native speakers.

Despite these many drawbacks, the long-range importance of a language spoken by over one fifth of the earth's inhabitants, and which has given rise to a flourishing literature and philosophy, cannot be minimized.

There are numerous hypotheses as to the origin of the Japanese language, but none of them is substantiated. The old belief that Japanese formed part of a vast "Scythian" or "Turanian" group, which included also the Ural-Altaic languages, is now generally abandoned. Hardly more plausible is the theory that Japanese was originally a Polynesian tongue, somehow related to the Malay of Indonesia, which has a similar system of sounds and syllabic structure. But the morphology of Malay has at least as many points of similarity with that of Chinese as with that of Japanese, while vocabulary correspondences are conspicuous by their absence. The Japanese legend concerning the descent of the Japanese people from the sun goddess Amaterasu is of as little help to the linguist and historian as the insulting Chinese story to the effect that the Japanese are a cross between Chinese shipwrecked youths and maidens and a tribe of monkeys.

Japanese written records begin in the seventh or eighth century of our era, when Chinese and Korean Buddhist missionaries brought the Chinese characters to the islands of Japan and put them into use by the very simple expedient of giving to each character a Japanese spoken-language value. The pictogram for "man," for instance, which is read *jên* by the Chinese, was read *hito* instead. But difficulties soon developed. Unlike Chinese, Japanese is an inflected language, with case postpositions for nouns and tense and mood endings for verbs. Written Chinese, relying exclusively upon word order, makes no provision for such variations in a word. The upshot was that in the ninth century a Japanese Buddhist priest hit upon the clever device of isolating a certain number of Chinese characters and giving them an invariable phonetic value, to cover all of the possible syllabic combinations of the Japanese language. If at this point the Chinese ideographs had been discarded and the syllabic symbols used exclusively, Japanese would have today a system of writing not too unlike that of the western languages. Instead, the next step taken by the Japanese was to combine the new syllabic characters with the Chinese ideograms, and this method persists to the present day. To render the spoken *hito no* ("of the man"), the ideogram for "man" is used, followed by the syllabic character that has the invariable phonetic value of *no*; *kakimashita* ("wrote") is expressed by the ideogram for "write" (*kak-*) followed by the syllabic characters *ki-ma-shi-ta*.

To the frequently asked question whether a Chinese can read Japanese and vice versa, the answer is that there is a limited measure of comprehension. The root words, though quite different in speech, are generally represented by identical symbols in both languages. But the Chinese will be baffled by the Japanese noun and verb endings expressed in syllabic characters, while the Japanese will be left in wonder as to the intricacies of Chinese syntax, which is quite different from his own.

Spoken Japanese, in contrast to Chinese, is decidedly a polysyllabic language. In fact, some of its verb forms run to unconscionable lengths, although the majority of the roots consist of two syllables. A few Japanese words are distinguished by tones, but for the most part tone plays no semantic role in the language. The syllabic structure is simple, being of the consonant-plus-vowel type, and the general acoustic effect of Japanese would be closer to that of Italian than to that of Chinese were it not for a certain guttural quality that distinguishes the tonality of most Far Eastern languages. There are long vowels and short vowels in Japanese, as well as vowels so reduced that they are practically silent, like the *-u* at the end of many verb forms (*arimasu*, "is" or "are," normally pronounced *arimas'*) and the *i* within words (*arimashita*, "was" or "were," pronounced *arimash'ta*). Double consonants appear and must be fully pronounced.

There is no strong stress in Japanese, the syllables of a word being about equally stressed: Yokohama is pronounced yókóhámá, not yokohámá. A certain amount of stress, however, falls on long vowels, as well as on vowels followed by double consonants. Within the sentence, case particles, or postpositions, are specially stressed, which gives the Japanese sentence a rhythm completely foreign to western ears.

Like many other languages, Japanese is lacking in grammatical gender. This does not mean that sex cannot be expressed: *inu* is "dog," *o-inu* "male dog," *me-inu* "female dog"; *ko* is "child," *otoko no ko* ("man-of-child") is "boy" and *onna no ko* ("woman-of-child") is "girl." But there is no such thing as agreement for gender, and even such suffixes as *san,* used after names, may indifferently express "Mr.," "Mrs.," and "Miss."

The Japanese notion of grammatical number is almost equally vague, though there are many (perhaps too many) suffixes that may serve to indicate plurality if one really wants to do so. *Ko* ("child") may be pluralized by adding *domo,* but strangely enough *ko-domo* may also express the notion of a single child.

Most striking is the Japanese insouciance with regard to grammatical person. One can, if he deems it necessary, say "I," "you," "he," "we," "they," but generally speaking these words are omitted. *Doko e ikimasu ka* (literally, "where to there-is-a-going?") is currently used for "Where are you, is he, are we, are they going?" The sensitive Japanese are slightly shocked by western insistence upon personalities; and the use of the subject pronoun, customary in Chinese, is in Japanese largely the mark of the foreigner.

All case relations are indicated by postpositions, of which a few common ones are *wa* and *ga,* which indicate the subject; *no,* which marks possession; *ni,* for the indirect object or location; and *wo* (more often pronounced *o*) for the direct object.

The word order is rigidly formalized and not too unlike that of Latin. Compare *tsukue no ue ni hon ga takusan arimasu* (literally, "table of top on book [subject mark] many are"; "there are many books on top of the table") with Latin *mensae in culmine libri-permulti sunt.*

The Japanese verb is in a class by itself. It offers the learner the advantage of being completely impersonal, so that there is no need of learning personal endings, but makes up for this simplicity by the intricacy of its familiar and polite forms, as well as by its numerous tenses and moods. *Taberu* is the verb "to eat" but can be used in this form only if one is speaking familiarly. The polite form generally used among equals is *tabemasu.* If one wishes to go beyond the polite stage and use an honorific form, which implies super-politeness, he uses an entirely different verb, *meshiagaru*. The foreigner would ordinarily have little use for the familiar form, were it not for the fact that it must be used in subordinate clauses even though the verb of the main clause is polite. The polite past is formed by the suffix *-imashita*, an indefinite future by using *deshō* after the familiar root, the conditional by the suffix *-imasureba*, and there is a large assortment of participial forms, one of which appears in the imperative, where "please buy" takes the form of "buying, please." There is no change of word order for the interrogative, but only the addition of the questioning particle *ka*, while negative forms often take the ending *-imasen*. These are only a few of the many complexities of Japanese verbs, which are joined by many adjectives that take on verb endings and then acquire the meaning of "to be" plus whatever quality the adjective denotes.

Japanese numerals come in two series, one of which is borrowed from Chinese while the other is native. These numerals change their form according to the nature of the noun with which they are used, becoming true determinatives or classifiers. "Five," in the numeral series borrowed from Chinese, is *go;* but "five pens" is not *pen go*, but *pen gohon* ("pen five-round-object"); "five men" is *hito gonin* ("man five-person"); "five dogs" is *inu gohiki* ("dog five-animal"); "five birds" is *tori gowa* ("bird five-fowl"). There is some doubt as to whether this concept of classification was borrowed from Chinese along with the numerals or formed part of the original Japanese linguistic equipment, but the former supposition seems more likely.

Japanese expressions are fully as picturesque as the Chinese. Where the Chinese say "afternoon peace," "evening peace," the Japanese use simply "it is afternoon," "it is evening" (*konnichi wa, komban wa*). The Japanese "good morning," on the other hand, sounds like the name of one of our States, *ohayō*. The Japanese "good-by," *sayōnara*, literally means "if it must be so." Two extremely common phrases are *shigata ganai* ("it can't be helped") and *ano ne*, which serves to attract attention, express futility, wonder, sorrow, regret, appreciation, or astonishment at the high price of an object.

The intricacies of Japanese polite forms are bewildering. In addition to the honorific verbs, there is a particle *o*, prefixed to nouns, which is erroneously translated by "honorable" but in reality glorifies the person addressed. *O mizu kudasai* means not "honorable water, please," but "You, honorable person, please bring water." Names of relatives differ radically according as it is the speaker's relative or that of the person addressed that is referred to. "Wife" is *tsuma* or *kanai* if I refer to my own wife, but *okusama* if I am speaking of yours; "husband" and "son" are *shujin* and *segare* if they are the speaker's, but *dannasan* and *musukosan* if they are his interlocutor's.

Japanese words that have entered English are not very numerous: *kimono, geisha, samurai,* the medieval feudal retainers of Japan; *jūjutsu* and *judo,* Japanese forms of wrestling (the former means "soft art"). *Banzai, kamikaze, bushidō,* came with World War Two.

Japanese, on the other hand, has borrowed heavily from English. Names of western-style foods (*bifuteki, choppu, hamu, beikon, chīzu*), tableware (*naifu, fōku*), wearing apparel (*nekutai, hankechi, botan*), military terms (*raifu, tento*), writing implements (*pen, inki*) have entered the Japanese vocabulary, along with the majority of our sporting terms, particularly in the field of baseball, which is Japan's most popular sport.

It is already a far cry to the days when Japan held control over territories inhabited by 500 million people. The linguistic penetration effected by the Japanese in the lands they temporarily conquered was not very deep. Only in Korea, which was held by Japan for some decades before World War Two, did the Japanese language take a real foothold. Today, Japanese is restricted to the islands. Still, it is the tongue of nearly 100 million people who have shown great genius in assimilating and adapting many aspects of the more ancient Chinese culture as well as of the modern civilization of the West. It would indeed be a pity if the study of Japanese, which took root and flourished in America as a war necessity, were to be forgotten or neglected, now that Japan is our ally in the battle for peace.

In both Chinese and Japanese, the adoption of a fully phonetic western alphabet to replace the pictographs and ideographs has long been under discussion. Communist Chinese language scholars are at work on a double project, one prong of which involves the simplification of the written Chinese characters, so that they may be produced with a reduced number of strokes and be easier to read, write, and print, the other prong involving the complete discarding of the logographic system and its replacement by a modified Latin alphabet, called *Latinxua,* scientifically constructed and adapted to North Mandarin phonology. Both projects are still in the experimental stage, but both have already given good results from the standpoint of increasing literacy. The Japanese *Romaji* movement, older than the Chinese, aims at the use of Roman characters of the conventional variety and is already widely used, though a more recent variant, called the Hepburn method, aims at using the Roman characters in such a way that they will correspond even more closely to the Japanese spoken sounds. In both cases, a terrific obstacle is posed by the existing body of Chinese and Japanese literature, which would have to be scrapped and reprinted.

Two Far Eastern languages that are not faced with the problem of phonetization are Korean and Vietnamese. The first, a language sometimes linked with Japanese for what concerns grammatical structure, has long enjoyed a native alphabet of ten vowels and fourteen consonants, known as *Eunmoon*, which is probably one of the most perfect in the world and quite adequate to represent phonetically the sounds of the language.

Vietnamese has possessed since the seventeenth century a Roman script, elaborated by Catholic missionaries and known as *Quoc-ngu,* which by a system of suprascript characters too complicated to be reproduced here indicates not only sounds but also the six tones of the language.

Vietnamese is in some respects a mystery tongue, being linked by some scholars with the Thai or Siamese of the Sino-Tibetan family (which would ultimately range it with Chinese, Burmese, and Tibetan), by others placed in a separate Austroasiatic family, with the Munda of India and the Mon-Khmer of Cambodia. With a speaking population of over 30 million, and the strategic position it holds in southeast Asia, Vietnamese is a language of interest to Americans. It has fully semantic tones (the same word pronounced with a different tone undergoes a complete change of meaning) and no inflections or derivations. It is basically monosyllabic and has a word order highly reminiscent of Chinese. Classifiers are used, as in Chinese, while clear-cut grammatical categories and parts of speech are absent. The verb meaning "to plow" may, by adding on the word meaning "thing," become "the plow"; by the addition of the word meaning "worker" it turns into "the plowman." Like Chinese, it makes frequent use of compounds.

It is a tribute to the power of Chinese civilization that both Korean and Vietnamese are replete with Chinese loan words, and that both languages may on occasion, despite their possession of a fully phonetic alphabet, revert to the system of Chinese ideographs for literary purposes. In the words of a Vietnamese scholar, "Educated Chinese, Japanese, Koreans, and Vietnamese were indeed able to carry on a 'pen conversation' without having to pronounce the Chinese written symbols in the same way; as a matter of fact, Chinese was the Latin of all the areas under the influence of Chinese culture."

— Chapter Nine —

THE WORLD'S OTHER TONGUES

Language, as well as the faculty of speech, was the immediate gift of God.

—Noah Webster

THE remaining languages of the earth are far too numerous to be described in a work of this sort. What they lack in commercial, political, or cultural importance they make up for in picturesque variety.

Chief among the secondary groupings of the world's tongues is the great Malayo-Polynesian family that stretches across the south Pacific and the Indian Ocean, from Easter Island, off the coast of South America, to Madagascar, off the coast of Africa, with stopping-off points in such diverse localities as Hawaii, Samoa, Tahiti, New Zealand, the Solomon Islands, the Philippines, Indonesia, and Malaya.

The number of speakers of Malayo-Polynesian languages comes close to 130 million. Among the languages we find tongues of widely different phonetic pattern. Some, like Hawaiian, are almost wanting in consonant sounds, others are relatively rich. Yet despite these structural differences and the enormous distances intervening, it is not too difficult to recognize their kinship. A word like "five" is *lima* in Indonesia, the Fiji Islands, Samoa, and Hawaii, *rima* in New Zealand and Tahiti, *dimi* in Madagascar; "nine" is *siwa* in Indonesia, *tsiwa* in Fiji, *iwa* in Hawaii and New Zealand, *iva* in Samoa, *sivi* in Madagascar.

For the sake of geographical rather than linguistic convenience, the Malayo-Polynesian languages have been divided into Indonesian, Melanesian, Micronesian, and Polynesian. The common suffix "-nesian" is Greek and means "pertaining to islands." Micronesia is "small islands," Melanesia "black islands," Polynesia "many islands."

Because of their general lack of a written form and cultural tradition, many of the languages of the Pacific have in the past been subject to rapid and drastic change. There is an unauthenticated story to the effect that English traders visiting an island in the Pacific in the eighteenth century recorded the native speech, but that another party visiting the same locality in the following century found the language changed beyond recognition; however, the population may have changed, or perhaps it was not the same island. At any rate, the Malayo-Polynesian tongues illustrate the principle of similarity combined with diversity. On the single island of Guadalcanal, which is about eighty by twenty-five miles, twenty Melanesian dialects are spoken. On the Philippine island of Leyte, the inhabitants of the eastern portion speak Samarino, those of the western half Cebuano, and interpreters are needed between the two. The Philippines, with 31 million people, have over fifty different languages and dialects, chief among which are Visaya, Ilocano, Moro, and Tagalog. Many Filipinos still speak Spanish, a relic of pre-Spanish-American War days, when the islands were a Spanish possession.

Maori is the original Polynesian tongue of New Zealand, still spoken by nearly 100,000 natives. Many Maori words have penetrated the English of New Zealand (*paheka* for "stranger," *mana* for "prestige," *tenakoe* for "hello," *rangitira* for "big chief," *kai* for "food," *kia ora* for "good luck"). In like manner, Hawaiian words like *hula, ukulele* (literally "jumping flea"), *luau* or *hukilau* ("banquet"), *lei* ("wreath"), *pilikia* ("trouble"), *haole* ("white man"), *kamaiina* ("old timer"), *hoomalimali* ("boloney") have entered Hawaiian English. *Aloha* is in Hawaiian almost anything you want to make it, from "hello" to "good-by"; it can even mean "I love you" if you add *mi loa* to it. *Kapu* is Hawaiian for "taboo" and illustrates the consonant shifts that are made necessary by Hawaiian's poverty of consonant sounds.

Malagasy is the Malayo-Polynesian tongue of Madagascar, spoken by nearly 5 million. Among its interesting words are *hova, zarahova,* and *andevo,* the names of three of the island's many castes, which are said to outnumber those of India.

Leading among the Malayo-Polynesian tongues is Malay, a language of common intercourse for Indonesia, British Malaya, and adjoining regions. The creation of this *lingua franca* was rendered necessary by the vast number of Indonesian languages spoken in the area (over 300 languages and dialects appear in the Indonesian area alone). Even on the comparatively small island of Java, where Javanese is the tongue of the 45-million majority, there is a 14-million minority that speaks Sundanese, and Javanese itself assumes a three-fold form, Ngoko for the common people, Krama for the aristocracy, and Madya for interchange between the two, with practically every word differing either completely or in the endings.

By reason of its musical quality, Malay has been styled the "Italian of the Orient." It has no harsh sounds and very few difficulties of a grammatical nature, with no conjugations or declensions, roots mostly of two syllables, a consonant vowel arrangement, and loan words chiefly from Sanskrit and Arabic. When Malay speakers became Mohammedans in the thirteenth century, they adopted the Arabic alphabet with a few modifications, but today the language is for the most part written in Roman characters. *Bahasa Indonesia,* the official tongue of the Indonesian Republic, is substantially a polished and standardized Malay.

From Malay there come to us a few words: *orangutan,* literally "jungle man"; *Mata Hari,* "eyeday," for "sun"; *cherutu,* "cigar," which Malay had previously borrowed from one of the languages of southern India; even "so long," which is the Malay *salang,* borrowed from the Arabic *salaam,* "peace."

A recent theory concerning the languages of the Pacific is that the islands were settled by overseas migrations of pre-Inca Peruvians from the mainland of South America (or perhaps vice versa). Kon-Tiki, the name of a mythical Peruvian leader, reappears as Tiki in the Marquesas, with a similarity of tradition concerning the Pacific odyssey. *Kumara* is a name for the sweet potato common to both Polynesian and Peruvian Indian. The implications of this theory are such as to give comfort to the believers in the monogenesis of language, but the evidence so far is quite scanty.

The original inhabitants of Australia, Tasmania, and the interior of New Guinea speak languages which do not seem connected with the Malayo-Polynesian family. Native Australian languages number at least 200, although they are spoken by fewer than 50,000 people, and while the original tongues of Tasmania are now extinct, there seem to have been at least five. The precise number of Papuan languages of New Guinea has never been accurately determined, though the Reverend Frank Laubach asserts that at least eighty-two are definitely known to exist. The dying tongues of the Australian natives show remarkable diversity and extraordinary features. One of them, Aranta, displays such complexities of structure as nouns that have to be rendered by verbs, combined with extremely primitive concepts. *Unta,* the equivalent of "you," literally means "one lying down"; *alirra,* "child," means "one walking in front"; *talpa,* "moon," is "something stable that returns." Mowung, in the Darwin region, is described as having only three vowel and nine consonant sounds. Such words as "boomerang," "kangaroo," "billabong," and "cooee" have come to us from the Australian languages, but there are many others locally used, like the *woomera* (possibly a variant of "boomerang") that describes the base of the throwing spear used by some Australian aborigines, the *wap* of the Murray Islanders, the *dugong,* or seacow of Torres Strait, and the *bunyip* that is applied to a mythical animal reported to have been seen in certain localities of the interior.

The continent of Africa south of the Tropic of Cancer is the homeland of some 700 African Negro languages, in their three great divisions, Sudanese-Guinean, Bantu, and Hottentot-Bushman. These families are subdivided into very numerous languages, of which a few (Ruanda, Fula, Yoruba, Luba, Mandingo, Ibo, Somali, Galla, Zulu, Fanti, and Xhosa) number from 1 to 6 million speakers. The two great African Negro languages that serve as tongues of common intercourse for their respective areas are the Hausa of Nigeria and the Swahili of the east coast. The latter has reached such a stage of development that the comedies of Molière have been successfully translated into it and presented, with an all-African cast, in the city of Dar es Salaam. In this tongue, which is to some extent representative of the Bantu group, nouns are placed into distinct classes (man, tree, water, etc.), each of which receives a special distinguishing syllable or sound associated with the nouns. A shift from singular to plural is attended by a complete shift of prefix. Thus, *m-thu m-zuri* is "handsome man," but *wa-thu wa-zuri* is "handsome men"; adverbs often take the same prefix as the verb they modify: *ku-fa ku-zuri* ("to die beautifully"). *Uhuru* is the Swahili term for "freedom," and *jamhuri* for "republic." The Bantu languages are infinitely expressive (consider, for example, *mumagamagama,* "one who loses other people's things"; *muwavi,* "a good-looking woman who can't cook"; *muvumizi,* "a yes-man"; *muwandoloci,* "one who growls when waked up in the morning"; *mutolatoli*, "one who is constantly divorcing and remarrying").

From the native languages of Africa there come to us such words as "okra," "gumbo," and "juke," said to be from a Guinean *jugu*. Several Swahili words have reached us through the language of safari, but, like "safari" itself, most of them are of Arabic origin (*simba*, "lion," for instance). But *bwana*, the title of respect, is native.

The total number of speakers of African Negro languages is roughly estimated at about 160 million. It would not be surprising if one of the two leading Negro languages (Hausa, with its estimated 13 million speakers, or Swahili, with its estimated 10 million) were one day to take the lead and become the universal tongue of common intercourse for all of Africa's black populations, in the same fashion that Hindi is trying to assume that role in India. The fact is, however, that for the time being the Africans are voting down all native languages and prefer to continue in the official role the old tongues of colonization, with English predominating in countries that were formerly British possessions and French in lands that once were French or Belgian.

The languages of the American Indians have aroused perhaps more controversy than all others. On the one hand, they display the most infinite diversity of structure and forms of expression, which would lead linguists to deny all common kinship among them; on the other, they show certain features of similarity (like the form *na* for the expression of the first person singular in both North and South America) which encourage some linguists to continue seeking a common origin. The best we can say at the present moment is that at least 100 seemingly different linguistic stocks, each subdivided into separate languages and dialects, appear among the Indians of North, Central, and South America. Those of the United States, of whose speakers less than a quarter of a million survive, are divided into about sixty-five families, but at least 40 per cent of the original Indian tongues of the United States have become fully extinct since the coming of the white man. The groups that remain, after a long decline, are now slightly increasing in numbers, but with the original languages largely lost to the new generations.

Uncertainty prevails concerning the prehistory of these languages. Estimates as to the number of American Indians in the Western Hemisphere at the time of the coming of the

Europeans vary from 15 to 40 million. Today, the figure is roughly 12 million, of whom 2 million live on North American soil (U. S., Canada, Mexico), the balance in the Antilles and in Central and South America. Links have been advanced for various Amerindian groups with the Ural-Altaic and Paleo-Siberian tongues of northern Asia, with the Sino-Tibetan languages (the evidence for this is supposed to appear in a manuscript of the great American linguist Sapir, which was lost at the time of his death and for which search is still being made), with the Melanesian tongues, even with the little-known languages of Australia. The distribution of the Amerindian languages is such as to give evidence of great wandering and dispersion: Athapaskan languages, which cover western Canada, also straddle the Mexican border; the Iroquois, whose force was concentrated in upstate New York, had a southern offshoot in Cherokee; the Siouan tongues of the midwest have disconcerting east-coast branches. The diversity of the Indian tongues, even on U.S. soil alone, is illustrated by the word for "papoose carrier," which is *waltsol* in Navajo, *gaonseh* in Iroquois, *ullosiajohka* in Choctaw.

South of the Rio Grande, the American Indian languages enjoy far greater vitality than in the United States or Canada. The Aztec tongue is still spoken by nearly 1 million people in northern and central Mexico and is quite alive in Mexican place names. Characteristic of this language is the *tl* group found in names like Tlaxcala and Nahuatl, the *coyotl*, *chokolatl*, and *tomatl* that give us "coyote," "chocolate," and "tomato." "Aztec" means "crane people," "Toltec" "skilled workers" (this is an Aztec name; the Toltecs' own name for themselves is Aculhuaque, or "strong men"). Montezuma is a Spanish shortening of *Montecuzumai thuicamina* ("When the chief is angry, he shoots to heaven"). South of the Aztecs and Toltecs are the Mayas of Guatemala and Yucatán, who dominated Central America during the first twelve hundred years of our era.

In South America, all of the original Indian languages, from the Carib of the Antilles to the Araucanian of Chile, are very much alive. Chief among them is Quechua, which extends from Ecuador, across Peru and Bolivia, to northern Argentina, with about 6 million speakers. In Paraguay, the everyday language of the population is Tupi-Guaraní, though Spanish is official. Illustrative of the continued vitality of the South American Indian tongues are the very names of two nations, Paraguay and Uruguay, both of which are Tupi-

Guaraní; one means "parrot river," the other "snail river." *Jaguar* and *carioca*, from the same source, have the original meaning of "that which consumes" and "white man's house."

Any attempt to describe the American Indian languages *en bloc* would be futile. Some of them are polysynthetic, which means that words have little if any individual status but become meaningful only when placed in a sentence; or, putting it another way, the entire sentence forms one meaning-unit, with none of its component parts enjoying true separate existence. Oneida *g-nagla-sl-i-zak-s* ("I am looking for a village") illustrates this structure: *g-* carries the meaning of "I"; *nagla* conveys the idea of "living"; *sl* is a suffix that gives *nagla* the force of a noun (therefore, *nagla* plus *sl* conveys the idea of "village") *i* is a verbal prefix, indicating that *zak* is to carry a verbal idea; *zak* has the general meaning of "look for"; *s* is the sign of continued action. None of these parts would convey any very definite meaning if used by itself. Polysynthetism, however, is characteristic of other language families, notably the Basque and the Eskimo-Aleut, while many American Indian tongues do not display it to any appreciable degree.

Closely linked with the Indian languages are those of the Eskimos, both in Alaska and Greenland, and of the Aleuts. Here we have good samples of the polysynthetic type of tongue, with a phrase like "in the great country" rendered by *nunarssuarme* (*nuna*, "land"; *-ssuak*, "great"; *-me*, "in"). "Summer" is often rendered by a compound which means "season of inferior sledding."

A linguistic curiosity in connection with American Indian names is the different spelling they assume according as they were first transcribed by English or by Spanish speakers. The name of a tribe like Tihuanaca, in South America, would appear as Tiwanaka in English transcription, while Quechua would be Kechwa if we had gotten there first.

The Caucasian language group of the Caucasus region in the Soviet Union has perhaps 5 million speakers, distributed among such tongues as Georgian, Lesghian, Avar, and Circassian. Strabo, the ancient historian, stated that there were seventy tongues in this region, and modern linguists, curiously enough, find the count to be the same today. The medieval Arabs called the Caucasus "the Mountain of Tongues." One of these languages, Stalin's native Georgian, enjoys a fairly long tradition, with a fifth-century A.D. translation of the Bible as its first document.

Some linguists hold a theory concerning the kinship of a widespread "Mediterranean" group of tongues, said to include Caucasian, Iberian, Basque, Etruscan, and Sumerian. It is true that a region in the southern Caucasus once bore the name of Iberia, like the peninsula consisting of Spain and Portugal, but outside of this the evidence is slight.

The present-day Basque that straddles the northern Pyrenees is said to be the descendant of an ancient Iberian tongue once spoken throughout the Iberian Peninsula and in Aquitania. According to the tradition, the hardier Iberians who refused to submit to Roman rule retreated into the mountain fastnesses of the Pyrenees and continued to speak their language, while their weaker brethren succumbed to Romanization and became Latin speakers.

Today about 1 million people speak Basque, on both sides of the Franco-Spanish border. The Spaniards use four different names for the Basques (*basco, vizcaíno, vascuence,* and *vascongado*), but the Basques' name for themselves is *Euskar.* The Basque language enjoys a tradition of difficulty which the Basques themselves do nothing to dispel. They have even created a legend to the effect that at one time the devil spent seven years trying to learn their tongue, so he could tempt them, but finally had to give up in disgust; but there is another story to the effect that Basque is used by the devil to fight with his mother-in-law. The structure of Basque is reminiscent of the polysynthetism of some American Indian languages (*echeco-jauna,* literally "house-of-master-the," "the head of the family"), and this has at various times given encouragement to those who believe in the lost continent of Atlantis, joining what today is Europe with America. But to the best of our present knowledge, Basque is unaffiliated, and will probably remain so.

The Ainu of the white-skinned dwellers of Hokkaido, the northernmost of Japan's islands, the Hyperborean or Paleo-Asiatic tongues of northeastern Siberia and Kamchatka, and many other language groups too numerous to mention round out the world's linguistic picture and the 2,000- to 3,000-language total.

To the average person, Kamchadal and Yukagir, Cheremiss and Votyak, Cambodian and Kachin, Chibcha and Arawak are mere names to be glanced at and forgotten. To the linguist, they are problems which often contain their own solution, along with the partial solution of that bigger, broader problem: "What is language?"

One final, major consideration may here be offered. There is no human group, however backward and primitive, that lacks speech. Like structural anatomy and functional physiology, language is among the fundamental proofs that all men are brothers under the skin.

— Chapter Ten —

SELF-DESIGNATION

You speak Middle Country language? (Literal translation of the Chinese phrase for "Do you speak Chinese?")

THE question sometimes comes up whether it would not be desirable to standardize, for geographical and official documents at least, names of countries, nationalities, and languages. Outside of traditionalism, there are two rather important points that are normally overlooked in such discussions: the matter of pronunciation and that of transcription, particularly from such writing systems as the Cyrillic, Greek, Hebrew, Arabic, Sanskrit-Hindi, Chinese, and Japanese. In addition, account must be taken of the fact that there is constant change in the names of political units: that occasionally there is little or no link between the name of a country, that of its people, and that of its language. Occasionally, also, there is a considerable spread between the popular, semipopular and official name of a political unit (witness "Russia," "Soviet Union," "Union of Socialist Soviet Republics"). Again, the name of a political unit may vary, even officially, according to the languages which are official within it (Belgium is *Belgique* to its French speakers, *België* to the Flemish; Switzerland is *Schweiz* to its German speakers, *Suisse* to the French, *Svizzera* to the Italians; South Africa and *Zuid Afrika* are both official).

Among official names of countries that would normally be quite unrecognizable to English speakers are *Shqipni* (Albania), *Druk-Yul* (Bhutan), *Chung-Hua Min-Kuo* (Nationalist China), *al-Misr* (Egypt), *Suomi* (Finland), *Magyarország* (Hungary), *Bharat* (India—this is the modern designation of the country; the older name of *Hind* or *Hindustan,* though originally Persian, did not present difficulties); *Daehan Minkuk* (Korea), *al-Urdiniyah* (Jordan), *Maghreb-al-Aksa*

(Morocco; the literal meaning is "the Far West," justified by the fact that Morocco is the westernmost of the Arab lands). *Pyee-Daung Su Myanma Naingngan* is the official designation of Burma, and possibly one American out of a million, outside the State Department, is aware of the fact. Constant practice, with stamps and literature, has perhaps made us aware of *Deutschland, Oesterreich, Hellas, Éire, Polska*.

For names of languages the situation is, if anything, worse. Try yourself out on this list: *Vlaams, Cymraeg, Hrvat, Hayeren, Euskara, Nihongo, Chosenmal, Yueh, Breiz, K'art'veli*. They are, in sequence, Flemish, Welsh, Croatian, Armenian, Basque, Japanese, Korean, Cantonese, Breton, Georgian. There are confusing and even misleading names: *Gaeilge* and *Gaelig* are both Gaelic, but one refers to the Irish, the other to the Highland Scots variety. *Slovenski* is Slovenian, *Slovensky* is Slovak. *Serbski* is not, as one might think, Serbian (which is *Srp*); it is. the Sorbian or Wendish of the small Slavic group in the region of Cottbus and Bautzen in Germany. You may use Afghan for the tongue of Afghanistan, but its official name is *Pashto. Chung Kuo* is the Chinese name of China, but its official language is *Kuo-yü*. The tongue of the Basques is *Euskara*, but the people are *Euskaldunak*. The state is Israel, but its present-day Hebrew language is *Ivrit. Lietuva* is the country we know as Lithuania; its language is *Lietuviškai*. And, of course, there is no Swiss, Yugoslav, or Belgian language.

In the case of lesser groups that do not form national units, there is greater justification for the spread between the name of the group (often conferred by outsiders) and that of the language, which is more often native. *Nama* is the tongue or group of tongues of the Hottentots and *San* that of the Bushmen. *Inuit* is the leading variant of the tongue of the Eskimos (or would you rather spell it Esquimaux?). Of interest is the prefix *ki-* which comes before the names of Bantu tongues (*ki-Swaheli, ki-Ndongo, ki-Rundi;* the people themselves take another prefix, which ranges from the *ba-* of *Bantu* and the *wa-* of *Wa-Swaheli, Wa-Tuzi*, to the *ama-* of *Ama-Zulu*).

We have already seen how national, group, and language names are often bestowed by others than the ones to whom they become attached. Hungary and Hungarian are misnomers, for the Uralic tribe that settled in the central valley of the Danube, though related to Attila's Huns, who had passed through some centuries before, were Árpád's Magyars. Welsh and Erse are names bestowed by the hated Sassenach upon Celtic groups whose self-designation was and is quite different. Many Indian tribes received their present official names from English and French explorers (Blackfeet, Nez Percés). Occasionally, the name was merely the echo of a commonly used phrase (Iroquois, the form given by the French to a group that in councils made frequent use of the phrase *hiro koué*, "I have spoken with joy"—notice that the spelling even reflects the French pronunciation of the period, when French *oi* had not yet shifted from *weh* to *wah*). Bantu and Navajo both mean "the men," "the people," but the former was bestowed by European missionaries, while the latter is native. Kaffir, Arabic for "infidel," is resented almost as much by South African Blacks as is "nigger" or "nigra" by American Negroes. The Lapps do not care for their name, which is Scandinavian for "simpleton"; they prefer their own *Samis*.

On the other hand, there are names of non-national groups which are self-bestowed and viewed with pride. One branch of the Quebec Canadians, who stayed behind in spite of British conquest, proudly call themselves *Habitants*, the "inhabitants" of the province *par excellence*. The other branch, whose deportation to Louisiana forms the subject matter of Longfellow's *Evangeline*, nostalgically continued to call themselves *Acadiens* or Acadians (Acadia was the name of the original French settlement in Canada), and this has finally turned into Cajuns, a name that puzzles most visitors to the New Orleans area.

For these many reasons it may be impractical to seek too much precision and uniformity in our nomenclature of nations, groups, and languages.

❧ PART FIVE ❧

An International Language

— Chapter One —

"EASY" AND "DIFFICULT" LANGUAGES

What is healthy to a Russian is death to a German.
— Russian proverb

No man fully capable of his own langauge ever masters another.
— G. B. Shaw, *Maxims for Revolutionists*

THE process whereby a child learns his own language, first imperfectly imitating sounds, then words, then thought concepts, has been interestingly and thoroughly described by such famous linguists as Jespersen and need not be repeated here, all the more since its aspects are largely noncontroversial. On the other hand, the way in which a half-grown or full-grown adult assimilates a tongue other than the one with which he started out in life has of late given rise to acrimonious debates that have overflowed the pages of professional journals and found their way into the popular press and the conversation of cultured laymen.

It has been previously stated, and can never be sufficiently repeated, that intrinsically there is no such a thing as an "easy" or a "difficult" language. Every tongue, no matter how intricate it may seem to the outsider who undertakes to learn it, is easy to its own speakers, who have acquired it by the "natural" process—by direct imitation of their elders, in meaningful contexts, through a sequence of almost infinite trial and error, at the rate of sixteen hours a day, seven days a week, fifty-two weeks a year, for all the years of their lives.

This sweeping statement is subject, however, to several qualifications. In the first place, it applies to the spoken tongue but not at all to its written counterpart. The minute a language learner, native or foreign, undertakes to learn the written form of his own or another language, features of intrinsic ease and difficulty will at once present themselves, ranging all the way from the absolute ease of a quasi-phonetic written system like that of Finnish, through various gradations of increasing difficulty in languages like Spanish, Italian, or German, to the spelling complexities of French and English, and ultimately to the extremely difficult mnemonic features of ideographic systems of writing such as the Chinese. It may be emphasized that this characteristic of ease or difficulty in apprehending a language in its written form applies in equal measure to the native and to the foreign learner. The latter, if anything, has a slight advantage over the former, born of the possibility of comparing the system of the language he is learning with his own. In my early experiences with the intricacies of English spelling, for example, I found it a decided advantage to be able to memorize the written form of an English word in the phonetic pronunciation that such a written form would have had in my native Italian.

Secondly, the matter of a language's ease to its own speakers is subject to certain cultural restrictions inherent in the language itself. It definitely applies to the sounds of the language, its basic grammatical forms, and its vocabulary of common use. It does not apply to those more intellective, artificial features which find their expression in refined syntax and style and in an overextended vocabulary. All other things being equal (which they are not), a Bantu speaker will have a better chance of learning to speak Bantu perfectly than an English speaker of learning English in the same fashion, for the very simple reasons that the Bantu vocabulary is far more limited than the English, and that English, in the course of its literary history, has developed certain intricacies of literary syntax which Bantu, perhaps luckily for itself, has never had a chance to elaborate. Here, however, we tread on dangerous ground; the complexities of syntactic structure and the vocabulary range of supposedly inferior tongues are often such as to astonish linguists who chance to delve into them.

Since the feature of natural or inherent ease or difficulty is removed from the current spoken tongue of any given community, what is it that constitutes the element of "ease" or "difficulty" so often attributed to individual languages? What causes a high school student to say: "I'm going to take Spanish because it's easier than French or German," or an adult to remark: "My! How did you ever learn Russian? It's such a difficult language!"?

The answer lies in the purely subjective aspect of the individual background that each and every one of us begins to acquire from childhood. "We are creatures of habit" is a somewhat trite saying, but few of us realize to what a tremendous extent it is true. From the moment we are born (some say even before) we start acquiring habits—physical, mental, and psychological—and these habits tend to become permanent and remain with us through life. They color all our future experiences with psychological reactions based on earlier experiences, which make us like certain things and dislike others, consider some easy, others hard.

Language definitely falls under this heading of habit. From earliest youth, we begin acquiring certain habits of expression, which include the utterance of certain sounds in preference to a far greater number of sounds which at the outset are potentially as easy to produce; the shaping of certain ideas into certain thought-and-language patterns in preference to others; and the attachment of certain semantic connotations to certain sound groups which, however arbitrary at the start, gradually come to color our entire thinking with an almost indelible tint.

Viewed in this light, our habits, linguistic or otherwise, originally acquired at the cost of infinite pain, difficulty, and experimentation, ultimately turn into a series of almost mechanical reflexes. Today, after driving a car for thirty years, I do not consciously think of my clutch, my brake, my gas pedal, my steering wheel; but how consciously, even painfully, I thought of them when I was first learning to drive! If today I were to direct my attention to a new but kindred activity, such as flying an airplane, I would find it easier than if I had no knowledge whatever of guiding a vehicle, even though my transfer of mental habits might occasionally lead me into error by mechanically causing me to try to operate the plane as I would a car. The more the new vehicle resembled a car in its mode of operation, the easier I would find it to handle; the more it differed, the harder it would be.

Here lies the crux of "ease" and "difficulty" with learning another language. The tongue will impress me as "easy" insofar as it runs close to my already established linguistic habits, and "difficult" to the extent that it diverges from them. Languages whose structural pattern, basic vocabulary, general mode of expression resemble those of English strike the English speaker as relatively easy, those which differ radically as hard. Germanic and Romance tongues, which have many points of contact with English, are normally the easiest for us to learn. But a Czech would find it easier to learn Russian than English, because Russian is closer to his own language habits.

Again, this matter of ease or difficulty, based upon previous linguistic habits, must be placed in the perspective of numerous other factors. Children can master, without apparent effort and with great fluency and a flawless accent, several languages at once, if they are in direct contact with their speakers. This seemingly simple mastery is, of course, predicated not upon the written but upon the spoken form of the language, within its more ordinary conversational reaches.

The problem of language learning is often misunderstood because it is too often oversimplified. "Learning" a language can mean a dozen different things to as many persons. It involves not one but half a dozen diverse physiological and psychological processes. It is a matter of speaking, understanding, reading, and writing, the four language-learning functions generally recognized by the pedagogues; but each of these faculties represents a complex of acquired abilities and functions. In speaking, we must control the vocal organs so as to produce the proper sounds, at the same time that we work with the memory, the understanding, and the faculty of coordination. "Understanding" means at once a physiological process of accurate hearing and an intellective process of semantic selection. In both these processes the time element is essential, while it ordinarily plays a minor role in reading and writing. But reading again brings into play the element of semantic selection and that of coordination, while writing calls for a power of memory and discrimination which appears nowhere else.

Too often the purpose of language learning is left unclear. Do we learn a foreign language because we are primarily interested in its literature? If so, it is the reading processes that will have to be stressed, with considerable attention devoted to the more abstruse portions of the syntax and vocabulary. Or do we want a facile conversational ability, permitting us to "order a beer in Singapore," inquire how to get to the railroad station, or demand a lower price for what is offered for sale? In this case, we must cultivate our ability to produce a few sounds, attune our ears to them, and concentrate on a given number of basic words and expressions. Or we may wish to gain a writing and translation knowledge of the foreign tongue, whereupon its spoken features again drop into the background and its morphological characteristics come to the fore. Language teachers and others often speak somewhat glibly of a complete, well-rounded knowledge of the foreign tongue, the ability to converse in it fluently, to understand all that is said in it, to read it with facility, to write it gracefully. This, we beg to submit, comes close to being a lifetime job and is certainly not to be acquired in two years at the rate of three hours a week, or even in six months at the rate of eight hours a day. There should indeed be a striving for perfection, but perfectionism in language learning should be avoided, or at least tempered with the realization that the primary function of all language is to convey meaning; if that function is fulfilled, the means and methods may well be unorthodox, unconventional, or downright "incorrect."

Once the intrinsically complex nature of the language-learning process is understood, it will be simpler to deal both with the problem itself and with the claims of those who assert that it can be integrally applied in record-breaking time with a complete duplication of the natural function, or who rail at immature and uninterested students for their lack of spectacular achievement in foreign-language learning.

— Chapter Two —

THE TRANSLATION PROBLEM

Interpreting is not everybody's art.
—Luther

"Egad, I think the interpreter is the hardest to be understood of the two!"
—R. B. Sheridan, *The Critic*

THE Biblical account of the Tower of Babel is probably the first recorded instance of man's longing for an international, universal tongue. Like many other things that man longs for in vain, this particular boon was at first freely vouchsafed by a bountiful providence but later withdrawn because of man's own misuse of it.

When man realized that he could no longer communicate with his fellow man by reason of the confusion of tongues, he began to seek ways and means of circumventing the will of his Creator. Translators and interpreters were the outcome. Their inefficiencies and insufficiencies are at times disheartening.

The Italians have a saying about this: *Traduttore—traditore* ("A translator is a traitor"). Our State Department is said to have been at one time vastly disturbed by a note received from the French government which began: *Nous demandons.* "What right do they have to demand that?" said the irate officials. Then it was pointed out that the French expression had the more modest meaning of "we request." If the account is true, it was the fault of the original translator that we almost had a diplomatic break with France. Once, at the UN, there was considerable dither over a passage describing the threatened collapse of western Europe as "brutal." This was a literal rendering of the French *brutal,* but the tension lessened when it was explained that in idiomatic usage the French word corresponded much more closely to the English "serious."

English-Russian difficulties of translation are forever cropping up. There was the Russian phrase *ne budyet miritsya* in connection with West German rearmament, which was at first translated "will not tolerate" and caused a flutter of excitement. A more exact and less warlike translation was soon found: "will not reconcile itself with."

There is a story that the Japanese verb *mokusatsu* was responsible for the loosing of American atom bombs on Hiroshima and Nagasaki. The verb can mean either "no comment" or "to kill with silence" and was used in the Japanese newspaper accounts of the Japanese government's reaction to the American demand for unconditional and immediate surrender. By the time reports reached the Allied authorities, the second meaning was accepted, so it seemed that Premier Suzuki had contemptuously rejected the ultimatum as "unworthy of notice." What the Premier had actually said, so the story goes, was that his government had decided to postpone action and withhold comment pending clarification of the demand for surrender.

Translating and interpreting require a perfect command of two languages, and most of us do not command even one. Dictionaries are of limited help, because most words in one language have a dozen possible translations in another, which means that to use a dictionary properly you must first have command of the two languages, in which case you may not need the dictionary.

What can be accomplished with dictionaries, or with a literal knowledge of equivalent words, is illustrated by a couple of cases. A French teacher once found in a composition the expression *plateau de frêne*, which on the face of it means "container made of ash wood"; after racking her brain for a time, it finally occurred to her what the student had meant; he had sought "ash tray" as two separate words and had correctly gotten both. On another occasion, an English bridge player was trying to explain to an Italian kibitzer that he had a "leg toward rubber." It came out, literally enough: *"Ho una gamba verso la gomma,"* but what the puzzled Italian got out of it was: "I have a limb toward the eraser."

Translation boners and howlers come from all fields. Balzac's *Contes drolatiques* may be translated as "Droll Stories," but that's not precisely what the title means. *Erzieher*, literally "one who draws out," was at one time decried in educational circles as containing overtones of force and brutality. Actually, it has precisely the same formation and semantic value as its English counterpart "educator": "one who draws or leads forth." "The Brave Bulls" is meant to translate the Spanish *Los Toros Bravos; bravo* in Spanish has overtones that carry it beyond English "brave"; as evidenced by the phrase *se puso bravo*, "he got mad," "he got nasty," it conveys the added idea of meanness and ferocity: "Mean Bulls" or even "Ornery Critters" would have been more to the point. In the old days of Model-T-Fords, some got to Russia with instructions for their proper care. The booklet recommended "denatured alcohol" for antifreeze and "Ivory Soap" to wash the car. By the time the instructions emerged from the Russian translation bureau they read: "In the winter time fill your radiator partially with alcohol deprived of its natural qualities. When washing your car it is recommended to use soap made of elephant tusks." One of the more recent examples supplied by Berlitz is Cleveland's slogan, "the Matchless City," which got around to a few European countries as "Cleveland, the City without Matches." Some of the boners, however, are of the tongue-in-cheek variety, as where the reviewer of a dictionary of idiomatic expressions suggests that our "good clean fun" be rendered as *divertissement bien nettoyé.*

Exactness of translation is often hampered by diversity of national customs. A "dish of vegetables" could be translated literally into Japanese but would evoke a vision not of beets, peas, carrots, corn, and string beans so much as one of bamboo shoots, water chestnuts, mushrooms, watercress, scallions, and onions. The Singapore newspapers had difficulty with the title of Queen Elizabeth: the Chinese papers called her *Nye Huang,* "a queen in her own right"; the Tamil and Malay ones found that their languages lacked the term, and they could only call her "wife of the king"; Tamil editors bowed to the language and custom difference and called her *Maharani Elizabeth*; Malay editors used her English title untranslated: "Queen Elizabeth."

Often a literal translation *seems* to make sense. What is wrong with translating "School of Law" into Italian as *Scuola di Legge?* Nothing, except that that's not the way the Italians say it. They use *Facoltà di Diritto,* "Faculty of Right." In America, we speak of "the man in the street," "the Smiths and the Joneses"; is there an equivalent term in Chinese? Yes, *lao pai hsing;* but it literally means "the old hundred names." Can you say "to liberate" in Chinese? Yes, *chieh fang;* but the literal meaning is "loosen-let go." Can you say "Stick 'em up!" in Japanese? Yes, *he o agero*; but literally it means "hand raise."

Again, what is one to do with "untranslatable" words, like the German *Schadenfreude*, which may be rendered by "malicious pleasure," "gloating," but has more specifically the sense of "rejoicing over the downfall of another, particularly a former superior"? It was discovered in the course of UN gatherings that French has no real equivalent for "trusteeship," Chinese no way of expressing "steering committee," Spanish no way of distinguishing between "chairman" and "president." The UN finally had to establish a program of linguistic research to devise dictionaries of exactly equivalent words and phrases in its five official languages. But even without going into the specialized language of diplomacy, what can one do with such current German words as *Stimmung, Gemütlichkeit, Weltanschauung*, with French words like *éclat* or *demi-tasse*, even with English words like "pet" and "to miss"? They can all be translated after a fashion, but "domestic animal" will never carry the true meaning of "pet," any more than *le echo de menos* or *sento la sua mancanza* carry the full import of "I miss him." An expression like the American "How much is he worth?" leaves the translator floundering, and gives the foreigner mistaken notions of intellectual or moral qualities. During the war, the Italians got one of their few laughs out of the literal translation of the British "Home Fleet" (*Flotta di Casa*), which sounded like a domesticated tomcat. No word list is long enough to give all the possible meanings of the ubiquitous English "get."

When it comes to technical, commercial, or literary translations, the situation is even worse. Each technical field has its own linguistic domain, and the would-be translator of a technical document must command that technical field as well as the two languages, under pain of sending out disastrously wrong directions for the use, say, of machinery. The commercial language must be based on coincidence of consuming habits as well as on satisfactory translation. When the Coca-Cola concern hired a staff of linguists to translate "Have a Coke" into fifty foreign languages, all they got was a series of national forms of greeting; the literal rendering of "have a Coke" would simply have made no sense. In the literary field, a critic scornfully points his finger at an English translation of the intensely dramatic *Stabat Mater* and remarks that "when something great has been said in Latin, it has been said once for all."

The problems that arise in connection with translation are

infinite. Shall the author of a book translate passages quoted from a foreign tongue, or not? One critic says of an author that "he translates his quotations, so that his readers are embarrassed neither by his learning nor their ignorance." But there is widespread controversy on this point.

What to do with slang and colloquialisms? Lose their racy flavor by translating them into correct terms, or seek equivalent colloquial expressions in the foreign tongue? When George Gershwin's "Ain't Misbehavin' " was beamed to Russia, it was unimaginatively rendered by "I don't do anything bad"—proper and correct, but hardly flavorful.

To what extent should untranslated foreign expressions be allowed in connection with things in common use, such as restaurant menus? One journalist, tired of *entrecôte bonne femme* and *raie au beurre noir,* voices a serious complaint about "chow cards in ancient Gasconese" and admits he would like to eat without having to show a Berlitz certificate. But how would he anglicize *bouillabaisse* and *cassoulet*?

If one decides to translate, the question of overlapping meanings comes up for solution. English "wish" is French *désirer* if you wish something, but *souhaiter* if you wish someone something. English "engineer" is Italian *ingegnere* if you mean a civil engineer, but *macchinista* if you mean the engineer on a train, as the Italian war bride of an American G.I. who claimed to be an "engineer" found out to her disappointment. "Fire" is *fuoco* if you mean fire in the absolute, but *incendio* if you mean a fire to which firemen respond. Conversely, German and Russian find it difficult to make a real distinction between "national" and "popular" (the proper translation of *Volksepos* has sometimes worried me). French uses *serviette* for "towel," "napkin," and "brief case." Spanish *esperar* means both "to hope" and "to wait," and Italian *piano* means "piano," "softly," and "slowly." Even Latin *altus* means both "high" and "deep." A French professor always brought grins to the faces of his students when he inquired whether those in the "bottom of the room" could hear him; French *fond* normally means "bottom," but *le fond de la salle* is "the back of the room."

The use of the proper word combination in translation is an art in itself. In English you "pay" a visit, but in the Romance languages you "make" it. In English you "take" a walk, but in French you "make" it and in Spanish you "give" it. In English you "take" an examination, but in Italian you "give" it, in French you "undergo" it, in Spanish you "suffer" it.

Idiomatic expressions are, of course, what they are. The

Russian "How much to you of summers?" or the Spanish "How many years have you?" impress us as peculiar renderings of "How old are you?" On the other hand, "The child is two years old" sounds quite funny to Romance or Slavic speakers; how can a child of two be "old"? A "round-trip" ticket is incomprehensible to Romance speakers, who wonder what can be "round" about a trip; they use "ticket of going and coming." A simple, idiomatic, semicolloquial expression like "playing hookey from school" has the following renderings, among others: a French boy "goes to the bush school"; an Italian boy "salts away" or "pickles the school"; a German boy "goes behind the school"; a Russian boy "hoboes the school"; a Turk "avoids the school"; a Chinese "hides from school"; while a Spanish boy "plays the calf." Anyhow, "school" is etymologically "leisure," "unemployment," or "free time."

Deceptive cognates, like our *demander* and "demand," or words that merely sound or look alike, have ever proved to be pitfalls to translators. *Large* in French means "wide," while Spanish *largo* is "long." French *fermer* is "to shut," while Italian *fermare* is "to stop." *Lard, figure, douche, marine, crayon, plume, billet, coin, travail, placard, sale* and *type* are good English and good French, but in French they mean "bacon," "face," "shower," "navy," "pencil," "pen," "ticket," "corner," "work," "closet," "dirty" and "guy," respectively. *Gift*, a pleasant word in English, is "poison" in German, while *Lust* is quite harmless and means pleasure. *Burro* is "donkey" in Spanish, "butter" in Italian. An uncle of mine, traveling in South America, got himself into a ludicrous situation when he asked for *due uova al burro;* the Argentinian waiter went to great pains to explain to him that donkeys don't lay eggs—at least, not in Argentina. The Italian *sale* looks like the English "sale" but means "salt." My grandfather, on his arrival in this country, wondered why so much salt was advertised in the kind of stores where one would least expect it to be sold. *Merci* means "freight" in Italian, "thank you" in French. A French traveler coming to Italy for the first time remarked that the Italians must be an extremely polite people, since they had "thanks" in big letters on all their freight cars.

As a single example of what language diversity means in the field of science, we have a recent report from the National Science Foundation to the effect that it spends over two and a half million dollars a year for the purpose of producing English transcripts of some one half million pages of foreign scientific literature. This project has included, since 1959, the complete translation of thirty-seven Russian, one Chinese, and two Japanese science journals, along with numerous translations from the western languages.

Serious aspects of the translation problem, however, have come to light in the UN, despite its large staff of "simults" and "consecs" (the "simult" is a simultaneous interpreter, the "consec" is the translator who listens to a twenty-minute speech, taking notes in his own system of shorthand, then gets up and repeats consecutively the whole thing in another language, often making the meaning much clearer than when originally spoken). It was ascertained, for instance, that to translate into the five official languages the 20 million words spoken in the course of a seven-week meeting of the General Assembly, 100 million sheets of paper had to be used. A one-hour English speech made by a delegate is estimated to require 400 man hours put in by 124 different persons before it can be permanently recorded in English, French, Spanish, Russian, and Chinese. It takes on the average three translators eighteen man hours to get an English speech into Russian, and one translator thirty man hours to put it into Chinese.

The question of machine translation to speed up UN proceedings often comes up. But, as previously stated, machine translation is far from having reached a truly satisfactory stage for written material. For spoken material, it is as yet nonexistent.

The reaction of students who attended the UN proceedings was that these were insufferably slow, mainly by reason of the translations that had to be read, which retarded the work tremendously and caused everybody to fall asleep, including the original speaker. Mrs. Eleanor Roosevelt once made a similar observation and remarked that it would be wonderful if a single language could be used which would be understood by all the participants.

There is nothing novel about either the observation or the desire. Both have been expressed on countless occasions before. An international language eliminating the translation problem and all its attendant troubles has been envisioned for centuries. Such a language would at one stroke do away with all the linguistic difficulties encountered not only by diplomats but by technicians, scientists, missionaries, immigrants, businessmen, tourists, and students. It would place within the reach of all, without linguistic restriction, the world's science, political thought, and channels of trade. It would mean an end to the innumerable difficulties and delays by which men are beset as soon as they set foot beyond their own borders.

Is this solution of the world's translation problem and linguistic woes capable of achievement, particularly at this time, when modern means of communication have obliterated distances and made all the peoples of the earth potential next-door neighbors? What language, national or constructed, already in existence or yet to be created, would be suitable for the purpose? Before undertaking to answer these questions, it will be well to examine what has been proposed and what has been accomplished in the past, both on a limited and on a world-wide scale.

— Chapter Three —

UNIVERSALITY AND
INTERNATIONALITY, LIMITED

*Long Friday number one piccininni belong king belong
you and me 'e marry.*
—From pidgin English account of wedding of Princess
Elizabeth, published at Lae, New Guinea

WHAT may be described as a limited form of linguistic
universality has long since been achieved in several fields.
One often hears of the "international language of music,"
the "universal tongue of mathematical symbols," the "internationality of the language of science." The first is, of course,
a figure of speech when it is applied to the appeal that music
makes to all human hearts, whatever the color, race, or nationality of their owners. There is also, however, a more
literal application of the expression, for what concerns musical notation, directions, and terminology. In antiquity,
each nation had its own form of musical notation, but from the
eleventh century on, thanks chiefly to the inventiveness of
Guido d'Arezzo, a monk who lived in Italy but was probably
of French birth or origin, our present system spread to all
western lands until it is now indeed internationally used. The
first six notes of Guido's scale, *ut, re, mi, fa, sol, la,* were
taken from the initial syllables of the first six lines of a Latin
hymn to St. John the Baptist; the addition of *si* and the replacement of *ut* by *do* were later developments. Thanks to
Guido's scale, a musician of any land can today read or play
any composition from any part of the world. As for musical
directions and terms, these are 90 per cent derived from
Italian, the language that was first applied to the art of *il bel
canto.* While not quite so widespread as the use of the notation (German music often bears directions in German) this
terminology is internationally known and used. Not only

musicians and singers but even laymen throughout the world are acquainted with the meaning of *basso, contralto, tempo, falsetto, staccato, ritardando, con amore*. Two of many musical terms that offer linguistic curiosities are *glissando*, which is a hybrid compound of French *glisser* ("to glide") and the Italian gerund ending *-ando*, and *solfa*, which is the combination for vocalizing purposes of two notes of the scale but which Italian applies to any rigmarole, musical or otherwise.

However much we may admire the universality of the musical system, we cannot but be impressed by the fact that it is devised to serve one branch of human activity, and one only. The attempt made by Jean-François Sudre in 1817 to create an international language based on musical notes was a complete failure. A "musical Esperanto" devised recently to avoid conventional vocalizing uses pleasant-sounding nonsense syllables, but it can by no stretch of the imagination be termed a language.

Greater universality attaches perhaps to the system of mathematical notation and terminology in use throughout the civilized world. The Arabic numerals are very much in international use. So are Euclidian terms, as well as astronomical, chemical, and other symbols used by specialists in their respective fields. Of particular interest are the symbols of the chemical elements, which are based on abbreviations of Latin or Greek names (Na for *natrium*, the Latin name of "sodium"; F for *ferrum*, Latin for "iron"; Pb for *plumbum*, Latin for "lead"; Hg for *hydrargyron*, Greek for "water-silver," or "mercury"). Inspired perhaps by the international use of such symbols, a group of Massachusetts Institute of Technology scientists is at present actively engaged in an attempt to reform the scientific terminology of the major languages, so that they may all have corresponding terms. To give a very elementary demonstration of their procedure, the binary compound which is designated in English by the suffix *-ide* ("sulphide," "chloride," etc.) appears in Italian as *-uro* (*solfuro, cloruro*). If the suffix *-ide* or an easily recognized variant like *-ido* were adopted by Italian, or *-ure* by English, the confusion caused by these dissimilar endings would cease. In addition, many words which differ completely in two or more languages could be brought together in form. This system is devised to serve only scientific terminology and would not touch the everyday portion of the various vocabularies. But an extension of the principle has already been proposed, whereby semitechnical words such as "radiator" might be brought into line in the various tongues, thus leaving an ever-shrinking residuum of native terms for the learner to acquire.

In the matter of "radiator," French uses *calorifère* ("heat-bearer," from Latin roots), while Italian prefers the Greek *termosifone*. There is no intrinsic reason why English could not accept *calorifer* or *thermosiphon*, French *radiateur* or *thermosiphon*, or Italian *radiatore* or *calorifero* (the latter term is actually used in Italian side by side with *termosifone*). In this fashion, it is claimed, the international vocabulary of science and technology would gradually be extended to cover an ever-greater segment of everyday life, and the world's diverging languages would become more and more similar. Without entering into a discussion of the merits of the system for what concerns purely scientific terminology, it may be remarked that the extension of the scientific vocabulary would meet popular resistance at every step and would not at all solve the question of ordinary international understanding, particularly of the spoken-language variety.

The language of abbreviations is another excellent example of universality, limited. Such forms as *ca., n.b., e.g., i.e., viz., vs., etc., et al., lb., oz.* represent abbreviations of Latin words or expressions; degrees and titles like *Dr., Prof., LL.D., M.D.* are of the same nature. Perhaps the most widespread international abbreviation is the "&" or "ampersand" (*and per se and*), first devised, in 63 B.C., along with some 500 other abbreviations which continued to be used in manuscripts for over one thousand years, by Marcus Tiro, a precursor of Pitman and Gregg. While most of the Tironian shorthand symbols eventually dropped out of use, the "&" still survives in several hundred languages. The *Q.E.D.*, of mathematics (*Ouod Erat Demonstrandum*, "which was to be proved") and the ℞ and āā of druggists' prescriptions (the former is *recipe*, "take," with the subjoined symbol of Jupiter, which looks somewhat like a handwritten 4 but got changed in the course of centuries; the latter is for the Greek *ana*, "of each") are also part of our Classical heritage and remind us that at one time Latin and Greek were in truth universal, international tongues.

More modern abbreviations that have gained international currency are in the nature of "alphabet soup." UN, UNRRA, UNESCO, ECA are internationally known, though not everybody knows precisely what they stand for. U. S. S. R. stands for an English translation of the Russian S. S. S. R. but is accepted even by the Russians; so is U. S. A., though it stands not only for United States of America but also for United States Army and Union of South Africa. Among English abbreviations that have acquired some measure of international currency are O.K., B.O., I.Q., P.D.Q., and T.B.

The language of abbreviations is indeed international, but it can also be misleading. If you happen to be in a Romance country, do not turn on the "C" faucet to get "cold" water. "C" on faucets stand for "cold" in English but for "hot" in the Romance languages (French *chaud*, Spanish *caliente*, Italian *caldo*).

There is another sort of limited internationality that has already been achieved, represented by standard tongues which in the past have gained currency in certain areas and have served as media of linguistic exchange among people using different speech forms.

The role played by Latin and Greek in the ancient and medieval worlds is well known. In Classical antiquity, these two languages, ranged side by side, sufficed to care for the total needs of western civilization. It is rightly pointed out that during the so-called Hellenistic period Greek was the universal tongue of the eastern Mediterranean basin to such a degree that it served as the vehicle for the bulk of the New Testament. Latin, on the other hand, held sway over the west long after the fall of the Roman Empire. As the language of western Christendom and western scholarship, it was continued in international use until the Renaissance was well over. As late as the seventeenth century, international business was still carried on in Latin, and Grotius, when he wished to clarify international law, did so in Latin. Cromwell used Latin for his international correspondence, with a young man named Milton serving as his Latin secretary. As late as the nineteenth century, it was still fairly common for works of scholarship to appear in Latin, and those who claim that Latin is a dead language might well ponder on the English use of such words as "quota," "memorandum," "agenda," "maximum," "minimum," "medium," "data," "onus," "bonus," "prospectus," and "bona fide." Furthermore, Latin is still used as an international language by the Catholic Church, and Vatican Latin has evolved with the times.

It is a fascinating hypothesis that the very dualism of the two great Classical languages may have led to their downfall as international tongues. The death of Latin as the language of western diplomacy and scholarship did not come to pass until Greek had been rediscovered. But aside from such fanciful speculations, one may also point to the fact that, as the spoken vernaculars began to make headway, they very naturally tended to usurp the throne held by the ancient tongues.

In the thirteenth century, as a result of the Crusades in which France played a leading role, the French language enjoyed a European vogue that made it, in the words of some historians, a "universal vernacular of Christendom." Dante, at the outset of the fourteenth century, speaks of his rejection of Latin for his *Divine Comedy* as due to his desire to obtain a wider audience, including women, who could only be reached through the vernacular.

The rise of the national tongues has often been ascribed to the new, rising spirit of nationalism. But it is as often forgotten that the use of the vernaculars and the concurrent decline of Latin preceded nationalism, at least in its modern interpretation, by many centuries. There is more likelihood in the theory that it was the growing participation of the surgent bourgeois class in the affairs of the mind that robbed scholars and churchmen of their ancient linguistic prerogatives. In the century that followed the reflowering of the Ciceronian tradition under Cardinal Bembo, and while Grotius continued to use Latin, Comenius made the revolutionary pronouncement of advocating modern tongues for international use, Russian for the east, French or English for the west. It was this same seventeenth century, incidentally, that saw French forging ahead of the other western languages, by reason of military and political predominance, and beginning to occupy the role of the tongue of polite international intercourse that it still holds in part today. The use of English as an international language of trade and of German as an international language of science are comparative newcomers to the field, and their dominion has never won the general cultural acceptance that greeted French in the eighteenth century.

There is a possible parallel with the dualism of Greek and Latin in the tripartite role that these three great modern languages have played in recent times, and there is more than a hint that they may have acted as a check upon one another. With Spanish, Russian, and even Chinese entering the field as possible contestants, the emergence of one national tongue as the international language of the world seems more remote than ever.

Without any claim to universality, various semi-artificial tongues, partly the result of chance, partly of deliberate intent, have fulfilled the role of international languages in limited areas.

Some, like the *koine* which supplanted the ancient Greek dialects and the Malay of Indonesia, have managed to acquire the dignity and functions of national tongues. Others were curious literary devices, like the Franco-Venetian of the Middle Ages, created for the purpose of conveying the French *chansons de geste* to a population speaking another, but not too widely different, Romance language. The majority of these limited international tongues consists of the various pidgins in use throughout the world today.

Being a product of necessity pure and simple, and revealing crude, elementary processes of simplification, including baby talk, most of these tongues are regarded with scorn by all but professional linguists. Yet they are international tongues in embryo, with perhaps a touch of universality and, in the case of many, with definite literary strivings.

Among the oldest recorded pidgins is the *lingua franca* of the Mediterranean basin, a conglomeration of Italian, Arabic, French, Greek, and other languages, devised by medieval navigators and traders to supply a means of communication among multilingual populations in a state of constant warlike and peaceful interchange. It is common in *lingua franca* to find an Arabic verb root with an Italian verb ending, or a sentence consisting of five or six words, each taken from a different source. Yet attempts at literature and poetry in *lingua franca* were made by its users, with not too unpleasant results. Had some great literary genius taken up *lingua franca* seriously, it is likely that we would have today a masterpiece in that hybrid tongue.

Tupi, a South American Indian language, was used by the missionaries as a *lingua geral,* or tongue of common intercourse, for many of the tribes in Brazil and Paraguay. The Hausa and Swahili of Africa, the first of which serves as a medium of common intercourse for the populations of the Gulf of Guinea, the second for the eastern part of the Black Continent south of Ethiopia, seem to have been in origin pidgins concocted out of the numerous local dialects. But Africa has also many pidgins based on European languages. Afrikaans is in origin seventeenth-century Dutch which became semipidginized by use with the South African natives. It, too, turned into an official and literary language at the time of the Boer War.

The pidgin French varieties of West Africa and New Caledonia, the Gumbo or Creole French of the Louisiana Negroes, the pidgin Portuguese of India, Zanzibar, and Singapore, the Nigre-Tongo of Surinam in Dutch Guiana, called *taki-taki,* or "talkie-talkie" by the natives, the Papiamento of Curaçao, whose Spanish origin is easily ascertained (*kore poko poko* means "go very slowly"), the various American

Indian pidgins of North America, which have given us such distorted English forms as "paleface," "heap," and "firewater" along with the more indigenous "wampum," "squaw," "moccasin," and "tepee," are all samples of international languages deliberately devised for limited use. So are the many immigrant dialects now gradually dying out in the United States and other Western Hemisphere countries, like the *cocoliche* of Argentina, which is a perfect compromise between two already kindred languages, Spanish and Italian.

These languages of limited international currency point out a moral, and some linguists have not been slow to grasp it. If a tongue like Franco-Venetian or *cocoliche* can be created to serve speakers of kindred languages, why not others, on a more ambitious scale? Why not a universal Romance, or a universal Germanic, or a universal Slavic, reversing the historical process whereby the languages of these groups were formed out of the fragmentation of Latin, early Germanic, and early Slavic?

The Slavs, suffering perhaps from an inferiority complex due to the neglect their languages have suffered from language builders in the past, are at present hesitating between a national tongue like Slovak which, by reason of its geographically central position among the Slavic languages, is described as an ideal common tongue for all Slavs, and an artificially created Slovan, based on 440 root words common to all the Slavic languages and endowed with a simplified grammar, also common to all, and a phonetic spelling. But Slovan, elaborated by A. E. Zidek in Michigan, is an American product and shows little sign of being recognized by the Slavic nations of eastern Europe.

At this point the problem logically and legitimately reenters the broader field of world-wide currency. Why bother with a language, national or artificial, which will merely have wider acceptance than the languages it replaces? Why not give the problem an integral solution while we are about it? Why not create, devise, or select a language that will truly be universal and will serve all nations and all men without restriction or exception?

— Chapter Four —

UNIVERSALITY BY ARTIFICE

That language is the best which, at every single point, is easiest to the greatest possible number of human beings.
—Jespersen

WHILE Latin prevailed, there was no question of another international language. It is hardly an accident that the identical seventeenth century that witnessed Comenius' revolutionary pronouncement and the gradual ascent of French also gave rise to the first attempts at artificial, constructed languages. Sir Francis Bacon is said to have suggested a written system similar to that of the Chinese ideographs, which were then just beginning to be known in Europe. But this, even had it met with acceptance, would have represented only an international writing code.

In 1629 the philosopher Descartes outlined a scheme for a constructed language based on numbers that would represent words and notions. This suggestion, coming from one of the greatest minds of the period, really set the artificial language machinery in motion. Within a few decades, half a dozen international language systems sprang up, differing from the original ones in that they were meant to be spoken as well as written. Dalgarno's system, presented in 1661, consisted of an ingenious arrangement of Latin and Greek vowels and consonants, in which the first consonant of a word gave the key to the broader classification of the object denoted, the following vowel brought it down to a more restricted class, and so on. Almost at the same time, Bishop Wilkins offered, for philosophical writings, a set of symbols somewhat similar in appearance to those used in mathematics, but having spoken values. Practically contemporaneous were the international languages devised by Francis Lodwick (1647), Thomas Urquhart (1635) and Cave Beck (1657). The last-named used in writing combinations of letters and numbers, the numbers being replaced by spoken sounds in actual speech. A sentence like "Honor thy father and thy mother" appeared in writing as "leb2314 p2477 pf2477," but was read *"lebtoreonfo peetofosensen piftofosensen."*

As was quite natural, none of these systems, despite the fact that they were widely discussed, encountered success. To begin with, they were meant to be aristocratic languages for the use of philosophers and scholars, the very people who, having a broad linguistic culture, needed them least. Secondly, they were based upon an *a priori* foundation of logic and principles of philosophical perfectionism, quite at variance with the nature of language, which is neither logical nor perfect. Lastly, in a world still largely dominated by Latin and in which the national languages were beginning to make themselves strongly felt, there was little chance of acceptance for artificial newcomers.

Between the time of Bacon and the present day, it is estimated that some 700 attempts, in round numbers, have been made to construct artificial tongues for international use, a few extremely ingenious, the majority of them at best unimaginative blends of existing tongues or of previously devised systems. The early nineteenth century saw, among others, Sudre's attempt at a language based on musical notes. The late nineteenth century had a galaxy of forgotten tongues, including such picturesquely named ones as Bopal, Spelin, Dil, Balta, Veltparl, Langue Bleue, and Latinesce. The twentieth century has continued the tradition, with Idiom Neutral, Novial, Ido, Interlingua, Interglossa, Ro, Occidental, Arulo (later renamed Gloro), Monling, Suma, Neo, Loglan, Nordlinn, and a host of others.

Of all these many constructed tongues only two, Volapük and Esperanto, have met with some measure of success. The first, constructed by Monsignor Schleyer around 1880, had roots based mainly on English and Latin-Romance, with a grammatical structure strongly influenced by its inventor's native German. The word "Volapük" itself comes from the roots for "world" and "speak," both taken from English. The beginning of the Lord's Prayer in Volapük reads as follows: *O Fat obas, kel binol in süls, paisaludomöz nem ola; kömomöd monargän ola; janomöz vil olik, äs in sül, i su tal.*

The rising green star of Esperanto, the "language of hope," gave Volapük its death blow. The tongue constructed by Dr. Zamenhof of Poland in 1887 presented the advantages of extreme grammatical simplicity coupled with a fair degree of logic, utter ease of sounds, absolute correspondence between the spoken and the written form, and a vocabulary based mainly on the Germanic, Greek, and Latin-Romance elements of Indo-European. In accordance with the nineteenth century point of view, the Eastern languages were overlooked.

The Esperantists claim that their tongue is today the only living interlanguage, and their claim is substantiated by the fact that it has several million flesh-and-blood speakers scattered throughout the earth, as well as a flourishing literature which includes thousands of titles, both original and in translation (one of the most recent translations into Esperanto is that of the Finnish epic *Kalevala,* done in Helsinki). In addition, Esperanto has gained a measure of official acceptance. Along with Latin, it is the only language which by international agreement must be accepted in telegrams throughout the world. It is used by international associations of doctors, teachers, lawyers, scientists, and musicians, and by collectors of coins and stamps. Many business houses issue Esperanto catalogues of their products for foreign trade, and Esperanto tourist literature is issued by some tourist associations and by several governments. More than 100 newspapers and magazines in Esperanto are published throughout the world, and Esperanto programs are frequently broadcast by foreign radio stations. In 1921, the British Association for the Advancement of Science pronounced that a constructed language like Esperanto is better for international purposes than either a dead or a modern tongue.

But there is more. Some years ago, *Life* magazine, in an attempt to expand its international edition subscriber list, issued a four-page letter completely done in Esperanto and mailed it to all its European subscribers. Esperanto is used by the U. S. Army as the official language of the Aggressor Force in its war games. Members of the Aggressor Force are required to speak and understand it. Over 5,000 terms appear in the Aggressor Force linguistic manual. For the opening of the 1964 New York World's Fair, over 10,000 guide booklets in Esperanto were printed and distributed.

Over 600 schools all over the world teach Esperanto to some 20,000 pupils. In Whitburn, England, where one of the schools is located, the parents, noting that their children were communicating among themselves in a language which the parents did not understand, organized their own adult class in Esperanto so that they would know what was going on.

In view of these facts, it may be worth while to examine the basic structure of Esperanto, a simple task, since the grammar of the language can easily be condensed to fit into a single page. The Esperanto alphabet, which uses Roman symbols, has only one sound for each symbol. It omits *q, w, x,* and *y,* and uses a circumflex accent over *c, g, j, s,* and *h* to denote the sounds of *ch, j, zh, sh,* and *kh,* and a breve mark over *u* to indicate the sound of *w.* The accent of Esperanto is always on the next to the last syllable. The definite article is always *la.* All nouns end in *-o,* with a plural *-oj;* all adjectives in *-a,* with a plural *-aj;* all adverbs in *-e,* all infinitives in *-i.* The present of all verbs ends in *-as,* the past in *-is,* the future in *-os,* the imperative in *-u.*

Esperantists challenge people to test their own intelligence by offering them brief reading passages, which they claim anyone can understand. Here is an untranslated sample: *La inteligenta persono lernas la interlingvon Esperanto rapide kaj facile. Esperanto estas la moderna, kultura lingvo por la internacia mondo. Simpla, fleksebla, praktika solvo de la problemo de universala interkompreno, Esperanto meritas vian seriozan konsideron. Lernu la interlingvon Esperanto!*

The success of Esperanto aroused other interlinguists to redouble their efforts. In 1902 an academy of Volapük experts devised a radical simplification of their tongue, which they rechristened Idiom Neutral. The simplification process can be gauged by comparing the passage from the Lord's Prayer given previously in Volapük with the corresponding passage in Idiom Neutral: *Nostr patr kel es in sieli, ke votr nom es sanktifiked; ke votr regnia veni; ke votr volu es fasied, kuale in siel, tale et su ter.*

Just as Idiom Neutral is an offshoot of Volapük, Ido is an offshoot of Esperanto (Esperanto uses the suffix *-ido* for "descended from"; would-be improvers of Esperanto called their new language Esperantido, which was shortened to Ido). Somewhat similar to Esperanto is Novial, an artificial tongue devised by the great linguist Jespersen.

An interesting return to Latin was presented by the Italian linguist Peano in his Interlingua or *Latino Sine Flexione* ("Latin Without Endings"). In presenting it before a congress of linguists, Peano began his report in perfect Classical Latin; as he spoke of dropping the various endings, he actually dropped them in his reading; at the end of his report, what had started out as Classical Latin turned into "Endingless Latin."

Interglossa, devised by Hogben, author of *Mathematics for the Million* and editor of *The Loom of Language,* consists of Latin and Greek roots combined with a Chinese system of syntax. It may be remarked in connection with it that the system of Latin and Greek roots is not always easy even for those who use them in ordinary conversation; how many people who use "heterodyne" and "microphone" are able to analyze the former into "other" and "force" and the latter into "small" and "sound"? The Chinese syntax, on the other hand, presents its own peculiar drawbacks, as illustrated by *mi pre kine topo tendo un acte re*, literally, "I past go place purpose a do thing" ("I went there in order to do it").

Latecomers to the international language field are Monling, whose chief claim to fame is the exclusive use of monosyllabic words (*ling 't top pai ken ad ploi, il klar top bon* is Monling for "The language easiest to learn and use is obviously the best"), and the now completely formulated Interlingua devised by I.A.L.A. (International Auxiliary Language Association), a New York organization which is attempting to evolve an international language based on English and Romance; a sample of the tentative language thus far advanced, which is constantly being modified on the basis of questionnaires sent out to prominent linguists, is the following: *L'unita' quel permise action comun por le bono comun e contra le periculo comun es le sole metodo efective per quel, in tempor de pace, le nationes queles ama le pace pote garantir-se securita' e progreso ben regulate con liberta' e justitia.*

In addition to these true constructed languages, based on both writing and speech, one may also mention exclusively written-language codes which continue the tradition of Bacon and Descartes. The ingenious Gibson Code, compiled by a Coast Artillery officer, uses only numerical symbols. Nouns start with 1, 2, or 3, verbs with 4, adjectives with 5, adverbs with 6, pronouns with 7, conjunctions with 8, prepositions with 9; verb tenses are indicated by adding 10, 20, 30 to verbs; while even-numbered endings on nouns indicate the plural and odd numbers the singular. In Gibson Code a sentence like "The boy eats the red apple" would read as follows: "5—111—409—10—5—516—2013." This does not differ too much from cable codes in commercial use and has, unfortunately, the same limited application; it also fails to take into consideration structural diversities in the different languages of its prospective users. Sir Denison Ross, not too long ago, revived the Baconian plan of using Chinese ideographs internationally, but the limited use of such a system is obvious.

The major charges that are usually leveled against constructed languages are: 1) that they are "artificial"; 2) that they are not really "neutral," since they lean to one or another of the great language families; 3) that if adopted, each nation would tend to pronounce them with its own accent, so that in a short time an entire series of new languages would spring up.

The first of these charges is, of course, no charge at all. Granting the artificiality of a language like Esperanto in contrast with the natural qualities of languages like English or French is like granting the artificiality of an automobile as against the naturalness of a horse. Artificiality can be, and generally is, an expression of the human intellect, leading to an improvement over nature for the purpose at hand.

"Neutrality" is another overworked expression. As rightly pointed out by Hogben in his Interglossa, what will it avail the Zulus to have in a truly neutral constructed language two or three words from their own tongue, which is all that their numbers or importance would warrant? The fact that constructed languages are usually heavily weighted in favor of the great languages of civilization instead of endeavoring to give proportional representation to all the myriad language groups of the earth is an argument in their favor.

The third criticism is one that is easily met with a knowledge of linguistic history. Languages tend to break up into local dialects under conditions of isolation and lack of communications. When the factors that make for political, educational, and commercial unity are strong, it is rather the opposite process that takes place—dialects tend to vanish. Those who point to the breakdown of Latin into the Romance languages after the fall of the Roman Empire should look also at the earlier picture of the spreading and standardization of Latin over a vast multilingual area when conditions were favorable for the process of unification.

There are two additional criticisms of international languages, constructed or otherwise, which are not so frequently voiced but which deserve, perhaps, greater consideration than the ones enumerated above.

The first is that an international language, once adopted, would tend to displace the existing tongues and eventually obliterate them. That this threat is serious is evidenced by the fact that all international language advocates, without exception, go to great pains to inform us that their creations are not at all meant to replace national tongues but only to complement them for purposes of international communication.

The other point of criticism deals with the basic philosophy and methodology of the interlinguists. The older ones among them, including all the seventeenth-century scholars mentioned at the outset of this chapter and more recent ones down to Schleyer, were overwhelmingly preoccupied with logical perfectionism: as philosophers and logicians they could not conceive of an artificial product that would not be fully and completely logical and in accord with what the scholars of those days viewed as the universal, God-given system of linguistic and grammatical structure. Modern interlinguists, from Zamenhof on, swinging to the other extreme, seek not logic but ease of learning. Their major preoccupation is how to make their creation readily accessible to the world's masses, by a simplification of grammatical structure, which runs to the extreme of Chinese syntax, and by the selection of a vocabulary that will be most readily acceptable to the greatest number of people. It might fairly be remarked that we have moved from one swing of the pendulum to the other—from the concept of an aristocratic, philosophical language devised for the world's intellectual *élite* to that of a democratic, all-embracing tongue that will be favored by the world's masses. We still have perfectionism with us, but it is perfectionism of a different, more modern variety.

These two points of criticism are far too fundamental to be taken up in detail until we have examined the other wing of the international language movement—that which advocates the international use of a natural, national tongue like English, revised and modified in such a way as to meet the needs of a multilingual world.

— Chapter Five —

UNIVERSALITY VIA LINGUISTIC
IMPERIALISM

> *Here you have a very carefully wrought plan for an international language, capable of very wide transactions of practical business and interchange of ideas.*
> —Winston Churchill (*Speech advocating Basic English as a world tongue, September 7, 1943*)

THE only possible alternative, if one wishes to achieve an international language without recourse to artificial devices, is to adopt one of the existing national languages. Considering the number and variety of the latter, the only difficulty should be what the French call the *embarras du choix*. Which of the many shall we select?

As often as this question arises, the situation begins to resemble a national party convention at which each state delegation persists in voting for its own favorite son. Prominent Americans and Englishmen like Mrs. Roosevelt and Churchill somewhat naïvely cry out: "By all means let us have an international language! And by all means, let that language be English!" Unfortunately, speakers of other languages entertain precisely the same sentiments with respect to their own national tongues. Discussions, begun in an academic spirit, often turn acrimonious; or at best they are transformed into panegyrics on the merits of the various languages, their extent, their phonetic beauty, their grammatical simplicity, their literary achievements, their commercial or political importance. Not only the world's big languages, English, French, Spanish, German, Russian, Chinese, present their own candidacy, but even smaller languages, like Finnish or Swedish, are proposed on the same grounds by which dark horses are offered at political conventions.

Convincing people of the superior merits of a language

other than their own is on a par with persuading them that the pies produced by Mrs. Jones, whom they don't know, are better than those mother used to bake. Language is, after all, a very integral part of a people's way of life. A proposal to interfere with it can rub a sore spot second only to that created by interfering with people's religion.

An old lady of my acquaintance, knowing that I knew a few languages, would ask me how one said "bread" in French, Spanish, Russian, etc. Then, after listening attentively, she would shake her head and say: "But why do those people go to all that trouble? Wouldn't it be far simpler and easier for them to say 'bread'?"

Eisenhower, when in command of NATO forces, used to insist that war games be conducted in a single language—English. This directive was not invariably carried out.

More important than pointing out the advantages of the leading national candidates for the post of international language (which has all too frequently been done) is the task of pointing out their disadvantages—the difficult sounds of French and Chinese, the ponderous verbal apparatus of Spanish and Italian, the structural complexity of Russian and German. Of prime importance is the thankless chore of pointing out the drawbacks of English to American readers, who are all too prone to follow the mental pattern of the old lady in the story.

Yet before we do that, it may be well to review the advantages of English by placing it in juxtaposition with its leading national rivals. No other language with the exception of Chinese has so many speakers; no other language with the exception of French has its speakers so strategically distributed all over the globe; no other modern language has shown such mighty capacities for extension, growth, and colonization; none wields such far-flung political and economic power; none has at its command such enormous means of linguistic propaganda, of which one-half of the world's newspapers, two-thirds of the world's radio and TV stations, and three-fourths of the world's motion-picture industry are only samples; none, with the sole exception of French, has met such enthusiastic acceptance from broad segments of speakers of other tongues. The structure of English is a healthy compromise between the isolating morphology of tongues like Chinese and the agglutinative tendencies of languages like Russian. The English vocabulary combines, perhaps to an even greater degree than that of Esperanto, the roots of the major tongues of civilization. "Wondrous the English language, language of live men!" asserted Samuel

Johnson; and a great linguist to whom English was not native, Jakob Grimm, declared: "In richness, good sense, and terse convenience, no other of the living languages may be put beside English."

As against all this, English presents a mass of drawbacks of some of which even its own speakers are aware. Consonant combinations like those contained in "desks" and "pests," contrasting vowel phonemes like those of "hall" and "hull," "beat" and "bit," "caught" and "cut" baffle and irritate speakers of languages with simpler sound structures. While we need not take the evaluations too seriously, it is nevertheless true that a Spanish proverb says: "Spanish is for lovers, Italian for singers, French for diplomats, German for horses, English for geese," and that immigrants asked to describe the impression made on their ears by English when they first heard it compared it to "cats meowing." The phonetic difficulties encountered by foreign learners of English are illustrated by this Spanish phonetic rendition of a well-known American song: *"Iú most remémbar dis—e kis is stil e kis —e sáig is chost a sáig,"* etc. Add to this the very real discrepancy in pronunciation (and, to a lesser degree, in vocabulary and grammar) between the British and American parts of the English-speaking world, as well as within both countries, which leads many to advocate the creation of an English-language academy for the purpose of standardizing the language, at least for international use.

The very looseness and elasticity of English grammatical structure are a disadvantage in spots. In no other world language would it be possible to get newspaper headlines so full of misleading double talk as these: "Million in Gold Flies"; "June Tires at Peak"; "Hits Homer in Every Park."

What English can do to foreigners who try to use it is indicated by such phrases as *Correctly English in 100 Days* (the title of an English handbook for Orientals); "I was suddenly disemployed" and "May I have an interview with you, facial to facial?" (two of the phrases listed therein); as well as "Soldiers are refused to eat and drink here" (sign over a Shanghai shop) and "We are boys in the age of 17 years, ful from spirit of enterprise" (letter to a New York daily from Germany). The story, authentic or not, is told of an American technician employed in a Russian plant during the war who received a distressing wire from home about his only daughter: "Harriet hung for juvenile crimes"; the telegram had been translated into Russian, then retranslated into English; the original version was: "Harriet suspended for minor offenses."

In the field of vocabulary, it may be pointed out that "batter" is not only the man at bat and what you fry, but also the backward slope of a stone wall in gardening and what fire blight does to quince trees in horticulture. As for the attitude of the speakers of English toward their own language, G. B. Shaw said: "The English have no respect for their language, and will not teach their children to speak it."

By far the greatest drawback to the use of English on an international scale is the extraordinary spread between its spoken and its written forms. That the latter was fixed in the sixteenth century by printers who were more preoccupied with the problem of words to a line than with etymology or sound-for-symbol correspondence is an explanation, but not an extenuation. That we have gotten rid of such forms as "musick," "gheste," "strayt," "diuerse," "townge," is to our credit but does not answer the question why we did not complete the task. The growing use of "simplified spelling" forms like "nite," "donuts," and "thru" only adds to the general bewilderment, when "tight," "dough," and "enough" remain unaltered.

Advocates of English spelling reform are legion, ranging all the way from the late Senator Robert Owen of Oklahoma and G. B. Shaw to idealistic members of various obscure societies in all English-speaking countries. Some of them have the quaint notion that once English spelling is made phonetic the language will at once be adopted for international use, and that once this event occurs wars will become impossible. It is hardly worth while to controvert this point of view. What is of more importance is that none of the reformed-spelling advocates has ever undertaken to answer the question of what should be done with our existing stock of books and other literature if their proposals should be adopted. Reprinting would be a monstrous task, while continuing to use present books would compel everyone to learn two written languages instead of one.

There is little doubt that in the matter of facility of spoken sounds English is outstripped by a number of languages, notably Spanish and Italian; that for grammatical structure a slightly more complex but less misleading arrangement might be desirable; and that, for correspondence between sounds and spelling, English is at a decided disadvantage in the face of most of its competitors.

Add to all this the charge of cultural and linguistic imperialism raised by speakers of other languages every time English is mentioned, the opposing claims of a tongue like French, which has held for centuries a semiofficial position as the international language of diplomacy and culture, the clamor of speakers of more recently "arrived" languages, like Spanish, Russian, and Chinese, the outcry of the advocates of fully constructed "neutral" tongues, and you have a picture of the thorny way that must be trod by English before it can gain international ascendancy.

But while the controversies among national and constructed tongues were raging, a clever device was being prepared by two Englishmen, which was designed to combine the advantages of a national tongue with the desirable features of a constructed language.

Sporadically, in the late nineteenth and early twentieth centuries, there were suggestions and proposals that the structure of English be simplified even further to make the language acceptable to foreign speakers. Quite recently a form of "Simplify-ed English" has been advanced. But these attempted simplifications, bearing on the grammatical structure of the language, barely scratch the surface of the problem. Basic English goes to its core—the vocabulary. For proper use of a language involves possession of at least 10,000 words, and these, if one does not know them, must be learned the hard way, by constant repetition and memorization.

Though Basic English was brought out several years before the Second World War, it did not begin to receive widespread attention until it was advocated by Churchill when the war was drawing to a close. The later purchase of its copyright by the British Government for £23,000 and the appearance in Basic English of a book on international peace by one of its inventors have added interest to the proposal.

Basic English represents a radical departure from other language schemes in that it offers neither an artificially constructed language nor a modified dead language, but an actual living, spoken tongue. Its inventors, C. K. Ogden and I. A. Richards, while working on a semantical treatise, *The Meaning of Meaning,* were struck by the recurrence of certain common, frequently used words in the dictionary definitions of involved and abstruse terms covering all subjects. By reducing the longer, more complicated words to their definitions in terms of the more frequently used words, they concluded that it was possible to get along with as few as 850 words in the English language. This number, at the rate of a dozen a day, could be mastered in less than three months. The well-known simplicity of English grammar, its lack of endings, the fact that English is already the most widespread language on earth, led them to suppose that with the proper reduction in vocabulary it would be easy for anyone to acquire their creation and use it as an international tongue, at least for purposes of unpretentious self-expression.

The Basic English system calls for the elimination of all but eighteen verbs ("come," "get," "give," "go," "keep," "let," "make," "put," "seem," "take," "be," "do," "have," "say," "see," "send," "may," "will"). These basic words, combined with other "operational" words (prepositions and adverbs like "at," "before," "by," "to") or with nouns, can be made to replace any other verb in the English language ("keep up" for "sustain"; "take part" for "participate"; "go through" for "penetrate"; "have hope" for "hope"; etc.). Four hundred "general" nouns (such as "control", "government," "machine"); 200 picturable objects ("apple," "island," "monkey"); 150 adjectives ("full," "important," "ready") complete the scheme.

The process of using Basic English is primarily one of paraphrase. Without going to such extremes as defining a "beefsteak" as "a cut from the back end of a male cow kept on the fire long enough," we have such combinations as "small tree" for "bush," "without thought of others" for "selfish," "cruel government" for "tyranny." From the standpoint of logic and meaning, this is open to objection; the terms do not necessarily correspond, nor are the definitions altogether accurate.

Since Basic English has as its starting point a living, spoken tongue, it must be viewed in two lights: 1) from the standpoint of the native speakers of that tongue, who must acquire Basic in order to communicate with foreigners; 2) from the standpoint of non-speakers of English who wish to learn it.

English speakers may object to Basic English on the ground that it is confusing and involved, as seen from the examples above; that it is restrictive and negative, since it involves a process of "learning to forget" what has been painfully acquired and learning to "do without" a wealth of words accumulated by the language's speakers over centuries of experience and toil; that it is inaccurate, with "belief" used for "devotion," "true" for "brave," etc.; and that its claims are misleading and fundamentally dishonest.

The last charge calls for clarification. Basic, in its anxiety to cut down the number of verbs to an irreducible minimum, uses words like "stop," "jump," and "rest" as nouns ("come to a stop," "take a rest"). On the other hand, it permits the addition of *-ing* to such words, and their combination with "to be" ("I am resting"). But all that is needed to give us the complete English verb is the addition of "rests" and "rested." English verbs are extremely simple to use; is there need of a restrictive process whereby one can say "I am resting," "I was resting," but not "we rest," "they have rested"?

Basic also permits, outside the 850-word vocabulary, the formation and use of such compounds as "without" and "undertake." But "without" is not the same as "with" plus "out," nor is "undertake" the same as "take under." Extra sets of words are allowed scientists, economists, and other specialized categories; but scientists are not the only ones to speak of "kidneys," nor economists the only ones who have occasion to use "strike," "wholesale," and "budget."

Additional to the Basic English list are measurements, numerals, currency, calendar, and so-called "international terms requiring no translation." But "pound," "mile," "five," "sixteenth," "sterling," "Tuesday," "September" are certainly terms that will have to be learned, and while "beer" may be comprehensible to the German with his *Bier*, the Frenchman with his *bière*, and the Italian with his *birra*, it will not be readily understood by the Russian, who says *pivo*, the Spaniard, who uses *cerveza*, and the Portuguese, whose word is *cerveja*; in like manner, "cigarette," another of the "international" words said to require no translation, is *papirosa* to the Russian and *maki-tabako* to the Japanese.

By the time we come to the end of these special classes which are additional to the Basic list of 850 words, we find that we are closer to 8,000 than to 850; and since 8,000 words is generally a sufficient minimum for everyday expression in any language, one wonders whether it is worth while to do violence to the normal English tongue and the habits of thought and speech of its speakers. The elimination of verbs has been likened to "throwing the motor out of the car because that is where all the nuisances come from," while strong protests have been voiced over the choice of the Basic vocabulary. Why "monkey" and "sheep" and not "lion" and "wolf"? Why "heart" and not "liver"? Why "potato" and not "spinach"? Why "library" and not "bookcase"?

The normal English speaker would probably have at least as much difficulty learning to express himself in Basic as learning to use a foreign language, and the learning would be of the restrictive type, the very opposite of the expansive form of learning that the child goes through when he acquires words for concepts out of simple definitions.

The claim that the Bible is satisfactorily translated into Basic English is well substantiated (provided it is done by

Basic experts), but it is met by the objection that the English of today has traveled far beyond the King James stage. Attempts to render into Basic the very speech in which Churchill advocated its use for international purposes resulted in an entire series of ludicrous and dismal failures.

As for the claim that Basic is a ladder to fuller English, and that the ladder can be knocked down when its purpose is achieved, it has been remarked that it would be strange indeed if foreigners, having climbed the ladder, were to be left conversing in excellent English, while the original English speakers, having corrupted themselves with Basic in order to oblige them, walked down the ladder instead of up.

From the standpoint of a foreigner, it is objected that a Frenchman who at present wants to learn to say *égoïste* in English learns "selfish" and is at once assured that his newly acquired word conveys precisely the meaning he wants. Learning Basic, he must distort, just as the English speaker must, his concept of *égoïste* into "without thought of others," which does not mean the same thing, does not fit into his thought pattern, and involves the learning of four words, in a given sequence and context, in the place of one.

As things stand at present, a Romance speaker finds it difficult to use "get in," "get out," "get down" but easy to say "enter," "depart," "descend"; he has his choice of two locutions, one of which is close to his own mental outlook and speech pattern. "Give up" is meaningless to him, but "abandon," "desert," "resign," "surrender" are meaningful. English has combinations of Basic verbs and prepositions that are so highly idiomatic and unique that they have to be learned as separate word groups: "look out," for example, will be taken in its literal sense, "to look outside," but not in its more customary idiomatic meaning of "to be careful"; "go on" means "continue," but not literally; "get," by itself or in combination, is probably the most idiomatic and untranslatable expression in any language: "obtain," in any of a dozen fashions, "be obliged to," "cause to be," "induce," "become," "arrive," "procure" are only a few of its multifarious meanings. Yet it is one of the eighteen verbal mainstays of Basic.

English spelling is by far the worst, the most inconsistent, of all spellings on earth. In the course of the 850-word Basic list we find letters and combinations of letters having from two to ten different sound values. Other defects of English are its uncertain syllabification and unpredictable stress. No attempt is made by the inventors of Basic to repair these fundamental defects of English.

Foreign reactions to the Basic English movement are varied and interesting. There is no use denying that the overwhelming majority of Basic enthusiasts are English speakers, who view Basic as a means of spreading their own language and as a salvation from the necessity of learning other tongues. The results achieved by Basic English where it has been taught to foreigners are doubtful, if we make due allowance for the customary extravagant success claims of partisans and teachers with an ax to grind. Foreigners who favor Basic English are for the most part those who already know English. To what extent their support is due to nonlinguistic considerations is an open question.

Representatives of the governments of the minor United Nations declared against Basic when it was proposed as an international tongue. Foreign writers oppose it, either seriously, as an instrument of racial and economic imperialism, or jocularly, as a movement designed to debase the most important of existing world languages and to create a "black market in verbs and adjectives." On the other hand, some foreign linguists have taken it seriously to the extent of trying to duplicate it in their own tongues. Basic Spanish, Russian, and Chinese have been offered as world languages. A great French language scholar, Professor Georges Gougenheim of the University of Strasbourg, has brought out a Basic French which works on an essential vocabulary of about 1,000 words and has fascinating aspects. But it is obvious that if English cannot succeed in Basic form, neither can they, with their greater grammatical complexities, difficulties of sounds and tones, and vocabularies which are far less international in origin and scope.

— Chapter Six —

IT CAN BE DONE!

A world language is more important for mankind at the present moment than any conceivable advance in television or telephony.

—Lewis Mumford

AFTER all that has been said, the careful weighing of evidence for and against natural, modified, and constructed languages, it will seem strange that we suddenly reverse our approach and advocate a method that smacks of procedural anarchy. Yet that is precisely the position one is forced to take when faced with the labors and bickerings of the interlinguists, who are so laboriously trying to evolve a language for international use. This attitude springs from the fact that both labors and bickerings are predicated upon two fundamental linguistic errors, one of which follows logically from the other.

Interlinguists, including advocates of natural languages, apostles of modified modern tongues like Basic English, and constructors of purely artificial tongues, lose sight of the fundamental fact that every language, however intricate it may seem to those who try to learn it as adults, is simple to its own native speakers, who have learned it from childhood by natural speaking processes. As a result of this oversight, they proceed to plan not, as they should, for the future generations but for the existing adult speakers who will for the most part disappear within the next fifty years. They ignore the fact that the people now alive will be completely replaced, within less than a century, by other people whose habits, linguistic and otherwise, are not yet formed because the people are not yet born, and who can be given, with proper planning, any set of linguistic or other habits that it pleases their enlightened elders to impart to them.

This simply means that there is no rhyme or reason to the controversies now bitterly raging as to whether it would be better to use a natural, a modified, or a constructed language as an international medium of communication. Esperanto, Interglossa, Basic English, natural English, French, Chinese —it makes no difference which one is selected, provided all people now living agree to use it, not primarily for themselves but for their descendants. What is needed for the solution of the world's language problem is simply *a* language, any one of the world's 2,000 to 3,000 natural languages or one of the 700 or so constructed ones that have at various times been proposed, with, however, two qualifications: the language selected must have absolute correspondence of written symbols for spoken sounds, and it must be adopted, by international agreement, in all countries at the same time, not in the high schools or colleges or universities, but in the lowest grade of the elementary schools, side by side with the national tongue, so that it may be learned easily, naturally, and painlessly by the oncoming generations.

Let us consider for a moment the logic of these propositions. There is no linguistic expert on earth who will deny that all *spoken* languages are essentially "easy" to their own speakers. Chinese, Russian, American, and Zulu children speak their own tongues with approximately the same ease and fluency up to the time their schooling starts. It is when the speaking process turns into a conscious learning of grammatical rules and, worse yet, when it becomes a conscious tie-up of spoken with written forms that the difficulties begin; and these are greater (sometimes immeasurably greater) in one language than in another. If this is granted then it follows that any *spoken* tongue, natural, constructed, or modified, may be adopted with equal chance of success to be imparted by natural speaking processes to all the world's children as soon as they become old enough to go to school. We need not worry about the fact that they will previously have learned, in part, their own national tongues. The experience of bilingual countries like Belgium, Switzerland, Canada, and South Africa shows us that one language can be started at birth, another at six, and both come out equally well. And it does not matter what the languages are: "easy" or "difficult," "inflected," "isolating," "agglutinative" or "polysynthetic." All these terms represent conscious processes of language acquisition after linguistic habits are fully formed: that is, when we try to learn languages at the rate of three hours a week in high school or college, by the grammar method, which is simply comparing the language we are learning with the one we already possess.

On the other hand, the written form of the language we are acquiring has a great deal to do with true "ease" and "difficulty." In Spanish and Italian, where there are few exceptions to the sound-for-symbol correspondence, the process of learning to read and write and spell is a quick one. In the case of French and English, where there is strong divergence between spoken and written form, learning to read is much more complicated. In Chinese and Japanese, where complete spoken words are represented by arbitrary symbols, the process is still more involved. Consequently, the language adopted for international purposes must be written absolutely phonetically, which means that existing national languages, if they wish to present their candidacy for the post of international tongue, must be prepared to reduce their spelling to a system of absolute phonetic correspondence, at least for international use.

Outside of this, the problem rests not with the world's linguists but with the world's governments. Do they want an international tongue for international and possibly even national use, which will permit any inhabitant of the world to move about from country to country without ever encountering a language difficulty, since all the people of all the countries he visits will speak, in addition to their own national languages for home use, the international language which he himself has learned to speak since he first began going to school? If they do, the remedy for the world's linguistic troubles lies in their own hands.

As we have seen, some 700 international tongues have been evolved and proposed since the seventeenth century. In all of them, one outstanding preoccupation is evident: to make things as "easy" or as "logical" as possible for the greatest possible number of learners of the *existing* generation. Since the existing generation speaks a vast number of widely diverging languages, this preoccupation is doomed to sterility in advance. The Spanish, Portuguese, or Italian speaker who likes Esperanto's largely Romance vocabulary is still baffled by features that run counter to his habits. The French speaker who tries to use Basic English must give up words which to him are perfectly accessible and meaningful and learn compounds which are idiomatic, while the native English speaker finds himself beset at every turn by galling restrictions. The western scientist who tries to use Interglossa resents the Chinese syntax, while the Chinese scholar resents the Graeco-Latin vocabulary.

The real point, lost by all the interlinguists, is that the interlanguage of the future is for the future, not for the present generations; and that it does not have to be made "easy" or "logical" for anybody in particular, provided it is imparted in the right way at the right age.

It is sometimes advocated that further studies be made, either for the purpose of blending existing constructed languages into a single harmonious whole, or to determine what elements of grammar and vocabulary the European languages hold in common, or to investigate the known deficiencies in individual natural languages and the elements their speakers seem to feel the lack of so that the findings may be incorporated into yet one more constructed language still to be constructed, or even for the purpose of giving proportional representation to the earth's great language groups. All this would be largely a waste of time and effort and in any event could be done *after,* not before, the international language is chosen.

Either the world's governments are interested in giving the world's future generations the means of mutual understanding, or they are not. If the latter, nothing more need be said. The Tower of Babel, like its counterpart of Pisa, will continue to topple along for centuries as it has done in the past. People who want to travel or communicate in any way with other nationals will painfully learn foreign languages at the adult stage or get themselves interpreters, translators, and guides.

If the governments are interested, the solution is simple. A commission of international linguists can be set up for the purpose of selecting one language from the world's many natural and artificial ones to serve as an interlanguage. Which one they select is of comparatively little moment provided they do select it. Once it is selected, it goes into all the elementary schools in the world at the same time to be imparted (not "taught" as a foreign language) by natural methods, from kindergarten on, side by side with the national tongue and on an absolute parity with it. Within ten years, a new generation of interlinguists will crop up all over the world; within twenty, it will have grown to maturity; within thirty or forty, it will be ready to take its place at the helm of the world's affairs; within fifty or sixty, at least in civilized countries, the person that is not equipped with the interlanguage will be as rare as the illiterate is today.

The present generation? Let it do what it wants. It will be dead within a century anyway. Those who want to keep up with the times can take up the new interlanguage in special classes and acquire it painfully, the hard way, as they acquire foreign tongues today. Those who are too lazy, or haven't the time, or don't believe in the idea, can be left completely undisturbed. The world's linguistic picture will not change overnight, and by the time it does most of them will be enjoying their eternal reward. Is it callous to treat the present generation with so little regard? Certainly no more so than when we ask it to lay down life, liberty, and comfort in order that future generations may be assured of certain advantages, political or economic, which those same future generations may not view as advantages at all.

Is all this too simple to be true? Perhaps so; it is the same kind of simplicity as that which would put an end to all wars by the expedient of complete disarmament on the part of all nations, save for ordinary police forces, armed with clubs, revolvers, machine guns at the most, in all sovereign countries, and one international police force endowed with a few military planes, a few cruisers, and a few pieces of field artillery.

And yet perhaps it is not so simple. In the first place, the will to universal international understanding must be there, just as the will to peace must be there in the matter of disarmament. This means international government action—a concerted move on the part of all governments to make possible what is desirable. One government (possibly our own) may initiate the movement. It remains to be seen whether the others are willing to cooperate in the interests of those "children and children's children" concerning whom so many beautiful words flow but for whom so little is ever really done by any existing generation.

Secondly, there is the problem of the linguistic commission. Were all the governments to agree in advance to abide by the decision of the commission, the commission itself would have to be carefully picked and even more carefully watched. The number of delegates from each country would have to be determined in advance, and it could very well be determined not by population figures but by literacy figures. There is no reason why a country like China, with a population three times that of the United States but educational facilities that are only a fraction of ours, should exert a predominant influence in such a group, all the more since the immediate results of the commission's decision would in reality apply only to that portion of any country's population which has the possibility of schooling. (The principle of basing representation in international congresses on literacy rather than on population opens up interesting vistas, since it would encourage national governments to develop literacy within their borders; it might even be profitably applied to our own nation, where presidential conventions and elections go by states.)

Thirdly, the selection of representatives by the various governments is of some importance. Known advocates of one or another of the systems now vying for supremacy should *a priori* be excluded. The qualifications of every delegate should be passed upon by the body as a whole.

But even more important is the question of time and procedure. Left to their own devices, linguists might bicker forever, and since what language they select is not one tenth so important as their selecting it, a definite time limit should be imposed on their labors. While all languages, national, modified, and constructed, could be presented for candidacy at the outset, the procedure should involve a series of compulsory run-off elections, with weaker candidates gradually weeded out until an absolute majority for one tongue is reached. Lastly, it should be understood that the language selected, if a natural tongue, would immediately be given a phonetic spelling for international purposes. The charge of cultural imperialism against any national tongue that might be selected would be countered by two facts: the choice would have been made by an international commission, in which all nations would be fully represented on the basis of their literate populations; and its spelling would be changed to conform with phonetic requirements, thereby differentiating it, in written form, from the national tongue.

The process of training teachers in the international tongue would take a little time, but with educational facilities, teachers' colleges, and normal schools what they are today, it might be hoped that the actual process of imparting the international tongue in the kindergartens could begin within two or three years of the commission's decision. As the first batch of children moves on to higher grades from year to year, more and better trained teachers would also become available.

In view of the long record of civil wars, even in the recent past, it is extremely doubtful that an international tongue will end international conflicts. It might have to be coupled with some additional international reforms, such as the universal disarmament already suggested. There is little question, however, that it would make future wars a little more comfortable to their participants.

Will the rise of an interlanguage ultimately do away with existing national languages? All who are trying at present to sell us a particular interlanguage scheme assure us that it will not, that it is meant "only" for international communications, with the existing languages surviving and flourishing. My answer is that it assuredly will in the long run, though the long run may easily turn out to be a few centuries. In economics, bad money drives good money out of circulation, because everybody wants to hoard good money for future use. In languages, the opposite is true, because languages are for immediate, not future, use. The language that is good at all times and in all places will eventually supplant languages whose currency is limited to their own territory. The process will, of course, be gradual, but we may expect that the present spoken languages will, in due course of time, tend to become cultural relics, like Latin, until they are ultimately studied not for practical use but solely for literary values. This would happen under any circumstances, for even if they were continued in full use, in 500 years they would be so changed that the tongue of the twentieth century would be just as much a cultural relic.

What are the chances that the new interlanguage will dialectalize, just as the Latin of the Roman Empire broke up into the various Romance tongues? Under present conditions of communications and education, they are exceedingly slim. The Roman Empire's means of communication and education (roads, trade, military service, books, schools) were primitive as compared with those of today; yet while those rudimentary means endured, the language remained substantially one. It was only when communications failed after the Empire's downfall and each community became an isolated, self-contained unit that incomprehensibility arose. Our comparison, under modern conditions, should be with the Anglo-American of the English-speaking world rather than with the Latin of the Empire. The King's English and the American Language, which had been diverging more and more down to the turn of the century, began to grow together again with the advent of the radio, TV, and the talkies. These inventions, by bringing the pronunciation and intonation of one set of speakers to the other, caused each one insensibly to modify its own habits of speech in the direction of the other's. In the world of tomorrow there will be much more international travel than in the past, but even the obdurate stay-at-homes will get standardized inter-language radio, television, and movie programs.

This being so, there is little doubt that the interlanguage will spread with relative rapidity and, as it spreads, crowd out the world's spoken vernaculars. Were the plan we outline to be initiated in the 1960s, the universal tongue would be a living, powerful reality by A.D. 2050.

The story of language has carried us far afield, through the domains of history, of physical science, of anthropology, sociology, and geography.

We have witnessed the birth and growth of human systems of communication, chief among which is language. The nature of speech and writing are no longer closed books to us. The fundamental purpose and function of speech has become clear. We have seen what language and languages consist of. We have observed the intimate connection of language with all basic human activities. We now know enough about the location, affiliations, cultural and economic importance of the world's chief tongues to be able to discuss them intelligently. Even their appearance and structure are no longer mysteries.

The number of existing languages and the difficulty of mastering even a single one beside our own have been brought into sharp focus. The problems of language are not something for the pedagogues alone to worry about. They concern each and every one of us, if not in connection with foreign tongues with which we may at any time be thrown in contact, then at least in conjunction with our own mother tongue, over which none of us exercises absolute mastery.

The story of language is a phase, perhaps the most important, certainly the most enlightening, of the story of mankind. May it have a happy ending!

WORD LIST

A

a, 125, 317
-*abad* (place-name suffix), 72
abbot, 43, 221
Aber- (place-name prefix), 72
Aberdeen, 72
able Grable, 199
abnormal, 155
Abominable Snow Man, 272
about, 323
above, 323
abrams, 191
absinthe, 164
abyss, 221
Abyssinia, 69
Acadiens, 417
acanoptic, 177
a cappella, 165, 223
according to Hoyle, 214
accumulator, 325
ace, 190
acidosis, 292
acknowledge and confess, 221
acreage, 263
acro- (prefix), 268
acte authentique, 264
action, 248
-*acum*, (place-name suffix), 65
adamant, 164
Addis Ababa, 73
Adirondack, 64
Adolph, 79
Adonai, 267
Adonis, 287
aeroembolism, 293
aerothermodynamic border, 293
afghan, 416
Afghanistan, 72
-*age*, 176, 263
agenda, 437
Agnes, 80
agora- (prefix), 268
agravic, 177

aide mémoire, 264
ailurophobia, 268
aim to provide, 323
ain't, 183
air, 161
airtel, 175
aisle, 221
Akkadia, 252, 255
Al- (place-name prefix), 72
al- (prefix), 165
à la carte, 159
alas, 164
Albania, 415
Albert, 80
Albion, 66
Alcántara, 72
Alcázar, 72, 241
alchemy, 292, 387
alcohol, 165, 292, 387
alcove, 165
al dente, 235
Alexandria, 75
algebra, 165, 292, 387
Algernon, 81
alias, 263
alibi, 263
alibi day, 196
alkali, 165, 292, 387
Allah, 221
Allemagne, 68
Allemand, 68
aloha, 407
alpha, 372
alphanapthylthiourea, 295
al-qadi, 259
Alsace-Lorraine, 69
Alt- (place-name prefix), 72
Altai, 72
Altamaha, 72
altar, 220, 222
al-wazir, 259
am, 125
ama- (prefix), 416
Amazon, 66
Ama-Zulu, 416
amen, 221
America, 73
Americana, 176

Americanize, 221
American swindle, 278
American theft, 278
amongst, 323
amoronthologos-phorus, 179
ampere, 292
ampersand, 436
Amtorg, 247
an, 125, 318
-*ana*, 176
anacoustic zone, 177, 293
anathema, 223
Andes, 66
and how, 187
angel, 222
angel cake, 199
angel cake and wine, 193
Angeleño, 76
anger, 163
Anglos, 281
Anglo-Saxon, 222
animage, 171
animal control warden, 269
ankh, 389
anoint, 220
anonymous, 248
another pair of shoes, 329
An Poblacht Abu, 277
Antarctica, 70
ante bellum, 264
anthem, 220
anti- (prefix), 261
antibiotic, 292
anticipating, 269
antipasto, 233
antique, 150
antsy, 189
antu, 295
any more, 189
Ap- (name prefix), 83
apartheid, 281
apartment, 324
apocryphal, 220
apostle, 222, 223
apparatus, 196

grace, 91, 221
gracias, 91
gracious, 94
-*grad* (place-name suffix), 72, 362
graft, 329
Graham Land, 70
gram, 252
grand, 192, 226, 263
granddaughter, 228
grandfather, 226, 228, 229
grandmother, 226, 228
grandson, 228
Granfinos, 261
grapevine, 186
grasser, 194
gratis, 91
graupel, 292
gravel, 196
graveyard shift, 195
gravipause, 177
gravy, 190
gray, 190, 306
grazhdanin, 88
grazhdanka, 88
grazie, 91
great, 335
Great Bear, 305
great outback, 328
greats, 173
Great White Father, 258
Green Bay, 74
greengrocer, 324
Greens, 306
Greenwich Village, 72
gremlin, 182
Gretta, 81
grey, 323
gridiron, 328
grilled, 323
grip, 192
gripe, 185
grippe, 165
grismal, 177
groggy, 166
ground grippers, 197
grouse, 185
grunt, 198
gruntle, 172
Guad- (place-name prefix), 72
Guadalajara, 72
Guadalquivir, 72
Guadalupe, 72
guarani, 251
guard, 241
guest, 88
guidance worker, 269
guilty big, 198
guise, 44

guitar, 165
gum, 29
Gumbinnen, 70
gumbo, 410
gun, 194
gun play, 182
gurgle, 169
Gurk, 360
Gusev, 70
gut robber, 196
guy in my trunk, 189
gyrene, 197

H

ha-, 388
habeas corpus, 263
haberdasher, 324
habitants, 417
had, 125
Hadassah, 388
hadn't ought, 184
hair-do, 172
hair-pounder, 196
Haleakala, 67
ham, 192
-*ham* (place-name suffix), 241
hamateur, 175
hamburger, 176
ham-dog, 189
Hamlet, 286
hand, 252
handmuckers, 193
handout, 173
hang out one's shingle, 185
hang out the laundry, 197
hangar rat, 197
Hankuk, 69
haole, 407
happen, 163
happy shop, 190
hardware, 194
harem, 221
Harlequin, 287
harlot, 154, 270
Harwich, 322
hash, 174, 195
hate, 44
Hatikwah, 388
hatriot, 176
have, 125
have-got-wata-topside, 331
have had it, 182, 327
having a goosh, 195
hayburner, 196
head-end traffic, 196
headline, 173

heap, 440
heathen, 222
heaven, 220
heavy cream, 198
Hebrew, 278, 416
heck, 268
hectic, 182
hegira, 221
heir-conditioned, 269
Helen, 80
hell, 94, 220, 269
hello, 92, 161
helots, 282
Henry, 79
Herculean, 287
Hercules, 287
heresy, 221
hermetic, 287
hermit, 221
Herr, 88
Herzog, 259
Hesperia, 65
heterodyne, 445
hide, 198
hierarchy, 221
high old time, 185
highball, 196
higher-up, 173
him, 125
Hind, 415
Hindu, 73
Hindustan, 69, 72
Hindustani, 415
hire, 249
hire purchase, 325
his garden is green, 198
his'n, 181
Hispano, 274
hit and run, 195, 214
hit below the belt, 214
hitchhiker, 196
hit the bottle, 199
hit the road, 182
Hi, ya, Pop, 327
hoagy, 179
hoax, 282
Hoboken, 64
hocus pocus, 282
hodgepodge, 237
hog, 30
hogget, 59
hoi polloi, 164
hold-up, 166
holdupnik, 189
hole, 193
holiday, 222
-*holm* (place-name suffix), 72
home, 241

unbleached American, 187
unbuttoned, 329
uncle, 226, 228
uncurrent, 250
under dog, 166
underground, 323
underwear, 180
underworld, 182
UNESCO, 436
ungothroughsome, 179
Union of Soviet Socialist Republics, 415
Unitedstatish, 326
unmentionables, 269
unobtainium, 197
UNRRA, 436
unspeakables, 269
unutterables, 269
up, 151, 323
upcry, 175
uppercut, 166
uprightmen, 191
upsilon, 372
upstanding, 324
up-to-date, 166
urbiculturist, 172
urgle, 179
Ursula, 81
Urzad Bezpieczenstwa, 259
U. S. A., 436
U. S. S. R., 436
Usted, 90f
utensil maintenance man, 269
Utica, 75
utility car, 325
Utopia, 287

V

Valentine, 80
valuta, 249
vampire, 271
van (name prefix), 84
van, 185
-*var* (place-name suffix), 72
Vasconia, 65
vaseline, 246
vaudeville, 287
veal, 233
Veglia, 70
veld, 166, 338
venerable, 220
Venice, 74, 249
venire, 263
veniremen, 263

venue, 263
Venus, 287
Vercingetorix, 258
verbatim, 163
verge, 325
verge on heath, 325
vermicelli, 235
very, 161
vessel, 199
vet, 185
vetophobia, 174
video, 292
videogenic, 173, 195
videognosis, 177
videot, 177
Vienna, 74f
Viet Cong, 283
Viet Minh, 283
vig, 193
vigil, 221
vigorish, 193
villa, 241
villain, 155
-*ville*, 178, 242
vine, 190
viola, 165
virgin, 221
Virginia, 64
vista, 165
Vitelia, 66
viz., 436
vizier, 154
Vladivostok, 73
vodka, 362
volcano, 287
Volgograd, 70
volt, 293
von (name prefix), 84
voodoo, 272
vote down, 325
vote up, 325
vow, 221
voyage, 176, 221, 263
Vozhd', 91
vs., 436
vulcanize, 287
Vyatka, 70

W

wa-, 416
wad, 72
wagering, 325
wagon, 166
wait small, 331
walkie-talkie, 173f
wallop, 190
Walpurgisnacht, 271
wampum, 127, 440
wanhope, 162
want, 163

wappened, 170
warden, 199
warm up to, 195
war of nerves, 283
warp, 163
Washington, 64
wassail, 161
waste, 193
water, 336
watt, 293
Wa-Tuzi, 416
wed, 44
Wednesday, 255, 287
weed tea, 192
week, 255
weekend, 166
weigh into, 329
welsh, 278
Welsh, 278, 416
Weltanschauung, 429
Wendish, 416
weregeld, 250
werewolf, 271
west, 160
what's it in aid of, 187
what's with it with you, 199
what's with you, 199
whets, 233
whiffer, 198
Whigs, 233
whilst, 323
whiskey, 376
whistle and flute, 190
white, 306
white feather, 307
Whites, 306
white sound, 293
white supremacy, 260
whiz, 192
whodunit, 178, 182
whole caboose, 329
whooper-upper, 171
whoreson, 269
-*wich* (place-name suffix), 72
-*wick* (place-name suffix), 72
Wiener Schnitzel, 236
wig, 163, 185
wigwam, 162
wildcat strike, 195
William, 79
Windex, 247
windscreen, 325
wine, 29, 41, 238
wing, 163
wireless, 324
-*wise*, 178
witch hazel, 270
withdrawing room, 172

INDEX

A

Abbreviations, 87, 247, 270, 435 f
Ablative, 134 (see also Case)
Ablaut, 385
Academies, 142, 352, 450
Accusative, 134 f, 331, 359, 365, 373, 386 (see also Case)
Achaean, 59
Ach-laut, 339
Action, complete and incomplete, 138
Adams, J. Donald, 179, 203
Adige River, 346
Adjectives, 130 f, 133, 318, 338, 340, 348, 359, 365 f, 387, 402, 444, 453
Adverbs, 130, 356, 409
Advertising, 18, 156, 161, 245
Aegean Islands, 370
Aeneid, 50
Aeolian, 371
Affiliation of languages, 255
Affirmative conjugation, 138
Afghanistan, 36, 377 f, 416
Africa, 82, 91, 99, 121, 276, 312 ff, 317, 329, 344, 383, 409, 439
African Latin, 384
African Negro languages, 32, 37 f, 50, 158, 160, 225, 233, 312, 327, 409
Afrikaans, 34, 328, 333, 338, 439
Age, concept of, 227
Agglutinative languages, 389, 449, 458
Agreement, 133, 142, 243, 355, 387, 390
Ainu, 37, 256, 413
Air Force terms, 197
Air lines, 245
Akkadian, 28 f, 217, 383, 393
Alaska, 412
Albania, 298, 370
Albanian, 30, 32, 34, 36, 160, 218-19, 370, 374 f

Albigensian Crusade, 345
Aleutians, 412
Algeria, 300, 344
Algerian-Tunisian-Libyan Arabic, 386
Algonquian, 64, 133
Alias, 85
Alien words, 162
Allophones, 117
Alphabet, 97 ff
  Arabic, 99, 101, 219, 221, 377 f, 391, 408
  Armenian, 99, 376
  Black Letter, 98, 339
  Cyrillic, 98, 101, 218 f, 356, 359, 361, 368, 370, 415
  Devanagari, 96, 99, 220, 378
  Etruscan, 98
  Greek, 98, 370, 372
  Hebrew, 339, 347
  Phoenician, 98
  Roman, 98 f, 101, 219, 300, 359, 366 f, 370, 374 f, 391, 404
Alphabet soup, 436
Alpine race, 279
Alsace-Lorraine, 333
Altaic, 36, 389 f
Alto Adige, 276
Amalfi, 244
America, 166, 214
American Bible Society, 300
American Board of Foreign Missions, 299
American English, 53, 55 ff, 63, 79 f, 182, 250, 320 ff, 339, 450, 463
American Indian languages, 19, 32 f, 37, 51, 63 f, 96, 127, 137, 142 f, 158, 160, 162, 224, 235, 241, 272, 281, 302, 312, 328, 410 ff
American Institute of Foreign Trade, 244
American Revolution, 283, 298, 327

487

SIGNET SEE IT AND SAY IT Language Books

(50¢ each)

A series of word-picture language texts to enable the beginner to learn a foreign language without a teacher. Each book includes a pronunciation guide and traveler's dictionary.

SEE IT AND SAY IT IN GERMAN
by Margarita Madrigal and Inge Halpert
(#D2184)

SEE IT AND SAY IT IN FRENCH
by Margarita Madrigal and Colette Dulac
(#D2185)

SEE IT AND SAY IT IN ITALIAN
by Margarita Madrigal and Guiseppina Salvadori
(#D2002)

SEE IT AND SAY IT IN SPANISH by Margarita Madrigal
(#D2001)

Other SIGNET and MENTOR Books of Interest

ENJOYING MODERN ART   by Sarah Newmeyer
A vivid account of the development of modern art, tracing the major movements of the past hundred years. Includes reproductions of 80 famous paintings. (#MP389—60¢)

STORIES OF FAMOUS OPERAS (revised and expanded) by Harold Vincent Milligan
The plots, casts of characters and highlights of over 50 of the world's great operas.   (#T2746—75¢)

MUSIC AND IMAGINATION   by Aaron Copland
The world-famous composer explains the role of the imagination in composing, performing, and listening to music.   (#MP502—60¢)

MODERN MUSIC by John Tasker Howard and James Lyons
A handbook explaining the new harmonies and rhythms—including jazz—presenting a history of 20th century developments.   (#MP396—60¢)

Other MENTOR Books You'll Enjoy Reading

THE USES OF THE PAST   **by Herbert J. Muller**
> The civilizations of the past, how they flourished, why they fell, and their meaning for the present crisis of civilization. (#MT521—75¢)

THE ANVIL OF CIVILIZATION   **by Leonard Cottrell**
> This fascinating history of the ancient Mediterranean civilizations reveals the long-buried secrets of the early Egyptians, Hittites, Sumerians, Assyrians, Babylonians, Greeks, and Hebrews, brought to light by archaeological discoveries. (#MT649—75¢)

PREHISTORY   **by Jacquetta Hawkes**
HISTORY OF MANKIND, Cultural and Scientific Development, Volume One, Part I)
> This first volume in the UNESCO history describes primitive man from his beginnings in Africa to the Neolithic Age. (#MQ632—95¢)

THE BEGINNINGS OF CIVILIZATION
      by Sir Leonard Woolley
(HISTORY OF MANKIND, Cultural and Scientific Development, Volume One, Part II)
> The second part of this UNESCO history describes the dawn of culture in the Bronze Age, and goes up to the splendid civilizations of Mesopotamia and the Nile at the end of the 13th century B.C. (#MY633—$1.25)

LOST LANGUAGES   **by P. E. Cleator**
> An absorbing investigation into writings of the past—how they were discovered, deciphered, and what they reveal about ancient peoples and civilizations. With photographs and drawings. (#MT427—75¢)

THE MEANING OF THE DEAD SEA SCROLLS
      by A. Powell Davies
> A fascinating interpretation of one of the most important archaeological discoveries of recent times, ancient documents which revolutionize religious teachings and beliefs. (#MP587—60¢)

To Our Readers: If your dealer does not have the SIGNET and MENTOR books you want, you may order them by mail enclosing the list price plus 10¢ a copy to cover mailing. (New York City residents add 5% Sales Tax. Other New York State residents add 2% plus any local sales or use taxes.) If you would like our free catalog, please request it by postcard. The New American Library, Inc., P.O. Box 2310, Grand Central Station, New York, N. Y. 10017.